UNDERSTANDING NAFTA

WILLIAM A. ORME, JR.

Understanding NAFTA

Mexico,
Free Trade,
and the New
North America

UNIVERSITY OF TEXAS PRESS *Austin*

For reasons of economy and speed, this volume has been printed from computer disks supplied by the author, who assumes full responsibility for its contents.

Requests for permission to reproduce material from this work should be sent to Permissions, University of Texas Press, P.O. Box 7819, Austin, TX 78713-7819.

⊗ The paper used in this publication meets the minimum requirements of American National Standard for Information Sciences—Permanence of Paper for Printed Library Materials, ANSI Z39.48-1984.

LIBRARY OF CONGRESS CATALOGING-IN-PUBLICATION DATA

Orme, William A.
   Understanding NAFTA : Mexico, free trade, and the new North America / William A. Orme, Jr.
      p.   cm.
   Includes index.
   ISBN 0-292-76046-9
   1. Free trade—North America. 2. Canada. Treaties, etc. 1992 Oct. 7.—Public opinion. 3. Public opinion—North America. 4. Mexico—Economic policy—1982– 5. United States—Commercial policy. I. Title.
HF1746.075   1996
382'.097—dc20
                                                            95-47521

To Deborah and David for their forbearance and support.

With affection.

CONTENTS

INTRODUCTION

After the Fall

With the North American Free Trade Agreement finally in force, Mexico was supposed to leave the South and underdevelopment behind. But the new *Salinista* Mexico of cellular telephones and stock options suddenly gave way to scenes of helicopter gunships and defiant guerrillas. On New Year's Day 1994 Mexico was supposed to start looking like Texas. Instead, it looked like El Salvador.

By 1995, after the trade pact had been in effect for a year, the Mexican economy was hardly the dynamo NAFTA boosters had depicted. It seemed more like a smoking ruin. Economic achievements that NAFTA was supposed to consolidate and accelerate had instead been abruptly reversed. Inflation was roaring back from single digits to 50 percent or worse. An economy that was expected to expand by four percent yearly now faced a savage four percent contraction. Unemployment was rising, wages were falling, and money was flowing north, not south. Rocketing interest rates made new business ventures impossible and mortgages unpayable. The green eyeshades at Moody's, once expected to reward post-NAFTA Mexico with investment-grade securities ratings, had instead demoted Mexico to the risky ranks of the ex-Warsaw Pact economies.

The post-NAFTA reality north of the border didn't look much better. The fat U.S. trade surplus was evaporating, and along with it prospects for NAFTA-driven U.S. job growth. Halfway through 1995, when this new introduction to *Understanding NAFTA* was written, the United States was already $8 billion in the red in its Mexican trade account.

On the Mexican side, the new bilateral trade surplus was a setback falsely hailed as an economic triumph: it was accomplished not by a surge in exports, but by a drastic cut in imports. An industrializing nation like Mexico needs to buy a lot of foreign consumer products and capital goods. This is both healthy and efficient. NAFTA ensures that most of those imports will come from the United States. When Mexico is again posting regular deficits in its U.S. trade, it will be a solid indicator of recovery.

Mexico's climb out of this very deep and swiftly dug hole will take years. NAFTA makes the ascent easier, but critics of the pact could properly point out that NAFTA did not and could not prevent the fall.

NAFTA supporters (this author included) said the pact would propel Mexico into the first ranks of newly industrializing nations, creating a booming market for U.S. exports and raising Mexican incomes in the process. They expected the peso to hold steady or even strengthen as inflation stabilized in the middle single digits. NAFTA's architect, outgoing President Carlos Salinas de Gortari, was expected to graduate to a second career as an international economic statesman.

Detractors said NAFTA would simply prop up a venal political monopoly, triggering a massive loss of U.S. manufacturing jobs to low-wage workers who couldn't afford the goods they produced. They dismissed recent Mexican economic growth as an illusion built on borrowed dollars and an inflated peso; they said NAFTA's ratification would be followed by a steep devaluation, the disappearance of the U.S. bilateral trade surplus, and continuing economic hardship for most ordinary Mexicans.

■ The opponents were wrong about a lot of things, but they can certainly claim to have come much closer to describing post-NAFTA Mexico than NAFTA supporters did. Mexico remains a struggling nation of "grave needs and wants," as President Ernesto Zedillo has acknowledged. Half of the potential workforce is unemployed or underemployed. With the domestic market contracting, export manufacturers spending more on machines and less on labor, and a million new job-seekers coming of age every year, the employment problem is more acute now than it was when the NAFTA negotiations started. Those Mexicans who do have jobs are earning less in real terms than they were when NAFTA was ratified. In January 1994, when NAFTA legally came into effect, per capita income had passed the $4,000 mark, putting Mexicans in the upwardly mobile company of the East Asians and Southern Europeans. By January 1995, Mexico's per capita income had slid brusquely backwards to $2,600, erasing the gains of the previous three years. The destruction of wealth among ordinary Mexicans is retroactive as well: Inflation is savaging the savings of the middle class, while rewarding the moneyed minority who keep their cash in banks across the border.

Mirroring this drastic economic reversal was the spectacular decline in the personal and political fortunes of Carlos Salinas. The former president left Mexico for Europe not as the triumphant new chief of the World Trade Organization, as he had once confidently expected, but as a virtual fugitive, blamed by his countrymen for the collapse of the peso and the assassination of two of his closest political allies.

Does all this mean that NAFTA was a terrible mistake?

No. But it does show that many arguments made on NAFTA's behalf were flawed or specious, and many of the questions raised by critics were entirely valid. It is not enough to point out that Mexico's latest crisis was caused not by free trade, but by disastrously mismanaged currency policies. It is not enough to argue that without the trade pact Mexico's plight would be far more severe, to the detriment of all three North American economies. Supporters of NAFTA should acknowledge that NAFTA was never going to be a quick fix for a country whose problems are fundamentally social and political, not economic. Nor was NAFTA ever the key to making the giant U.S. economy "competitive" in the international marketplace.

NAFTA's supporters should also acknowledge that building a continental market requires constant attention, creativity, and a willingness to run risks. The new North American institutions created by NAFTA—the dispute resolution boards, the tripartite labor and environmental commissions, the border agencies and development bank—have only barely begun to function. Yet they have already forced environmentalists and their adversaries to sit at the same table in alliances that cut across national lines. American unions are now defending and collaborating with their Mexican counterparts, and together they have made cross-border employers more accountable for their labor practices. States and communities on both sides of the U.S.-Mexican border are beginning to work cooperatively on infrastructural planning and pollution control.

North America needs more of this, not less. The peso crisis of late 1994 underscored the urgency of better institutional communication and cooperation on monetary matters. The ugly backlash against Mexican immigrants in California dramatized the need to address migratory issues bilaterally, if not trilaterally. Continuing friction with Canada on anti-dumping allegations underlines the importance of eliminating anachronistic dumping rules within the NAFTA market. The passage of NAFTA signaled only the starting point of a process that will take decades. The North American Free Trade Area should be deepened before it is broadened: Chile and its Southern Hemisphere neighbors are being invited into a house that hasn't been built yet.

The political and economic crises of 1994 and 1995 highlighted NAFTA's importance as well as its shortcomings. Tellingly, Mexico's response was to push the NAFTA process faster—exporting more, privatizing more, bringing foreign capital more quickly into its banking system. In a truly revolutionary change, the Mexican government began releasing economic data—to its NAFTA partners, as well as to its own citizens—on a more regular and credible basis. In Washington and Ottawa, officials were jolted into the realization that after NAFTA they would have to pay even closer attention to Mexico's travails. The Clinton rescue package for Mexico, with its onerous conditionality, served to bind the North American economies even more tightly together.

Better communication and further policy coordination are essential if all three NAFTA nations are to maximize the benefits of interdependence and minimize cross-border economic shocks. The lesson of the new Mexican crisis was not that NAFTA didn't work, but that it didn't go far enough.

■ *Understanding NAFTA* was written during the two years that NAFTA was being negotiated and debated, and it chronicles the twists and turns of that public policy spectacle. Resisting the temptation to edit in retroactive prescience and excise undue economic optimism, I have left the text in this edition essentially intact. Despite Mexico's latest descent into recession, little of underlying importance has changed—except that NAFTA is now a fact.

The book's original intent was to scrutinize arguments and dispel myths propagated by NAFTA proponents and adversaries alike, while examining Mexico's motives for redefining its relationship to the United States. I tried to follow the NAFTA negotiations in the contexts of each country's vastly different political reality and to assess the agreement's likely impact on the North American economy. It was clear from the start that this impact would be felt first and most profoundly in Mexico. Changing Mexico, after all, was the pact's real purpose. The effect of

NAFTA on the United States (and, more distantly, on Canada) would be the indirect repercussions of the Mexican economic transformation that NAFTA helped make possible.

That is why a book about the "new North America" is mainly about Mexico. What is new about North America after NAFTA is that Mexico has switched continents, leaving "Latin" America in order to enlarge and enrich the industrial societies of Canada and the United States. The United States and Canada were tightly interwoven long before Brian Mulroney and Ronald Reagan wrote new ground rules formalizing and liberalizing this relationship. Mexico, despite its deep dependence on U.S. markets and investment, had been a country proudly apart. Its membership in a North American free trade zone is more than a simple, structured acceleration of an ongoing integration process. It is a revolutionary attempt to integrate a poor developing economy and an industrial superpower. For Mexico, it marked the end of its 20th century, a century of great suffering, but also of celebratory nationalism and economic self-sufficiency. In a historic gamble, Mexico was willing to trade autonomy for prosperity. In the short term, it was left with neither. Yet NAFTA still gives Mexico an opportunity to prosper that it would never have had on its own.

In the Washington debate over NAFTA, both sides argued as if the pact's effects would be instantaneous. Opponents contended it would precipitate a mass southbound exodus of U.S. manufacturing jobs. Advocates suggested NAFTA would transform Mexico overnight into the Latin equivalent of an East Asian tiger—with the odd variant that it would contentedly rack up large and continuing trade deficits. NAFTA was always about something more difficult, and much more significant: the slow immersion of a great but poor nation into the economic mainstream of the planet's biggest industrial superpower.

In retrospect, it seems unsurprising that this radical experiment would prove less popular in the richer of the two markets. But it did not look that way in 1990, when President Salinas first decided to accept Washington's long-standing invitation to join a continental trade pact. He was braced for bitter resistance at home. Not only was he abandoning Mexico's long history of zealous protectionism, he was challenging the conventional wisdom that Mexico could survive anything except Uncle Sam's embrace. He expected his political opponents to accuse him of economic treason, and many of them did. Remarkably, though, most centrist Mexican politicians came to accept free trade with the North as the country's best strategic alternative, and NAFTA never became a bitter partisan issue.

Neither Salinas nor his American partners anticipated that the fiercest opposition would come from north of the border. But the more Americans heard about NAFTA, the less they liked it. When the negotiations began in late 1991 the free trade pact enjoyed broad but shallow support. Two years later, as the actual vote approached, few members of Congress were willing to campaign for the accord, and more than a hundred were working actively against it—most of them Democrats, despite their president's vigorous if belated support for the pact. For NAFTA's supporters, the most encouraging news in the fall of 1993 was that after nearly three years of negotiations half of all Americans surveyed were still unclear what NAFTA was all about. When the House of Representatives finally approved the pact, narrowly, after a contentious debate, it was more a tribute to President Clinton's persistence and horse-trading skills than to the success of the NAFTA lobby in selling the agreement to the country on its merits.

The great NAFTA debate of 1993 was not really about the agreement itself, or even about Mexico, but about competing domestic political agendas and irreconcilable world views. Appeals were made not to rational economic interest but to nationalistic fears. On one side, there was calculated alarmism about accelerating immigration and purported alliances between anti-NAFTA leftists and drug traffickers; on the other, there were crude appeals to the most xenophobic strains of American populism. Critics exaggerated the risks of more rapid economic integration while minimizing its rewards; advocates, no more responsibly, did just the opposite.

Discussions about Mexico itself degenerated into a war of caricatures. NAFTA boosters painted a picture of a country saved from destruction by Americanized reformers who would teeter and fall without Washington's support. Critics described a two-dimensional society where industrial peons work for inbred billionaires in factories spewing toxic waste. On both sides, the agreement's true purpose and likely effects were distorted and obscured.

When Presidents Salinas and Bush unveiled the trade initiative, each man was at the height of his political power. Salinas used all his domestic strength to build a public case for the agreement. Bush did not. North of the border, pro-NAFTA salesmanship was confined to politicking with business councils and editorial boards; the American people—increasingly worried about stagnant incomes and global competition—were largely ignored. And though Clinton was a much more forceful salesman for NAFTA than Bush, he also left NAFTA to low-ranking subalterns until the final critical weeks.

NAFTA's opponents exploited this leadership vacuum, turning NAFTA into a potent symbol for everything they disliked about American politics: the influence of foreign lobbyists in Washington; the cult of executive secrecy; the intrusion of international responsibilities in domestic affairs; the disregard of inside-the-beltway pundits for economic hardship in America's heartland. And they made Mexico itself a cunning metaphor for the problems America faces in adjusting to global competition from low-wage labor.

But Mexico isn't a metaphor. It is a country, it is not going away, and NAFTA is going to make it and us different.

As this book argues with perhaps tiresome insistence, NAFTA's success or failure can only be assessed fairly in a decade or more. Forecasts of dramatic instantaneous benefits and of immediate economic disaster were always equally wrong. Every serious analysis of NAFTA agreed that NAFTA's short-term economic impact on the United States would be marginal. It was also obvious to anyone who knew Mexico that its evolution into a modern industrial society would take decades, not years. But I still expected NAFTA to have a quick, visibly positive impact on Mexico's standard of living. Despite this book's warnings about the fragility of the Salinas free-trade experiment, I still overestimated Mexico's fundamental economic strength, and underestimated the skittishness of American institutional investors.

I also underestimated the commitment of policymakers in Mexico and Washington alike to the stability of the peso. The December 1994 devaluation not only slashed the currency's value in half, it made it much harder for Mexico to take advantage of NAFTA's potential for sustained real growth. As this book shows, NAFTA was the cornerstone of the Salinas sound-money strategy, which depended on a constant influx of foreign (mainly American) portfolio capital. This was in turn organically linked to the Salinas anti-inflation policy, which required stiff price competition from the imports permitted into the country by free trade.

As described within (see "1992: The Year of Living Dangerously"), the inevitable result was a ballooning current-account deficit. Mexico had been walking a monetary tightrope for three years. At the end of 1994 it lost its balance and fell.

The critics said they told us so. And they had. It wasn't just that NAFTA was followed by a drastic devaluation, as Ross Perot and other pact opponents had predicted. NAFTA's own champions based their economic claims on two central premises, each of which, just one year later, had seemingly been proven empirically wrong.

The first premise was that NAFTA would raise Mexican wages. This would create a vast new consumer market south of the border while reducing low-wage competition for manufacturing jobs. Critics of NAFTA were skeptical, so Salinas promised Clinton that after the pact's approval Mexico would boost its minimum wage in real terms for the first time in a decade. Instead, his successor ended up slashing wages in order to contain the inflation generated by his mismanaged devaluation—a strategy *demanded* by the Clinton Administration as a price for its financial aid. The devaluation already represented a steep salary cut for a workforce that was told it would regain the purchasing power it briefly enjoyed during Mexico's oil boom 15 years earlier. Now, by keeping wage increases far below the increase in the cost of living, the government was compounding the damage to family incomes.

In the long term, NAFTA will in fact help Mexican incomes rise. But the gap between U.S. and Mexican wages that had been narrowing for five years opened up anew to a ten-to-one chasm. More jobs will migrate south as a result.

The second premise was that free trade with Mexico would be a huge net producer of jobs within the United States *because* the United States would maintain a strong positive balance in this bilateral trade. That assumption was the sole basis for most pro-NAFTA job creation estimates. The Department of Commerce, private business lobbyists, and even independent sources such as the Institute for International Economics propagated the notion that NAFTA-generated employment could be extrapolated directly—so many billions of dollars equaling so many thousands of jobs—from projected bilateral trade surpluses. At the end of 1994 that surplus inconveniently disappeared. By mid-1995 Mexico was deepening the U.S. trade deficit by $1.5 billion monthly.

NAFTA advocates were reminded that their argument had a corollary: if the U.S. posted a deficit in its cross-border trade, that presumably meant more jobs were being eliminated under NAFTA than were being created. In the auto industry, for example, the devaluation sabotaged hopes that U.S. plants would soon be shipping yearly 100,000 or more vehicles south of the border. The United States could no longer count on a surplus *even if the Mexican economy recovered;* the rescue strategy fashioned by the U.S. Treasury was predicated on *Mexico* racking up continued surpluses. As if nothing had been learned from the debt crisis of the 1980s, Mexico was again forced to sign on to the standard International Monetary Fund layaway plan: recession, inflation, and fat trade surpluses stretching into the sunset.

The obsession with the trade balance has distorted the NAFTA argument on both sides. Before the December peso collapse, NAFTA boosters were claiming vindication because U.S. exports to Mexico had climbed 22 percent as of the close of the year's third quarter. Critics, meanwhile, groused that imports of Mexican goods had risen even faster, climbing by 23 percent—as if that fractional difference made the United States the loser in the deal.

NAFTA opponents cited as further evidence the claims put forward by unemployed U.S. workers who blamed the loss of their jobs on Mexican competition. Only a few thousand of the labor movement's estimate of 60,000 lost jobs in 1994 due to "NAFTA" could be convincingly documented, and those jobs would have likely left America with or without a trade pact. (Even 60,000 is equivalent to a week's fluctuation in the U.S. job market, and would have to be balanced against the 200,000 or more jobs that NAFTA created that year.) And these claims were evidence not of economic distress, but of the existence of NAFTA-linked provisions for job-training compensation to people who are unemployed because of imports coming from or jobs moving to Mexico. There is, after all, no analogous program for people thrown out of work because of competition from China or Japan, and therefore no point of comparison.

What is more significant is that despite Mexico's rocky year, cross-border trade still surged ahead in 1994, creating jobs in both countries. That was a direct result of NAFTA's elimination of trade barriers. Yet it was logical and defensible for NAFTA critics to judge the success of the pact by charting variations in the trade balance, since that was the measure used by proponents to sell the pact. Now, with the peso devalued and the U.S. facing a deficit in its bilateral trade, the NAFTA lobby would seem to have some answering to do.

■ They could find some of those answers, paradoxically, in the peso crisis of December 1994, which dramatized precisely why NAFTA is so crucial for Mexico, and so strategically useful to the United States.

Even among NAFTA supporters the devaluation debacle has been mythologized in retrospect as an economic morality play, an object lesson in the evils of currency overvaluation, current account deficits, and "speculative" foreign capital. A subplot of this fable features American and Mexican officials deliberately inflating the peso just to ensure NAFTA's safe passage.

This indictment is wrong in its premises, and in almost all its particulars. The real mistake the Salinas regime made was to stanch an outflow of cash in 1994 with massive sales of short-term dollar-pegged bonds. This was reckless, a big and ultimately bad gamble. But the Salinas administration was right to try to avoid a sudden devaluation at all costs. The key to Mexico's long-term recovery was *and still is* building confidence in the peso at home and abroad. By late 1994, when a devaluation was clearly unavoidable—because inherently unpredictable political shocks and a narrowing interest-rate gap were chasing both Mexican and American money back to the United States—astute monetary management and prearranged international financial support could still have kept the peso from falling more than 20 percent. Not even the most zealous devaluationists proposed chopping the peso in half. There was nothing inevitable, and certainly nothing desirable, about the massive devaluation triggered on December 20, 1994.

One new NAFTA myth is that Mexico deliberately set out to court portfolio capital while spurning long-term direct investment. To the contrary: the entire NAFTA enterprise was designed as an enticement for the kind of direct investors who think in terms of decades. Once it was clear that the Salinas government was serious and that NAFTA was likely to be approved, the strategy began to work. During the three years of the NAFTA negotiations direct investment—most of it American—rose by nearly $15 billion, double the inflow of the previous three years.

Stock and bond funds poured in far faster, however. Mexican officials were going to take whatever investment they could get, but they were acutely aware of the volatile imbalance between highly liquid and fickle portfolio capital and long-term investments in fixed assets. Mechanisms used by Chile and some Asian countries to control similar investment surges—including quantitative limits and repatriation rules for stocks and bonds bought by foreigners—were rejected as both unenforceable in a U.S. border economy and antithetical to Mexico's quest for economic integration with North America. Not unreasonably, the Mexicans saw the solution as attracting more direct investment, not as chasing portfolio capital away. NAFTA was the way they intended to redress this imbalance.

A free trade agreement was only half the equation, however.

■ The Salinas government originally sought a trade pact with Washington because it needed foreign investment, and there were limits to what it could accomplish on its own. Mexico had already given investors the three things they need most: political stability, a growing market, and predictable, intelligently managed macroeconomic policies. But it could not unilaterally guarantee access to the U.S. market, or even the long-term survival of Salinas's economic reforms. NAFTA did both.

Trade treaties cannot prohibit rude surprises, however. The painful irony of 1994 was that with NAFTA safely in place, Mexico could suddenly provide neither political stability nor economic predictability.

Assassinations and armed uprisings had not been part of Mexican political life for half a century, but the events of 1994 showed that the government remained extraordinarily vulnerable to such violent shocks. Equally unnerving to investors was the strategic ineptitude displayed by Mexico's financial managers in the period leading up to the December 20 devaluation. One thing these Ivy League technocrats had done, their political opponents would have then readily conceded, was master the inner workings of a modern international economy. Yet in those crucial weeks they bungled both the technical challenges of currency crisis management and the even more critical tasks of communication and coordination with the international financial markets.

There were ironies within ironies. The new finance minister responsible for handling the peso problem was Jaime Serra Puche, the chief negotiator of the free trade agreement. Serra saw the finance ministry as the final stepping stone in a career-long quest for the presidency. But his reputation was destroyed in a fortnight because he flagrantly disregarded the rules of the new borderless economy that he himself had painstakingly engineered. In the old days of prideful autarky, Mexico could conduct its economic affairs behind closed doors. The finance minister convened key players in business and government and together they would plot their course and strike their deals. Outsiders—foreigners, political antagonists, ordinary Mexicans—would be informed in due time, at least in part, on a need-to-know basis.

After NAFTA this was no longer possible. Mexico wasn't autonomous any more. Wall Street was more important to the Mexico City Bolsa than

Monterrey. And, unlike Mexico's moneyed elite, the foreign investors who bought billions in Telmex ADRs through New York stockbrokers could afford to walk away. And walk away they did—with a vengeance.

■ Nothing mattered more to investors in Mexico than a sudden fall in the value of the currency. Yet Serra played his policy cards close to the vest, in the old PRI style, failing to forewarn allies at the U.S. Treasury and International Monetary Fund and refusing even to return the calls of foreign money managers who controlled billions in Mexican stock and bonds. The devaluation option was discussed by top officials with local labor and business leaders even as they issued steadfast denials of such plans. New York mutual fund managers listened nervously in early December to insider tales of savvy Mexican oligarchs moving hundreds of millions offshore. Yet they believed the reassurances of Mexican officials, largely because they had never been deliberately misled on such matters by the Salinas economic team. After NAFTA, they expected Mexican policymakers to be more forthcoming, not less. So when Serra suddenly volunteered on a local radio call-in show that the peso was being "adjusted," New York money managers were infuriated. They considered it a deliberate deception, a betrayal. They couldn't believe that Mexico City taxi drivers heard the news before Merrill Lynch did. They didn't care that Mexico's budget is balanced, that its banks and phone company are now privately owned, that oil dependence is a thing of the past. Irrationally or not, they withdrew foreign private money from Mexico en masse, making intervention with foreign public money unavoidable.

Within Mexico the devaluation was even more damaging. It is a rule of Mexican economics that peso devaluations are much more destructive than conventional analysis would suggest. Panic sales of the devalued peso drive its value down still further, accelerating inflation and scaring local savings into dollar havens across the border. The cheaper the peso gets, the more Mexicans wanted to sell them; the more pesos they sell, the less their remaining cash is worth. Smart money leaves quickly, then returns for undervalued bargains. Less smart money—more abundant in any society—leaves much later, much more expensively, and stays away for a long, long while.

This devastatingly self-perpetuating cycle kept Mexico impoverished for most of the 1980s. The Salinas team, anchored by Finance Minister Pedro Aspe and central bank president Miguel Mancera, had tried to break the pattern, keeping the peso strong, and fending off the pro-devaluation lobby of export manufacturers and IMF apparatchiks. Because of political shocks, rising U.S. interest rates, and Mexico's own policy errors, this strategy became unsustainable in late 1994.

This time, however, Mexico was working with a net: NAFTA. The trade accord gave solid guarantees to investors who would have worried about other economic policy reversals after a sudden devaluation. By the middle of 1995 foreign capital was flowing back into Mexico, despite an acute and deepening recession.

As critics correctly insisted, NAFTA was more an investment agreement than a trade agreement. It was designed to convince investors that Mexico was a safe place to do business. A paradoxical side-effect of the protracted NAFTA debate was that potential investors stayed away from Mexico; they weren't about to spend millions on a new factory until they knew exactly what the new rules were. The political upheavals of 1994 and the economic debacle of 1995 kept these investors on the sidelines. In that sense, NAFTA hasn't even started yet.

The Salinas Administration sought economic union with the United States because it foresaw the increasingly acute global competition for capital. Mexico badly needed private investment, in the tens of billions of dollars. So did scores of other emerging industrial nations. What distinguished Mexico from the rest of the developing world was its special relationship with the world's largest and richest economy. Yet its history of expropriations and debt troubles made Mexico unattractive to most U.S. investors. Mexican exporters, meanwhile, feared being shut out of the U.S. market through punitive tariffs or other barriers. Mexico needed to provide clear rules and guarantees to U.S. investors while securing permanent and privileged access to the U.S. market.

Ultimately, Mexico could prosper only by restoring the confidence *of the Mexicans themselves* in their own economy. From his days as economic czar in the De la Madrid administration, Salinas was intent on breaking the cycle that saw every recent presidency end with the peso shattered and money fleeing offshore. His strategy was built on two mutually reinforcing goals: reducing inflation and stabilizing the peso. The free-market opening to trade and investment codified by NAFTA could accomplish both these things through price competition from imports, and the influx of investment capital needed to pay for those imports. And it was working: the transition from the De la Madrid to the Salinas administration was marked by currency stability and economic policy continuity. The disadvantage of the Salinas strategy—that it made Mexico beholden to Wall Street—was also part of its appeal, in that it brought both huge cash reserves and the threat of market discipline to an economy that needed both. The unsentimental speed with which investors later yanked their money out of Mexico showed how ruthless that discipline could be.

■ Far from proving Perot right, the events of December 1994 gave us a taste of what would have happened if the Clinton administration had lost the battle for the North American Free Trade Agreement in November 1993.

If NAFTA had been defeated, the Mexican currency crash would have been instantaneous and far more severe. NAFTA kept the peso's slide from accelerating into a free fall. Without NAFTA, not only portfolio investors but most direct investors in Mexico—including Mexicans— would have sought safe refuge in dollar holdings. There would have been no assurances that Mexico would not halt or reverse its economic open- ing. Since this would have been a crisis directly triggered by Washington, it could have prompted a nationalistic backlash against further reliance on American capital and policy counsel. The Clinton administration, mean- while, would hardly have been able to justify a $20 billion bailout to a Congress that had just rejected the entire concept of a special economic relationship with Mexico. (In January 1994 the administration didn't dare subject the emergency loan package to a vote in Congress even with NAFTA in place, and six months later a majority of the House went on record opposing further such aid to Mexico.)

The response to the peso crash dramatized anew how the Mexican and U.S. economies have become inextricably intertwined. This interdepen- dence is not new, but the market opening encoded in NAFTA multiplied our cross-border connections and made them both more binding and more visible.

The Mexican debt crisis of 1982 posed a far more acute threat to the U.S. economy: Leading American banks faced a real risk of insolvency, and the possible repudiation of debts by Mexico and other third world borrow- ers would have destabilized the entire international financial system. Yet it was a crisis that could be (and was) managed by fifty men in suits in a Manhattan board room. This time the cast of characters numbered in the thousands. The U.S. Treasury was forced to intervene, massively, not just to keep Mexico from sliding into default on dollar debts, but to protect the Big Three carmakers, the new industrial corridors of Texas, and the Middle America mega-investors who had bet big on Mexican stocks and bonds.

Nervously watching the rescue efforts were tens of thousands of mom-and-pop stockholders who had turned Telmex into the Ma Bell of the 1990s. Few of them would have known the name of Mexico's president a decade earlier; now many wished they never had.

The political dynamics had also changed. The NAFTA battle left the White House and pro-NAFTA Congressional leaders with a vested interest in Mexican economic success. NAFTA's opponents, though seemingly vindicated by Mexico's distress, had no desire for a deeper crisis, since they too saw that depression in Mexico would mean recession in cities and industries throughout in the United States.

Critics charged that the Clinton administration was bailing out Wall Street. This was unquestionably true. But it was also bailing out Main Street. A collapsing peso threatened not only the financial markets but hundreds of thousands of American manufacturing jobs.

And the damage would not have been confined to Mexico. The spillover when the peso first went skidding south—what money traders sardonically termed the "tequila effect"—affected not just the cruzado and the quetzal, but the zloty and the bhat. Without American financial intervention in Mexico, the domino effect of collapsing currencies throughout the developing world would have put a swift end to global American export growth.

This, again, was fallout from the free trade pact. NAFTA represented a radical policy reversal by a repentant former exponent of economic nationalism, plus an equally radical U.S. commitment to reciprocate with open market access and capital. This was seen instantly around the world as a viable new development model. The NAFTA negotiators made the third world safe for bond salesmen: Mexico became the locomotive pulling a whole string of developing nations onto the trading floors of New York and London.

Private capital flows into developing nations nearly trebled between 1990 and 1993, as it seemed that country after country was converting to free-market economics. Mexico was the biggest single beneficiary, but this historic policy shift was transforming most of Latin America, most of the former Soviet bloc, and many poorer Asian nations that had only recently industrialized. The assumption was that capitalist virtue would be rewarded with cash. Now, however, if Washington abandoned Mexico in its first post-NAFTA crisis, that implicit bargain was off. Foreign capital would stampede out of all these fragile markets, and local policy makers would be tempted to reimpose tariff barriers and exchange controls. And the United States would lose critical ground in its newest and fastest-growing markets. The U.S.-I.M.F. $50 billion rescue package of early 1995 was essential; if it had been assembled faster, though, it would have been both cheaper and more effective.

The only redeeming aspect of the peso disaster was the marginal enhanced competitiveness of labor-intensive Mexican export industries. Without NAFTA, even that advantage would have been lost. The free trade pact gives Mexico assured access to the all-important U.S. market—a market where most of Mexico's competition comes not from North America, but from exporters in Asia and Latin America. Factoring in Mexico's newly reduced labor costs, NAFTA's competitive edge may prove decisive. The peso devaluation accelerated the NAFTA-induced relocation of labor-intensive export manufacturing from Asia to Mexico, a trend that is beneficial to the United States as well. With Mexican assets suddenly cheaper in dollar terms, the devaluation also encouraged needed investment in tourism, real estate development, and natural resource industries.

Still, the effects of devaluation on post-NAFTA investment were overwhelmingly negative. Foreign investors will come to Mexico when they see it as a solid, growing market; the world is awash with cheap export platforms, and Mexico can never compete with Asia on wages. Mexico's domestic market is now paralyzed, with few prospects for quick revival, and its government is again considered ingrown and erratic. The kind of investment that a cheap peso typically attracts is not the kind that Mexico needs: it is predicated on low-paid unskilled labor, and does nothing to turn Mexico into a competitive industrial society. Mexican industrialists had been noisily urging devaluations for years, because it always seems easier to compete on cost than on quality. The Salinas administration wisely resisted—and manufactured exports still climbed by a remarkable 20 percent or more yearly. More importantly, the most successful exporters were the most technologically advanced. Now Mexico may revert to the low-tech *maquiladora* model, competing with Haiti and Bangladesh instead of Spain and South Korea. Disturbingly, *maquiladora* employment was rising quickly in 1995, when unemployment elsewhere grew more acute. Most of the export growth of which Mexico boasted after the peso crash was from this quick-turnaround border reassembly trade. This is precisely the fate NAFTA was intended to help Mexico avoid.

■   But there is one unquestionably positive outcome of the peso devaluation. We are now witnessing the withering away of the PRI, and NAFTA is speeding its demise. The transition to a new democratic Mexico is now unstoppable. This is the most profound effect of the free trade pact, and the most surprising.

Of the many arguments against NAFTA the most cogent was the case made by many Mexican opposition activists: that it would artificially prop up a decadent political monopoly, delaying democratic reform and ultimately making it harder for Mexico to modernize. This presumed that NAFTA would in fact spur economic growth and that the PRI would reap the rewards. Many students of Mexico (like their counterparts in Asia) saw democracy and economic dynamism as diverging choices, not mutually reinforcing goals. Even if that were true, it was hardly smart geopolitics for the United States to provoke an economic crisis in a friendly bordering nation on the off chance that it might accelerate the emergence of pluralism. Besides, business interests were more interested in stability than democracy. And many Mexicans who loathed the PRI were not ready to make the great leap of faith and vote in an opposition government of untested and largely unknown amateurs.

Now, however, such a leap seems like the only way to escape disaster. The present government's political incompetence and direct culpability for the current economic disaster has created a national consensus for change. Every state election now is bitterly contested, and the PRI under Zedillo is too weak and too closely watched to brazenly steal what it cannot cleanly win. By the midterm elections of 1997, nearly half of Mexico may be living under opposition state or municipal rule—a dramatic turnaround for a country that didn't have a single opposition governor until 1989. And by the presidential election of 2000, the PRI's opposition will for the first time in its history be able to field a slate of experienced politicians with strong local constituencies and national name recognition. With NAFTA's trilateral guarantees firmly in place, a change of government is no longer worrisome to investors. The descent may be turbulent, but the PRI is finally coming in for a soft democratic landing.

This was not the script NAFTA's architects had in mind. They had looked forward to 1994 as the year of free trade and of Luis Donaldo Colosio's long march to the presidency. José Angel Gurría, the debt negotiator who later became Zedillo's foreign minister, reminded a group of Japanese executives in December 1993 that the Salinas inner circle had already been running Mexico for twelve years. Gurría expansively assured them that he and his colleagues would stay in power for at least twelve more. Not only was the PRI's triumph a foregone conclusion in 1994,

Gurría promised, but in the year 2000 as well, when the next president would also emerge from the cabinet. "Continuity in economic policy for 24 years ought to give you confidence," he said, "even for you Japanese, who tend to views things over such a long term."

Gurría's confidence sounds a bit ludicrous in retrospect, but it was rational enough at the time. Mexico was finally emerging from a decade of zero growth. The central bank held a record $26 billion in foreign reserves, more than enough to keep the peso aloft during the minor turbulence of an election campaign. With the passage of NAFTA one month earlier, the single great uncertainty about Mexico's economic future had been triumphantly resolved. Investment was surging, and the opposition remained conveniently fractured between right and left. The great 1988 threat, Cuauhtémoc Cárdenas, never a dynamic campaigner, seemed weary and wooden and out of ideas. The old confessionalist right, represented by the National Action Party, appeared uninterested in a real run for power now that Salinas had enacted most of its program. The PRI had never lost an election. And Colosio, the hand-picked heir, was beginning to emerge from Salinas's long shadow.

Chiapas ended all that. The presidential campaign was knocked off the front pages by the rebel forces led by *Subcomandante* Marcos, whose ski-masked visage was not the face Mexico had hoped to present to the world in 1994. Even secondary characters in the Chiapas drama became more compelling public figures than Colosio and his rivals. (First among them was Salinas's designated negotiator and former everything Manuel Camacho, Colosio's theoretically vanquished PRI rival, who courted dissidents and still openly pined for the presidency.) The Chiapas confrontation was the surprise first act in a national drama that would turn the election into a sideshow.

Objectively, the insurgency was a joke: a ragtag band of post-Marxist rebels seizing control of a few Maya villages and declaring "war" on the Salinas government. With their wooden rifles and green recruits, the self-styled Zapatista National Liberation Army never had a prayer of controlling the Chiapas highlands, much less of posing a military threat to the central government. (And for all their vaunted sophistication, they would have destroyed NAFTA, their avowed target, if they had staged their uprising just three months earlier.) But the Zapatistas punctured the hubris of the PRI technocracy like expert marksmen. They forced Mexico City to acknowledge that the Salinas industrial revolution was leaving the rural poor behind. At the very instant that Mexicans officially became

North Americans, they had resurrected the defiantly Mesoamerican mythos of Zapata and Sandino.

The lightly armed insurgents became instant folk heroes, delighting Mexico City intellectuals and Tijuana street kids alike as they outwitted government negotiators and held the system hostage to its own revolutionary rhetoric. With the help of a surprisingly cooperative press corps, the Zapatistas became the standard-bearers of popular resentment against the PRI elite. For all the talk (from people like me) of the long-term democratizing benefits of freer trade, it took the shock of an armed challenge to force the PRI a few more begrudging steps towards political reform. Within one month the Zapatistas had forced concessions out of the government that the democratic opposition had been unable to achieve in ten years of electoral battles and peaceful street protests. The PRI agreed to stricter limits on campaign spending and independent scrutiny of election returns. Salinas, after initially opting for a ham-handed counterinsurgency response, was forced to restrain the military and their hard-line supporters within his increasingly unstable coalition. (Fidel Velázquez, the apparently immortal PRI labor patriarch, wanted the rebels "exterminated.") Salinas had to replace his strong-armed state security chief with Jorge Carpizo, a respected former attorney general and human rights ombudsman. The government even vowed to honor the Zapatista demand for more balanced television election coverage—an extraordinary acknowledgment of its control over private broadcasting and systemic refusal to let the opposition take its case to the country.

The Chiapas uprising also exposed how NAFTA had fundamentally changed Mexico's relationship with the United States. Wall Street investors pulled funds out of the Mexico City Bolsa when the rebellion first erupted and the government seemed poised for an army-led crackdown. As the Mexican exchange plummeted, Salinas switched strategies and sought to negotiate. When talks started and the fighting stopped, much of the money flowed back in: fund managers abhor instability above all.

But in 1994, instability would prove the order of the day. Money fled anew following the March murder of PRI candidate Colosio, the first such political assassination since the ruling party consolidated its power six decades earlier. The murder exposed the vacuum of power at the top of the PRI pyramid, and the pathological corruption of the country's criminal justice system. With his hand-picked heir dead and other contenders ineligible, President Salinas was forced to pick a far weaker candidate as the PRI standard-bearer. (To preclude internecine electoral challenges, sitting cabinet members cannot become candidates once the campaign is under way; Ernesto Zedillo had resigned his ministerial post months before to work on Colosio's campaign.)

Zedillo, the politically clumsy technocrat that Salinas was once incorrectly assumed to be, became an accidental president in a system that loathes surprises.

In a curious way, NAFTA helped legitimize Zedillo as a candidate and as a president. Unprecedented U.S. scrutiny of the 1994 presidential election focused overdue attention on the enormous advantages—slavishly favorable television coverage, total control of public works spending—that had sustained the PRI in power for 65 years. Because this spotlight made brazen fraud impossible, Zedillo's 50-percent victory was far more convincing than Salinas's identical claimed margin six years earlier.

With the August election behind them, the PRI hierarchy and the financial markets were enjoying a rare and heartening calm. Funds were returning, the peso strengthening. NAFTA was working.

Then came a new shock: the assassination of the new PRI majority leader and close Salinas associate, José Francisco Ruiz Massieu. Airbrushed after his death into a democratic reformer, Ruiz Massieu was (as noted in the chapter "Lead or Silver") a hard-edged power broker determined to preserve the PRI's franchise. His brother's sensational accusation that the murder was an internal PRI plot shook the country further. Even more fantastic and disruptive was the subsequent charge by the Zedillo government that the murder's mastermind was the former president's own brother, Raúl Salinas, and that both Carlos Salinas and Ruiz Massieu's brother connived to cover up this extraordinary fact. If nothing else, this was a soap opera of epic proportions, revealing the PRI's *familia política* to be even more rapacious and inbred than its critics had dared suggest, and making the Salinas regime in retrospect seem more a product of Palermo than Cambridge. The Ruiz Massieu assassination scandal directly precipitated the peso crash of December. More important than the political drama, though, was the fact that at every stage of this unfolding crisis, Mexican leaders had to take into close account the reactions of Washington, and New York, and Dallas, and Los Angeles.

Mexico had been dependent on U.S. trade and investment for decades before NAFTA. The fundamental change in the relationship since NAFTA was not economic but political. In 1994 Wall Street put Mexico's central bank on notice that it had lost its autonomy. Many powerful U.S. investors were vocal in their disappointment about the Zedillo cabinet—they wanted their confidant, Pedro Aspe, to retain control of the treasury. The fear that NAFTA would be revoked by the U.S. Congress—as it has the power to do, and as several powerful Congressmen threatened to do during the Chiapas uprising—was another new and unaccustomed constraint on Mexican presidential power. So was post-NAFTA scrutiny by American media and by grass-roots labor and environmental activists. (Human rights abuses in Chiapas sparked protests at Mexican consulates in New York and Los Angeles and Chicago by Mexican-American demonstrators, a warning that Mexico would have to revisit naive assumptions that it could one day wield indirect power in Washington as an ethnic voting bloc.)

Despite their own second and third thoughts, Mexicans had become North Americans after NAFTA. Cross-border economic integration is irreversible. So is cross-border political influence. The Cardenista opposition, sublimating its reflexive nationalism, invited U.S. and Canadian monitors to observe the 1994 election, and has tightened ties since with its anti-NAFTA partners in the U.S. labor and environmental movements. The biggest opposition group, the conservative National Action Party, is forging new bonds with Sunbelt Republicans. The PRI itself, by engineering NAFTA's passage, cemented its own alliance with American business interests and U.S. foreign policy mandarins.

Part of the PRI's bargain was the promise of democratic reform: This pledge was made implicitly by Salinas and his emissaries in innumerable speeches throughout the NAFTA debate, and explicitly by NAFTA's defenders in the White House. Zedillo's declared intent to democratize and instill respect for the rule of law is now a new unwritten codicil to the NAFTA contract. Enforcement will be up to Mexican and American public opinion. It will be fascinating (to use a Perot word) to see how many of the energetically engaged U.S. critics and defenders of NAFTA remain committed to monitoring Mexico's political and economic progress.

The great fault line of the NAFTA debate in the United States divided those who saw the Mexican and American economies as complementary and those who considered them inherently antagonistic. Almost every NAFTA argument flowed naturally from one of these two positions. If the bilateral relationship is fundamentally adversarial, then NAFTA had to be viewed that way, with one side winning and the other losing. If the two economies are a natural fit, however, then free trade is collaborative, not competitive, and both sides benefit.

This book is a brief for the latter analysis. The United States has much to gain from a developed, industrialized Mexico. Despite the setbacks of 1994 and 1995, the North American Free Trade Agreement will help speed that transformation. It was essential during the NAFTA debate to expose the myths and half-truths that obscured the agreement's historic importance. That was the original goal of this book, and it is even more important now.

William A. Orme, Jr.
July, 1995
New York City

UNDERSTANDING NAFTA

CHAPTER 1

Overview: NAFTA Myths and Misconceptions

To be "for" or "against" freer trade in North America is like being for or against the weather. With or without NAFTA, the continent's economic integration was fast becoming a reality. The North American Free Trade Agreement clarifies how this integration will proceed, at what pace, and for whose benefit. Ultimately, NAFTA should help Mexico become a fully industrialized country. But NAFTA did not determine whether or not the U.S. and Mexican economies would become more deeply intertwined. That process was already well under way, and it cannot be reversed.

In a dense thicket of lawyerly prose, ridden with caveats and codicils, NAFTA sets the ground rules by which cross-border trade would be liberalized. Within 10 years, nearly all restrictions on manufacturing trade will be removed. After 15 years, the last tariffs and quotas on agricultural goods will disappear.

But NAFTA does more than strike down barriers to the movement of goods and services: it commits Mexico to a deepening of its free-market investment policies. By staking so much of its future on a trade agreement with its powerful neighbor to the north, Mexico has consciously rejected a legacy of autarchy and populism. It knows that it must compete in the world economy, and it wants to do so as an integral part of North America. This, in turn, has forced it to address deep flaws in its economic and political systems—problems that transcend the formal agenda of the free trade agreement.

Even more significant, Mexico is ending a long chapter of proud and defiant nationalism. Entering into an economic concordat with the immensely powerful neighbor that once stole half its territory and that has only sporadically seemed to accept its independence is a dramatic event. From Mexico's vantage point, as from Canada's, NAFTA marks the foundation of a common market in which it can never be more than a secondary power. That Mexico has taken such a step at all shows great confidence in its own political cohesion and cultural resilience.

By codifying the Salinas economic liberalization program, NAFTA gives American companies privileged access to the fast-growing Mexican market. As a practical matter, NAFTA makes these reforms irreversible. No future Mexican government is likely to risk the confrontation with Washington that a return to protectionism would entail.

Yet what is driving this process is not U.S. trade policy, but domestic Mexican economic policy. The dramatic liberalization that Mexico started a decade ago had already made the country attractive to foreign manufacturers—even without NAFTA. The Salinas government (and its successor) would surely have continued down this pro-business path—regardless of how NAFTA was ultimately disposed. Privatization will shear off big chunks of the state energy monopolies and open ports, railroads and the media to direct foreign investment. Deregulation, tough fiscal policies, and linkage with foreign capital markets should stabilize the currency and speed the flow of credit to private business. Trade growth and the decentralization of investment decisions will spur new cross-border economic alliances from Baja to the Yucatan, forcing local improvements in physical infrastructure and health and education services. A new foreign investment law will put in statute form the exemptions and presidential decrees that have already allowed these changes.

What NAFTA adds to this process is the predictability of a negotiated tariff reduction schedule, a guaranteed edge for American companies in the Mexican market, and the fire-breathing vigilance of Washington trade lawyers.

Without NAFTA, Mexico would probably have pursued most of this agenda—without, of course, giving preferential access to American companies. But NAFTA's rejection would have set Mexico back hard. NAFTA's defeat would have provoked capital flight, weakening the peso and pushing Mexico back in the direction of a low-wage, export-assembly strategy. And that, in turn, would have left little margin for enforcing strict environmental and workplace safety rules. The dangers of protectionist measures on both sides of the border would have discouraged trade and investment.

In concept, NAFTA is both simple and—from an American stand-point—seemingly unobjectionable. Mexico agrees to do almost every-thing of an economic nature that the United States ever wanted it to do. In return it gets reciprocal access to the American market, plus the steady influx of outside capital that the imprimatur of a trade treaty with Washington virtually guarantees.

That extra cash is crucial. It's the difference between a Mexico perpetu-ally dependent on low-wage assembly jobs and a Mexico able to develop its own markets and skills. It's the difference between economic growth that barely keeps pace with population and a sustained expansion that would propel Mexico into the first rank of newly industrializing nations. It's the difference, over time, between South Korea and the Philippines, between Spain and Morocco. And it's the key to Salinas's professed ambition to lead Mexico out of the third world and into the first.

The money that NAFTA "adds" to Mexico will only rarely be "sub-tracted" from the American economy—for the simple reason that little of this money would otherwise be invested in the United States. Yet much of the political opposition to NAFTA stemmed from just this sort of fixed-pie picture of how the economy works: if American money is invested in Mexico, it must be money that has been stripped out of the American economy. If jobs are being created by American employers in Mexico, they must be jobs that have been taken from Americans in Detroit, Cleveland or Minneapolis. If Mexico raises its standard of living, it must be because the United States has grown poorer.

Little orthodoxies of this sort littered the NAFTA debate. And in the hands of political barn burners like Ross Perot, they made it extremely difficult for ordinary Americans to sort through the conflicting claims and counterclaims and make up their own minds about what NAFTA might mean for America's future. Through the efforts of NAFTA oppo-nents, millions of Americans were persuaded that a prosperous Mexico would be a direct threat to their jobs and incomes.

This is simply wrong: NAFTA makes Mexican manufacturing an integral part of North American industry, not a rapacious competitor. Indeed, NAFTA neatly fits the accepted wisdom for coping with East Asian competition: it calls for investing to maximize economies of scale, for planning for the next decade instead of the next quarter, for replacing low-wage sunset industries with high-tech sunrise industries.

NAFTA critics labored hard to persuade Congress and the public that American negotiators were outdone by crafty Mexicans who better un-derstood the needs of their own economy. Since Americans have a natural predisposition to think the worst of their public officials, this may not have been so difficult. But it wildly misrepresents the substance of NAFTA.

Consider the example of the Mexican oil industry. Critics argued that Mexico's zealous protection of its state oil monopoly kept petroleum off the negotiating table. Yet no part of NAFTA is ultimately of greater benefit to the United States than the provisions affecting investment in Mexican oil development.

The oil majors have grumpily lamented Washington's failure to end Mexico's state control of its oil reserves, and Mexican negotiators have proclaimed triumphantly that they beat back American demands to privatize Pemex, the state oil monopoly. Yet what really matters is Mexico's long-term viability as an American oil supplier. And on that score, NAFTA succeeds—giving Mexico the money and technology it needs to keep production running ahead of domestic demand. Before NAFTA, the Mexican energy business was closed to American investors. Now the door is open—in petrochemicals, drilling contracts, natural gas supplies, power plant construction, and other potentially lucrative areas.

NAFTA virtually guarantees billions of dollars of new business for the American oil service and refining industries, which are based not far from Mexico's Gulf Coast oil fields. Without NAFTA, Mexico might have run out of exportable oil by the end of the decade. With NAFTA, the United States should be able to rely on its closest, most stable major oil supplier for many years more, avoiding increased dependence on the Persian Gulf and diminishing the attendant risks of another oil war.

Not bad for a negotiating "failure."

■ NAFTA is a blueprint for the more efficient reordering of industrial production on a continental scale. Granted, this requires some initial pain and disruption—mostly in Mexico, but also in vulnerable regions and industries north of the border. But much of this dislocation is inevitable in response to global economic competition and change.

NAFTA directs more American overseas investment toward Mexico. In Mexico, these funds will be recycled in the form of spending by Mexican consumers and businesses on largely American goods (something that doesn't happen to American funds invested in East Asia). Over time, this concentrated investment will make Mexico grow richer faster— and become an even better market for American exports. Without NAFTA, these funds—portfolio investments in stocks and bonds as well as direct manufacturing investment—would have continued to be dispersed almost randomly across the globe. (There is currently about $500 billion in U.S. overseas investment; Mexico receives about 5 percent.)

But U.S. officials did not make this argument. (It implies that the trade game has "losers" as well as "winners.") Nor did the Bush or Clinton Administrations exploit one of the most persuasive arguments for NAFTA: that it's North America's belated response to the consolidation of the European Union and regional production-sharing arrangements in East Asia. (That would have meant admitting that the United States is now doing what it has long chided its trading partners for doing.) Nor would American officials have openly said that Mexico is a special case. (Such candor might have offended sensibilities in Latin America's southern hemisphere.)

Yet Mexico plainly is a special case: even without NAFTA, it would be more closely linked to the United States—economically, culturally, demographically—than any other country except Canada. Unfortunately, making that argument means admitting that NAFTA is the precursor of a North American common market—which all three governments steadfastly deny.

For decades America has wanted Mexico to lift import barriers, stabilize its currency, scale back state industry, deregulate private business, and allow more extensive foreign investment. Under Salinas, Mexico has begun to do all of this unilaterally. But there were things Mexico could not do on its own. It needed U.S. assistance to reduce and restructure its debt. And it needed a bilateral trade treaty to guarantee continuing access to the American market and to assure investors that Mexico would not suddenly abandon its new reforms in the future.

The real problem with NAFTA is that it doesn't offer instant gratification. The benefits accruing to the United States will be largely a byproduct of Mexican prosperity and will not be felt fully for 20 to 30 years.

In the meantime, there are all those problems in Mexico that NAFTA's critics rightly pointed out. Water pollution and toxic waste along Mexico's northern border show the dangers of unchecked industrial growth and lax environmental controls. Although it keeps promising change, Mexico's ruling party maintains a chokehold on business, labor, the media, and the mechanics of elections. And then there is the ostensibly free-market economy, where entire industries are controlled by de facto monopolies and where the stock market is plagued by insider trading.

NAFTA's opponents forced these issues onto the Mexican agenda, and they deserve credit for speeding the pace of reform and for broadening the scope of the entire NAFTA enterprise. American criticism of

Mexico may have created diplomatic friction, but it also led to a more open market economy and a freer political system, changes that many Mexicans welcomed.

Nevertheless, in virtually every particular—environmental enforcement, labor conditions, democratic processes—Mexico's problems would have gotten worse if NAFTA had been defeated and will be easier to mend now that NAFTA has been passed.

Private sector NAFTA proponents—especially those on Mexico's payroll—rarely made that critical argument. That's because they were reluctant to acknowledge the authoritarian nature of Mexico's political system, the grotesque concentration of wealth that accompanied the Salinas economic reforms, the willful past flouting of environmental laws, the subversion of inflation controls to crush independent unions. Few of NAFTA's business defenders conceded that there were grave environmental and labor problems in the border maquiladora belt.

NAFTA's many critics forged a formidable coalition, reflecting both cynicism and idealism. Mexicans fighting for democracy and human rights found themselves working alongside "Paco-bashing" nativists who detest immigration and doubt the Mexicans' capacity for self-government. Union leaders and conservationists stood shoulder-to-shoulder with sugarcane growers, who have the most wretched environmental and labor records in American agriculture. Even the self-styled "consumer lobby" found itself opposing a pact that would lower consumer prices.

But there was something else driving the anti-NAFTA coalition: the inchoate yearnings of the American left for an alliance of mainstream labor, environmentalists, civil rights activists, populist farmers, human rights advocates, and the other splintered fragments of a broken movement. The left's search for a new post–Cold War agenda had bogged down in a general distrust of big business and a growing sense that American wages would increasingly be set by the international marketplace.

Then came NAFTA, which (to their eyes) combined the worst aspects of laissez-faire Republicanism with global capital mobility. Mexico was made a scapegoat for America's economic ills. For the formerly internationalist American left, anti-NAFTA-ism became the new anti-anti-Communism: a unifying ideology rooted in a personalized opposition to their adversaries, rather than in a coherent alternative vision of the future.

Critics didn't need to show that NAFTA itself was bad, merely that real problems existed and that NAFTA advocates seemed indifferent to those problems. This enabled them to sidestep the contradictions in their own coalition, which ranged from advocates of tougher environmental and labor laws to fierce opponents of such regulations. And so we had the curious spectacle of the American left providing foot soldiers for a crusade financed in part by the very sort of union-busting business combines they would normally have abhorred, fronted and led by a right-wing Texas billionaire. One might fairly ask: who was using whom?

■ From its inception, NAFTA suffered an identity crisis: was it a foreign policy initiative, a domestic jobs program, a border rehabilitation project, a pre-emptive strike in coming global trade wars, an attempt to halt Mexican immigration? NAFTA advocates variously promoted it as all these things.

The academic reports often seemed confusing and contradictory. Proponents pointed to studies claiming that NAFTA would expand trade and increase jobs in all three economies. Critics countered with studies of their own, arguing that the agreement would move manufacturing jobs from the United States to Mexico, drive down wages in the United States, and perpetuate the exploitation of unskilled labor in Mexico. Some trade analysts saw NAFTA as a way for North America to meet the challenge of Japanese competition; others said it would simply turn Mexico into a duty-free assembler of East Asian consumer imports.

The Bush Administration called NAFTA the first step toward a hemispheric common market—a goal which was applauded by some economists and criticized by others, but which again raised questions that were seldom answered. Would Canada and Mexico lose their relative advantages under such a scheme? Would the Europeans and Asians retaliate with new regional trade strictures of their own?

Cynics concluded that NAFTA's real objective was the exploitation of a cheap and convenient labor market. The Mulroney, Salinas and Bush regimes seemed to be ideological soulmates, united in opposition to organized labor, unconcerned about gaps in social-welfare safety nets, and dedicated above all to the freest possible movement of capital. Making matters worse, NAFTA owed its political life to Ronald Reagan, the first major American politician to propose it. That in itself guaranteed some persistent liberal hostility.

Even the name was misleading. The North American Free Trade Agreement is neither "North American"—in the sense of a genuinely trilateral endeavor—nor simply a "free trade agreement," inasmuch as the elimination of formal trade barriers was never the central purpose of the pact. What distinguishes NAFTA from the U.S.-Canadian free trade accord, obviously and dramatically, is Mexico. And what distinguishes NAFTA from all trade pacts before it is the attempt to regulate the domestic investment policies of a developing country through a pact with an industrial superpower. NAFTA extends industrial North America southward into the poorest and most protected economy on the continent. This, and the radical reshaping of the entire U.S.-Mexican relationship that it implies, is what makes NAFTA a genuinely historic accomplishment.

For that reason, Canada is discussed in this book only in passing. Though an essential part of the NAFTA triangle, it is ultimately a bystander to the North-South rapprochement that NAFTA represents. The St. Lawrence River, culturally and economically, is in no way equivalent to the Rio Grande. Americans didn't need to overcome ethnocentrism or fears of dollar-an-hour labor to sign a trade pact with Canada. A few provisions of the U.S.-Canadian agreement would have been simplified by NAFTA; others would have been liberalized further. Overall, however, the status of U.S.-Canadian commerce—already largely free, and representing fully a fifth of American global trade—will be little altered.

NAFTA—it cannot be said too often—is about Mexico. For Mexico, NAFTA is the difference between a higher-tech development strategy and the low-wage export assembly route it was forced to take in the debt-strapped 1980s. North of the border, the lasting benefits of NAFTA will be the indirect results of those changes in Mexico. Over time, in almost every instance, what's good for Mexico will also be good for the United States. NAFTA's ratification means that Mexico and the United States have independently recognized that fact. For the United States, treating Mexico as an equal and an asset is as revolutionary a concept as Mexico treating the United States as a reliable ally.

NAFTA Myths

Separating the facts about NAFTA from the fables of its enemies and friends is a first step toward a rational discussion of the NAFTA plan. This is no small chore: few public issues were engulfed in as much misinformation and utter nonsense as NAFTA. Herewith, then, a brief tour through just 25 of the most common NAFTA myths and misconceptions:

NAFTA creates the world's biggest and richest market—a $6 trillion market of 360 million consumers.

Journalists, NAFTA advocates, and even presidents uncritically recited this USTR mantra for the past three years. But NAFTA won't create a $6 trillion market. That already happened in 1990: the United States ($5.4 trillion in gross domestic product) plus Canada ($600 billion). More careful NAFTA boosters touted a $6.2 trillion market, but avoided noting that Mexico is the "point two." (Mexico's GDP has since grown past $300 billion, making it equal to an Ohio, or half a Canada.)

NAFTA makes the North American giant taller, but by just a few inches. Still, it can't be denied that NAFTA makes North America the biggest and most formidable of the new trading blocs.

It can be denied. Portraying NAFTA as a new colossus may be comforting to those steeled for post-Gatt interregional trade wars. But size alone doesn't matter that much. And even if it did, North America isn't the behemoth some people seem to think.

Our most tenacious competitor, Japan, has been spectacularly successful within and against the North American market while remaining little more than half North America's size. With its web of trade and investment networks in South Korea, Taiwan, Hong Kong, and the new Southeast Asian Free Trade Area (Indonesia, the Philippines, Malaysia, Thailand, Singapore, Brunei), Tokyo already presides over a de facto bloc with more people and manufacturing muscle than NAFTA has created. But this region is far from a unified trading zone. And with U.S. economic and military power counterbalancing Japanese influence throughout East Asia, a united Asian market remains unlikely for the foreseeable future.

A better comparison is with the European Union. In 1990, the combined gross domestic product of the 12 EC countries was $6.015 trillion. Growth and the absorption of East Germany have since pushed it past $6.3 trillion. Economically, then, North America and the EC are about the same size.

Population is a less relevant measure, but again the figures are close. North America has even more people than NAFTA boosters gave it credit for: by most independent counts Mexico's population recently passed the 90 million mark, pushing the tri-country total to nearly 370 million. About 345 million people live in the European Union.

The Europeans, on average, are wealthier, with a per capita GDP in 1990 of $18,365. With low-income Mexico diluting the mix, the per capita gross product of North America in 1990 was about $17,000. The difference is marginal, though, and would be quickly reversed by a strengthening of the dollar.

A tie, then. But not quite. When the European Union achieved economic union at the end of 1992, it was also absorbing the affluent European Free Trade Association: Sweden, Norway, Finland, Iceland, Austria, Switzerland and Liechtenstein. The EFTA Seven added 33 million people and an aggregate $900 billion economy to the wider Western European market. EFTA's free trade deal with the EC Twelve—creating the "European Economic Area"—will be consummated more quickly than will Mexico's phased entry into NAFTA. So Brussels already presides over a $7.2 trillion market with nearly 380 million consumers. And that isn't counting the EC's potential expansion into the post-Comecon East.

Exaggerating the scale of the North American trade area isn't just sloppy math. It slyly implies that we are gearing up for a global trade war, and, worse, that North America would easily prevail in such a conflict. That's quite wrong: NAFTA offers about the same incremental enhancement of North America's competitiveness that Scandinavia gives to Europe: it's an edge, perhaps, but hardly decisive.

Negotiated and championed by a Republican White House, NAFTA reflects a clear ideological preference for market forces over industrial policy, for free trade over managed trade. This puts NAFTA at philosophical odds with the more interventionist, fair-trade–oriented Clinton Administration.

This common formulation has it exactly backwards: if you like industrial policy, you should love NAFTA.

The North American free trade agreement unabashedly picks winners and losers—but on a generally rational basis, with more competitive, high-wage American industries favored over businesses dependent on subsidies or cheap labor. U.S. negotiators agreed to phase out protection for the labor-intensive apparel business, for example, but insisted on rules forcing Mexican garment-makers to buy their fabric from the capital-intensive American textile industry. NAFTA lets Mexico dominate much of the low-end glassware market in North America, but technologically advanced glass products throughout the continent will be supplied largely by the United States. NAFTA sets up Mexico as a competitive producer of light trucks, a strategy by Detroit's Big Three— who dictated most of NAFTA's auto industry rules—to regain a market largely lost to small Japanese pickups. In agriculture, Washington favored its grain growers, pressing for an end to Mexican subsidies and import limits on corn and beans; it sacrificed sugar and citrus producers, who would gradually face open competition for the first time.

NAFTA is filled with these calculated trade-offs. Even within highly specific import categories, such as steel pipe or cut flowers, some products will be immediately subjected to the full competitive force of duty-free trade, while others will be weaned from protection more gradually, with phase-in periods of five or 10 years. True, all of NAFTA's provisions are ultimately transitional: after 15 years for sensitive farm products and 10 years for almost everything else, trade and investment will be largely barrier free. But the terms of the transition could determine which industries will survive when North America's last trade barriers come down.

NAFTA's insistence on reciprocity, moreover, puts into practice the fair-trade argument that liberalization shouldn't be an end in itself, but a tool to force open markets. America's trade negotiators are horse traders, not free traders.

NAFTA isn't the trade-diverting mechanism some Asian and European critics make it out to be; its provisions are scrupulously "Gatt-legal," meaning that NAFTA doesn't impose new barriers on goods and investments from outside North America.

Partly true, but wholly irrelevant. There are several NAFTA provisions that might not survive formal Gatt review, but neither Tokyo nor Brussels is eager to put them to that diplomatically treacherous test. Yet even if NAFTA were written in the most impeccable Gatt-ese, its technical compliance with international norms is beside the point. The real issue is how NAFTA affects the price and availability of goods in the North American market.

Trade blocs are designed to divert investment and trade to the benefit of members and the detriment of outsiders. If NAFTA works as planned, widgets from the Yukon, Yonkers and the Yucatan should start displacing widgets from Tokyo, Toulouse and Taipei. With its strict rules of origin, NAFTA doesn't need to impose new tariffs on third-party goods; price competition is a better barrier. Indeed, if an Asian widget baron paying 5 percent duties were matching the American wholesale price of a Mexican widget tycoon paying no duties at all, the Asian would probably be hit with a dumping suit.

The widget trade, however, wouldn't be diverted nearly as much as will trade in the two products with the stiffest NAFTA content rules: textiles (including apparel) and autos (including parts). European car companies and Asian textile makers are already moving production to North America to protect themselves against NAFTA's strictures.

NAFTA's big impact will be in manufacturing, the marrow and bone of the North American economy; after that, its effects will be felt most strongly in the farm belt.

That's the impression one got from the NAFTA debate, which centered obsessively on the job creation effects of cross-border restructuring in traditional industries like steel, autos, textiles and consumer appliances— and even in such marginal manufacturing businesses as plastic toys, blown glass, and corn-straw brooms. In rural America the dialogue switched to parallel arguments about NAFTA's impact on agricultural trade.

But the real action after NAFTA will take place in the service sector, which is more important to all three economies than manufacturing and agriculture combined. In Mexico, services account for 60 percent of GDP and include the industries most closed to American trade and investment. By contrast, in the 23 percent of the economy that is in manufacturing, American companies are not only present but dominant. And for farmers, the United States is already overwhelmingly Mexico's biggest market, and Mexico is typically the second or third biggest buyer of American agricultural exports.

Disdain for the service sector as semi-skilled burger-flipping ignores its crucial role as a high-tech, high-wage American export earner. Mexican service industries that NAFTA fully opens to American companies include banking, communications, transportation, insurance, publishing, beachfront tourism, film distribution, retailing, educational training, civil engineering, software design, natural gas and electric power distribution, and scores of other highly competitive and lucrative businesses. This opening comes variously from NAFTA's removal of equity limits, patent and copyright rules, government procurement reforms, and investment guarantees.

The impact will be immediate. One service business that will benefit dramatically from NAFTA is construction. Mexico's infrastructure—ports, railroads, phone lines, power plants—lags behind not only American norms but such developing nations as Chile, Malaysia and Turkey. Getting it in shape will be a bonanza for the Bechtels and the Brown & Roots of this world: estimates of public works projects planned for the next five years exceed $100 billion. In the world market, American companies have a tough time competing for giant turnkey engineering contracts. But NAFTA gives American firms an inside track in Mexico, from bidding rights to financing to the barrier-free importation of material and personnel.

Free trade will spur a massive relocation of American factory jobs to Mexico.

This is the "big sucking sound from the south" that so unnerves Ross Perot. But what Perot hears isn't jobs moving south: it's Mexico vacuuming up all the American products it can buy. Exports to Mexico quadrupled over four years to $40 billion in 1992, giving the United States a $7 billion surplus. NAFTA opens Mexico's import doors even wider. Manufacturers want NAFTA not to secure production relocation opportunities, which they already have, but to open a long-closed market to their American factories.

Claims of massive job migration are based on gross exaggerations of the role of labor and environmental regulations in production costs—and gross underestimates of the costs of building new factories in a foreign country. Union-sponsored research has been able to document just 96,000 jobs that have been moved to Mexico over the past 15 years. That may sound like a lot, but it's less than the average monthly fluctuation in the size of the American work force. More to the point, if they hadn't been shifted to Mexico, most of these jobs would have been lost anyway to increases in productivity and competition, or would have migrated to even cheaper labor zones like China.

NAFTA doesn't lure any American employers across the border. If they were going to move south, they'd move with or without a free trade agreement.

The standard rebuttal of the Perot thesis also has it wrong. NAFTA is meant to make Mexico more appealing to American investors—giving them permanent rights to full control of Mexican subsidiaries and protecting them against any future reversal of Mexican investment rules. NAFTA's dispute resolution panels will in effect extend U.S. legal protections to American businesses on Mexican soil.

Under NAFTA, Mexico will be a better place to do business—with lower financial costs, an improved infrastructure, a larger pool of trained bilingual personnel. For outside investors, there will also be an intangible "comfort factor" in knowing that Mexico was somehow legally linked to the United States. In short, NAFTA removes many of the obstacles, perceived or real, that have kept hundreds of companies from ever considering expansion into Mexico. That's exactly what Mexico wants NAFTA to do.

But that doesn't mean Perot is right in predicting a massive relocation of American manufacturing jobs. Most of the Mexican investment generated by NAFTA will be in services (retailing, restaurant franchising, banking, software) and natural resource industries (mining, oil drilling, petrochemical production)—areas that have been off-limits to American capital. None of these investments imply a loss of jobs in the United States.

Only a small portion of overall investment will be in manufacturing. And even there, Perot and others absurdly misrepresent the ease with which a manufacturing plant can be boxed up and moved to Mexico. Moving a technologically advanced production operation is hugely expensive. Moreover, the movement of any significant number of jobs to Mexico would be political suicide for industries like steel and autos that depend heavily on Washington's trade favors.

But it's true that with NAFTA growing companies will routinely consider Mexican sites for new investments—investments that might have otherwise stayed in the United States. What kind of companies? Not the giant manufacturing conglomerates, which are already established there, which could defend their interests even without a free trade pact, and which are in any event contracting, not expanding, their North American operations. The real impact, both economic and psychological, will be on smaller, labor-intensive manufacturers with little international experience.

Despite the claims of Perot and other NAFTA-bashers, these companies seldom offer the kind of high-skilled, high-wage jobs that the United States needs to prosper and compete in the 21st century. And because their competition primarily comes from low-wage foreign producers, American wage scales will be increasingly hard to sustain. Even without NAFTA, many of these firms would have been drawn south by the prospect of sales within Mexico.

Under NAFTA, North American car production will shift to Mexico, which will become an Asian-style exporter.

Wrong again. NAFTA's immediate effect on the auto industry will be a flood of imports—*from* the United States *into* Mexico. Former Mexican rules allowed car makers to import only half as much in dollar terms as they exported. With NAFTA, they are now able to import 20 percent more into Mexico than they export: that's equivalent to about 400,000 vehicles yearly. The import ceiling will rise gradually to 55 percent above exports over 10 years, and then will be removed entirely.

What does this mean? Direct yearly exports of at least 100,000 American-made cars almost immediately, compared with zero a few years ago. Mexico is by far the fastest-growing auto market in North America: sales tripled in just five years to 750,000 vehicles in 1992, and could pass the million mark by 1995. NAFTA gives American car makers and their underused American plants an inside track: for years to come, the growth of the Mexican market will outpace the expansion of the Big Three's Mexican operations. That means job gains, not job losses, for American auto workers.

The workers who will suffer most under NAFTA are the high-wage members of the big industrial unions; that's why the AFL-CIO made NAFTA's defeat its leading legislative priority.

First, the number of unionized workers who are even exposed to competition from Mexico is relatively small. Less than 8 percent of American workers in competitive businesses (discounting utilities and other monopolies) belong to labor unions. Less than half of these people are directly involved in the production of tradable goods. Of those that aren't, many—teamsters, stevedores, airline mechanics, hotel workers—will benefit directly from increased cross-border commerce.

The minority within the unionized minority who build things that Mexicans also build are, by definition, better able to defend their interests than are their non-unionized brethren. And even there, traditional American manufacturers are not as vulnerable as commonly thought. (The auto, textile and steel businesses all enjoy large and growing trade surpluses with Mexico.) In many industries NAFTA will expand markets at a time when rising productivity would otherwise lead to layoffs.

The jobs most directly threatened by NAFTA are the non-unionized, minimum-wage assembly jobs typically filled by immigrants and the unskilled young. So why is labor so concerned? Because anything that makes it easier for an American employer to transfer production abroad will be opposed by the unions on principle: even the threat of such a move undermines the bargaining power of organized labor. Still, union opposition to NAFTA is far from monolithic, and other issues on labor's agenda—job training, say, or health insurance—are ultimately of much greater importance.

NAFTA is going to turn Mexico into one big maquiladora, with dollar-an-hour assembly plants from Chihuahua to Chiapas ravaging the environment and destroying American manufacturing jobs.

Critics can hardly be blamed for seeing NAFTA as an expansion of the maquiladora concept into the rest of Mexico. Many NAFTA advocates defended maquiladoras on the same basic grounds as NAFTA: American industry needs labor-intensive production options, and better to have the jobs go to Mexicans than to distant Asians controlled by Tokyo. Few

NAFTA supporters were critical of the classic maquiladora's failure to pay taxes, train workers, or raise wages above the legal minimum.

Yet NAFTA numbers the days of the maquiladoras—both legally (in-bond assembly plants have no place in a free trade zone) and economically (wage rates would rise and factories would become more capital intensive). With NAFTA, plants that depend solely on minimum-wage labor will be forced to move to cheaper areas in southern Mexico (and even further south, to Central America and Hispaniola). If you want to strike a blow against the maquiladoras, NAFTA is your club.

Still, with or without maquiladoras, dollar-an-hour Mexicans will be taking jobs from American workers. No manufacturer can resist that 10-to-1 or 20-to-1 wage differential.

Some will. Granted, wages are still about a dollar-an-hour in many border assembly plants and in the poorer districts of the rural south, such as the state of Yucatan (whose relentless advertising of its dollar-an-hour work force were a public relations windfall for NAFTA's American opponents).

But such wage scales are atypical. Mexico's median manufacturing wage, including mandatory benefits, is now approaching $3-an-hour, twice what it was five years ago. For the developed Mexican industrial states hoping to lure foreign manufacturing investors, the most direct competitors are the states of the non-unionized American South, where median wage rates in equivalent jobs average about $12-an-hour. A 4-to-1 gap is still a lot, but it isn't 10-to-1. And the gap is steadily shrinking.

The balance of cross-border trade over the next 10 to 20 years will ultimately determine whether NAFTA was good for the United States.

Pro-NAFTA economists have pointed to the swelling bilateral surplus as proof that free trade with Mexico is good news. Opponents have said it's a transitional aberration: Mexico is importing equipment to produce exports, they say, and once its new factories are in place, cheap Asian-style products will flood the American market, driving the trade balance back into deficit.

Who's right? It doesn't really matter: trade surpluses aren't inherently virtuous, and deficits aren't always a problem. In the specific case of the United States and Mexico, manufacturing trade has always favored the United States, and should continue to do so as long as Mexico remains a developing nation. If the bilateral balance goes a few billion dollars into deficit, so what? Countries can't maintain surpluses with every trading partner at once. If Mexico enjoys a surplus because it is exporting goods to America that we used to buy in East Asia, that's a positive development for the American economy: money paid for Mexican products will be recycled back as spending on American products, which won't be the case with trade dollars in Asia.

Economists on both sides of the NAFTA table perpetuated the trade-balance myth by equating trade surpluses with job creation. The equation was usually the same: the number of workers it takes to make a given volume of goods is multiplied by export projections to provide a gross job creation estimate; the more politically relevant net job creation figure is determined by subtracting import projections on the same worker-to-output basis. The great fallacy is that imports are usually not products that would have otherwise been made in the United States; moreover, marketing and distributing and utilizing those imports creates employment. Virtually all exports add jobs, but most imports don't subtract jobs.

Between 1987 and 1990, exports from the United States to Mexico more than doubled. Exports from Mexico to the United States grew even faster, giving Mexico a $2 billion surplus in this $60 billion exchange. In 1991 American exports grew more quickly than Mexico's, giving the United States a $2 billion surplus in this now $65 billion two-way trade. Does this mean that in 1990 trade with Mexico was destroying American jobs, while in 1991 it suddenly began creating American jobs? Foolish on its face, that's exactly the logic employed by those who warn against a bilateral trade deficit 10 or 20 years from now.

Sometimes, it's true, trade deficits can balloon out of control, jeopardizing the stability of the trading relationship. That's been a problem recently with Japan, China, and several smaller Asian exporters. NAFTA critics (particularly those employed by protected manufacturing interests) said that NAFTA would turn Mexico into an export tiger of the same voracious, predatory stripe. Yet these same critics also claimed that Asia's trade surpluses are the booty of unfair trading practices: dumping, hidden subsidies, domestic investment barriers, preferential purchasing, and so on. Under NAFTA, all these things are explicitly precluded. NAFTA is designed to avoid persistent, destabilizing trade imbalances.

NAFTA opens the gate to the Trojan Horse from Tokyo:
Japan will soon be busily building plants in Mexico, their new
duty-free "back door" into the American market.

Just because Mexico wants NAFTA to attract Japanese investment doesn't mean it is going to work out that way.

To begin with, Japan doesn't have much trouble getting into the

American market through the front door. And Japanese companies have never been that interested in Mexico: despite a zealous courtship, Japan contributes less than 5 percent of Mexico's foreign investment. NAFTA doesn't necessarily make them more interested. To comply with NAFTA's North American content rules, the Japanese need to do exactly what Washington used to urge (futilely): invest their trade-surplus dollars in a poor country that also happens to be a loyal American customer. And if that's not a sufficient deterrent, Washington is signaling Tokyo that it considers Mexico its own economic turf, and won't welcome an aggressive Japanese presence. For all these reasons, it's quite unlikely that NAFTA will lure the *keiretsu* south of the Rio Grande.

Mexico is a virtual dictatorship, with rigged courts, crooked cops, phony unions, and a sham legislature. We shouldn't do business with it until and if things change.

Let's assume this is at least half true; Mexican critics say far worse. We already do business with Mexico. The real question is whether a NAFTA-ized Mexico is more or less likely to democratize. Paradoxically, many Mexican oppositionists who opposed NAFTA on PRI-as-dictatorship grounds saw it as helpful to their own democratizing ends. The American media spotlight that NAFTA trains on Mexico makes electoral fraud more difficult and gives critics a public forum they are often denied at home. NAFTA's dispute-resolution mechanisms are forcing needed reforms in the Mexican judiciary. And in the long run, economic liberalization will loosen the central government's control over all aspects of national life, giving greater autonomy to states, regions and independent political forces, including antigovernment trade unions.

NAFTA strikes a blow for democracy: the Salinas gang of Harvard-trained reformers represent the forces of openness battling against an ossified authoritarianism. Once they consolidate economic reform, democratization is sure to accelerate.

For Salinas, economic growth is not the main thing—it is the only thing. Salinas thinks his job is to keep the PRI in charge, not to turn power over to opponents in the name of pluralism. (This is hardly surprising.) Consequently, he is opening up the system only where it is unavoidable or in the PRI's best interests. Meanwhile, he has kept every single arrow in his authoritarian quiver: a controlled press (monitored more closely than ever); pork-barrel election spending; co-optation of the independent right; harassment of opponents; central supervision of vote counts; even the ultimate Mexican presidential perk—the power to name his own successor.

That doesn't mean that NAFTA won't ultimately be a democratizing force. But democratic progress in Mexico will be the result of insistent pressure from below, not enlightened Lockean reforms bestowed graciously from above.

Won't NAFTA shore up the PRI, then, perpetuating its system of one-party rule?

Absolutely. Prosperity is incumbency's friend, and the whole point of NAFTA is to accelerate economic growth. NAFTA's ratification virtually guarantees the PRI presidential candidate's election in 1994. Conversely, if NAFTA had been rejected and the economy had gone into a tailspin, the opposition might again have pulled within striking distance, as it did in 1988. But a collapsing Mexican economy is not in the best interests of the United States.

Does that mean that America's interest in promoting democracy conflicts with the need to promote economic growth? In Mexico, in the short term, the answer is yes. There is no alternative to growth. Depriving Mexico of needed investment might induce a democratic revolt, but a more likely outcome would be a return to old-line PRI authoritarianism. Local pressure for democratic change can be supported without punishing Mexico economically.

So Washington, like it or not, has a stake in the PRI's continued success.

The United States has a stake in a stable, prosperous Mexico. Today that translates into a stake in NAFTA and conditional support for the Mexican government that negotiated the agreement.

But this does not imply that the United States has a vested interest in the perpetuation of PRI rule. Quite the contrary. The PRI's lockhold on power has kept capital out of the country for years. Indeed, NAFTA was drafted to provide the constraints on the PRI's autonomy that the Mexican system does not. There would be little need for such assurances if Salinas's economic policies had broad popular support—support that would survive any change in political command. The best way to forge this kind of consensus is through the give-and-take of democratic transitions: the opposition comes to power to alter but not overturn national economic policies. Witness Chile, where investment soared after Pinochet's opponents took office and showed that free-market economics could prosper without military rule. Similarly, if an opposition coalition came to power in Mexico and followed open economic policies, it would reassure investors and build a foundation for long-term stability and growth.

Bush and Salinas were moving too fast—trying to accomplish in two years what took the Europeans three decades. NAFTA should have been approached partially, and gradually.

Wrong again. If anything, European integration has been swifter. The European Economic Community was founded in 1958 by France, Germany, Italy and the Benelux countries, building on Jean Monnet's success seven years earlier in setting up a common market for coal and steel among the six neighboring countries. The North American equivalent to Europe's 1951 Coal and Steel accord was the 1965 U.S.-Canadian automotive pact, which expanded and restructured trade and investment in an industry that is still the continent's biggest item of cross-border business. Two decades later, Ottawa and Washington began working toward the liberalization of virtually all bilateral trade, culminating in the U.S.-Canadian free trade agreement in 1990. Mexico, meanwhile, started moving decisively toward free trade in the mid-1980s, entering Gatt and starting "framework" negotiations with the United States to discuss bilateral liberalization. Under NAFTA, many tariffs and investment controls won't be eliminated until 2004, with some sensitive categories delayed until 2009. A decade from now North America might be ready to take the next logical step, the creation of a customs union, something the Europeans did in the 1960s.

It's true that it took 40 years for the European Coal and Steel Community to evolve into today's European Union. But the EC's borderless marketplace, free internal immigration, movement toward monetary union, harmonized labor and environmental standards, and centralized bureaucracy (complete with a continental legislature) represent a far greater commitment to integration than anything proposed by NAFTA.

NAFTA is the first step toward a hemispheric common market.

A free trade zone from the Aleutians to Antarctica? Not if Mexico can help it. Or Canada, for that matter. Or the United Auto Workers. President Clinton, like President Bush before him, tells other Latin Americans that after Mexico, they will come next. But "next" could be a long time coming.

Domestic American opposition to NAFTA's annexation of the giant Mercosur bloc would be fierce—and few of the forces that have intervened so effectively on Mexico's behalf would be prepared to do battle for Brazil or Argentina. Unlike Mexico and the Caribbean basin, South America trades more with Europe (and in some countries more with Asia) than with the United States. Most of the trade and investment liberalization that remains to be accomplished in the hemisphere can be done unilaterally and, then, within subregional trading groups, which would at that point be ready to negotiate with NAFTA—and with the European and Asian blocs as well—as economic equals.

Even if Gatt should falter, a pan-American free zone would be unlikely to become a priority. The biggest growth area for North American trade would continue to be East Asia—the home of North America's most severe trade deficits. One way to keep trans-Pacific commerce flowing might be to negotiate a multilateral trade and investment agreement among NAFTA and the major East Asian exporters, with or without Japan.

Environmentalists opposed NAFTA because they fear that American companies will cross the border to avoid U.S. anti-pollution rules, fouling the Mexican environment while weakening the consensus for environmental enforcement at home.

In fact, most environmentalists didn't oppose NAFTA. After they forced negotiators to put environmental concerns on the NAFTA agenda, they began to see that NAFTA focuses resources on border and internal Mexican environmental problems in an unexpectedly effective way. NAFTA brings Mexico into the broader North American consumer economy, where environmentalists have enormous clout. And it gives Mexico's fledgling environmental movement real political leverage for the first time.

Mainstream conservation groups either backed NAFTA formally, though with caveats, or withheld support until the parallel environmental pact was complete. The more militant organizations—Greenpeace, Friends of the Earth, even the Sierra Club—remained unsatisfied. But even their opposition proved constructive: NAFTA is the first international trade agreement that addresses the environmental consequences of trade between developed and newly industrializing economies.

Most environmentalists now realize that there are very few industries where pollution compliance costs are so high that lax environmental enforcement would be a decisive investment incentive. Still, the side agreements provide sanctions against such abuses—providing environmentalists in a post-NAFTA world with leverage they would otherwise have lacked.

NAFTA is good for the United States because it will stop Mexican immigration: as President Salinas says, it will let Mexico "export jobs, not people."

This assumes that Mexican immigration is an economic problem for the United States, which it is not, and that immigration flows come more from the "push" factor of Mexican unemployment than from "pull" of American demand, which is also untrue.

Serious students of Mexican demography don't expect NAFTA to have any noticeable effect on Mexican immigration over the next five to 10 years. The cross-border networks that connect jobs and workers are so numerous and complex and so embedded in the fabric of both economies that the marginal effects of NAFTA will be impossible to discern. Far more important will be the overall economic performance of the United States and, to a lesser extent, the results of any change in U.S. immigration laws.

But in the long run Salinas is right. To the extent that NAFTA promotes industrialization and urbanization, it will accelerate the decline of Mexico's birth-rate. It will also further narrow the gap between U.S. and Mexican wage rates, reducing the incentive to emigrate. Higher Mexican wages will also force increased mechanization in California agriculture, which remains the biggest single importer of cheap Mexican labor.

Still, many people think that NAFTA will dramatically increase Mexican immigration. They point to the agricultural reforms that could push 1 million or more Mexicans off the land in the next 10 years. (The biggest change, the privatization of communal farms, is not part of NAFTA, but could fairly be seen as necessary for competition in an open North American agricultural market.) NAFTA itself strips away price supports and other subsidies for traditional corn-and-beans farmers, guaranteeing an exodus from overpopulated farmlands. Critics said that if NAFTA were passed, many of these displaced peasants would be forced to come north.

The problem with this argument is that Mexico would be taking these steps even without NAFTA. Mexican corn is a symbol of the national culture and self-sufficiency, exactly like Japanese rice. But Mexico, unlike Japan, cannot afford the subsidies and high food prices that result. Communal corn farms were not only an extraordinarily expensive way to feed the country, they trapped Mexican farmers in a self-perpetuating cycle of poverty and dependency.

If these changes were implemented without NAFTA, the disruption would be much more severe. NAFTA softens the blow in two critical ways. First, by trading off American access to the Mexican grain market for Mexican access to the American horticultural market, NAFTA makes it easier to substitute viable export crops for inefficient subtropical cornfields. Second, by expediting the flow of foreign capital into provincial Mexico, in both agricultural investment (once forbidden) and light industry (now rapidly expanding), NAFTA creates alternative local employment opportunities that would not have otherwise existed.

Without NAFTA, the rush from the farms to the north would be a stampede.

Canada's unhappy experience proves the critics were right: a free trade agreement leads inexorably to huge job losses, falling real wages, and pressure to reduce social welfare benefits.

The critics were wrong—but their Tory opponents were only half right. The real lesson from Canada is that Mexico's entry into the free trade area will be much less disruptive to American manufacturing workers than they seem to think.

Canada's recession wasn't caused by the U.S.-Canadian Free Trade Agreement: the real culprit was Ottawa's unsustainable budget deficits and declining competitiveness in key industries. American economic sluggishness made things worse.

Canadian unions say that after the FTA jobs were lured out of Canada by lower American wages and lower American corporate taxes. But wage differentials alone are far too marginal to be a factor. Many American companies say the health care savings in their Canadian subsidiaries more than pay for higher tax bills. (Indeed, some American auto production has been transferred to Canada to reduce overall payroll costs.) Exports from Canada to the United States have increased significantly since the FTA took effect in 1990.

But jobs have fallen even faster—by some estimates, a fifth of Canada's manufacturing work force has been laid off in the past three years. These job losses are largely the byproduct of Canada's deficit-spawned recession. Yet the FTA has clearly produced job losses of its own, particularly among the subsidiaries of American manufacturing companies, which can now supply the Canadian market from more efficient plants in the United States. That's what free trade agreements are supposed to do: increase productivity on a continental scale. In the short term, that usually means job losses as well as job gains.

NAFTA may be a fine idea, but it will punch a $40 billion hole in the federal budget. We simply can't afford it.

That $40 billion price tag is not the cost of NAFTA, but an expansive estimate of the cost of buying the votes that were needed to secure its ratification. Here's how it breaks down:

PUBLIC WORKS

Nearly half of it will go for public works improvements in border zones from San Diego to East Texas: bridges, roadways, sewage systems, new customs crossings, and the like. Partly, this is a standard public works wish list. But much of it is long overdue because of the growth of trade and border industry over the past 10 years, along with the continuing population shift to the sunbelt. It is quite true that the increased trade generated by NAFTA puts added strain on local infrastructure. But that's true of increased economic activity everywhere: it's perverse to oppose growth simply because it has associated infrastructure costs.

ENVIRONMENTAL CLEAN-UP

Another big-ticket item—estimated cost: $10 billion plus—is the overdue clean-up of toxic waste dumps and polluted waterways along the border. This is needed, but again not because of NAFTA. In fact, NAFTA helps prevent such abuses by improving regulatory oversight and discouraging further industrial concentration in the border zone. Some NAFTA critics, such as columnist Pat Buchanan, have said that American taxpayers shouldn't be expected to pay for the clean-up of the "pigpen" the Mexicans have made of their side of the border. But whose mess is it, really? Much of it was made by American companies manufacturing for the American market with toxic substances imported from the United States— pollutants that they were legally obliged to ship back to the United States for disposal. While Mexican environmental enforcement has often been deplorably lax, Buchanan's complaint might more properly have been addressed to American corporate lawbreakers. (It's as if he went camping in Yellowstone, left his garbage behind, and came back to Washington to bang out a column on the mess those bears had made of the woods.)

JOB TRAINING

Worker retraining is the other major expenditure associated with NAFTA. Export manufacturing in low-wage countries like Mexico has unquestionably hurt manufacturing job creation and pay scales in the United States. Targeted training programs, run properly, can alleviate this pressure. But Mexico itself is only one small part of the problem. NAFTA's net impact on the overall need for worker training will be undetectable. There will be more pressure on American jobs directly attributable to

Mexico, but not more pressure on American workers as a whole. The Clinton Administration wants to triple its worker retraining budget to $1.6 billion in 1994. These funds will aid nearly 1 million workers left unemployed for a host of reasons. Only a fraction of it can be considered a "cost" of NAFTA.

TARIFFS

That leaves the $600 million or so a year that Washington will no longer collect in tariffs under a free trade regime. This is NAFTA's only major direct budget cost. Yet tariffs are not intended as a revenue source (at least not in the 20th century), but as an import penalty. Tax revenues from new business and rising incomes will more than offset losses from canceled tariff collections. Mexico understands this, even though it will give up three times as much tariff revenue as the United States in absolute terms, and more than 30 times as much in terms of budget impact.

Still, we should be careful. Like Perot says, "measure twice, cut once." Let's follow his advice and implement free trade only partially and provisionally, before it's too late to turn back.

Either we have a free trade agreement or we don't. NAFTA's comprehensive nature—encompassing a broad range of industries in three large economies—is what makes it work. It can't be introduced piecemeal, sectorally or geographically.

Yet nothing is forever. If the warnings of NAFTA critics ever came to pass—falling wages and massive manufacturing unemployment north of the border, brutal environmental degradation and labor repression south of the border—the United States could (and would) withdraw. All that's required under NAFTA is six months' notice. Mexico and Canada are so acutely dependent on American capital and markets that an abrupt unilateral withdrawal would be unthinkable. In the United States the immediate economic impact would be minimal. The ability of the U.S. Congress to quit NAFTA at any future point puts industry on notice that the promises of NAFTA's supporters must be visibly fulfilled.

Mexico doesn't need NAFTA. If the agreement had been defeated or postponed, Mexico would have continued to enact economic reforms unilaterally. Since NAFTA's importance is more psychological than economic, it would have been better to avoid the risks of rejection and let Mexico liberalize on its own.

This is the most pernicious NAFTA myth of all. Curiously, it was promoted both by Mexico's government, which wanted to downplay its dependence on the agreement's success, and by NAFTA's American opponents, who argued that Mexican officials (a) "out-negotiated" their Washington counterparts, and (b) would continue to liberalize the Mexican economy even if denied preferential access to the American market. On both sides, these arguments are disingenuous.

As American public opinion began turning against the agreement, Mexican officials started to think the unthinkable: what if NAFTA fails? They knew they would need to reassure investors that free-market reforms would continue, NAFTA or no NAFTA. And they had little margin for error: Mexico's trade deficit had topped 5 percent of gross domestic product for the third straight year. A sudden loss of investor confidence could start a vicious cycle: portfolio capital withdraws, the peso is abruptly devalued, inflation surges, and investors start fretting about a possible return to state intervention and currency controls.

To dampen such fears, Mexican officials began to talk openly about accelerating investment reforms and trade liberalization if NAFTA failed. But this exposed them to a logical counterattack: if Mexico is ready to do all this on its own, why does America need NAFTA? Indeed, why should it give Mexico any economic concessions at all? And the critics didn't stop there: they argued that NAFTA wouldn't really give the United States *privileged* access to the Mexican market, since Mexico was planning to extend the same open investment invitation to companies from Japan, Europe and everywhere else.

Narrowly, the critics had a point. Mexico's planned new foreign investment law, replacing its restrictive 1973 statute, is designed to extend much of NAFTA's liberal investment regime to investors from outside North America.

Yet companies from the United States and Canada enjoy special privileges under NAFTA that they would not have gotten from domestic Mexican reforms. First, they are uniquely protected against a reversal of Mexican investment rules. Mexico could nationalize a Japanese plant or, less drastically, impose export performance requirements and foreign exchange controls. Under NAFTA, it forfeits the right to take similar action against American and Canadian firms.

Second, the abolition of border tariffs and non-tariff import barriers is critical to American investors in Mexico. Most bilateral trade in manufactures takes place among subsidiaries of the same (mostly American) companies. By making this intrafirm commerce cheaper and easier, NAFTA speeds improvements in efficiency and productivity. This offers few advantages to companies based outside North America, which generally depend on materials and components from Europe and Asia—goods that still have to pay tariffs.

NAFTA's local content rules give a clear edge to American and Canadian products, which, by definition, are largely North American in origin.

Without NAFTA, Mexico wouldn't have given American banks the first crack at its protected market, or guaranteed American companies a share of its government service and supply contracts. Without NAFTA, Mexico wouldn't have promised not to divert oil away from North America to alternative markets overseas. Without NAFTA, Mexico would no longer have felt any need to be "North American": it would have made every effort to attract Asian and European investment and would have pursued formal trade links with the Pacific Basin economic blocs.

But there were clear limits to what Mexico could have accomplished unilaterally. Otherwise, Salinas would never have risked negotiating a trade pact with Washington. By itself, Mexico could never have allayed fears that its present policies might be reversed by some future government. Nor could Mexico alone have attracted the steady stream of investment that would be lured by a trade accord with the United States—or have protected itself against an outbreak of American protectionism.

NAFTA does more than "lock in" Salinas's economic reforms. It guarantees that Mexico gets the capital and market access it needs to survive painful economic adjustments and develop skill-intensive industrial jobs. Without NAFTA, this restructuring process would have been much harder, and growth would have been much slower. Imports from the north would have been stifled not by tariffs but by contracting demand. The Mexico that American workers fear and deplore—the Mexico of $5-a-day assembly lines, of lax environmental and labor standards, of rigged bidding for state contracts—would have reappeared with a vengeance if capital inflows fell short of expectations and there were no NAFTA safeguards against such abuses. Mexico would have lost. But in some ways, the United States would have lost even more.

For some time now it has been clear that the American economy will thrive only through increased productivity and smarter strategic planning. The labor-intensive, low-skill jobs of the past must gradually be replaced by the high-skill, high-paying jobs of the future. The North American Free Trade Agreement offers a unique opportunity to take a purposeful step in that direction.

But NAFTA implies change, and real change is always unnerving. Politicians like House Majority Whip David Bonior tried to sway public opinion by citing government "studies" that allegedly forecast job losses of up to 40 percent in autos and steel if NAFTA were to go into effect. *There are no such studies.* In fact, business analysts think NAFTA will be a long-term boon for the heavy industries of the rustbelt.

It is true that NAFTA will cause some jobs to be lost: change means just that—change. It is also fair to view the costs and benefits of economic growth with some skepticism. But in NAFTA's case, the benefits dramatically outweigh the costs. If anything, the pact is skewed in America's favor. Official estimates that NAFTA will lead to as many as 500,000 lost jobs sound scary—until one realizes that these jobs will be lost not at once but over the course of a decade, and that most of them will disappear anyway because of productivity enhancements or import competition from other low-wage countries. Meanwhile, some 20 million new American jobs will be created over the next 10 years—including at least 1 million through sales to the expanding market in Mexico that NAFTA helps create.

The political impediment is this: over the next few years, the pain of change will be more immediately visible than any compensating gains. The factory shutdowns and other dislocations that NAFTA might accelerate will have almost no measurable effect on the economy as a whole. But in affected communities the impact could be traumatic. That most of these jobs would disappear even without NAFTA doesn't lift the obligation of NAFTA supporters to see that people suddenly unemployed through no fault of their own have guaranteed access to health care and training for the new, better jobs that NAFTA helps create. America's need to help its people make the transition to a new, higher-skill economy is every bit as great as the need of business to gain access to foreign markets. The NAFTA debate usefully focused attention on this fact.

But to oppose growth because it has associated costs is tantamount to a Luddite withdrawal from the modern industrial world—a world the United States still dominates. NAFTA's rejection would have marked the advent of a New Age defeatism—an outlook that combines the worst traits of 19th century isolationism with a new sort of 21st century economic cowardice. NAFTA's most prominent opponents live in a universe where naive Washington negotiators are perpetually outwitted by wily foreign opponents, where core American industries like steel and cars can survive only through subsidy and protective tariffs, where the United States can brake its slide to inevitable economic decline only by shutting its borders to goods and immigrants and by disentangling itself from foreign economic alliances.

This is a crabbed, distorted picture of a nation that is still, despite its problems, the biggest, most varied, and most creatively dynamic economy in the world. It is a view that overlooks the reality of American automakers' regaining market share with better and cheaper cars, of high-tech American steel mills exporting to eager customers in Mexico and beyond, of the continuing American entrepreneurial domination of the computer science, biotechnology and communications industries that will shape the global economy of the 21st century. There is a reason why a country like Mexico wanted to forge an economic union with the United States. For America to have turned Mexico down would have been to acknowledge that it had lost faith in its own future.

CHAPTER 2

The Origins and Importance of NAFTA

It was February 4, 1990, and President Carlos Salinas de Gortari had just returned from his first state tour of Europe. Waiting on his desk was the document to which he had devoted most of his first year in office: an agreement cutting payments on his government's $48 billion foreign debt.

That afternoon, in a televised ceremony, with Treasury Secretary Nicholas Brady looking on approvingly, Salinas and the chairmen of Citicorp, BankAmerica, and the Bank of Tokyo would sign the landmark accord, calling it "the concluding chapter" of Mexico's eight costly, frustrating years of debt negotiations.

It was an important achievement, negotiated collaboratively—and essentially bilaterally—with the U.S. Treasury and the American money center banks, led by Citicorp. For the first time since the 1982 debt crisis, Mexico's payments would begin to decline in real terms and, more dramatically, as a share of its dollar earnings. The first practical application of what became known as the Brady Plan, the agreement represented a conceptual breakthrough in third world debt management. Previous agreements had merely refinanced a country's existing debt—"rolled it over," as the bankers put it. The Brady Plan actually reduced Mexico's outstanding commercial loans.

It also insulated Mexico against oil price and interest rate shocks, permitting long-term planning of a kind that hadn't been possible in years. Mexico could now talk credibly about a return to non-inflationary growth. The great gains it had made in stabilizing the peso and erasing the government deficit no longer seemed ephemeral, but permanent reversals of practice and policy. Equally important, so did the strides it had made in clear-cutting tariff barriers and promoting the expansion of export manufacturing.

Above all, the debt restructuring had symbolic importance. In a demonstration of commitment and confidence that no other debtor country could equal, the deal was collateralized with $5.4 billion from the World Bank, the International Monetary Fund, and the Japanese Ex-Im Bank, which in turn financed an unprecedented special issue of $33 billion in U.S. Treasury zero-coupon bonds.

This first world financial imprimatur had already bestowed practical benefits. Over the previous 12 months, as it became clear that the complex negotiations were moving toward a successful end, Mexico had launched Latin America's first international bond issues in a decade. Real domestic interest rates had plunged by 30 points. The value of Mexico's debt on the secondary market reversed a five-year free fall, climbing from 33 cents to 40 cents on the dollar (it never slipped back: three years later it was above 70 percent of face value). These new signs of creditworthiness had propelled the first non-inflation-driven economic expansion—better than 3 percent—since the debt crisis began.

Now, as Salinas signed the 30-year debt pact, the benediction of the U.S. Treasury Secretary and the chairmen of three of the world's most powerful banks dramatized how far Mexico had traveled in the eyes of the international financial community. For eight years money had been flowing out of Mexico. Now it would at last start flowing in.

It wouldn't be enough, however, and Salinas knew it. His negotiators were disappointed that the debt savings weren't deeper: only $1 billion had been cut from the $10 billion Mexico had to pay in annual debt service. New borrowing to finance the package added nearly as much debt as the relief mechanisms had erased.

More critically, it was soon clear that the Brady accord—and the stabilization of the debt problem that it implied—would not be the magnet for private capital that Mexico had hoped. In 1989 Mexico posted its first net capital inflow since 1981: it came to just $3 billion. To achieve its moderate economic growth goals of 3 to 5 percent—double population growth—Mexico needed $5 billion to $10 billion in fresh capital every year.

Making matters worse, Mexico was seeking this money at a time of global slowdown. Multinational firms were halting overseas expansion plans, and the suddenly free economies of Eastern Europe were clamoring for investments and financial aid. Salinas was forcefully reminded of this competition during his European tour, when business groups listened politely but noncommittally to his tales of Mexico's transformation. He worried aloud that all of Latin America was being overlooked in the euphoria about the collapse of the Warsaw Pact. "Don't forget about us," he beseeched one British audience. When Salinas spoke to the annual World Economic Forum in Davos, Switzerland, he had trouble filling the room, while presentations by Poles and Russians were packed.

Despite Salinas's salesmanship, Mexico hadn't shaken its bad name. Investors wondered whether it had really abandoned its populist ways. After all, it still maintained tight restrictions on foreign capital and a huge state industrial complex. Then, too, there was Mexico's troubling history of erratic policy swings and property seizures. Even if Salinas was sincere in his commitment to free-market reform, what was to keep some future government from reversing course?

These concerns were voiced not only by foreign investors, but by rich Mexicans with billions of dollars stashed in offshore bank accounts. Mexican officials themselves thought at least $20 billion was concentrated in relatively few hands, and could be lured back with the right incentives and guarantees.

But they also realized that more—much more—needed to be done to attract foreign and offshore money into the Mexican economy. So as Salinas sat down to sign the debt deal, he had already resolved to take two additional steps—actions that ultimately would prove to be the most important of his presidency. The first was the privatization of Mexico's banks. The second was the pursuit of a free trade pact with Washington.

Famed among colleagues for his methodical habits, Salinas is not given to impulsive choices—in politics or economics. He himself stresses that the decision to pursue a free trade agreement was not made hastily: "It was such an important decision, with such serious repercussions in the medium and long term, that it demanded careful analysis of a wide range of issues that we had been considering."

Now, with the debt accord signed, there was no reason to wait.

Salinas knew that bank privatization had to come first. To begin with, it was easier, in that it could be accomplished unilaterally. The free trade decision, by contrast, marked a reversal of policies Mexico had vigorously sustained for most of its history. But the two initiatives reinforced one another, symbolically and economically, sending the message to private capital—domestic and foreign—that Mexico was irreversibly committed to free-market economics.

Salinas had already revealed his intention to sell the government's majority stake in Telmex, the state telephone monopoly. But privatizing Mexico's 18 commercial banks would have far greater impact, financially and psychologically. By overturning the 1982 expropriation by former President José López Portillo, Salinas would begin to mend the corporatist bond between the private sector and the PRI. The money that the bank expropriation had driven offshore would be invited to repurchase those confiscated properties—albeit at prices 10 times higher than what the government had paid as compensation.

Eventually, the Salinas Administration would sell 18 banks for more than three times book value, double the market rate for an American bank. Without the simultaneous commitment to a free trade agreement, and its promise of economic expansion and an increasingly open investment regime, the bidding would never have risen that high. Similarly, the prospect of NAFTA had made the privatization of the phone company far more lucrative, as American investors snapped up Telmex shares as proxies for the Mexican economy itself. The growth expectations and long-term policy assurances attached to NAFTA also drove up the market value of state airlines, steel mills, fertilizer factories, and scores of other divested properties. By mid-1992 the Salinas government would take in $19.5 billion from privatization sales, far more than it could have hoped for without the NAFTA premium.

In contrast to the privatization program, the pursuit of a free trade deal with the United States was far more complex and politically risky.

Salinas first needed to verify that George Bush—who had privately reiterated the Reagan Administration's free trade invitation in their first conference—had really meant what he said. So he dispatched two of his closest aides—José Cordoba, his chief of staff, and Jaime Serra Puche, the trade minister—to confer with their U.S. counterparts. Overall, Bush and his aides were surprised but supportive. Then, a month later, the *Wall Street Journal* published a leaked story about the Cordoba-Serra mission. This forced Washington's hand and allowed bureaucratic momentum to shift in Mexico's favor. Bush officials agreed to announce their intention to seek an agreement in June, when Salinas was scheduled to visit.

Then came the Iraqi invasion of Kuwait—and for six months Mexico disappeared from Washington's strategic map. It was not until February 5, 1991—exactly one year after Salinas had returned from Europe to sign the debt agreement and begin the pursuit of a free trade pact—that Bush formally notified Congress of his intention to negotiate a trilateral free trade agreement with Mexico and Canada. It marked the beginning of a political battle such as no Mexican government had ever seen.

'El Padrino'

If Salinas and Bush are the parents of the North American free trade agreement, Ronald Reagan is the godfather—*el padrino*.

When Reagan first began advocating a North American common market in his 1980 presidential campaign, few took the idea seriously. Canada, then under Pierre Trudeau's social democratic leadership, was attempting to forestall further encroachment by American culture and investment. It seemed an unlikely candidate for an open-borders initiative.

On the Mexican side, Reagan's free-market proposal seemed even more far-fetched. Heady with its new oil riches, Mexico appeared certain to reject such ideas out of hand. In most developing nations—and especially in Mexico—it was widely agreed that reciprocity in trade relations with an industrial superpower would bring disastrous results.

Moreover, after a bitter internal cabinet fight, Mexican President José López Portillo had only recently reversed an earlier decision to join the General Agreement on Tariffs and Trade. On both the left and the right, critics had argued that Gatt membership would force Mexico to buy more manufactured imports from its oil customers, while restricting the domestic use of petrodollars for industrial promotion and decentralization programs. Not surprisingly, they prevailed: Mexico was chalking up record growth rates, oil exports had given it unaccustomed leverage in dealings with Washington and the rest of the world, and the president himself had said that his biggest economic problem was "managing abundance." That Washington wanted Mexico to join Gatt had been a windfall for the plan's nationalist opponents. As the largest Western economy still outside Gatt, Mexico was unable even to contemplate the radical trade steps Reagan was proposing—even if it were willing to seek an economic partnership with the United States, which it clearly was not.

The idea of a continental economic bloc had never been part of the Reagan canon. In 1979, however, when he was organizing his third run for the presidency, Mexico's profile had risen notably as both a strategic asset (oil) and a problem (drugs, immigration, and the perceived threat of leftist insurgencies). The California background of Reagan and his campaign team gave them an appreciation for Mexico's importance, if no special insight into its problems or political culture. Indeed, the under-pinning of Reagan's criticism of Carter's Nicaragua policy was the pur-ported leftist threat to Mexico's stability and resources. Martin Anderson, an economist who later became Reagan's first domestic policy advisor, recalls a conversation in early 1979 with John Sears, the Reagan campaign's first manager. Sears saw an economically unified North America as "a colossus" resistant to subversion from the south and commercial assault from the east and west. He knew that Canadians and Mexicans alike might take this vision as an expansionist ploy for oil and other natural resources. But he felt it could be made palatable to them if American doors were opened to their goods and workers. In dealing with Mexico, especially, Sears argued, American conservatives had to move beyond knee-jerk references to the Monroe Doctrine and construct a market-driven appeal to mutual self-interest.

Sears and Anderson dubbed this idea the "North American Accord" and took it to Reagan, who was immediately receptive. "What we were talking about went way beyond free trade," Anderson recalls. "Reagan embraced it as a way to resolve illegal immigration and a lot of other problems."

Before advocating the North American Accord publicly, Reagan broached the idea privately with American business leaders, Canadian Conservatives, and influential Mexicans. In July 1979, he traveled with Sears to Mexico City for a talk with Mexico's president. As recounted in López Portillo's memoirs, Reagan talked at length about his proposal for an open border and open markets. He stressed that his intent was a comprehensive agreement on labor and capital movement as well as trade, and carefully avoided mentioning oil until the Mexican president himself raised the topic. López Portillo wrote later that he was impressed by Reagan's direct, cordial manner and apparent conviction in his "three or four fixed ideas" about Mexico, the first and foremost of these being its eventual inclusion in a North American common market.

López Portillo was open to the idea of a broad new approach to bilateral economic relations. With foreign borrowing and government spending outpacing its petroleum income, Mexico faced a growing trade deficit with the United States—an unusual problem for a leading oil exporter. Mexican negotiators had failed to persuade Washington to remove restrictions on products ranging from tomatoes to hot-rolled steel. Acrimonious negotia-tions with the Carter Administration over natural gas exports had recently collapsed, with Washington reneging (in Mexico's view) on a previously agreed sales price. American initiatives to restrict immigration worried Mexican officials as well. They saw "labor mobility" and some $2 billion a year in expatriates' remittances as vital to stability in rural Mexico. López Portillo was still preoccupied by the internal cabinet debate over Mexico's membership in Gatt, with the Americans warning that unless Mexico joined, the United States would be obliged to stiffen countervailing duties and other restrictions on Mexican imports.

From Mexico's viewpoint, all these bilateral issues were part of a single, larger problem. "There are no isolated problems; everything is part of everything else," López Portillo had complained. "If, for example, we want to solve the problem of undocumented workers, we must understand that the problem lies in Mexico's economic situation. This will improve if we achieve a better balance in our very unfavorable trade relations with the United States."

But López Portillo was not ready to embrace a proposal for U.S.-Mexican economic union. Sears recalls that the president told his visitors that while he would promise not to attack the proposal publicly, Mexican political reality precluded an endorsement—and would continue to do so for a long time. "He told us that our children, and probably our grandchildren, would never see the day," Sears recalls.

This pessimism was shared north of the border. Despite a generalized sympathy for closer (and fairer) economic ties with Mexico, few economists, Latin Americanists, or foreign policy specialists thought much of the free trade proposal's real-world prospects. Not only was it assumed that Mexico would be hostile, it was also felt that a bilateral approach to regional issues would undermine hemispheric institutions (such as the Organization of American States) and contradict the U.S. commitment to multilateral trade negotiations under Gatt.

But Reagan was as indifferent as ever to received wisdom. He issued his call for a North American Accord when he declared his presidential candidacy in November 1979. In political and diplomatic circles, the proposal was seen as an easy way to soften Reagan's hard line on Latin America. Reagan had made Latin America a prime focus of his attacks on the Carter Administration. Yet most of his own prescriptions for the region were defined by negatives: opposition to the Panama Canal Treaty, arms to combat leftist insurgencies, and hostility toward a foreign policy that gave precedence to human rights. The common market idea might not go anywhere, but it had the distinct virtue of sounding constructive.

For those who thought about it at all, the question was whether Reagan fully understood the implications of his own proposal. Its off hand radicalism was stunning: he was proposing a frontal assault not only on Mexican and Canadian nationalism, but on deep-rooted protectionism in all three

HOW NAFTA WORKS:
Tariff Elimination 1994–2004*

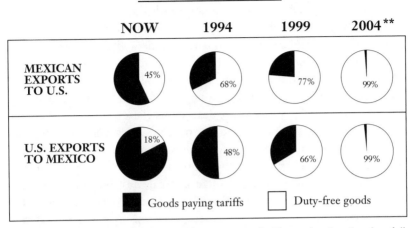

	NOW	1994	1999	2004**
MEXICAN EXPORTS TO U.S.	45%	68%	77%	99%
U.S. EXPORTS TO MEXICO	18%	48%	66%	99%

■ Goods paying tariffs ☐ Duty-free goods

* Percentages represent the share of exports exempt from tariffs. They are based on the value of all goods traded bilaterally in 1990. American tariffs on Mexican goods now average about 3.5 cents on the dollar; Mexican tariffs on American goods average about 10 cents on the dollar.

** In the final five years of the Nafta phase-in calendar — from 2004 to 2009 — tariffs would be removed on the remaining one percent of eligible goods, most of which are agricultural products.

Source: International Trade Commission

countries—and, far beyond that, the eventual elimination of barriers on media and migration as well. It was classically Reaganesque: bold in its reframing of a policy problem, ideologically faithful to market economics, yet bereft of detail and seemingly unmindful of practical difficulties.

A hemispheric free trade zone was not a new idea. In the 19th century, any number of American commentators had proclaimed that Latin America's salvation lay in economic absorption into the United States. Such proposals were angrily dismissed by Latin American leaders from Simon Bolívar to José Martí, whose admiration for U.S. political freedoms was tempered by deep distrust of U.S. economic ambitions.

Mexico was the least receptive of all. It had long felt that it was already far too close to the United States. Under the iron-handed capitalism of Porfirio Díaz, the dictator's scholarly economic advisors—the *científicos*, seen by Mexican oppositionists today as the spiritual forbearers of Salinas's technocrats—sought to lure European investment as a deliberate counterweight to American power. The Díaz government spurned early American offers to extend rail networks south to Mexico City. Between the United States and Mexico, the dictator is said to have replied, we want not the sound of the locomotive, but the sound of the desert.

Despite this, Mexico's foreign trade was increasingly dominated by cross-border commerce. After the 1910 Revolution, Mexico repeatedly tried to diversify trade and investment towards Europe, and later Asia. All the while, it grew steadily more dependent on the United States. American efforts to expand and reorder bilateral trade in the New Deal "Good Neighbors" era were derailed temporarily by the 1938 expropriation of Mexico's oil industry. But the breach was short-lived. The United States' entrance into the second world war, with Mexico as a nominal ally, brought the first big wave of Mexican industrial exports to the United States. The next big wave came during the Korean war, which again increased American demand for Mexican steel, glass and other products. The suspension shortly after the Korean war of the *bracero* migrant worker program, a flawed experiment in legalized labor movement, led indirectly to U.S. customs rules allowing duty-free imports from border-zone assembly plants. The success of these maquiladoras led their American owners to press for more cross-border tariff exemptions.

Throughout this period, some two-thirds of Mexico's foreign trade and investment was tied to the United States. And regularly, some American academic or policymaker would propose some form of trade compact with Mexico. Just as regularly, the proposals would be hooted down.

Even in more recent times, Reagan was not alone in his advocacy of open U.S.-Mexican trade. In the Nixon Administration, Treasury Secretary John Connally had toyed with the idea, suggesting the creation of a cross-border free zone to generally unreceptive Mexican visitors. Robert McNamara, while head of the World Bank, urged closer trade ties with Mexico as a way to foster both economic development and border security. Reagan's successor in Sacramento, Jerry Brown, also urged the elimination of border barriers to immigration and trade.

In 1979, another undeclared presidential aspirant, George Bush, chaired an American Enterprise Institute study group that called on policymakers to reexamine the entire U.S.-Mexican economic relationship, not simply Mexico's role as an exporter of oil and people. "Mexico's ability to utilize its oil resources effectively and to sustain a rapid growth rate in its economy will depend on its ability to expand non-oil exports to the United States," Bush wrote. University of Texas President Peter T. Flawn argued in the Bush group's report that it was "to the long-term advantage of the United States . . . to work toward a more integrated bilateral economic policy or perhaps, over time, a common market."

Within the Carter Administration there was also support for a liberalized trade relationship. At the urging of Robert Pastor, a National Security Council advisor on Latin American affairs, Zbigniew Brzezinski asked the USTR to investigate possible sectoral agreements with Mexico in manufacturing and agriculture in preparation for a 1979 meeting between Carter and López Portillo. But no action was taken.

It took Ronald Reagan to bring the idea to life. Ironically, Reagan himself never really pursued his free trade vision with Mexico. In Canada, he had to wait for the 1984 election of the like-minded Brian Mulroney to begin free trade talks. With Mexico, the inauguration in December 1982 of the economically orthodox Miguel de la Madrid should have provided a similar opportunity. But Mexico City and Washington first had to address the unfolding drama of Mexico's debt crisis, never imagining that it would stretch on for the next six years.

Yet it was Reagan's championing of the notion on the stump that introduced the concept of a North American trade pact to the broader public. Equally important, he put it on the agenda of the Republican Party. And it was his conclusion of a bilateral deal with Canada that laid NAFTA's structural foundation. Most important of all, it was Reagan who told Mexican leaders that if they wanted to join a continental free trade zone, it was their move. That was the invitation—repeated by Bush in 1988—that Salinas, to Washington's great surprise, accepted.

Managing "Free" Trade

One of the many ironies of the North American free trade agreement is that its American critics tended to favor government intervention in support of strategic industries, while its architects—from Reagan onward—complained about the danger of letting bureaucrats pick winners and losers. Similarly, critics—such as Ross Perot and House Majority Leader Richard Gephardt—tended toward the managed trade school, which favors tactical protectionism to force open foreign markets.

Yet NAFTA is not the monument to unbridled capitalism that it is often made out to be. Formal integration with an adjacent but radically different economy has forced free marketeers in both countries to focus on basic questions about the future of important industries.

Not that the negotiators had much choice. A broad-ranging trade and investment agreement, by its nature, demands an orderly transition schedule to allow businesses to gear up for new markets and new competitors and to phase out investments based on outdated economic assumptions. It also demands deals that favor some businesses at the expense of others.

Industrial policy, like the devil, is in the details: the trade-offs, the

U.S.–MEXICO TRADE:
GROWTH & BALANCE

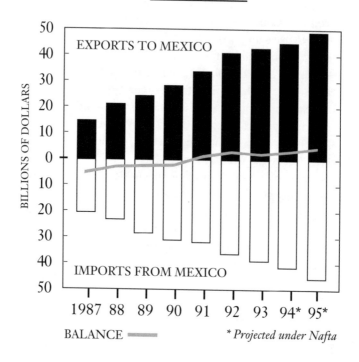

phase-ins, the industries on both sides that have managed to opt out of NAFTA's free trade and investment rules. Ten years after NAFTA comes into effect, almost all trade and investment will flow freely across the borders. But the transition period will determine which industries will be best situated to take advantage of this eventual free trade regime: steel in the United States, light truck assembly in Mexico, textiles in the United States, sewn garments in Mexico, natural gas in the United States, fertilizer plants in Mexico, mortgage marketing in the United States, Spanish-language news broadcasting in Mexico.

That's why the sectoral trade-offs and phase-in calendars in the agreement are critical. In aggregate, this detail determines whether NAFTA is a positive-sum game—adding to the continent's output and competitiveness—or, instead, a fundamentally protectionist initiative that encourages retreat from the world economy.

The crucial test centered on the rules of origin: could they promote competitive industrial restructuring without distorting trade flows and discouraging Asian and European investment in Mexico? In the most divisive areas, cars and textiles, negotiators came to a reasonable compromise, avoiding the extreme protectionist demands of affected companies in all three countries. Still, in both cases, NAFTA's content rules are stricter than those in the original U.S.-Canadian free trade agreement (USCFTA). In textiles and apparel, the USCFTA required eligible goods to be made from North American fabric. NAFTA takes matters back a step, demanding that the goods be woven from North American thread or yarn. In autos, the USCFTA required at least 50 percent North American content for duty-free car imports. The NAFTA standard raises the minimum immediately to 56 percent, and then to 62.5 percent four years later. The requirement for auto parts was hiked from 50 percent to 60 percent.

The agreement is protectionist in other ways as well. Costly, anticompetitive barriers against many third-party products—from clothing to refined sugar to pickup trucks—are maintained by NAFTA, and in some ways strengthened. During the protracted 15-year transition period, new duties will be applied to a host of politically sensitive farm products: orange juice, sugar and peanuts on the U.S. side, corn, beans, pork and apples on the Mexican side. The agreement is riddled with "snapback" and "surge" provisions that allow the reimposition of tariffs on imports that prove too successful too quickly. Many influential industries were allowed to opt out of NAFTA's open investment rules: Canada's so-called cultural industries, Mexico's oil monopoly, American defense contractors. In all three countries, majority foreign ownership is still banned in telecommunications, airlines, the merchant marine, and the nuclear power, broadcasting and fishing industries.

The greatest anomaly in this "free trade agreement" is its elaborate provisions for anti-dumping penalties. Building on the USCFTA's juridical structure, NAFTA sets up trinational dispute resolution panels with the power to impose countervailing duties on products deemed to have been sold below cost. In a true free trade regime, like that among the 50 states, there would be no call for such a mechanism. A cement producer in Texas can't take a cement producer in California to court for alleged underpricing: the presumption is that a tariff-free market is itself the ultimate arbiter of price competition. When that competition is especially vigorous, the beneficiaries are the cement companies' clients. Yet as the USCFTA experience has shown, the very existence of these anti-dumping rules and panels ensures that they will be exhaustively used. NAFTA won't end conflicts over dumping, but it will channel such disputes into an institutionalized forum.

Perhaps the most intellectually coherent case against NAFTA was that it isn't a free trade agreement at all. Milton Friedman and other conservative economists argued that NAFTA could set a dangerous precedent for managed trade in other international economic relationships. The most disturbing possibility was that NAFTA might have been adopted along with new protectionist barriers on non-North American steel, cars, and textiles. Protests that NAFTA is "Gatt-legal"—that is, it doesn't impose new barriers on extracontinental imports—are meaningless if the net effect of its ratification is a more protectionist North America. The United States is four-fifths of the NAFTA market, and U.S. import rules would tend to set a minimum threshold for Canadian and Mexican quotas and tariffs for non-NAFTA goods.

■ NAFTA, like the U.S.-Canadian trade agreement it replaced, is "a way of formalizing a de facto integration that was already substantial," notes Sidney Weintraub, a University of Texas economist and former diplomat who is widely considered the leading American authority on cross-border trade. "The Mexican trade relationship with the United States is similar to that of Canada, in that each country sends about two-thirds of its total exports to the United States and an even higher proportion of its manufactured exports. Each country feared increased protectionism, particularly through non-tariff measures, so it moved to secure access to the market."

What the free trade agreement is unlikely to do—at least over the next several years—is produce much of a measurable impact on the United States. The first detailed macroeconomic study of NAFTA, by KPMG Peat Marwick, the accounting and economic analysis firm, found that the immediate American effects of NAFTA will be minimal. (The study was commissioned by the strongly pro-NAFTA Mexico-U.S. Business Council.) A slight rise was projected in American wages and employment in beneficiary sectors, with "limited adverse affects" in select industries, especially sugar refining and the garment business. In Mexico, by contrast, employment and industrial output will surge in a spectrum of industries, led by sugar refining (a projected 32 percent increase), apparel makers (up 19 percent), and electronics assembly (up 16 percent).

But if NAFTA is so economically marginal, why is American business so enthusiastic about it? The answer is simple: NAFTA gives access to the domestic Mexican market. Export-hungry American businesses see enormous sales potential in a population of 90 million, half of whom are under 18. Per-capita purchasing power, now about one-fifth that of the United States, has nearly doubled in the last five years—greatly expanding Mexico's middle class.

NAFTA opponents claimed that there "is no Mexican middle class." But the leading experts on middle-class consumerism disagreed. Retailers like WalMart and Home Depot and franchise operations like Blockbuster Video and Pizza Hut are rapidly expanding their Mexican operations. Auto sales—Detroit's Big Three hold the same market share in Mexico that they do at home—have more than doubled since Salinas took office. Manufacturers like General Electric, Kodak and IBM report that most sales from their expanding Mexican operations are made locally.

There is tremendous pent-up demand for such basic services as telephones, sewage systems, power plants, modern ports, and railways and highways—all areas where NAFTA gives American industry an inside sales track. Civil engineering firms see NAFTA as paving the way for more exotic industrial megaprojects. And Pemex, the Mexican state oil monopoly, will be spending an estimated $6 billion or more annually for the rest of the decade on outside goods and services, and NAFTA opens that procurement market to American companies for the first time.

NAFTA supporters often exaggerated the agreement's benefits while neglecting its costs. But the case for free trade is ultimately strengthened if the legitimate concerns of critics are fully acknowledged. And there is no getting around it: in the short run, NAFTA hastens the elimination of tens of thousands of jobs. The absolute number may be dwarfed by the number of new jobs created elsewhere by the pact—but that is no comfort to those thrown out of work.

The free trade agreement hurts glass blowers in West Virginia, apparel workers in the Carolinas, and sugarcane farmers in Texas and Florida, to mention a few. Ultimately, this is a price that Americans should be willing to pay. Salinas could hardly justify an accord that did not give Mexico access to protected American markets, and the American economy is better able to absorb the blows of restructuring.

Thus far, most of the pain has been felt on the southern side of the border. Mexico has lost more than 200,000 permanent jobs due to American apparel and textile imports. Another 200,000 oil and steel and airline workers have lost their jobs through privatization. The once-thriving Mexican toy industry has been devastated by import competition. Even the maquiladora assembly business has stopped growing after a decade of constant expansion. In the most severe dislocation of all, the free-market reform of Mexico's land tenancy laws could eventually push more than 1 million peasant farmers off the land.

Despite these disruptions, NAFTA will create many more jobs in both countries than it will destroy. It will also bring real benefits to consumers in both countries. Fierce competition and greater economies of scale will keep manufacturing costs down. In most cases, consumers will have to take the economists' word for it: savings will primarily be embedded in such big-ticket items as cars. Chryslers may be cheaper because their engines are made in Mexico, but the typical Chrysler buyer won't know that.

But consumers will see more tangible changes—some trivial, others profound. In the United States, avocados will become as cheap and plentiful as potatoes. Mexican superstores will sell Wisconsin butter, Quebec maple syrup, Massachusetts cranberry juice, and Washington State apples. Seafood will be more abundant and affordable in both countries as pisciculture enterprises populate Mexico's protein-rich shore-lines. (These businesses will in turn give Mexico an economic incentive to protect—and restore, in many cases—the ecology of fragile mangroves, estuaries and coral reefs.)

Consumer choice will be broadened in unlikely ways: farmers will ship jalapeños from Texas to Chihuahua, vintners will sell Baja California Chardonnay in Northern California. The biggest coals-to-Newcastle business will be almost literal: oil-rich Mexico will become a huge buyer of hydrocarbons (natural gas, refined fuels, low-sulfur coal) from both Canada and the United States. Entrepreneurs from north of the border will help build strings of rest-stop Mexican gas stations, while Pemex will buy into gasoline distribution companies in the United States. Joint ventures between the Mexican state oil monopoly and private American oil giants—in refining, pipelines and primary petrochemicals—will take root in both countries.

Collaboration between computer program writers in both countries will make software routinely available in Spanish as well as English, building a new market beyond North America. Sierra Maestra villages will pump and purify potable water with solar panels from California. Mexico City will edge toward Los Angeles-type standards on air emis-sions, creating a binational market for electric and natural gas-powered cars—cars that could be designed in Detroit and Monterrey, assembled in Toluca and Torrance, and sold around the world.

Overnight car ferries will ply the Yucatan straits, linking Merida to

Miami, much as Portland, Maine is connected to Halifax, Nova Scotia. Cancun and Chichen-Itza will become Winnebago destinations. Motorists from Chiapas and Tabasco will use the boats to drive to Disney World. This two-way tourism will be underwritten by roll-on, roll-off freight traffic.

Some of these developments are likely even without a free trade accord. But it is NAFTA that is driving events. NAFTA changes the bilateral trading relationship in a profound and permanent way: with NAFTA, the burden is on American competitors to show why a Mexican product should be kept out.

Take the contentious question of Mexican avocado imports. For decades, all Mexican avocados have been banned from the American market. The U.S. Department of Agriculture (USDA) justifies this by claiming that some Mexican avocados carry a pest that could destroy the avocado orchards of California. Mexican officials have argued that on-site or border inspection could easily isolate contaminated avocados (a routine process with other agricultural products). They have also suggested restricting Mexican exports to areas like New York and New England, far from any native avocado groves.

In the past, the USDA always rejected such proposals. This reinforced Mexico's conviction that the avocado ban was a blatant non-tariff barrier protecting California growers from a superior product that could be sold for half the price. While some USDA officials were willing to acknowledge protectionist pressures from California—and even label the American avocado industry "a dentists' tax shelter" and a "consumer rip-off"—they also complained that Mexico hadn't tried hard enough to eliminate the pest. So the impasse continued.

But as the free trade negotiations intensified, agriculture officials from both countries began to seek a compromise. Mexico suggested partitioning the country by growers' region and stepping up pest eradication measures. This would allow U.S. authorities to permit direct exports from Michoacan, the heart of Mexico's commercial avocado industry, without sanctioning imports from other states with weaker sanitary enforcement. The USDA, in turn, accepted a long-standing Mexican proposal to ship Mexican avocados to markets far from any native avocado orchards. As a test case, Mexico recently began sending avocados to Alaska—a comically small and distant market, perhaps, but a breakthrough in a policy that has kept Mexican avocados out of the United States for half a century. It shouldn't be long before Mexican avocados are seen in more temperate parts of the American north.

For more than a decade, U.S. envoys have piously assured their Mexican hosts that the U.S.-Mexican relationship is the most important bilateral relationship in the world. They then raced back to Washington to attend to Middle East peace talks, trade frictions with Japan, the disintegration of the Soviet bloc, and a succession of shorter-lived crises in places like Panama, Grenada, Nicaragua, Kuwait and Somalia. Absent a clear and present danger, Mexico—like Canada— never received much attention. The embassy in Mexico City wasn't considered a plum assignment. In the Reagan Administration, the ambassador in Tegucigalpa was more of a policy-making personage than the ambassador in Mexico City. Lawrence Eagleburger, after stepping down as Secretary of State, was asked whether he agreed with his successor's assertion that the Tokyo-Washington axis was the most important bilateral relationship in the world. Well, he demurred, Japan is important, but so is Russia, and the United Kingdom, and Germany, and China . . . He never mentioned Mexico.

Yet no other bilateral relationship cuts so broadly across bureaucratic lines. When American presidents schedule state visits to Mexico, the interagency preparatory meetings fill entire auditoriums. The hundreds of officials who deal routinely with Mexican issues are concentrated not only in such expected places as the Commerce and State Departments, but in Treasury (customs, tax conflicts, foreign debt problems), Justice (including the semi-autonomous drug enforcement and immigration bureaucracies, for which Mexico is the biggest foreign preoccupation), Agriculture (Mexico is the third biggest market for American farm exports and biggest source of imported fruits and vegetables), Energy (Mexico is consistently one of the three essential American oil suppliers), the Export-Import Bank (its biggest exposure, by far, is in Mexico), and the Environmental Protection Agency (the EPA's only foreign posting is Mexico City). Immigration and job training issues are also putting Mexico on the agenda at Labor and Education. Indeed, there is no cabinet department not engaged in some bilateral dealings with Mexico. Even purely domestic agencies such as the Departments of Interior and Housing and Urban Development face land management and urbanization problems that are unique to the border area.

The enormous complexity of the bilateral relationship is reflected in the number of U.S. government employees working within Mexico itself. The embassy in Mexico City, with about 1,000 employees, is the second biggest U.S. diplomatic post in the world (only Cairo is larger). The embassy's nearly 400 U.S. employees (the remainder are Mexican nationals) represent the largest and most varied detachment of civilian officials in any foreign posting. Their paychecks come from 37 different government departments, agencies and commissions. No more than 60 of these diplomatic passport holders are from the State Department itself. A Mexican desk officer characterizes State's receding role in bilateral affairs as a "concierge service"—providing advice and logistical support for an increasingly diverse interagency work force. In addition, there are more than 100 consular employees posted throughout Mexico, plus scores of transient contract researchers and consultants who are also working for the U.S. government.

This deployment is mirrored by Mexico's personnel in the United States. Though the Mexican foreign service has a long tradition of worldwide representation, more than half of its foreign-posted employees are in the United States. Most work in one of Mexico's 39 U.S. consular offices, which constitute a formal diplomatic network unequaled by any other country. In the past, the consulates were sleepy sinecures for over-the-hill political appointees. Under Salinas, they have been energized by ambitious young technocrats with a mandate to promote free trade and provide legal assistance to the immigrant communities the consulates had once seigneurially ignored. As in the United States, responsibility for the bilateral relationship has widened far beyond the diplomatic corps. Mexico's Commerce and Industry ministry has its own Washington office. Pemex, the oil monopoly, has concentrated its foreign purchasing, marketing and financing operations in offices in Texas and New York. The Mexican embassy's senior economic advisor is a central bank attaché. The Mexican finance ministry's international affairs department devotes most of its negotiating energies to dealings with the U.S. government and American commercial banks.

In contrast to the United States, however, the bilateral relationship is for all Mexican agencies the preponderant share of their international responsibilities. Once Salinas committed himself to the pursuit of a free trade agreement, the marketing and negotiating of NAFTA became the central organizing principle of his entire government.

On the U.S. side, NAFTA means that it no longer took an emergency to impose some order on bilateral affairs. Not only does NAFTA regulate the expansion of cross-border trade, it provides a basis for resolving the trade and investment disputes that have in the past led to unnecessary diplomatic friction. NAFTA also provides a way to address labor concerns and environmental issues, on the border and beyond. This coordination could be extended to other bilateral concerns, including transportation investment, narcotics enforcement, and monetary policy. NAFTA could also provide a non-confrontational framework for discussing immigration issues, the single most complex and difficult aspect of the bilateral relationship.

Still, economic partnership does not eliminate diplomatic friction; it might even exacerbate it. By seeking closer economic ties with the United States, Mexico is subjecting itself to closer political scrutiny. PRI ward bosses aren't the only Mexicans who don't like that idea. But it is entirely legitimate for U.S. politicians to ask whether the Mexican opponents of NAFTA were being cheated out of election victories. If they were, resistance within Mexico to a free trade pact was underestimated by its American proponents, and the future of the Salinas free-market experiment was far more precarious than its supporters contended.

The judicial system also opens itself to scrutiny. Mexico bristles about criticism of its cops and courts, yet with closer economic ties now, this antagonism will surely increase. Any legal discrimination against American or Canadian investors will become a full-blown trade dispute subject to review by NAFTA's independent panels. So will any evidence that judges bend the law at the will of the executive to favor Mexican individuals or companies. The Salinas government was already forced in the NAFTA negotiations to let trinational tribunals take precedence over Mexican courts in intellectual property rights cases and other disputes. Mexico also agreed to restructure the upper tiers of its judiciary to create appellate courts analogous to the U.S. and Canadian systems. These appellate courts will be handling sensitive foreign investment matters, under the scrutiny of U.S. and Canadian officials and high-priced corporate lawyers, with their decisions subject to trinational NAFTA review boards. They will be held to a standard of independence and professionalism unprecedented in Mexico's legal history. The contrast with Mexico's criminal courts and the fecklessly obeisant Mexican Supreme Court will be glaring, and salutary.

All of these changes will place great strains on the country as Mexico's north grows richer at the expense (critics would say) of its impoverished south, as domestic fights over human rights and environmental degradation and electoral reform spill messily across the border, as Mexico surrenders some of its fiscal and monetary sovereignty only to become further entangled in U.S. economic policy problems. But NAFTA means that there is no looking back. North America is redefining itself for just the third or fourth time since Columbus. And this time, Mexico is determined to be an actor, not a victim.

The Canadian Exception	When Brian Mulroney announced in late February 1992 that he would be stepping down as Canada's prime minister, the Mexican stock market wobbled in despair. Of the founding NAFTA triumvirate, only Carlos Salinas now remained.

Mexican investors worried that Mulroney's resignation would mean critical delays for NAFTA. And every time NAFTA stumbled, the Bolsa would fall.

But the skittish investor response to Mulroney's resignation was misplaced. If anything, Mulroney's resignation exposed Canada's marginality in the entire NAFTA process. Canada, the country where opposition to NAFTA was most entrenched, is also the country where NAFTA matters least.

Mulroney retired as the least popular prime minister in Canadian history, but his misfortunes had little impact on the ultimate fate of his trade policy. Kim Campbell, his better-received successor, backed Mulroney's decision to push NAFTA through the House of Commons before the fall election. She also supported Mulroney's reluctant decision to sign on to Clinton's side agreements, which the Tories had previously opposed as infringements on Canadian sovereignty and obstacles to freer trade. Campbell's cosmetic insistence on a limited Canadian exemption from NAFTA's labor and environmental sanctions procedures only underscored Canada's lack of leverage in the negotiations. Ottawa, unlike Washington, cannot simply walk away. That choice had been waived a decade earlier, when Mulroney first sought a free trade pact with the United States. That 1984 decision was irreversible, committing Canada to a regional integration process that could not now be stopped. If Washington went ahead with NAFTA, so would Ottawa.

Ratification, however, wasn't painless. Canadian public opinion still solidly opposed the accord. Washington's aggressive anti-dumping claims against Canada since the 1989 ratification of the U.S.-Canadian Free Trade Agreement (USCFTA) had led even hard-core free-traders to distance themselves from NAFTA. Conflicts over everything from beer to leather to wheat had disabused Canadians of the notion that the agreement would end cross-border haggling and ensure permanent American market access for Canadian products.

In the most transparently politicized case, U.S. customs inspectors, under pressure from Detroit, reinterpreted the USCFTA's rules of origin in a way that cut the U.S.-Canadian content of Canadian-made Hondas from more than 50 percent (the USCFTA minimum for duty-free treatment) to less than 20 percent. This reassessment was based on the novel premise that parts built in North American plants with Japanese owners—such as the Canadian Honda's Ohio-made engine—should henceforth be considered Japanese, not North American, for the purpose of U.S. customs classification.

Still, these conflicts obscured how well the USCFTA was really working: it had increased the volume of trade while reducing the frequency of trade conflicts. The dispute resolution panels gained respect for their professionalism, with rulings aimed roughly equally against each side. (In an encouraging precedent for NAFTA's various panels and commissions, the nationalities of the USCFTA panelists bore little correlation to their judgments.)

Most notably, Canada was tallying record trade surpluses with the United States as a result of the accord. It might seem odd that America's trade deficit with Canada was rarely acknowledged by critics who claimed that NAFTA would create a trade deficit with Mexico. But for the anti-NAFTA lobby, Canada was supposed to be proof of free trade's folly, and its bilateral surplus interfered with that thesis.

There is no question that Canada is suffering, despite its surplus. After the FTA passed, Canada bogged down in its worst recession since the 1930s. Growth lagged a point or more behind the sluggish American economy. Unemployment hovered around 10 percent. Many Canadians concluded that free trade was not only failing to deliver prosperity but was threatening to tear Canadian society apart.

Yet even Canadian economists agree that the recession wasn't caused by the FTA, but by unsustainable budget deficits, high interest rates, and the inability of basic industries to meet the challenge of competition from outside North America. Global and American economic slowdown made things worse.

Yet the FTA did deepen the recession in traditional industrial centers like southern Ontario, a fact which too many free-traders chose to ignore. The FTA's architects had oversold its short-term benefits, and then denied its short-term dislocations.

But job losses from free trade weren't as great as Canadian unions claimed. Nor were they generally attributable to the causes, such as lower American wages and taxes, that the unions cited. Manufacturing wage differentials are too small ($17.31 versus $15.45 in 1991) to justify the relocation of an entire industrial plant. Lower health care costs in Canada generally compensate for higher wages and tax bills. (Some jobs also go north: General Motors closed Southern California's last auto plant in August 1992, and started building all its Chevy Camaros in Quebec—prompted in part by a $600-a-car savings in health-care costs.)

Still, there were losses. The biggest FTA-related cuts came in the American manufacturing companies—including GM—that could supply the Canadian market from larger, more modern plants in the United States. Transportation costs also dictated new marketing arrangements, which often penalized Canadian plants. No longer would customers in Vancouver be supplied by a factory in Quebec if the company had an equivalent plant in California. The result is that smaller, less efficient plants geared for the Canadian market were closed or converted to more specialized product lines requiring fewer workers.

The free trade agreement was intended to do just this—increase productivity on a continental scale. But that invariably translates into short-term job losses. Not that Canada had any long-term choice: the FTA simply accelerated its inevitable reckoning with the inefficiencies of producing exclusively for a market smaller than California. The Canadian economy should emerge from this transition chastened, but strengthened.

Even if the Tories had failed to get NAFTA through the House of Commons, and were then trounced in the general election, that still wouldn't have meant that NAFTA was doomed in Canada. After several impressive showings in provincial elections, the ferociously anti-NAFTA National Democratic Party has more recently seemed spent as a national force; at the time of Mulroney's announcement, the NDP was running behind even the Tories in the Gallup poll. Far ahead of both was Jean Chretien's Liberal Party.

Chretien had an artfully fudged, Clintonesque take on NAFTA: endorsing free trade generically, but criticizing the agreement itself. He said that he favored "renegotiation," not abrogation. Yet renegotiation as he defined it seemed to mean little more than the addition of the side agreements that the three countries have since concluded. Aimed at the broad Canadian center, the Liberals didn't want to alienate the Canadian business organizations, which were strongly behind the agreement. And Quebec, always the exception to the Canadian rule and critical to a Liberal majority, was the one province where NAFTA had considerable popular support. So it suited Liberal purposes to let the Tories pass NAFTA as their final legislative act, lament (but accept) its passage as a now-binding sovereign commitment, and tinker around the edges with the labor and environmental accords. The Clinton parallel is plain.

The cold truth is that the United States and Mexico started their trade talks without consulting Canada and were quite willing to continue on their own if Canada dropped out. Ottawa had demanded a place at the table to defend its interests. A U.S.-Mexican accord would alter the terms of North American trade, and Canada is even more dependent on the American market than Mexico. Mulroney had predicated his risky free trade strategy on the presumption that a special relationship with the United States would have compensating rewards. He never expected Salinas to seek his own FTA barely a year after Canada's was ratified. And, not unreasonably, once Mexico made its request, Mulroney expected to be consulted by Washington. But the Bush Administration never called.

In some ways, Mulroney deserves as much credit for NAFTA as anyone. When the Progressive Conservatives swept to victory in 1984, winning a record 211 of the Parliament's 282 seats, Mulroney asked to start free trade talks with Washington almost immediately. In 1988, with the agreement largely negotiated but not yet ratified, he centered his re-election campaign on a defense of the controversial pact. The Conservatives won again, but their majority dropped to 169 seats. After the free trade deal's signing in 1989, however, Mulroney's fortunes slid downhill. The economy sagged, and the government became embroiled again in Quebec's demands for autonomy. Against this background, many Canadians feared that open trade would slowly push Canada toward dissolution, with the provinces drifting into the orbits of their immediate American neighbors.

Salinas, for his part, worried that Canadian participation would only complicate and prolong a difficult process. He preferred to strike a separate deal with Ottawa, building on the Mexico-Canada framework accord that Mexico had just negotiated. But the Mulroney government wanted to influence the terms of Mexico's agreement with the United States, and the only way to do that was through trilateral negotiations.

Once the talks got under way, the American and Mexican negotiators found Canadian participation unexpectedly constructive. The trilateral format kept disputes from becoming polarized along predictable U.S.-Mexican lines. There were shifting alliances. Canada backed Mexico's demands for transitional protection for domestically controlled industries, but supported U.S. pressure for liberalized Mexican state procurement practices. Canada's staunch protection of its media industries helped Mexico in its fight to require some of its movie theaters to show Mexican films. With Detroit's backing, Canada and Mexico fought to keep used American cars out of their markets. (They succeeded: used cars can't be imported freely into either country for 25 years, NAFTA's longest phase-in period.) Canadian companies backed American efforts to open up investment in the Mexican telecommunications and banking industries.

But Canada was not a full NAFTA partner. The fact that Ottawa could insist that penalties for labor and environmental violations be assessed in Canada's case alone by Canada's own national courts—for Mexico and the United States, the sanctioning body would be the new labor and environmental commissions—proved again that the real negotiations were being conducted between Washington and Mexico City. Earlier, Canada had successfully resisted NAFTA's sweeping liberalization of the textile trade, preferring to update existing bilateral arrangements. On agriculture, it stayed out of NAFTA entirely, retaining its original USCFTA terms for the farm trade and striking a limited parallel deal directly with Mexico. Canada's bargaining weakness was most evident in the critical area of rules of origin. Over Canada's strenuous objections, the North American content threshold for cars was ratcheted up from the 50 percent minimum laid down by the USCFTA to 62.5 percent, a level that Ottawa feared would keep the Japanese and Europeans from building car plants in Canada. Canada also unsuccessfully fought NAFTA's tougher "yarn-forward" rules of origin for textiles and apparel. Still, its Tory advocates came out of the talks insisting that NAFTA is a good deal for Canadian business.

And it is, despite Canada's negotiating disappointments. In itself, trade with Mexico is unimportant to Canada, barely reaching $3 billion a year. Some predict it will double to $6 billion by the year 2000. But that is minuscule compared to Canada's $180 billion yearly trade flow with the United States. Even pro-NAFTA economic studies show the accord boosting the Canadian GDP by less than one-quarter of 1 percent.

But integration with the broader U.S.-Mexican market could still prove critical for important Canadian industries. The combined southwestern American and northern Mexican market is already attracting a wide range of exporters, from Nova Scotia fishermen to Ottawa telecommunications firms to Alberta natural gas companies to British Colombian coal mines. Canada's withdrawal from NAFTA now would penalize its shrinking automotive industry, which would find itself excluded from the continent's fastest-growing car market. It would hurt Canadian wheat growers, who have quietly become Mexico's biggest suppliers, and the lumber exporters who are hungrily eyeing the timber-scarce Mexican construction market. Most dangerous of all, it would make Canada less attractive to Asian and European investors.

But, finally, NAFTA is about Mexico. NAFTA extends North American industrial society south into a relatively closed and much poorer economy. Canada is necessarily a bystander in this process. It never sought Mexico's inclusion in the free trade area, and it was powerless to prevent it. NAFTA is ultimately bilateral, a pact between Mexico City and Washington to which Ottawa, under any government, must reluctantly subscribe.

CHAPTER 3

'Via
Positiva'

Hermann von Bertrab, the dapper former priest who ran Mexico's Washington trade negotiating office, was speaking to a group of California newspaper editors, trying to convey a sense of NAFTA's importance. Instinctively, he reached for a theological analogy. His Jesuit instructors, he recalled, used to teach that there were two paths to God: the slow, tortuous *via negativa* of suffering and duress, and the more gratifying *via positiva* of clearly sustained faith. For Mexico, he said, NAFTA represented the assured, "positive" route—not to salvation, perhaps, but to economic success.

The editors listened politely. Von Bertrab decided to try a more prosaic metaphor. He likened the newly liberalized Mexican economy to a loaded 747 leaving the runway. NAFTA's rejection, he said, would be "catastrophic," like a vicious and unexpected downdraft. The jumbo jet would crash on takeoff, and he and the rest of Salinas's pro-American reformers would have full responsibility for the wreckage.

Does NAFTA matter? Mexican officials like Von Bertrab may find the question offensive, but other NAFTA advocates like to claim that it doesn't.

There were three distinct phases of the NAFTA debate, each with its own set-piece arguments. In the first phase, when George Bush fought for fast-track negotiating authority, a trade pact with Mexico was portrayed as a border-cum-foreign policy initiative and, later, as the cornerstone of a hemispheric common market. In the second phase, during the 1992 election campaign, the newly drafted agreement was promoted as a mammoth domestic jobs program. Then, in the third phase, with a tepidly pro-NAFTA Democratic White House confronting a protection-ist-minded Democratic Congress, the case for ratification was made with a new modesty. The new wisdom was that NAFTA didn't really matter much: it's a marginal economic event for the United States, advocates argued, while for Mexico it simply represents the codification in treaty form of policies it was already implementing unilaterally.

This minimalist spin had a certain political logic. NAFTA advocates (including the USTR negotiators themselves) had tired of defending the Bush Administration's overheated job creation claims. By overstating NAFTA's short-term impact on the United States, Bush had opened the door to critics who could argue that this gain wouldn't come without commensurate pain.

By downplaying NAFTA's domestic impact, American proponents were trying to vent emotional steam out of the free trade debate. By stressing that U.S.-Mexican integration was well advanced, and already substantially liberalized, advocates could portray NAFTA as merely the continuation of an existing reality, rather than as a bold but possibly perilous step into the unknown.

The minimalist argument had the additional political virtue of being technically true. In acknowledging that American job growth resulting from NAFTA would be statistically insignificant, advocates were reflecting their own economic research. Trade with Mexico represents a scant 7 percent of the American export market. The entire export sector represents a narrow sliver—about 10 percent—of the American economy. Sales to Mexico add less than a percentage point to the American gross domestic product.

Mexico's dependence on the United States, moreover, has long been apparent, and will continue with NAFTA. Even in the specific matter of bilateral tariff reductions, trade experts pooh-poohed NAFTA's significance: tariff barriers on the American side were already quite low, averaging less than 4 percent. Mexican duties had already fallen from 100 percent in 1981 to 10 percent 10 years later. Taking the last step to zero over 15 years would only extend an ongoing process. Some Mexican officials, eager to assure investors that not everything in Mexico was dependent on NAFTA, also became late converts to the no-big-deal doctrine. Mexican finance officials began telling Park Avenue business conferences that NAFTA, as the final entry on a long list of Salinas economic policy accomplishments, was merely "the icing on the cake."

At least the Mexican finance ministry knew better. For the Salinas Administration, NAFTA wasn't the icing on the cake—it was the cake itself. Without NAFTA, Mexico couldn't gain the kind of market access it needs or be confident that American policy wouldn't change in the future. As a result, Mexico's economy could not hope to attract the billions required to sustain its dynamic growth. Salinas's adversaries have no doubt that NAFTA is the linchpin of the government's strategy: Senator Porfirio Muñoz Ledo, one of the president's bitterest opponents, noted gleefully as NAFTA came under attack in the U.S. Congress that Salinas's "whole economic theater will collapse the day that it is known that there will be no free trade treaty."

Mexican economists are right to say that NAFTA itself doesn't guarantee growth: only sound money, open investment policies, and macroeconomic stability can do that. Mexico also remains dependent on forces beyond its control, such as dollar interest rates and oil prices. Increasingly, moreover, maintaining confidence in the country's future won't be simply a matter of astute economic stewardship, but of adept and flexible political management. But having NAFTA in place makes it far easier for Mexico to take full advantage of economic opportunity and withstand external economic shocks.

For Mexico, however, NAFTA isn't just a trade pact. It's a seal of good economic housekeeping for investors. The potential power of NAFTA's imprimatur was dramatically illustrated by the cascade of capital into Mexico during the period in which NAFTA was negotiated. Foreign portfolio investment in Mexico—most of it in equities, and most of it from the United States—quadrupled in 1990 and more than tripled in 1991. The moment it became clear that NAFTA would be slowed or even stopped by the U.S. election, the flow of portfolio funds dried up. Economic growth fell from 4 percent to less than 3 percent, as authorities struggled to contain inflation and a trade deficit that was no longer self-financing.

NAFTA is more important to Mexico than it is to the United States by a factor of at least 10: even its critics agree on that much. And the impact on Mexico will be immediate. Foreign capital will again flow into the stock market, followed by the many direct investment projects that have been delayed by companies that first wanted to see how NAFTA's rules would affect their specific industry.

Judging from recent Mexican experience, NAFTA could bring in $10 billion in portfolio funds and $5 billion in direct investment in its first year alone. Moody's and Standard & Poor's could be expected to bestow investment-grade status on Mexican government and blue chip corporate bonds, widening their appeal in the huge institutional investor market in

Europe, Japan and the United States. The potential impact on Mexico is enormous. American and European institutional investors now have less than one-fifteenth of 1 percent of their $5 trillion bond portfolio invested in Mexico. Under NAFTA, that share might rise to perhaps one-half of 1 percent by the end of the decade. This seemingly small advance would translate into a $25 billion endorsement of Mexico by the world's most conservative money managers.

No longer will Mexico need to struggle to maintain an annual growth rate of 3 to 4 percent. Conservative calculations of NAFTA's impact on Mexico predict that it will add up to a percentage point of growth. The difference between 4 and 5 percent is hardly trivial. Sustained over two decades, this will represent an additional $200 billion in gross domestic product, an amount equal to the size of the entire economy when Salinas took office in 1988.

More optimistic economists believe NAFTA will let the Mexican economy grow by at least 6 percent a year. That will put the GDP at $500 billion in 10 years—making Mexico's economy as big as Canada's is today.

NAFTA might easily propel Mexico toward a steady growth of 6 to 7 percent. After all, Mexico sustained that pace from the 1940s through the 1970s. Economic integration should drive inflation down closer to American norms, letting Mexico's hypercautious finance ministry take off the fiscal brakes. By some calculations, Mexico doesn't have much choice: factoring in the growth of the job market and projected improvements in productivity, its economy has to grow by more than 6 percent a year just to keep unemployment under control. At that rate, the Mexican GDP will approach the $600 billion mark by 2004, when most of NAFTA's liberalization is fully in force.

Students of East Asia and the recent Chilean experience suggest that faster growth in the 7 to 8 percent range is perfectly feasible. Yet even at 6 percent, Mexico will have a trillion-dollar economy by 2010, after NAFTA is to remove the last remaining barriers to free cross-border trade. That is five times bigger than the economy Salinas inherited, which hadn't grown in real terms for almost a decade. And the Mexicans who live in that NAFTA-expanded economy in the year 2010 will be twice as rich in real per capita terms as Mexicans are today.

It is that brute increase in the size and wealth of the Mexican economy—growth that would be paralleled by a steady surge in bilateral trade—that is the real story of NAFTA for both Mexico and the United States. Niggling over whether the trade balance would be a few billion dollars in surplus or deficit in 2010 is pointless when the volume of that two-way trade will have tripled to $150 billion over the previous 20 years. Even less relevant is NAFTA's marginal impact on the enormous American job market for the next five or 10 years—the far horizon of any credible mathematical modeling exercise. The issue in the short term isn't the American job market, but the Mexican job market. The right time frame for assessing NAFTA bilaterally isn't five or 10 years, but 15 or 25 years.

It is quite wrong to view NAFTA as simply the culmination of an inevitable process. There was nothing inevitable about a free trade and investment agreement with the United States. Mexico's trade liberalization strategy was adopted on an emergency basis in the throes of the debt crisis to control inflation and stabilize the currency. The decision to seek a free trade pact was prompted by a continuing cash flow problem at a time of great concern about competing demands for capital from Eastern Europe. Mexico's leader happened to be an academically trained economist whose political disposition and years in American universities had left him open to the idea of a closer relationship with the United States. He was surrounded by a cohesive team of similar background and training.

The American and Mexican economies have been interlocked for generations. Mexican statistics from a century ago describe the same degree of dependence that characterizes the economy today, with American trade and investment each representing more than 60 percent of Mexico's transactions. Despite the tumult of the Mexican Revolution and varying Mexican economic strategies, these percentages barely budged. Yet it wasn't until Mexico joined the General Agreement on Tariffs and Trade in August 1986 that the scale and scope of that interrelationship was radically enlarged. In just five years American export sales to Mexico tripled to $40 billion. Direct investment in Mexico, three-fifths of it American, nearly doubled to $22 billion, and foreign portfolio investment, also mostly from the United States, soared from near zero to $30 billion, representing the biggest short-term redirection of American capital outflows in recent years.

These changes were not just quantitative but qualitative, with two-way trade flows reflecting the integration of Mexican subsidiaries into broader North American manufacturing networks, and the increased investment resulting from new access to the stock market and once-protected "strategic" industries. As with the earlier U.S.-Canadian integration, most of this increased manufacturing commerce is taking place within companies with plants on both sides of the border. Intracompany trade and restructuring on a continental scale is raising productivity and lowering costs to consumers—precisely the changes that NAFTA promises to encourage over the long term.

Mexico's economic strategy in the years since the debt collapse is often treated as a single period of market-oriented reform. In reality, the 1980s divide into two distinct phases, reflecting fundamentally different strategies and results. In the first years of the financial emergency, Mexico was forced to follow the International Monetary Fund's three-step program for recovering debtors: first, turn the trade deficit into a surplus by drastically devaluing the currency; second, eliminate the budget deficit by any means necessary; and third, keep up interest on the foreign debt by borrowing more and more from the same banks that are demanding those interest payments.

This formula deepened the debt disaster everywhere it was applied. It "worked" in the short term, in the sense that it kept both debtors and creditors technically solvent. But it condemned already poor countries to a politically unsustainable regime of constant real wage cuts—Mexican salaries fell 40 percent in five years—and ever-rising debt payments. The devaluation strategy fed ruinous inflation, encouraged capital flight, and made essential imports prohibitively expensive. It artificially prolonged the life of inefficient local manufacturers, who were spared from competition at home while selling abroad only on the basis of low labor costs and a cheap currency. Worst of all, it undermined public faith in the local currency, which in most smaller economies is a surrogate for the economy itself. The peso, which in early 1982 had traded at 26 to the dollar, had plummeted within a year to 150-to-1. By the end of 1987, when the Mexican central bank could no longer afford to intervene on its behalf, the peso had tumbled to 2,300 to the dollar.

After five years of IMF medicine, Mexico was suffering from the highest annual inflation in its history—160 percent. Real wages had fallen heavily. Tens of billions of dollars of Mexican flight capital remained stubbornly offshore. Emigration was soaring to record levels. Oil prices had collapsed, reminding Mexico how dependent it was on crude sales and how urgently it needed new sources of revenue. The only growing source of investment, local or foreign, was the maquiladora assembly industry, low-tech and transient by nature, wholly dependent on supplies and markets in the United States, with sharply limited benefits for Mexico due to the low wages on which the business was predicated.

The De la Madrid Administration, led by its planning and budget minister, Carlos Salinas de Gortari, was plotting a new strategy. In August

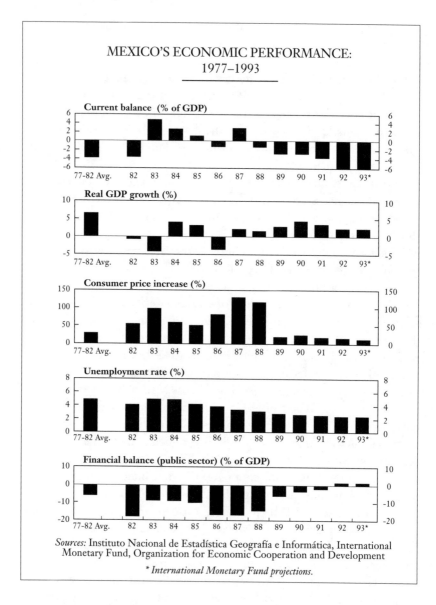

MEXICO'S ECONOMIC PERFORMANCE:
1977–1993

Sources: Instituto Nacional de Estadística Geografía e Informática, International Monetary Fund, Organization for Economic Cooperation and Development

* *International Monetary Fund projections.*

1986, fulfilling a commitment it had made a decade earlier, Mexico at last joined the General Agreement on Tariffs and Trade. The import liberalization that forcibly accompanied Mexico's Gatt entry was prompted less by an ideological devotion to free trade than by the urgent need to control inflation: only brutal competition from foreign goods would keep local producers' prices in check.

Mexico's trade surplus soon vanished, threatening the country's dollar reserves. The Mexican economic team began pushing for a new approach to the foreign debt, which would shrink the stock of outstanding debt and halt the growth of the interest bill that had been transferring 6 percent of Mexico's economy to creditors abroad every year since 1982. They sought ways to balance the budget—not by slashing deeper into social welfare spending, but by preparing an ambitious privatization campaign that ultimately would net the treasury nearly $20 billion in hard cash.

The new strategy had, at its core, a commitment to containing inflation and stabilizing the peso. A strong peso was essential to restoring investor confidence, raising living standards, and recapturing billions in flight capital. As chief economic strategist in the De la Madrid Administration, Salinas had grown accustomed to resisting pressure from Mexican manufacturers who wanted to compete simply on the basis of a cheap currency. The radical combination of unilateral trade liberalization and the deliberate strengthening of the currency may have been a shock to inefficient local producers, but it was a boon to investors who banked on long-term recovery.

The long-term goal was sustainable growth of 5 to 6 percent a year, with inflation in the single digits, a declining debt service ratio, and a current account deficit of 2 to 3 percent of GDP—a profile not unlike that of many East Asian economies in the 1980s. That strategy implied a slow but steady increase in productivity and real wages, with an ambitious campaign to attract technologically advanced foreign investment and to prod complacent local manufacturers to export and invest abroad.

It was a plan to escape the maquiladora trap of the 1980s, which condemned Mexico to investments based on low wages and lax environmental standards. But to work, it needed a steady net influx of billions of dollars a year to finance imports and investment. And as the government discovered, only the promise of permanent domestic economic reform and access to the crucial American market could guarantee the capital flows on which it relied.

As Mexico waited for NAFTA, the experiment became increasingly difficult. The peso was becoming gradually overvalued, with the incremental slippage against the dollar not keeping pace with the 10 to 15 percent spread between the U.S. and Mexican inflation rates. The trade deficit was steadily widening.

The Salinas regime had amassed a record $18 billion in foreign reserves, giving the peso a strong but temporary buffer. The only real solution was to have Mexico's economic reality catch up to where the peso already was—and the 5 percent growth needed to make that happen wouldn't materialize until and if NAFTA were ratified.

Again, Mexican exporters began clamoring for a quick devaluation. But that would have been a cure worse than the disease: the economy would shrink instantly in real terms. The entire Salinas experiment would suddenly appear disturbingly ephemeral to private and foreign investors alike. For Mexican workers, a sudden devaluation would be like an across-the-board wage cut in a company that offers neither job security nor profit sharing. Moreover, a devaluation would have made Mexico appear unstable to outside investors, undermining the case for NAFTA in the rest of North America.

What If NAFTA Fails?
The best way to appraise NAFTA's importance is to contemplate the consequences had it been rejected.

One immediate result would have been the collapse of the peso. A sharp devaluation would have provoked an upsurge in inflation and multibillion-dollar capital flight, devastating the stock market and crippling at least a few of the country's newly privatized banks. Pressure to impose currency controls and limit foreign debt payments would quickly have grown intense. Either move would have destroyed the credibility in world credit markets that Mexico has worked so hard to regain. Yet there would have been few alternatives.

Even more serious than the economic upheaval would have been the breakdown of public confidence. So thoroughly had the government persuaded people that NAFTA was vital to solving Mexico's problems that a rejection would have had calamitous results. Persuading people to look optimistically toward the future—to invest in their homes, educations and savings accounts—would have been much harder. Meanwhile, fears of a new economic downturn would have driven waves of jobseekers northward across the U.S. border.

Critics argued that this scenario was valid only because Salinas had put the economy in a precarious position. His entire strategy, they charged, was built on the imprudent assumption of NAFTA's passage. Fair enough. Only an influx of speculative portfolio capital had allowed the country to sustain its widening current account deficit, which ended 1992 at a record-setting 6 percent of gross domestic product. But that was the position that Mexico was in—and it got there largely because it had followed U.S. advice. And since NAFTA enjoyed the declared backing of the leadership of both American political parties, assumptions about its eventual ratification were hardly irresponsible.

It is true that NAFTA's impact has been exaggerated by both critics and opponents of the agreement. It is also true that for Mexico the agreement simply formalizes and accelerates a process of economic integration that can be traced back to Mexico's entrance into Gatt in 1987, the collapse of its dollar-indebted treasury five years earlier, and its emergence as a leading oil exporter five years before that. Commerce Minister Jaime Serra likes to say that the reforms Mexico has already undertaken voluntarily are more profound than anything NAFTA obliges it to do, and he is probably right. He and his colleagues have also been careful to stress that even with a free trade accord, they have every intention of pressing ahead with economic reform.

Indeed, throughout the NAFTA talks Mexico moved forward on its own on a range of related issues, and without exception it moved in directions welcomed by U.S. negotiators. By reducing Pemex's role in the petrochemical industry, by opening transportation bottlenecks, by its landmark rewriting of agrarian property laws, the Salinas Administration unilaterally opened Mexico's doors to American trade and investment. And it has not demanded reciprocity. To the contrary, the Salinas contention is that these measures are sovereign decisions, essential for international competitiveness, taken for Mexico's own good. The Salinas team has been careful to assert at every opportunity that Mexico's prosperity is not dependent on a free trade deal with the United States, but on such fundamentals as sound fiscal policies, clear investment rules, and better public education.

There is a great danger, though, in underestimating what NAFTA ultimately means to Mexico. The stakes are too high. The promise of a free trade agreement lured billions in stock investments and new factory installations: the Salinas economy became a prisoner of its own success. If NAFTA had been defeated in the U.S. Congress, the economic upheaval in Mexico would have dwarfed the dimensions of the 1987 stock market crash. The repercussions would have approached those of the debt emergency of 1982, which stopped the economy cold for almost five years.

A NAFTA defeat would also have unnerved the rest of Latin America. Touted by both Bush and Clinton as the first part of a pan-American free trade zone, NAFTA is the cornerstone of what many Latin Americans have welcomed as the most constructive U.S. initiative toward their region since the Alliance for Progress. As a result, U.S.-Latin American diplomatic relations are now at their most cordial and cooperative in decades. But if neighboring Mexico were rejected in its attempt to erase bilateral trade barriers, there would be little hope for any other country in the hemisphere. A NAFTA defeat—especially when coupled with stepped-up economic aid to the former Soviet bloc—would have shown Latin America all too clearly where it stands in the list of U.S. priorities.

Equally important, a rejection of NAFTA would have been a humiliation for the only Mexican president to ever stake his career on a closer relationship with the United States—"a slap in the face," one Salinas aide said, wincing at the possibility. No Mexican politician would make that mistake again.

Even if NAFTA had been postponed beyond 1993, Salinas would have lost valuable maneuverability in the selection of his successor. This was Mexico's principal argument for an early NAFTA decision, or so asserted Salinas's closest advisor, José Córdoba, who met with Samuel Berger, Clinton's chief foreign policy advisor, a month before Clinton's inauguration.

Plainly, the mechanics of the Mexican presidential succession are the PRI's problem, not Washington's. Indeed, for those who feel that Mexico is urgently in need of democratization, there was a case for protracting the NAFTA debate through the PRI candidate's selection and into the early months of the general election campaign. The process of pursuing a free trade deal had already pushed the government toward political reform. Continued attention from American critics would have made the PRI more likely to introduce some measure of internal democracy, and less likely to rig the general election of 1994 with the blatant use of state resources and control of Mexican press coverage.

Yet it is a telling irony that the American debate over NAFTA gave such resolute nationalists as opposition leader Cuáuhtemoc Cárdenas valuable leverage in the domestic political process. Cárdenas, who shares Mexico's deep traditional aversion to foreign intervention, had at one point suggested that NAFTA should wait until Mexico held new elections vetted by foreign observers (he stressed that he didn't oppose NAFTA in principle, however, and wouldn't repeal it were he to reach the presidency after its ratification).

This begs a question: if seeking NAFTA was good for the Mexican political and economic system, why not have protracted the process indefinitely? The short answer: Salinas and his crew might not survive, and the opportunity could be lost forever. The long answer: bilateral conflicts would not instantly cease after NAFTA's approval, and neither would U.S. leverage over Mexico's behavior. Inevitably, there would be trade and investment disputes. Narcotics control could resurface as a point of friction. The foreign debt could again become a bilateral problem, especially if Washington grants more lenient repayment terms to other debtors than it was willing to give to Mexico.

The counterargument for NAFTA as a democratization instrument departs from the premise that the PRI will engineer a transition to Salinas's chosen successor, no matter what their opponents or American critics think about it. The issue then becomes the identity of that successor.

With NAFTA, foreign investment flows will be largely guaranteed, and Salinas will be free to pick an heir who will concentrate on political restructuring. NAFTA also will make it easier for a future government to pursue a higher-wage strategy, allow greater union freedoms, devote resources to environmental concerns, and tolerate a critical press. And NAFTA will make it harder to concentrate political and economic power in Mexico City.

Without NAFTA, Salinas might have felt forced to choose a technocratic lieutenant whose selection would have assured foreign investors and the local financial community that the free-market program would continue. Such a choice, however, would have delayed essential political reforms. Only an astute politician with intimate knowledge of the PRI's internal machinery could orchestrate the transition to a representative and competitive electoral system.

That is not to say that democratization is the PRI's goal. Salinas, who has all the necessary skills, chose to rebuild the PRI juggernaut, not dismantle it. But the selection of a pure technocrat would make such reforms almost impossible. It would make the election itself much more difficult, discouraging any impulse toward a transparent and credible vote count. And once in office, a president with scant political skills tends to become a prisoner of entrenched interests, making risk-filled reform even more unlikely.

The longer-term implications of a NAFTA rejection were even more troubling.

The most common scenarios sketched for Mexico's non-NAFTA future missed the mark. Many NAFTA studies departed from a false premise: that without NAFTA Mexico would have returned to the economic strategies it employed in the past—protectionism, state management, import substitution. At its most extreme, this scenario had Mexico reverting to populism with a vengeance, with a new anti-Salinas government shirking debt obligations and re-expropriating petrochemical plants. Capital would again have fled, followed by a stream of newly unemployed manufacturing workers.

But even if that were the Mexican Left's intent, which it's not, that manner of economic nationalism simply isn't viable anymore. Virtually every country across Latin America, Southeast Asia, and Eastern Europe has concluded that there is no alternative to foreign investment and competitive export industries. Most Mexicans understood that reality long before NAFTA was proposed. Similarly, the lesson of countries like Peru is that the repudiation of foreign debts is self-defeating. Debts can be renegotiated almost endlessly, but to remain eligible for credit countries must at least try to encourage investment and maintain their interest payments. Mexico, hypersensitive about its image abroad, is not a nation that takes easily to pariah status. For Mexico to abandon the community of financially responsible nations would be both counterproductive and out of character.

The question for Mexico would be how to attract foreign capital and build up export industries without a free trade agreement. The answer can be found on the American border: the maquiladora. Without NAFTA, Mexico would feel compelled to compete for investment however it could, and low-wage, low-tech assembly industries would be the quickest and easiest way to do that. Most foreign investment restrictions would be removed and labor-intensive manufacturers from East Asia would be lustily courted. Plans for rigorous enforcement of environmental laws would be quietly deferred in the search for new investors.

None of this is theoretical: this is exactly the strategy Mexico followed in the throes of the 1980s debt crisis, when it was desperate for investment and had few viable choices. The maquiladoras not only paid badly, they were transient by nature. They leased their buildings, and their machinery could be unbolted from the factory floor and shipped out to a lower-wage country in the course of a long weekend.

Now, however, with NAFTA's long-term guarantees to American investors, the risks of building high-tech industrial installations are minimized. The stock market can attract funds from American institutional investors. A modernized banking system can lure flight capital back home and lower the costs of private investment. Export-oriented agribusiness ventures look feasible for the first time.

With NAFTA, the underpinnings of a high-wage, industrially selective development strategy are firmly in place. Without it, Mexico would have had to work harder for much less. And if the crises of the past are any indication, the government would once again have had to postpone political reform. Wage controls and democratization aren't a good mix.

A defeat of NAFTA could have led to exactly what opponents said NAFTA would create: a low-wage, authoritarian, pollution-tolerating economy living off the low end of the American textile, garment, and electronics markets. The devastating combination of a cheapened peso and a moribund trade pact would have driven Mexico back to the dead-end alternative of labor-intensive export assembly: the maquiladora strategy writ large, exactly the path that NAFTA's bitterest opponents wanted to keep Mexico from taking.

Thinking Too Hard

The minimalist view of NAFTA, when advanced in good faith, is a classic example of thinking too hard about what is ultimately a simple issue.

Would it be good for the United States to have a southern neighbor with a larger and faster-growing economy than Canada's, with an equivalent dependence on American markets and goods? With NAFTA's capital flows and productivity gains, the Mexican economy could be bigger than the Canadian economy by the time the trade agreement is completely phased in—15 years from now. Without NAFTA, it would have taken Mexico at least another 10 years to approach Canada's economic size, if it ever managed to catch up at all.

Would it be good for the United States for Mexico to become a bigger market for American exports than Japan? Under NAFTA, that could happen within a year or two. The bilateral trade surplus with Mexico ballooned from $1.4 billion in 1991 to $7 billion in 1992, with a similarly large gap projected for 1993. Without NAFTA, however, Mexico could not have sustained the expansion of its American import bill at anything close to its present pace.

The real economic benefits of NAFTA for the United States will be the indirect result of Mexican prosperity. NAFTA almost guarantees that the past five years' surge in bilateral trade and investment will be sustained over the next 15 years. Without NAFTA, that would not have happened: Mexico couldn't afford it. Indeed, it can barely afford it now.

The Salinas economic experiment was always far more precarious than its architects admitted. Without the large capital flows drawn by the promise of a trade pact with Washington, his shaky new free-market edifice might have already collapsed. Even with that money, the Salinas program has run into trouble. The most serious and celebrated problem is the current account deficit, which soared from $5 billion in 1991 to $20 billion in 1992—a sobering 6 percent of gross domestic product—and remained threateningly high in 1993.

This import binge was financed largely by private American investment in Mexican stocks and bonds, an invaluable but fickle resource. Officials argued that most of these imports were industrial machinery and other capital goods essential to the development of Mexico's manufacturing base. But a lot—more than the 15 percent share in Mexico's official trade statistics—came in the form of a flood of non-essential, foreign-made consumer products, as any visitor to a Mexican department store or middle-class household could readily attest. This wasn't all bad. The imports kept consumer prices low—a boon to the Salinas anti-inflation program and to middle-class living standards—while challenging Mexican competitors to improve the quality of domestic goods.

Without an avalanche of compensatory foreign capital, however, this import spending couldn't be sustained. Mexico's non-petroleum exports had stayed at a stubbornly flat 7 percent of gross domestic product after a spectacular mid-1980s ascent. Substantial gains would have to wait on the new investment and long-term American market access that only NAFTA provides.

The current account deficit was only part of the problem. Economic growth lagged far behind the 5 to 6 percent annual expansion the government had originally forecast for the latter half of the Salinas Administration. Despite a record influx of foreign investment, growth peaked in 1990 at 4.5 percent (up from 3.3 percent in 1989 and 1.3 percent in 1988). The GDP expanded by just 3.5 percent in 1991 and 2.6 percent in 1992, with a projected return to 3.5 percent for 1993. While faster than Mexico's 1.9 percent annual population growth, this performance should more properly be measured against the 3 percent annual expansion of the work force, the delayed consequence of the 1970s Mexican baby boom. And job creation was even more anemic than the growth in economic output. By most estimates, fewer than half of the 1 million job-seekers who have entered the labor market every year during the Salinas Administration have managed to find permanent employment paying minimum wage or better. Mexican manufacturers reported the net creation of just 173,000 jobs in 1992, a small gain that was more than offset by rural unemployment and state industry layoffs. Over the course of 1992, the number of workers registered with the social security system—considered the best measure of full-time wage-earners—actually declined by 2 percent.

Mexico, like the United States, is living the paradox of productivity improvement in a slow-growth economy: gains in corporate profits are paralleled by the steady loss of jobs. The biggest and most successful Mexican manufacturing companies—Vitro, Cemex, Alfa, Grupo DESC, and many others—have been cutting payrolls while their overall sales and export earnings continue to rise. So have the Mexican subsidiaries of American companies, like Zenith and General Motors. Most dramatically, so have public sector behemoths like Pemex, the oil monopoly, which dismissed more than 100,000 workers in the first half of the Salinas term.

If the economic advantages were slight, why would Salinas have risked seeking a trade pact in the first place, knowing that he would be accused of selling out to Washington? Why did his trade negotiators say with unfeigned vehemence that it would be a catastrophe if NAFTA were rejected? Why did economists on both sides of the border say that NAFTA's rejection would sabotage the peso, triggering an outburst of inflation and capital flight? If NAFTA didn't matter, why did the stock market abruptly contract in June 1992, erasing its gains for the year, when investors worried that Ross Perot's then-surging presidential candidacy would doom the agreement? Conversely, if NAFTA was such a marginal event, why had the promise of a trade pact lured billions of American institutional dollars into the Mexican market in the first place? And why did the PRI and its opponents both say that NAFTA would ultimately determine the outcome of the 1994 presidential race?

Without NAFTA, it would have been impossible to maintain the flow of foreign capital. And without that money, Mexico's export-led, open-borders experiment could not have been sustained. That this money started flowing to Mexico before NAFTA's approval does not make it any less a part of the NAFTA process. The 1991 decision to seek the agreement was the clearest signal Salinas could send that he intended, with Washington's backing, to institutionalize his economic policies. Private investors got the message.

Even more important, the commitment of the White House to the trade pact confirmed the deepening of the close, collaborative relationship Mexico had developed with Washington during the negotiation of the Brady Plan. The promise that this relationship would shield Mexico against a revival of U.S. protectionism was invaluable to potential investors, be they multinational manufacturers considering expansions of their Mexican subsidiaries, or portfolio investors eyeing purchases of Mexican stocks and bonds. An accord with Washington would also prevent some future Mexican government from rewriting the country's foreign trade and investment rules. The details of the pact mattered less than the liberalization process itself, which began the moment that the Bush and Salinas governments started negotiating. Portfolio capital began to flow, as did funds for the expansion of existing multinational operations.

Mexico could, of course, have liberalized unilaterally. But it could not, on its own, have secured long-term access to the American market. Without that guarantee, many investors, domestic and foreign, would not even have considered building the technologically sophisticated manufacturing plants needed to compete in world markets. The fear that Mexican companies could have lost access to the American market was hardly an academic concern. Their empirical experience is that whenever they gain a respectable share of the American market—the only significant successes so far have been beer, cement, steel and glass—they immediately confront higher tariffs, countervailing duties predicated on dubious dumping allegations, demands for "voluntary" export reductions, or some combination of the above. They had little choice but to comply: the United States is the bulk of their export market, and a prolonged legal battle in Washington is rarely worth the expense or political risk.

Nor could Mexico unilaterally have provided the guarantees that investors seek against any future uncompensated expropriations, profit repatriation constraints, export performance requirements, the mandatory sharing of patented technology, or the many other perceived risks in Mexican investment. By banning such measures, NAFTA moves Mexico under the umbrella of U.S. jurisprudence and, more to the point, American political and economic influence, protecting private capital against any future reversal of trade and investment policy. The unwillingness to make new long-term investments in Mexico without those kinds of external assurances applies not only to American and Canadian investors, but to many rich Mexican industrialists as well. Often omitted from the NAFTA equation is the critical importance of repatriating the huge sums of private Mexican capital—at least $20 billion, and possibly double that amount—that remain stashed in foreign accounts, mostly in the United States.

The effect of economic liberalization on Mexican incomes is also already clear. Since 1987, the gap between American and Mexican median manufacturing wages has been cut in half, from 13-to-1 to 6-to-1. In the 15 years that it would take to fully phase in NAFTA, that gap should be halved again. And it could easily close more: if industrial wage increases consistently average 7 percent more in Mexico than in the United States, the ratio would close to 2-to-1 by 2010. That is an ambitious but attainable goal. In every year of the Salinas government except one, the base wage was hiked by 7 percent, though those increases were undercut by inflation. After NAFTA, capital inflows should keep inflation in single-digit check, allowing real wages to keep pace with rising productivity.

If wages in the northern Mexican states where competitive manufacturing is concentrated are compared with wages directly across the border, the earnings gap is narrower still. Median salaries in Texas border cities have stayed about a third below the U.S. national average for many years. Just south of the border, in the industrial districts of Chihuahua and Nuevo Leon, wages are more than a third higher than the Mexican average and are rising faster than Mexican wages elsewhere.

A steady reduction in the gap between U.S. and Mexican wages will gradually eliminate the risk of plants relocating to exploit labor savings. The existing incentives for Mexicans to emigrate to the U.S. will fade. At the same time, rising Mexican wage levels will build a broad-based consumer market, where American companies will enjoy privileged access. But this depends on a strong peso, constant improvements in productivity, and a steady influx of foreign capital and technology—a package that only NAFTA provides.

Two-Way Barriers

NAFTA supporters, trying to allay fears that the agreement would flood the American market with cheap Mexican imports, often claimed that NAFTA would affect southbound trade almost exclusively. Their argument was straightforward: Mexico maintains much higher import barriers than the United States, while most Mexican goods already enter the United States with virtually no duties at all. NAFTA, therefore, will open Mexico's doors to American products, while barely altering market access for Mexican goods into the United States.

That's wrong. The removal of import barriers will have a profound effect on trade moving north as well as south. That is because the American economy, while far more open than Mexico's, is a far more protected market than most Americans realize.

It's true that the average U.S. charge on dutiable Mexican imports is an extremely low 3.5 percent, compared with the average 10 percent tariff collected on American goods entering Mexico. It is also true that nearly half of Mexico's imports pay no duties at all, thanks to the Generalized System of Preferences (GSP). Yet these average tariff figures are deceptive. There are many product categories—about 750 in all—where U.S. duties are extremely high, ranging up to 800 percent in some extreme cases. These categories embrace many products where Mexico could be extremely competitive. Average tariff figures also disguise the impact of seasonal tariff barriers on farm products. Duties on Mexican tomatoes, for example, jump to prohibitive levels only during the Florida and California harvest months. With NAFTA, these fluctuating tariff barriers will be phased out entirely.

There are some products where imports have been banned entirely. "Take brooms—a simple product, perhaps, but one we could produce quite efficiently," Jaime Serra, Mexico's trade minister, noted in an interview. "We were told that the United States wouldn't import brooms because this is a product reserved for the blind, which seemed unusual, but perhaps reasonable. Then we investigated and discovered that only 5 percent of the brooms made in the United States are made by the blind. The rest are made by machines. The machines are blind, it is true. But they are machines."

The duty-free status of many Mexican exports under the Generalized System of Preferences is also misleading: goods get GSP treatment only if they are not imported in significant numbers. Once the goods arrive in enough volume to worry American competitors—as has happened with Mexican beer, bathroom tiles, blown glass, and myriad other products—they are taken off the GSP list and forced to pay import duties.

Nor do tariff averages reflect U.S. quotas on products like sugar and textiles, or theoretically "voluntary" limits on other imports. Eliminating these restrictions—and precluding their future application in other sensitive industries, such as auto parts—was one of the most powerful incentives for Mexico to seek a free trade agreement. In most cases, it should be stressed, the special access that Mexico gains under NAFTA in these categories comes at the expense not of American companies but of other developing-country producers in Asia and Latin America.

Mexican steelmakers, for example, were never allowed to supply more than a tiny fraction of American steel imports, even though there was no formal restriction of steel sales on the books of either country. The steel quota system imposed by the Reagan Administration was based on historic American import market share. This perversely penalized the Mexicans for having been the best foreign customer of American steelmakers in the 1970s, while rewarding net steel exporters like South Korea and Brazil. After the debt collapse of 1982, when the domestic market vanished in a matter of months, Mexican steel companies were prevented from steering their excess re-rods and pipeline sections to willing customers north of the border—even though they would have been competing with largely foreign producers. In other words, American trade policy was helping to bankrupt Mexican hard-currency earners at the same time that the Federal Reserve was strug-gling to keep Mexico and its American bank creditors solvent. Eventually, both nations recognized that these anomalies were in neither country's interest. This led to the bilateral trade talks of 1984 and 1985—which ex-panded Mexico's steel quota and, much more important, helped lay the foundations for NAFTA.

The steel saga taught Mexican planners two important lessons: first, leading industries must always be ready to shift markets quickly, and second, for most Mexican manufacturers, these shifts are feasible only within the greater North American market. With steel, Mexico missed its chance: plants that were modern and efficient 15 years ago have been technologically leapfrogged by new American mini-mills and the cutting-edge foundries of Korea and Malaysia. The United States once again enjoys a fat surplus in the bilateral steel trade, with traditional powerhouses like Pittsburgh's USX (now a supplier for Pemex) and non-unionized sunbelt firms like Birmingham Steel Corporation (which is expanding capacity in Phoenix to meet Mexican import demand) enthusiastically backing the notion of North American free trade. Even American steelworkers have realized that duty-free trade with Mexico is in their long-term interest.

Still, Mexico expects that under NAFTA its steel industry will develop competitive niches in the American market, probably with joint-venture production and marketing assistance from American investors. The result will be a genuine integrated market in steel. To the maximum extent possible, buyers in the United States will replace steel imports from China with steel from Mexico, while Mexican buyers will have compelling reasons to choose suppliers in Pittsburgh over suppliers in Osaka.

In some cases, of course, Mexican producers will be competing directly against American companies. They see NAFTA as essential to their goal of becoming North American corporations, just as Chrysler is a North American corporation, with markets and integrated manufacturing facilities on both sides of the border. Without NAFTA, their ability to coordinate sales and production across national lines could have been sabotaged at any moment by new voluntary or involuntary import restrictions from Washington.

A good example is Vitro, a bare-knuckles competitor in the glass business, with a rising North American market share in everything from beer bottles to windshields. Vitro's $820 million purchase of Tampa-based Anchor Glass—the first hostile takeover of an American firm by a Mexican company—made it the continent's leading producer of glass containers. (That isn't as predatory as it sounds: Anchor, which had been plundered in an early 1980s LBO raid by former U.S. Treasury Secretary William Simon, regained jobs and its former technological edge as a result of the Vitro acquisition.) Vitro then signed a joint marketing and development agreement with Corning, the industry's technological leader, strengthening its market position. Without NAFTA, the Vitro empire would have rested on a precarious foundation: its American sales could have been stopped dead at any point by quotas, prohibitive tariffs, or (the most likely scenario) costly dumping suits filed by competitors in the American market, who need not even have been American in origin.

This is not as crazy as it may sound: consider the experience of Cemex, a Monterrey company that has recently become the fourth largest cement company in the world. Its young American-educated management team bought out its biggest domestic competitors. They then purchased distribution companies in Corpus Christi, Houston, Albuquerque, Phoenix and Long Beach. Cemex became the largest cement supplier in the southwestern United States and the largest cement exporter anywhere. "The economic border between Mexico and the United States has disappeared," Cemex's president proclaimed. But not completely: the steady increase in Cemex's American sales triggered an onslaught of dumping accusations by American-based cement manufacturers.

Some of these complaints were later reviewed and found baseless by Gatt panels in Europe. But the damage had already been done: countervailing duties are imposed immediately, even before final rulings are handed down by the U.S. International Trade Commission. Cemex had to cut its exports by nearly half, and paying for specialized Washington counsel cost it millions more. Yet who were the litigants? The foreign-owned producers who control the American cement industry: Gilford-Hill & Co. of Dallas, which belongs to Britain's C.H. Beazer Holdings; Ideal Basic Industries, the Denver-based subsidiary of Holderbank Financiere; Virginia's Lafarge Corp., which is controlled by France's LaFarge-Coppee; and the American affiliates of companies from Australia, Italy and Japan. And what was the result? Construction companies in Texas and California paid up to 50 percent more for cement, while Cemex paid millions to the U.S. Treasury that under Gatt rules should rightfully be returned. Under NAFTA, Cemex would have had its case decided in a trinational panel less beholden to its competitors and more sensitive to the economic impact on consumers.

NAFTA won't preclude spurious dumping accusations, but it would make it easier to deal with them fairly. And in the long run, as economic integration across the continent deepened, dumping suits and countervailing duties will be eliminated as the anomalous obstacles to free trade that they are.

Playing the Washington Game

Since early 1990, the Salinas government focused all its external resources—specialized subsections of the economic secretariats, plus External Relations and its vast U.S. consular network—on the fight for NAFTA. Though still attentive to security issues, foreign policy is now driven by national economic interests.

This new pragmatism was first discernible during bilateral debt negotiations that preceded the Brady Plan. In the protracted course of those discussions, the Salinas team learned a few invaluable lessons.

First, the United States was broke. In earlier debt deals the Treasury would ante up billions for bridge loans and oil purchases. Now it could only try to wring concessions from banks and obtain credits from Tokyo.

Second, American psychology had been radically altered by the change from creditor to debtor. Where once a supplicant could play to Washington's sense of guilt or inclinations to charity, it could now get help only through blatant appeals to American self-interest (such as the solvency of American banks and the preservation of America's third largest export market).

Third, it was better to be an actor than a victim, a partner than a pleader. By crafting and then forcefully advocating a beneficial compromise (such as slight but real debt reduction), Mexico was openly and confidently defending itself on American turf. This was not only more dignified, but a better strategy. Peers get a fairer hearing than dependents. (Washington quickly learned that Mexico's doctorate-toting technocrats were more persuasive advocates of the Brady Plan than its eponymous author.)

Fourth, blaming economic distress on "external factors" is tactically inept, even when such complaints might be justified. In pushing first for the Brady bailout and later for NAFTA, Mexico saw that it was smarter to take responsibility for past policy mistakes and profess adherence to the new religion of the market.

This revisionism has gone far indeed. A decade ago Mexico exaggerated its victimization by dollar oil prices and interest rates. Today, officials explain the 1980s debt morass by pointing to domestic errors such as high tariffs and deficits. In truth, external factors contributed as much to the crisis as domestic errors, but blaming outsiders has become politically incorrect.

The new party line is useful. Like most people, bankers and politicians would rather be flattered than chastised (though they may deserve it less). The free trade agreement, like the Brady scheme before it, was portrayed to American audiences not as an end in itself, but as a tool to help Mexico remake itself in a more North American image.

Mexico had quite a story to tell: an inflation rate chopped from 100 percent to 10 percent, a vast privatization campaign, radical unilateral trade liberalization, and the elimination of what had been one of the world's fattest budget deficits. Mexican officials learned to tout their achievements in terms readily grasped by American audiences. (The dramatic fiscal turnaround is invariably measured in "Gramm-Rudmans"; at first it was two Gramm-Rudmans, then two-and-a-half, graduating recently to four with the wry kicker that, in Mexico's case, the budget freeze is real.)

They also learned to burnish Mexico's image in ways that ultimately make negotiations easier. With art exhibits, writers' colloquiums, tourism campaigns, video and publishing projects, they tried to highlight Mexico's rich mestizo culture—without appearing overly exotic. This corrective high-culture vision of Mexico adds subtle weight to the image of a nation offering itself as an equal-footing trading partner.

Mexico also realized that it must play the Washington lobbying game—a game that requires not just money but powerful contacts and an astutely crafted message.

And Mexico has hired some of the best. Among the 38 registered agents of Mexico in Washington are the public relations firms Burson-Marsteller and Daniel J. Edelman, the giant law firms Steptoe & Johnson and Shearman & Sterling, and such prominent lobbyists as Charls E. Walker Associates and the Keefe Company. Mexico has also hired former U.S. trade officials to press its case around town, including former U.S. Trade Representative William Brock and former USTR officials James Frierson, Stephen Lande, and Timothy Bennett, who drafted the 1987 U.S.-Mexico framework agreement that is NAFTA's underpinning. The Mexicans also recruited prominent Mexican-American politicians, a few former diplomats, and a former top aide to Treasury Secretary (then-Senator) Lloyd Bentsen.

Critics estimated that Mexico spent upwards of $30 million in Washington pushing the treaty. More of this went to legal counsel—trade law is complex, and competent advice is expensive—than to lobbying for political support for the accord. And Mexico's entire bill for American legal services was still dwarfed by what Japan spends in a typical year. Yet Mexico, which had long been criticized by American diplomats for its standoffish refusal to argue its case in Washington as other big trading partners did, was now playing the lobbying game for the first time. And it was playing it at a point when lobbying—particularly foreign lobbying—had become a potent symbol of Washington's greed and corruption. Mexicans protest that they didn't invent political action committees, trade courts, or the Washington revolving door.

Nor did Mexico ever expect to be seen as a crafty, formidable negotiating adversary; its main concern in hiring help was demonstrating negotiating competence and overcoming political prejudice. In the end, its hired guns not only failed to convince the general public of NAFTA's merits, they became themselves an additional reason for public hostility to the pact.

CHAPTER 4

The Year of Living Dangerously: 1992

When Carlos Salinas de Gortari visited George Bush at his Maryland mountain retreat on December 14, 1991, it was the eighth meeting of the two leaders since their elections. No Mexican president had ever had such close, continuing contact with his U.S. counterpart.

In contrast to the relaxed ambience of previous summits, this session was fraught with diplomatic tension. The political future of NAFTA, seemingly assured by the Congressional fast-track victory in May, was suddenly in doubt. In Pennsylvania, the come-from-behind victory of an openly protectionist Democrat in a special Senate election had unnerved White House strategists. Unemployment was rising, and Bush's approval ratings were falling. The primaries were just two months away, with Pat Buchanan raising the anti-NAFTA flag on the Republican right and Democrats Tom Harkin, Douglas Wilder, and Jerry Brown attacking the agreement from the left. From here forward, NAFTA's future would be tied to the unpredictable dynamics of American presidential politics.

At Camp David, Salinas pressed to accelerate the talks, arguing that a premature pact was preferable to no agreement at all. He was now at the midpoint of his six-year term, and Mexico's membership in a North American Free Trade Association was the great unfinished work of the Salinas *sexenio*.

More than pride was involved. Salinas needed tangible progress to reassure anxious investors and smooth the transition to a successor administration. After a decade of zero growth, Mexico's gross domestic product was expanding by 4 percent a year, double the rate of population growth. Without NAFTA, this momentum would be difficult to sustain.

Mexico's political calendar also required forward motion. The PRI was preparing for unusually strong opposition challenges in two mid-year gubernatorial races. Salinas would also soon be engineering the selection of a new PRI standard-bearer, who would run and take office in 1994. By party tradition, the selection of the PRI's nominee would be decided in the autumn of 1993. But the fierce internal politicking of cabinet *presidenciables* was already making governance difficult.

All of this would be infinitely easier with NAFTA in place. From the start, anti-Salinas nationalists had felt that the Mexican leader was liberalizing too quickly and too unilaterally. They contended that it was naive, if not reckless, for Salinas to count on real reciprocity from Washington—either in the substance of the agreement or in political commitment to it. If the White House decided now to put NAFTA on hold, or, conversely, to speed up the talks only to have NAFTA rejected by Congress, these arguments would appear vindicated. It would become far more difficult, if not impossible, for a future Mexican government to pursue cross-border economic integration.

Salinas's own window of opportunity was about to slide shut. Once his successor was named, he would be relegated in traditional Mexican fashion to lame-duck status. By the standards of most chief executives he would retain tremendous influence. But he would no longer be able to impose a new economic agenda singlehandedly. And even before that point, his autonomy in the candidate selection process would be constrained by NAFTA's political odyssey north of the border. Many Mexican political observers once thought that Salinas had forfeited the right to name his successor with his weak showing in the 1988 presidential election. Now, as the most popular and powerful Mexican president in a generation, Salinas had reclaimed that traditional privilege. The irony was that even as he wrested power away from his own party's chieftains, he was losing it to their counterparts in the U.S. Congress and executive branch.

Analysts in Mexico were already viewing the succession question through NAFTA's lens. If the trade pact were not concluded soon, some reasoned, the Salinas economic program would by definition remain unfinished, and he would have to pick an heir who could be trusted to continue his work. This scenario favored either Finance Minister Pedro Aspe or Budget-turned-Education Minister Ernesto Zedillo, the cabinet's leading economists. But if NAFTA were ratified, continued market liberalization and capital inflows would be assured, and Salinas could then choose a skilled politician, such as Mexico City Mayor Manuel Camacho or PRI Chairman Luis Donaldo Colosio, whose task as president would be a political reform modeled on Salinas's systematic opening of the economic system. Other observers saw matters differently, and assumed that democratization would be needed only if Mexico was still trying to shepherd NAFTA through the American Congress. But if the pact were finished quickly, there would be no need to keep pandering to foreign critics, and Salinas would be free to hand over control to a fellow member of Mexico's economic mandarinate.

Still other succession theorists warned of a nationalist backlash in the event of NAFTA's suspension or rejection, with Salinas losing control of the PRI nominating process. And critics who saw NAFTA as a Trojan horse for multinational domination worried that Salinas would have his candidate vetted not by PRI unions and interest groups but by American corporate CEOs. For PRI traditionalists, the prospect that the president might pick his successor on the basis of trade concerns was all the proof they needed that the advantages of closer ties with Washington were outweighed by the risks.

Waiting until 1993 would be equally tough in Canada. As a committed free-trader, Brian Mulroney belonged to Canada's most beleaguered minority. On the provincial level, a majority of Canadians were now governed by the social democratic opposition, which not only opposed NAFTA but called for the abrogation of the 1990 U.S.-Canadian trade accord. Legally, Mulroney had to call elections by the fall of 1993. Politically, it was clear that he couldn't hold out that long. Disputes with Washington over timber subsidies, beer imports, border meat inspections, and other trade issues had eroded support for NAFTA even among pro-American business people. Yet were Canada to walk away from NAFTA, Canadian interests would suffer most. Mexico's original intention had been to strike a direct deal with Washington; it would happily revert to bilateralism. The United States was also willing to proceed with a U.S.-Mexico pact without Canada. Ottawa's absence at the negotiating table would have little effect on an agreement primarily concerned with Mexican investment rules and calendars for the elimination of U.S.-Mexican tariff barriers. For political as well as economic reasons, the Canadians wanted to move quickly.

The negotiators themselves had been working nights and weekends for six months. They had a professional investment in a successful outcome, and they worried about the consequences of a loss of momentum. NAFTA lobbyists also urged faster movement, fearing that procrastination would play into the hands of their disorganized but highly motivated opponents.

Still, not everyone in the White House was persuaded. This caution was understandable, and not necessarily at odds with Mexico's best interests. The worst-case scenario for Salinas, after all, was not delay, but the outright rejection of NAFTA by the U.S. Congress. Bush aides knew they had won negotiating authority from Congress only because the president was still basking in the afterglow of the Persian Gulf war. Even so, the Bush Administration had carefully promoted NAFTA as a bipartisan initiative, courting border-state Democrats and the House Democratic leadership, and volunteering accounts of its difficulties with Northern Republicans. Now, a year later, Bush's popularity was waning. Sympathetic Congressmen warned that a presidential sales pitch would be seen as irrelevant to the needs of an economy in recession. It might even harden Democratic opposition. Sending NAFTA to Congress in an election year could also make it a target for activists disgruntled with Administration policies on a host of other issues—worker retraining, environmental protection, foreign aid, immigration, tax policy. "Trade," remarked Michigan Senator Carl Levin, a NAFTA critic, "is a metaphor." And metaphors acquired unusual power in presidential campaigns.

As Mexico had feared, the Camp David summit was inconclusive. Negotiators were told to produce a preliminary draft by February, with unreconciled policy positions juxtaposed in brackets. The timetable for the pact remained open, and Washington showed no real sense of urgency. Administration officials played down the Salinas visit—in contrast to their lobbying effort earlier that same week for economic aid to Boris Yeltsin's new commonwealth.

Bush aides insisted that NAFTA would go forward, hinting that it would be a part of the economic recovery plan unveiled in the January State of the Union message. Yet a month later, NAFTA would merit no more than a passing reference in the State of the Union speech. No firm timetable was offered nor was any mention made of the promised parallel pacts on labor and environmental standards. In the following weeks, the Administration did little to counter criticism from textile companies, fruit growers, computer manufacturers, shoemakers, auto parts suppliers, and other powerful industries fearful of the pact. There was almost no effort to promote—or even to explain—NAFTA before national audiences. Bush himself never devoted a single major speech to the pact. Although the negotiations continued, Bush's own commitment to the product of the negotiations seemed in doubt.

NAFTA's new difficulties highlighted the limitations of reliance on the U.S. executive branch. From the beginning, Salinas saw the Bush presidency as a unique opportunity to strengthen relations with Washington. The two presidents worked well together, knew each other's countries better than any of their predecessors, and shared a genuine conviction that free trade would benefit both economies. Bush understood Mexico well enough to appreciate the audaciousness of Salinas's tilt towards Washington. And Salinas felt confident that the Texas-dominated Bush Administration would deliver on its promises.

But Salinas did not have to sell his program to an opposition-controlled legislature. Like many foreign leaders before him, he tended to overestimate the autonomy of the American presidency—and underestimate the clout and complexity of the Congress. Despite his sophistication about American politics, Salinas still viewed the world from the near-monarchical vantage point of the Mexican presidency. Mexico's first sustained experience with Congressional lobbying—the fight for fast-track NAFTA negotiating authority—had only reinforced its natural inclination to rely on executive power. At the time—May 1991—Bush enjoyed the approval of four-fifths of the electorate. His re-election was taken for granted by Mexico's paid consultants in Washington (and by almost everyone else). Bush operatives had secured support for fast-track from prominent editorial boards, most business associations, leading Hispanic political associations, and Congressional committee chairmen from virtually the entire western half of the country. House Majority Leader Richard Gephardt and several environmental organizations were persuaded to drop objections and sign on. Fast-track had prevailed not on its merits but on the sheer strength of presidential power.

Still, in retrospect, the dangers were apparent. The fast-track roll call in the House had been close. If Gephardt hadn't backed Bush at the final hour, NAFTA would never have gone forward: at least two dozen NAFTA votes ended up in the pro column only because the tough-on-trade majority leader provided political cover. Even so, two out of three Congressional Democrats voted against fast-track. And many fast-track supporters, echoing Gephardt, warned that they would oppose NAFTA's ratification unless the Bush Administration kept its promises about labor and environmental protection. Now, with Gulf War memories fading and the Administration's critics newly emboldened, NAFTA was one of the few specific Bush policy initiatives available for attack.

At the bargaining table, the USTR tried to turn this domestic political uncertainty to its advantage. Prospects for a tough ratification fight in

Congress let the Bush Administration press Mexico for further concessions. From a U.S. vantage point, this good cop-bad cop routine between the White House and Congress on trade policy became an effective way to extract concessions. Salinas was in an impossible position. If he dug in and fought against additional concessions, he would be held accountable in Washington should the agreement fail to pass Congressional muster. If he gave in to U.S. demands, he would be accused at home of selling out. That was the paradox of negotiating with the United States: if Mexico defended its interests too well at the bargaining table, it heightened its chances of defeat on Capitol Hill.

From Washington's viewpoint, a hard negotiating line was needed to hold Mexico to its promise of a radically liberalized economy. Negotiators readily admitted pressing for more fundamental free-market concessions than the Mexican team had expected. Many of these concessions, it should be said, were in Mexico's own long-term interest. Granting national treatment to American banks lowers financial costs for Mexican business. Ending buy-Mexico policies for state industries heightens efficiency and saves money. Deregulating transportation is a boon to tourism. To make a real impression on Congress, Mexico was pressed on such hot-button issues as rules of origin, where the U.S. position tilted more towards "fair" than "free" trade. (Detroit wanted North American content levels of 65 percent or higher; Mexico, worried that this would discourage new foreign investment, wanted to keep the 50 percent threshold set by the U.S.-Canada agreement.) Mexico was also pushed to accept a protracted 15-year phase-in for duty-free sales of fruits and vegetables, delaying the infusion of investment desperately needed by its newly privatized communal farms.

The most sensitive subject for Salinas was petroleum. Washington began pressing for American investment in the constitutionally sacrosanct business of oil exploration and production. But Mexico knew that even something like that—a dramatic, politically costly policy reversal—wouldn't guarantee NAFTA's success in Congress. And if the first NAFTA draft failed to pass muster with U.S. legislators, Mexico could hardly toughen its position a second time around. Its initial stance would be taken as a starting point for further concessions.

Mexican business leaders began to complain that negotiators were conceding too much in financial services, textiles, auto parts, petrochemicals, and other sensitive industries. But the negotiators had a problem: the sudden prospect of a Bush re-election defeat meant that if Mexico didn't conclude a deal now, it might never get one at all.

In remarks to reporters immediately after the Camp David summit, Salinas played down the effect of postponement, calling NAFTA simply "one instrument more in a broad reform process." This was disingenuous. Perhaps there was a time when it could have been credibly argued that NAFTA was desirable but dispensable. But now Mexico was fast becoming a victim of its own success. Capital was pouring in, drawn by the promise of free trade with the United States. So were imports, at an even faster rate, as consumers enjoyed foreign luxury goods and manufacturers invested billions in new production machinery. As a result, Mexico's current-account deficit had swollen to a record $13 billion in 1991, a hefty 5 percent of GDP. This meant Mexico was in sudden, desperate need of the compensating investment flows an agreement would bring.

This foreign capital influx would virtually assure continued growth in the 4 to 5 percent range. Yet if NAFTA's prospects appeared endangered, growth could slow below 3 percent, barely keeping pace with population expansion. Mexico's other hard-currency choices were limited. Industry, from manufacturing to vegetable farming to oil extraction, was already close to peak capacity, and, as always, subject to the vagaries of world prices and markets. The previous year's loan restructuring, which stabilized Mexico's debt problem but only marginally reduced interest payments, had the effect of precluding any further reduction of the foreign debt. A million young people were entering the work force every year; but at current growth rates, only half could expect to find permanent full-time jobs. Though hailed worldwide as an economic success story, Mexico was still balanced on a financial tightrope, gingerly negotiating the transition to free trade.

The irony was that the current-account gap was widening dangerously—not as the result of anything in the agreement itself, but from the structural changes Mexico was implementing on its own to prepare for open competition. Tariff reductions, foreign investment liberalization, reformed securities markets, manufacturing investments—all essential, but each with immediate negative consequences for Mexico's balance of payments. The current account had been restored to rough alignment in the past decade only through painful public spending cuts, real wage suppression, and constant currency devaluation. Now the deficit was widening to a degree unseen since 1982.

For a newly industrializing economy, there is nothing inherently bad about a trade deficit, so long as the imports are predominantly durable goods purchased by private business for sound competitive reasons. A decade before Mexico had been an egregious counterexample. Its deficit had been financed by foreign borrowing, sustained by overvaluation, and squandered on white-elephant industrial monuments. In the 1990s, though, it had become a textbook case of the virtuous deficit-trader, investing in essential imports and paying the bill out of rising export earnings. Record dollar reserves averaging well above $10 billion provided a ready buffer against any sudden drops in export sales.

But the current-account gap had widened beyond the planners' expectations. Consumers reacted to falling import barriers and the strengthening peso by stocking up on once-forbidden foreign clothing, stereos, appliances, fancy foods, and other imported luxuries. At the same time, Mexican trade associations and chambers of industry began gearing up for free trade in 1990 by commissioning comprehensive inventories of each sector's strengths and weaknesses—and comparing the results to their business competitors in the United States. The comparisons weren't flattering. For the first time, many leading firms looked in detail at the product niches they could exploit in an open North American market. This prompted an immediate round of capital expenditures as entire industries faced up to the need to upgrade equipment and expand product lines. Billions in orders were placed for foreign-produced parts, materials and production equipment (about 70 percent of it American). Mexican business was responding to the NAFTA challenge far faster than its own leaders or the government's economists had expected. This import spending bolstered the country's long-term competitiveness, but placed severe short-term strains on the balance of payments.

Similarly, the surge in direct foreign manufacturing investment— much of it prompted by NAFTA—also widened the current-account gap. Companies building export-oriented assembly plants would spend a year or two importing parts and machinery before the operations began making money. In one example often cited by Finance Minister Pedro Aspe, Daimler-Benz decided in 1991 to build a Mercedes plant in Mexico— only its second in the world outside Germany. The decision was based on Daimler's belief in the potential of the local luxury-car market, but its timing was prompted by the desire to benefit from preferences that might be granted existing car makers under NAFTA's still-to-be-negotiated automotive rules. The arrival of the prestigious auto firm was a coup for Mexico's foreign investment board, but it was bemoaned with mock ruefulness by the finance minister, who noted that its imports of German components and assembly machinery would add a half billion dollars to the current-account deficit.

Aspe's intent in this tale was to put the current account gap in perspective and to remind nervous analysts that the long-term benefits of manufacturing investment more than justified the short-term difficulties of financing a trade deficit. Indeed, any economy newly exposed to global competition should logically find it marginally harder to sell its products abroad than to pay for the imports that consumers and industries demand. And the record pace of investment by foreign manufacturers like Daimler-Benz was testimony to their underlying confidence in Mexico's economic direction. Propelled by the prospect of NAFTA, foreign investment, like investment by Mexico's own private sector, was expanding more quickly than the Salinas team had expected. At the beginning of his term, Salinas had set an ambitious-sounding goal for his six-year term of $24 billion in new foreign investment. The entire stock of foreign investment in Mexico at that point barely reached $14 billion. Now, after just three years, Mexico had already collected $18 billion more, bringing total foreign investment to $32 billion.

On Wall Street, meanwhile, where investment in foreign stocks was soaring to record levels, there was no hotter foreign market than Mexico. Private American investment in Mexican stocks jumped by a net $2 billion in 1992's first quarter, a huge increase over the $146 million invested in Mexican companies in the same three-month period of 1991. Mexican stock sales surpassed net purchases in the second most popular foreign market, Japan, by $300 million and represented more than a quarter of the total $7.8 billion in net foreign stock purchases by American investors for that period.

Still, many observers worried that the deficit was widening past the point of prudence. In the first quarter of 1992 it would balloon to a record $4 billion, more than double the $1.8 billion registered in the same period of 1991. Foreign investment, remarkably, was still almost keeping pace, with a $3.4 billion inflow in 1992's first quarter. But more than half of this money—indeed, the majority of all foreign investment since Salinas took office—was American portfolio capital, highly liquid and committed only to high yields, with no deep knowledge of or faith in the Mexican economy. If the stock market stumbled, much of it would flee Mexico in an instant.

This was the risk of a NAFTA-propelled market boom. The prospect of a free trade deal with the United States—and Mexico's commitment to economic liberalization—had enticed American institutional investors into an undervalued stock market that was starved for capital and open to foreign money for the first time. From a starting point of zero when Salinas took office, foreign capital inflows to the Bolsa had climbed from a modest $493 million in 1989 to $1.99 billion in 1990 and a remarkable $7.54 billion in 1991.

When the accumulated appreciation of these investments is taken into account, foreign investment in the Mexico City stock exchange hit a stunning $18 billion at the end of 1991, up from $4 billion just one year earlier. Foreign shareholdings now surpassed 30 percent of the market's total capitalization and constituted a solid majority of all tradable stock. The bulk of this investment—more than $11 billion—was concentrated in a single company, Teléfonos de México, the newly privatized telephone monopoly.

Mexican critics disparaged the speculative nature of this capital influx, comparing it unfavorably to the direct industrial investment that many of these same commentators had long deplored. They also faulted the market's potentially dangerous dependence on foreign investment in a single stock. This new pool of portfolio funds proved invaluable, however, as a source of financing for Mexican businesses that were gearing up for foreign competition for the first time in their cosseted lives. More critically for the government, this hard-currency inflow compensated for the billions of dollars flowing out of Mexico to pay for production machinery and tariff-liberated consumer goods. In the view of the Salinas team, comparisons between portfolio capital and direct investment were invidious—both were needed, both were welcome, and discouraging the former would do nothing to attract the latter.

The East Asian tigers had also tallied big current-account deficits while covering the gap with foreign portfolio investment. But the best analogy was with Spain, Europe's fastest-growing economy. In 1991, it posted an even more lopsided ratio between portfolio and direct foreign investment ($19.4 billion versus $5.7 billion, compared with Mexico's $7.5 billion versus $4.8 billion). Like Mexico, Spain was criticized for relying on these portfolio inflows to finance a growing trade deficit and prop up an overvalued currency. As in Mexico, foreign money was lured by the prospect of economic unification with the richer nations to the north. But there was a big difference: Spain's inclusion in a borderless European market would be a reality by the end of 1992. The free trade agreement between the United States and Mexico, by contrast, remained very much in doubt.

Another distinction between Mexico and Spain was that Mexico, far poorer and less developed, needed the money much more. José Cordoba, Salinas's chief of staff and top strategist, calculated that simply to sustain current growth Mexico needed $150 billion in capital inflows over the course of the decade. Other official estimates ranged higher, to a net $1.8 billion monthly. That is to say, as remarkable as 1991's foreign investment flows were by Mexican historical standards, this performance needed to be bettered with each passing year. A free trade agreement was the only way Mexico could attract investment on that scale.

But the more immediate challenge was to keep the money flowing while the NAFTA talks continued. The Mexican stock market index had jumped 98 percent in dollar terms in 1988, 68 percent in 1989, 37 percent in 1990, and a record 104 percent in 1991. Would investors stay if returns slowed? What if oil prices dipped or American import demand softened? Even worse, what if NAFTA were crippled by the pressures of American politics? A withdrawal of foreign portfolio dollars could push Mexico's balance of payments into unsustainable deficit, undermining the peso and reviving inflation and capital flight. Most nerve-wracking for Mexican planners was the realization that this balancing act could no longer be maintained simply by adjusting their domestic economic policies—now they also had to react, nimbly and quickly, to the unfamiliar shifts and twists of American electoral politics.

Primary School
Happily for Salinas, the American presidential primaries begin in New Hampshire, not Pennsylvania. Despite their anger at the recession, and despite several poignant examples of local factories shuttered by companies that opened new plants in Mexico, New Hampshire voters remained—as they have been historically—stubbornly unreceptive to protectionist appeals.

Some of Mexico's advisors began pointing out that a Democratic victory wouldn't necessarily doom the agreement. The leading candidates, Arkansas Governor Bill Clinton and former Massachusetts Senator Paul Tsongas, both backed NAFTA, albeit with labor and environmental codicils. The Buy-America campaign of Virginia Governor Douglas Wilder fizzled before it began. Senator Bob Kerry of Nebraska, who had supported fast-track, hastened his candidacy's end by airing protectionist-tinged television ads. Former California Governor Jerry Brown's initial take on NAFTA was that free trade with Mexico wasn't inherently flawed in theory but was being corrupted in practice by PAC contributions and business lobbyists. If NAFTA's terms were dictated by the multinationals, the average worker would suffer, Brown argued.

Among the Democrats, only Tom Harkin stood steadfast against

NAFTA from the start. Yet even he would not make NAFTA a defining issue. When Democrats flirted with protectionism, Japan was the target of early 1992, not Mexico.

The only New Hampshire candidate directing sustained fire at the free trade accord was Pat Buchanan, whose anti-NAFTA and anti-immigration messages were tailored to trade on nativist and populist sentiments. Yet even Buchanan began to soften his protectionist rhetoric when his pollsters found it added little to his insurgent appeal.

On March 5, in their last televised debate before the March 11 Super Tuesday primaries, the Democratic candidates addressed NAFTA at length for the first time. The debate highlighted Clinton's studied ambivalence: while he stressed his guarded support for the agreement, he also listened carefully to the arguments of NAFTA's strongest opponent in the debate, whose views he would later echo in the fall campaign against George Bush.

Harkin, the purest exponent of anti-NAFTA sentiment, pressed hardest. He noted that he was the only candidate who had actively opposed fast-track negotiating authority. He hoisted aloft a 1990 trade-magazine ad urging businesses to invest in El Salvador—not Mexico, El Salvador—where, the ad stated, they could hire one Rosa Martinez, a sewing machine operator, for 57 cents an hour. Harkin then displayed a 1991 ad offering Ms. Martinez's services for 33 cents an hour. "What happened?" he asked. "Fast-track passed the Congress. And what does that got to do with Mexico? Because they can ship it into Mexico and then ship it right into this country."

This was simply demagogic: Central American garments don't need a Mexican back door into the United States. They enter with minimal duties, as the Salvadoran ad courting American manufacturers implied. Moreover, NAFTA expressly prohibits the duty-free transshipment of goods from third countries; setting strict North American rules of origin was the heart of the NAFTA negotiating process. And neither NAFTA negotiations nor the fast-track vote had any direct effect on wage or tariff rates in Mexico, El Salvador, or anywhere else.

Harkin added that the magazine ad "doesn't tell you that Rosa Martinez lives in a tin shack with a dirt floor, no health care, no education for her children, and no hope." What Harkin didn't say was why or whether he expected free trade to make matters worse. Was Harkin urging some prohibition on American investment in those countries? Or was he merely lamenting Central American poverty? It wasn't clear.

Rosa Martinez had no real connection to NAFTA or Mexico, but politically she would prove useful. The Salvadoran investment promotion agency that underwrote the offending ad had received financial support from the U.S. Agency for International Development as part of the Caribbean Basin Initiative, a regional economic development program started by the Reagan Administration with bipartisan Congressional support. Combined with NAFTA, this indirect use of taxpayer funds to lure American manufacturers south of the border could be portrayed as an overarching Republican-cum-Big Business plan "to ship American jobs overseas," as Harkin thundered on the stump. Harkin's rhetoric, Rosa Martinez and all, would be recycled almost verbatim by Clinton in his fall presidential campaign.

Harkin was sounding a theme common among NAFTA critics—that free trade should be opposed not just because it harms American labor interests, but because it hurts workers south of the border as well. The implicit presumption was that to hire a Latin American worker—at least at prevailing wage rates—was to exploit her. This line of argument was meant to make anti-NAFTA militancy more palatable to people who might otherwise be sympathetic to the economic ambitions of Latin American job-seekers. As the campaign progressed, however, it proved hard to sustain, both logically and politically. The issue for American voters wasn't living standards south of the border, but the preservation of jobs at home.

Jerry Brown's rejection of NAFTA was framed in similar terms. He said he would support a trade pact "negotiated by people who represent working people" but not one dictated by "million-dollar-a-year executives who want to move their plants to Mexico." Brown had a history of advocating tighter economic ties with Mexico—including explicit calls, contemporaneous with Reagan's a decade earlier, for a North American Common Market. Now he depicted NAFTA as a perverse variant of a potentially worthwhile project. Brown said he favored a free trade model more along European Union lines, with higher levels of adjustment assistance and government support for high-wage employment in both countries. The NAFTA negotiated by the Bush Administration, Brown argued, would be bad for both Mexico and the United States.

The usual caveat of NAFTA opponents was that free trade accords would be welcomed "with Mexico and with everyone south of our border if they first start raising their standards—wage standards, social security, health standards, have a fairer taxing system, and raise their environmental standards." Paul Tsongas, the only ardently pro-NAFTA Democrat in the race, might have responded that NAFTA was a good way to raise those standards; instead, he made the protectionist case for the pact as "our defense against what other nations are doing." Tsongas claimed NAFTA was needed to avoid American isolation in the global economy—a gross exaggeration of both Mexico's economic importance and Japan's interest in East Asian integration.

Clinton, characteristically, began by agreeing with everybody. He allied himself with the two critics ("I agree with Tom Harkin that we have to be tough on labor and environmental standards"; "Governor Brown has a point: if you go back and look at the poor countries being brought into the EC, you get an idea of things we might do to protect our wage base") and with the other supporter ("Senator Tsongas is also right: we need growth in Latin America"). He then said he doubted that he would support any agreement that Bush would negotiate, yet noted that he had favored giving him the authority to negotiate. Nodding towards voters in south Texas ("where you'll see some real benefits of increasing two-way trade"), Clinton said the "only way we can grow richer as a country is if our trading partners grow richer." In the next breath, he proposed undefined new tax rules that would discourage General Motors from building plants in Mexico.

This basic policy approach—a generic endorsement of the NAFTA concept, studded with ambiguous disclaimers and caveats—would define Clinton's stance for the rest of the campaign.

As Buchanan and the protectionist Democrats faded, so did the Administration's political fears about NAFTA. Inside the Bush Administration, a new strategy began to take hold. The fight in Congress could be delayed until after the election, but the agreement would still be signed, with full pomp and ceremony, before November. The president was obliged by law to give at least 90 days' notice before signing the agreement, a period for legislative consultation. As a practical political matter, the negotiations among the three countries had to be concluded and an agreement codified at the moment of notification. The only real deadline for concluding NAFTA was the end of March 1993, the outside date for starting the mandatory 90-day advisory period before the president could sign the agreement under fast-track authority, which expired on June 1, 1993. As long as it was signed before then, the agreement and its enabling legislation could be submitted under fast-track's yea-or-nay procedure at any point after that. The Congress would then have up to 90 legislative days to discuss the measure. But there was no real need to wait. If negotiations could be wrapped up in July, the 90-day advisory period would still allow a signing by the three chief executives before the American presidential election. This would avert an election-season battle in the House and still satisfy Salinas's and Mulroney's quest for a quick approval by their legislatures. In Mexico, as in Canada, legislative opposition was not an issue, and 1992 offered both governments convenient lulls in their federal electoral cycles.

But the real point of this new calendar was to give Bush a way to exploit NAFTA in the final days of the campaign. The 90-day advisory period was only the legal minimum. If public reaction to the trade deal promised to be unfavorable, the president could always delay the signing until after the election. But that wasn't the plan. Some Bush strategists thought a trilateral signing ceremony in late October would make the President appear forward looking and statesmanlike. Robert Mosbacher, who pushed NAFTA as Commerce Secretary before becoming a Bush campaign chairman, championed it as a "wedge issue" that could split the normally Democratic Mexican-American vote, while appealing to the free-market spirit of Western independents. The race card could also be subtly played: Hispanics would be reminded of the northern Congressional Democrats who embraced free trade with Anglo Canada but were fighting against an equivalent association with Latino Mexico. However the Democrats reacted, there seemed to be little danger in accelerating the negotiations—and potential gains for an Administration eager for concrete accomplishments. Either way, it appeared, the political risks of NAFTA had dramatically diminished.

Then came Perot.

'El efecto Perot'

In his February appearance on CNN's Larry King show, where he first proclaimed his willingness "to serve," Ross Perot cited just one specific disagreement with the Bush economic program: he opposed the free trade pact with Mexico, he said, because it would chase jobs south and "implode" the tax base.

This wasn't the first time Perot had lashed out against NAFTA. A few weeks before, in a Dallas radio broadcast, Perot had gone out of his way to attack NAFTA vigorously, even though the issue hadn't been raised by his interviewers. His pithy summation of the generic argument against free trade with a low-wage economy was laced with an offhand East Texas disdain for all things Mexican. "When the Mexican free trade agreement was announced," Perot told KLIV listeners, "I called a Who's Who of manufacturing and asked, when will you build your next plant in the U.S.? They said 'Ross, we won't.' Mexican labor, bad luck, is $1.55 an hour; good luck is 75 cents, average is about a dollar. Hire a young work force down there, build a new plant, pay off the local police chief. It's a rotten place to do business. I won't go to Mexico—I've told 'em, they've been after me—I told them that when the police chief in Mexico City doesn't live in the biggest house in town, call me. They haven't called me yet. The point is, if they can hire labor that cheap, little or no health care, little or no retirement, no pollution controls—dump it in the air, dump it in the river. Here's the bad news folks, the wind blows from the south. Guess who's gonna get it—Texas.

"To make a long story short, we won't be able to make anything up here. The guys in Washington don't understand business. See, they say 'free trade.' Philosophically, we are all for free trade, right? But we don't want to implode our economy, going to one step above slave labor wages. And the long story is, if you handled it and orchestrated it just right, what you would have is Mexican wages going up and our wages going down. Every other house in the country would be for sale, our tax base would be imploded—and that's if you handled it right."

Perot's comments to Larry King repeated much of this nearly verbatim. (So much for shooting from the lip.) As support for his freelance candidacy began to build, Perot kept citing NAFTA as an example of Washington-gone-haywire. After the artful blurring of positions where Perot's views had once seemed clearly defined—gun control, abortion funding, means-testing for entitlements—his anti-NAFTA stance became one of his few clear disagreements with Clinton and Bush. Despite the consistency of his remarks, many campaign observers questioned Perot's commitment to the anti-NAFTA cause. Perot himself always accompanied his criticisms with the claim that he was not a protectionist. He even implied that he hadn't made up his mind, telling the *Los Angeles Times:* "We need to think this through very carefully. In carpenter's terms: measure twice, cut once." But his overall position remained hostile, deeply worrying NAFTA strategists in Washington and Mexico City. Perot had put trade back into the campaign, and he was becoming a formidable opponent.

Opinion polls showed Perot beating Bush and Clinton not only in national surveys, but in exit polls of party-loyalist primary voters in states as dissimilar and strategically important as California, New Jersey and Ohio. Perot's take on NAFTA encapsulated the concerns of the pact's mainstream opponents in the labor, human rights, and environmental movements, while feinting folksily towards Buchanan's Paco-bashing nativism. A Texas billionaire couldn't easily be accused of anti-business bias, nor of ignorance of Mexico's strategic and economic importance, nor of covert alliances with radical ecologists and union militants. His carefully tended persona as a plain-talking yet worldly businessman lent an air of common-sense authority to his economic opinions. And it was hard to tag him as a special pleader: his own family's business interests—data processing, Texas real estate, an all-freight Metroplex airport—seemed like natural beneficiaries of freer trade with Mexico.

Perot began attacking NAFTA as the very model of special-interest, PAC-funded, inside-the-Beltway policy-making. This paralleled his assault on trade policy toward Japan and what he considered the treasonous pro-Tokyo lobbying of revolving-door Washington bureaucrats. It also gave him an opportunity to replay his old grievances against General Motors and other big American firms for "downsizing"—just a euphemism, he said, for "going out of business"—while investing and subcontracting abroad. With astonishing sleight-of-hand, Perot recast the standard terms of trade debate: free-traders were now out-of-touch ideologues who passively accepted America's decline, and protectionists were simply can-do patriots out to rebuild the national industrial base.

There was no mistaking Perot's position. If "protectionist" has any meaning in American politics, Perot fit the bill. Despite his advocacy of an industrial policy favoring capital-intensive technology over labor-intensive assembly lines, Perot seemed to want U.S. trade negotiators to seek to preserve jobs in virtually every domestic industry ("Do we need to make clothing in this country? Of course we do. Do we need to make shoes in this country? Of course we do"). The fear in both parties was that Perot would inherit the protectionist vote that had been courted by Buchanan from the right and by Brown from the left—a constituency that would otherwise stay home in November. He would be a centrist populist, drawing from both sides and the alienated middle.

Meanwhile, it was proving harder than expected to close the NAFTA deal. Carla Hills continued to insist that the talks wouldn't be hurried to meet "political" deadlines, while her boss began to wonder whether he would have an agreement in hand by November. (Asked by the *New York Times* in late June to cite the accomplishments of his first term, Bush listed arms reduction agreements with Russia, the reunification of Germany, Desert Storm, the Middle East peace talks, and "pushing for, but not having accomplished, free trade agreements.") At the negotiating table, the Republican National Committee's desire to turn NAFTA into a Bush campaign event gave Mexican negotiators a little unaccustomed leverage. With the USTR under pressure to wrap up an agreement, the

Mexicans could afford to be a little intransigent and they were, taking a hard line on oil (oil exploration and production would remain off-limits to foreign investors) and corn (like rice in Japan and lager in Germany, maize would be spared from free trade for cultural as much as economic reasons). But they bowed to the inevitable in other crucial issues—financial services (letting American banks acquire eventual control of Mexican banks, brokerages and insurance companies), apparel (accepting American textile industry demands for "yarn-forward" rules of origin), North American content rules for cars (agreeing to the 62.5 percent threshold demanded by Detroit), and environmental standards (letting individual U.S. states impose tougher limits on pesticide levels in Mexican food imports than the USDA). Salinas was still intent on getting an agreement concluded as quickly as possible.

On the Democratic side, meanwhile, NAFTA supporters worried that a three-way contest would drive Clinton closer to labor and inner-city constituencies and away from free trade. The Democratic Party platform draft blandly declared that Washington should work to expand world trade and make it "fair." It endorsed NAFTA, but guardedly, stressing that the agreement must reflect "our legitimate concerns about environmental, health and safety, and labor standards." It also said that workers displaced by the pact "must have the benefit of effective adjustment assistance." These caveats satisfied most of labor's concerns, while still giving Clinton the best of both NAFTA worlds: he could avoid being labeled a simple obstructionist, while retaining the right to block the agreement on labor and environmental grounds. Accusing the Bush Administration of failing on the ecological and workplace fronts would be a credible posture even to many NAFTA proponents—especially if Clinton vowed to implement the agreement once those conditions were satisfied. As president, Clinton could then focus Congressional energy on border clean-up and worker retraining programs. There would be no need to tamper with the NAFTA text itself, which could still be ratified intact under fast-track rules.

NAFTA advocates in both parties, meanwhile, continued to eye Perot warily. Perot's anti-NAFTA stance disturbed some of his own supporters, especially in his home state. In Texas, vocal opposition to free trade with Mexico had been confined to a strange-bedfellow minority of oilpatch populists, labor leaders, fringe nativists, environmentalists, and some younger Chicano professionals sympathetic towards Mexico's democratic opposition. None of these groups had much natural affinity for Ross Perot, nor he for them. Among Texas Republicans and businessmen, support for NAFTA was nearly universal. Nowhere was enthusiasm stronger than in the neatly groomed suburbs of North Dallas, Perot's home turf, where Mexico's thirst for imports was already helping to lift the area's high-tech industrial parks out of recession. But Perot's own instincts seemed rooted not in Dallas but in Texarkana, where Mexico is as distant—geographically and culturally— as it gets in Texas. His views reflected an earlier, more provincial Texas that saw the border not as an opportunity but a problem, a bias some Hispanics detected in Perot's criticism of bilingual education during his 1983–85 crusade to revamp Texas schools.

In early June, Perot told the *New Republic* that "if I can build a factory in Mexico, pay my labor a dollar an hour, hire a 25-year-old work force, have little or no health care, little or no retirement, have no pollution or environmental controls, then if you are the greatest businessman in the world, if you are an Einstein in business, trying to compete with me in the United States, you can't even get into the ring with those numbers." Perot went on to sketch out an apocalyptic scenario where people lose "the equity in their homes, their kids can't go to college, they can't support their families, you've got chaos in America, because all the jobs went to Mexico."

In a lead editorial on June 15, the *Wall Street Journal* cited those anti-NAFTA remarks and claimed that Perot was undermining Mexico's stock market. Suggesting that the Texan hadn't thought his "idle comments" through, the *Journal* advised him that "part of being a real candidate is that people and markets take you seriously."

Mexicans have a saying: *no me defiendas, compadre*—roughly, with friends like these, who needs enemies? The *Journal*, the most stalwart free trade proponent in the American press, had stiffened Perot's anti-NAFTA resolve while rattling the Mexican market to its core. The day the editorial appeared, the market dropped 67 points, a 3.7 percent loss. The following day, as reports about the editorial and Perot filled Mexican newspapers, the plunge continued, with a 2.9 percent loss. The next day, as American brokers placed more sell orders, the Mexican market index slid a stunning 5.9 percent, its steepest single-day decline since the scary days of October 1987. The spiral of defensive profit-taking pulled down 96 of the 105 stocks on the Mexico City exchange and every Mexican stock and fund listed in New York. The state investment bank, Nafinsa, intervened heavily in the market to keep prices from sliding farther. The Mexican central bank raised short-term interest rates to keep liquid capital from flowing out. Even so, perhaps $2 billion left the country in the second half of June.

Adding to the market's jitters was a confrontation between Washington and Mexico City over the U.S. Supreme Court's ruling that U.S. drug agents had acted legally in their abduction of a Mexican criminal suspect from Mexican territory for prosecution in U.S. courts. The ruling infuriated and humiliated the Salinas Administration. At issue was more than the abrogation of an extradition treaty. For a government that had staked its reputation on the premise—revolutionary for Mexico—that a mutually respectful relationship with the United States was both possible and beneficial, the Justice Department's defense of the kidnapping was an unexpected rebuke. Even worse for Salinas was the premise of the Supreme Court's decision: that since the U.S.-Mexico extradition agreement did not specifically preclude abduction, it had not been breached. The implications for NAFTA were seized on immediately by Mexican critics: how, they asked, could Mexico still assume Washington would scrupulously abide by the letter of a free trade agreement? Because of its stake in NAFTA, the Mexican government restrained its impulse to expel the DEA and ordered the U.S. agents to simply "suspend" activities in Mexico. Even this mild protest was rescinded a day later after prodding from the U.S. Embassy and Mexico's own NAFTA negotiators. The incident left Salinas vulnerable to nationalist criticism at home, while reminding American observers that such friction had long been the norm of the bilateral relationship, not the exception.

What Mexican brokers would later label *el efecto Perot* was a classic self-fulfilling prophecy. As Mexican economic commentator Sergio Sarmiento noted in his column: "Although Perot was virtually unknown among Mexicans, foreign investors, who now account for about one-fifth of total capitalization on the Mexican Stock Exchange, reacted sharply and negatively to [the] article in the *Wall Street Journal* emphasizing Perot's anti-NAFTA attitude at a time when all opinion polls were already showing him as the front-runner in the presidential contest." And market analysts who were following the Perot-NAFTA link thought that his hard-line trade views were helping him in the polls. A *Wall Street Journal*/NBC News poll at the time showed Perot (at 33 percent) with a statistically meaningless margin over Bush (31 percent) and Clinton (28 percent). Yet respondents overwhelmingly rated Perot the better leader on economic issues generally (37 percent versus 16 percent for each of his opponents) and on "protecting America's interests on trade" specifically (also 37 percent, compared with 27 percent for Bush and 9 percent for Clinton).

Perot had clearly tapped into a deep populist unease about the conduct of U.S. trade policy.

In San Diego on July 14, as Democrats convened in New York for the second evening of their nominating convention, and as the American League prepared to humiliate the National League in a game where he would be the honored foreign guest, Carlos Salinas held his second formal encounter of the year with George Bush. The White House had already quashed hopes for any definitive statement on NAFTA; President Bush told reporters beforehand that the negotiators weren't bound by "artificial timetables" and should "get politics out of the way if any is in there." Before heading off to Jack Murphy Stadium, the two presidents issued a statement saying that the talks were entering "the top of the ninth inning." Bush's introduction at the start of the game elicited the traditional round of lusty boos. The union-backed Fair Trade Campaign distributed mock baseball cards to the All-Star crowd depicting a Yankee-pinstriped Bush and Salinas with the legend, "Don't let them throw you a curve—Strike out NAFTA." Salinas could see that Bush's growing political weakness might force the NAFTA negotiations into scoreless extra innings.

The NAFTA timetable was hardly artificial or apolitical. Hopes that the San Diego summit would include an announcement of NAFTA's completion had evaporated a week earlier. Now, with the next ministerial session planned for July 25, U.S. officials put out the word that they didn't expect to have a finished agreement even then. If a complete, vetted text—with all sections fully lawyered and scrutinized by the mandatory private sector advisory committees—could not be readied for initialing within a few days of the ministerial gathering, it would be too late to have a signing ceremony before the November election. The three ministers held secret preliminary talks in the United States over the July 18–19 weekend, where the Canadians aired complaints that they were being railroaded into an early agreement due to American domestic politics. Back in Ottawa on Monday, Trade Minister Wilson told reporters that Canadian interests still "have to be met on a number of issues." A provincial counterpart was more blunt: "Helping to get George Bush elected by signing on to a dubious free trade deal is not part of Canada's economic agenda," declared Ed Philip, trade minister for Ontario's opposition government.

While Salinas and his advisors nervously monitored the Democratic Convention for hints about Clinton's NAFTA policy, they received unexpected but extremely welcome news: Perot, exactly one month after his inadvertent trashing of the Mexican stock market, had abruptly with-drawn from the race. In two frantic hours jubilant Mexican traders pushed up the Bolsa index by 3 percent. In New York, Telmex, still considered a proxy for the Mexican economy, was the most heavily traded issue of the day, rising $1.50 to nearly $50 a share. Mutual funds specializing in Mexico soared an average of 10 percent. Mexican brokerage houses hoped that *el efecto Perot* was safely behind them.

■ The June 1992 stock crash was a wake-up call, suggesting what might happen if NAFTA were rejected by the U.S. Congress. Nervous Mexican brokers accused the Salinas government of overselling investors on the importance of NAFTA. Since the beginning of the year, however, when it first became clear that NAFTA might be delayed, Mexican officials had been working hard to downplay the agreement's immediate importance. Their carefully coordinated speeches to foreign business audiences stressed Mexico's impressive budget-balancing accomplishments and liberalized investment rules. At home, they pointed to the spectacularly successful privatization of the banks as evidence of underlying business confidence. After June, they also minimized the cost and importance of the sudden market retrenchment, noting—correctly—that such downswings in the past had usually preceded sustained recoveries.

But the new pattern was different. Domestic economic fundamentals were now less important than foreign political beliefs—and foreign political realities. Foreign capital now held more than half of the Mexican market's most commonly traded issues. The defensive and amateurish reaction of Mexican companies and market officials to the downturn reminded investors abroad that this was still a young, thin and unpredictable market. For Wall Street, the bloom was off the Mexican rose.

The current account deficit, meanwhile, continued to balloon out of control. Economists began forecasting a $20 billion shortfall for the year, equal to 6 percent of Mexico's GDP, a financial chasm that could only be filled by foreign capital. The critical new importance to Mexico of American portfolio investors—and their skittishness at any signs of trouble in the trade talks—had been unnervingly exposed. So had the danger of trying to conclude a watershed trade accord in the middle of an American presidential campaign. The market plunge dramatized Mexico's dependence on NAFTA's success and its inability to affect—or even foresee—the political developments that ultimately would determine its fate.

■ The Mexicans took some small comfort from Clinton's vice presidential choice. Tennessee's Al Gore was among the minority of Democratic Senators who had voted in favor of fast-track negotiating rules. He was a free-trader of the industrial policy school and would provide invaluable environmental cover if a Clinton Administration had to push NAFTA through a recalcitrant Congress. They were also reassured by Clinton's economic advisors, who favored NAFTA for a variety of philosophical and practical reasons. (Robert Reich saw it as making the case for American specialization in "knowledge-intensive" industries, while Robert Rubin, as co-chairman of Goldman, Sachs & Co., had reaped millions as an advisor in the privatization of Telmex, a deal propelled by optimism about Mexican free trade.) Many pro-NAFTA lobbyists enjoyed close access to the Democratic campaign. Joseph O'Neill, a former top aide to Senator Lloyd Bentsen now on Mexico's NAFTA payroll, was advising Clinton strategists on lessons learned from the 1988 vice presidential campaign. The campaign's chief advisor on Latin American issues, Richard Feinberg, was a committed NAFTA advocate, as was Clinton counselor Bruce Babbitt, the former Arizona governor and an astute student of Mexico's economy and politics.

Clinton's own close attention as governor to Arkansas business interests also argued for a sympathetic view of the agreement. From poultry packers to rice farmers, many Arkansas exporters stood to benefit from NAFTA-smoothed inroads to the Mexican market. The state's biggest corporation, WalMart, had recently entered the Mexican market in an ambitious joint venture with Cifra S.A.—a project that depended on trade liberalization and the simpler cross-border transport logistics that NAFTA would permit.

NAFTA negotiators rushed to finish their work before the August Republican Convention in Houston. Republican operatives planned to spotlight the agreement as one of George Bush's most important and creative achievements both in foreign policy and domestic economic policy. The USTR staff and its Mexican and Canadian counterparts worked around the clock, and on August 12, Bush announced that the agreement had at last been struck. With Carla Hills standing behind him on the White House steps, Bush read a brief statement saying her work would "create jobs and generate economic growth in all three countries. Increased trade with North America will help our nation prepare for the challenges and opportunities of the next century. The Cold War is over. The principal challenge now facing the United States today is to compete in a rapidly changing, expanding global marketplace. Open markets in

Mexico and Canada mean more American jobs." In Ottawa and Mexico City, Mulroney and Salinas made similar announcements.

In truth, NAFTA wasn't quite finished. It would take nearly three weeks more to get the lawyered text to Congressional committees. Still, the announcement had come in time for the Administration to declare victory in Houston. Praise for NAFTA became a staple of the convention, led by a strongly partisan speech by Carla Hills, who had resisted earlier pressure to make the USTR and NAFTA part of the Bush campaign. It was too late legally to sign the finished treaty before the November election, so the White House scheduled a ceremonial initialing of the NAFTA text by the three trade ministers in San Antonio in mid-October, inviting both Salinas and Mulroney to attend. Despite the clear indications that the function would be a Republican campaign event, Salinas could not easily refuse. Without George Bush, there would have been no NAFTA. And most Mexican officials still expected Bush to be re-elected.

Several of Clinton's top political advisors had warned that a NAFTA endorsement could cost him as much as five points in the election. Perot was now back in the race and blasting the agreement in the presidential debates. Labor leaders and Majority Leader Dick Gephardt urged Clinton to make his support conditional on a radical upgrading of Mexican labor and environmental standards. But most of his advisors argued strongly that NAFTA should be backed on its merits, and Clinton agreed. If NAFTA "is done right, it will create jobs in the United States and in Mexico," Clinton declared in a 19-page speech at North Carolina State. "If it is not done right, however, the blessings of the agreement are far less clear, and the burdens can be significant. I'm convinced that I will do it right. I am equally convinced that Mr. Bush won't."

That speech outlined what would four months later become official U.S. policy.

Clinton's most important pledge, from Mexico's view, was his vow not to renegotiate what had already been negotiated, and to address his concerns with parallel accords. But Clinton went on to propose a long list of side agreements which the Salinas team saw as an infringement on Mexican sovereignty. Doing NAFTA right, Clinton said, would require that an "environmental protection commission with substantial powers and resources to prevent and clean up pollution . . . is up and running when the free trade agreement is up and running." He said it would also require a dispute resolution mechanism giving Mexican and American workers the right to sue for Mexican violations of Mexican labor standards. "Each agreement should contain a wide variety of procedural safeguards and remedies that we take for granted here in this country, such as easy access to the courts, public hearings, the right to present evidence, streamlined procedures and effective remedies," Clinton said. "I will negotiate an agreement among the three parties that permits citizens of each country to bring suit in their own courts when they believe their domestic environmental protections and worker standards aren't being enforced." He said he would urge the Congress to pass legislation giving American citizens "the right to challenge objectionable environmental practices by the Mexicans or the Canadians," even though Mexicans and Canadians would not enjoy reciprocal rights. Despite his promise not to reopen the NAFTA text, Clinton proposed additional restrictions on Mexican truckers and potential "surges" in Mexican exports.

As discomfiting as this was to the Salinas team, they were still confident that a Democratic White House would not reject an agreement signed by a lame-duck Republican president. Shortly after the November election, Salinas's chief of staff approached Clinton's foreign policy advisors to seek assurances that the president-elect wouldn't object to a final, binding signing of the NAFTA text by Bush, Salinas and Mulroney in December, the earliest moment permitted by U.S. fast-track rules. The Salinas emissaries were told that Clinton wouldn't mind. George Bush's wild ride was now over, and NAFTA was halfway toward becoming a legal reality. The Mexican economy was yet to recover from the body blows of the summer, and Mexican stock prices still veered downward at any new sign of negative NAFTA news. But the risks of free fall seemed averted. Mexico again began thinking of NAFTA as a matter of when, not if.

■ Looking back, the Salinas government began to see a lovely symmetry in the NAFTA saga. Only a Republican administration, they said, would have responded so readily to Mexico's request for a free trade agreement, yet only a Democratic president could sell the finished product to a skeptical Democratic Congress.

But the real challenge for President Clinton was not getting NAFTA through Congress. It was persuading the American public that NAFTA was a good idea.

Mexico—zealously nationalistic Mexico—was the only country in North America where trade integration enjoyed broad public support. And even in Mexico, after an expensive two-year pro-NAFTA public relations campaign, there were nearly as many opponents of the pact as supporters. North American integration was embraced with more resignation than enthusiasm; few Mexicans welcomed the idea of surrendering their economic sovereignty. But many saw no alternative, given the collapse of the old national economic order and the inescapable reality of Mexico's dependence on northern markets and capital.

In Canada, pro-NAFTA sentiment fell into the teens amid fears that it would deepen a recession that was already widely blamed on bilateral free trade. The harder Mulroney pushed for NAFTA, the more Canadians rebelled. After Mulroney announced his retirement in February 1993, support for NAFTA in Canada registered a slight rise. Still, opponents outnumbered supporters by 3-to-1, and every party except Mulroney's Conservatives was either critical of NAFTA or flatly opposed.

In the United States, support for NAFTA declined in inverse proportion to media coverage. When free trade emerged as a theme in the Democratic presidential primaries, polls reported opposition rising. Focus groups conducted by political professionals in both parties showed that attacks on NAFTA by Ross Perot and Jerry Brown had hit their mark: the more people heard about NAFTA, the less they liked it. In July, a *New York Times* poll showed twice as many people labeling NAFTA a "bad idea" as a "good idea." The Republican campaign decision to make NAFTA a focus of the Bush re-election strategy only increased popular antipathy. By election day, exit polls showed a majority of voters opposing NAFTA—even in the Texas and Southern California districts where Bush had tried hardest to capitalize on the issue. A *Wall Street Journal* poll at the time showed that only 21 percent of American voters endorsed NAFTA; two months later, when the issue had receded from the front pages, support had risen to 28 percent. Only a handful of the newly elected members of Congress actively supported NAFTA; scores had campaigned energetically against it, and the rest were carefully ambivalent. Despite the pro-NAFTA posture of both candidates, the 1992 election could not be taken as a mandate for North American free trade.

NAFTA was the first modern trade agreement to be subjected to sustained debate in a presidential campaign. Unsurprisingly, it came out bloodied. Public support for free trade is always broad but shallow. Grass-roots opposition is highly focused and motivated, and more conversant with the issue's details. With unemployment high, economic growth faltering, and incomes stagnating, criticism of the pact had an easy constituency. NAFTA became the protectionist fault line between pro-business "New Democrats" and the traditional urban and labor coalitions to which the party was still beholden.

Free trade also remained an emotional issue for the fifth of the electorate that backed Ross Perot, the country's most prominent anti-NAFTA politician. Perot had demonized NAFTA as a symbol of American industrial decline and of Washington's corruption by lobbyists. Democratic strategists had persuaded themselves that they needed to win over Perot voters to maintain control of Congress in 1994 and re-elect Clinton in 1996. So there was understandable resistance to any great expenditure of political capital on NAFTA's behalf. NAFTA could not be credibly sold as a short-term American jobs program, the political professionals reminded the White House. Couldn't NAFTA wait?

The answer was no, it couldn't, even though Clinton didn't owe Salinas a thing. Postponing NAFTA beyond that session of Congress would have been seen by the Mexican public and the international financial markets as tantamount to rejection. It would have been the biggest body blow to the Mexican economy since the 1985 earthquake. For the United States, in the long term, it would have meant missing a historic opportunity to raise Mexico out of poverty and lay the foundation for a true continental economy. And for the Clinton Administration, in the short term, it would have meant accepting responsibility for the likely collapse of the peso, a rise in illegal immigration, the revival of the low-wage maquiladora industrial strategy in Mexico, the loss of export jobs in the United States, and a resurgence of anti-American sentiment in a proudly nationalist country that had defied its deepest political traditions to propose a permanent economic partnership with its superpower neighbor.

CHAPTER 5

Jobs, Jobs, Jobs: The NAFTA Numbers Game

Ross Perot, NAFTA's most visible and voluble opponent, liked to tick off the figures: Mexican workers had their incomes cut by 65 percent in the 1980s. They now earned just 58 cents an hour, with no benefits. Nearly 600,000 Americans had already lost jobs to this cheap Mexican labor. Now NAFTA threatened to destroy 5.8 million more American manufacturing jobs.

These were compelling numbers. And all of them were wrong.

To begin with, Mexican industrial workers average better than $2 an hour, more than they did in 1980. In northern Mexico, they do even better. Fewer than 200,000 American jobs have been lost to Mexico over the past decade, and most of these jobs would have been lost anyway—either through bankruptcy or a production shift to East Asia or some other offshore site. Meanwhile, more than 600,000 jobs have been created by U.S. exports to Mexico. As for those 5.8 million industrial workers, the real threat they faced was is Perot's scare-mongering arithmetic. His advisors simply tallied up every small labor-intensive manufacturing operation in the United States and declared each one of them "at risk" of being moved to Mexico by predatory investment bankers.

What was missing from this claim was any sense of realism (call it "business sense," if you like) about what such a mass exodus would entail. It takes investment of at least $50,000 in plant and equipment to create one new Mexican manufacturing job. So the cost of moving all these jobs south would require investments of about $300 billion—more than all the net capital investment in the United States in a given year. If 100 Ross

Perots decided to exhaust their entire personal fortunes uprooting American light industry, and if Mexico were prepared to forcibly employ every one of its people over the age of 10, and if the managers, technicians and marketing experts working in these companies were prepared to relocate, this might be a plausible scenario. But it hardly seems likely.

Nor were NAFTA's critics the only ones playing fast and loose with numbers.

Mickey Kantor, the U.S. Trade Representative, says NAFTA will create 200,000 new jobs by 1995, bringing the total number of American workers employed by exports to Mexico to 900,000. His predecessor, Carla Hills, who negotiated the agreement, was even more enthusiastic, claiming that with NAFTA more than 1 million Americans will owe their jobs to exports to Mexico by 1995. Yet their numbers were nothing more than an extrapolation based on the recent growth of American exports to Mexico—jobs that the United States could have expected to have with or without NAFTA.

Unfortunately, the numbers cited by figures such as Perot, Hills and Kantor tended to be accepted by the press and the public as established facts—however speculative they may have been.

Economic Numbers, Economic Models
It would be nice if objective economic models could be used to settle the political score. But they can't. Economic models, no matter how complex and expensive, ultimately depend on the quality of their raw data and the assumptions they reflect about the future. As a result, their projections are rarely objective and often wrong.

Even in the best of circumstances, economic data are of doubtful reliability—particularly when dealing with such a small overall perturbation to the economy as that created by NAFTA. In the month the NAFTA negotiations concluded, the American labor force had more than 126 million people, including 9.7 million unemployed and 6.3 million part-time workers who said they wanted full-time work. That month, total employment fell by 167,000, including a 97,000 decline in manufacturing. In an economy where month-to-month changes are this large, the impact of NAFTA is almost impossible to discern.

All types of economic models were used by both sides in the debate. At one extreme were the complex computable general equilibrium (CGE) models. KPMG Peat Marwick, working for the Mexico-U.S. Business Committee, a pro-NAFTA group, published the results of their model—

based on 12,000 interlocking equations in early 1991. They predicted that NAFTA would produce, in the near-term, an $18 billion expansion in American exports; but they also forecast a negligible overall impact on American output, wages and jobs (a net gain of just 40,000). "Limited adverse affects" were noted in three areas: apparel, sugar and electronics. KPMG modelers stressed that the pact's real impact would be felt within Mexico—and that the impact would come not from trade liberalization but from investment. In the long term, Mexico stood to gain as many as 1.46 million jobs.

The problem is, computer programs can't easily foresee the effects of something that has not been tried. After all, their underlying premise is that the economy will respond in the future much as it has in the past. But if NAFTA works, it will make the Mexican economy a qualitatively different entity: a swelling stream of private capital will accelerate and redirect its growth in a higher-tech, higher-wage direction. Such a sea change does not lend itself to mathematical modeling.

Much simpler, and more widely quoted, were studies by two rival Washington think tanks, the Institute for International Economics (IIE) and the Economic Policy Institute (EPI). IIE reflected mainstream economic thinking: its board is studded with past members of the Council of Economic Advisors (and future aspirants), and its directors range from David Rockefeller and ex-President of Mexico Miguel de la Madrid to the United Auto Workers' Douglas Fraser. EPI, which supplements its foundation support with checks from labor unions, is primarily an advocacy group. Its founders include Labor Secretary Robert Reich, and several of its staffers, including Director Jeff Faux, were among NAFTA's most—effective opponents.

IIE estimated NAFTA would create 170,000 American jobs, while EPI calculated that it could eliminate as many as 480,000 jobs. Both numbers were based on fairly weak analysis.

IIE's forecast was made by two American trade specialists, Gary Clyde Hufbauer and Jeffrey J. Schott. The "model" that they used to make this often-cited forecast was based on neither NAFTA nor the Mexican economy—nor was it in fact even an economic model. It was merely an historical analogy—one that superimposed the experience of other successful developing economies on Mexican statistics. Macroeconomic projections were derived from averages contained in a 1991 World Bank survey of newly industrialized countries in Asia and Europe, even though most of these nations have economic profiles and strategies quite different from Mexico's. The IIE analysis took Salinas's first year in office as a base, then projected the data forward for five years. NAFTA-ized Mexico gained $12 billion more in foreign capital inflows than it would otherwise have received.

Although this type of analogy appeals to common sense, it has one egregious flaw. Job creation estimates are derived mechanically from trade balance projections, rather than from any projection of the specific consequences of cross-border economic integration. The IIE economists simply translated America's trade surplus with Mexico into American jobs, with $1 billion in surplus equaling 19,600 jobs.

Yet IIE's "non-model model" seems a paragon of analytic rigor next to the work of the Economic Policy Institute. EPI assumed that NAFTA would exert a "common market effect" on industrial job location. It then extrapolated its conclusions from statistics on American investment in Ireland during it first years in the European Economic Community. On this basis, EPI said, NAFTA would bring Mexico up to $53 billion in additional American investment through the year 2000, creating 490,000 jobs in Mexico that might otherwise have stayed in the United States.

But EPI's Irish analogy was wildly inappropriate. There are vast differences—in scale, resources and investment history—between Mexico and Ireland. And over the period in question, American investment increased almost everywhere in Europe, not just in Ireland and the other new EC members. Moreover, given EPI's claim that NAFTA would—create some muscular new threat to American manufacturing, the example of perennially distressed, emigrant-hemorrhaging Ireland seems almost perverse.

It is plainly wrong to argue that all funds invested in Mexico (or Ireland) are funds that would otherwise have been invested in the United States. It implies, in extremis, that America would be far richer if no investment funds had ever left the country. Yet many of the plants that now span the Mexican border would have failed or moved to southeast Asia had they not had access to cheap Mexican labor. Two recent examples: the decisions by Smith-Corona to move typewriter production from New York State to Tijuana and by Zenith to relocate its last American television assembly line from Missouri to Chihuahua.

Zenith had been relocating its assembly operations to Mexico for two decades—well before NAFTA was debated and long before Zenith's Japanese competitors shifted production from East Asia to Tijuana. That Zenith has no surviving American competitors lends credence to its argument that the move was vital to its survival. Zenith (which calls itself the last American television manufacturer) has fully three-quarters of its work force in Mexico. If those 18,000 employees were earning American wages, its annual wage bill would be $400 million higher—a crippling difference for a company that hasn't posted a good profit in years.

NAFTA critics often cited Zenith as an example of a company that has abandoned United States for the low wages and lax regulatory standards of Mexico. Yet in many ways the company provides a textbook case of how NAFTA is supposed to work. Zenith recently closed subsidiaries in Ireland and Taiwan and shifted production to Reynosa, Matamoros and Juarez. The transportation and payroll savings from this consolidation were crucial to the preservation of Zenith's prize operation, a high-tech picture-tube factory with 3,200 workers in Melrose Park, Illinois. Under NAFTA, Zenith will be able to sell directly in Mexico for the first time; but its competitors, also making televisions in Mexico but using Asian-made picture tubes, will face steep new tariffs in the United States. Meanwhile, its new Mexican employees live and shop along the U.S. border, generating growth in the American economy.

The relocation of a Smith-Corona typewriter plant from New York to Tijuana provides a similar story. Often identified as the last American typewriter company, it is actually British-owned, with much of its production in Singapore. Its New York plant made technologically outdated typewriters. This forced the company to compete by slashing prices, and that meant eliminating its American payroll. Had Smith-Corona invested in better electronic technology and leaner manufacturing techniques, it might have flourished with an American work force. But given the accumulated neglect of the company's management, the move to Tijuana may have rescued Smith-Corona from marketplace oblivion; if so, at least the jobs of its American suppliers and retailers will be saved.

The Mexican Market

NAFTA's ultimate benefit to the United States is a stable, prosperous Mexico. Typical forecasts show 500 jobs created in Mexico for every 100 jobs in the United States. That doesn't mean that NAFTA is a better deal for Mexico. It merely reflects the realities of an industrial superpower and a poor economy one-twentieth that size that depends on its neighbor for three-fifths of its trade and investment. Nor does it mean that Mexico will have an easy time of it: some Mexican academics have forecast gross domestic job losses of 500,000 or more from NAFTA's removal of corn subsidies and the collapse of uncompetitive textile and apparel companies. Indeed, there is little dispute that both the pains and the gains from NAFTA will be more pronounced south of the border.

In both countries, the pain will come first. Companies will not wait until the last possible moment to consolidate production lines, build market share, or abandon uncompetitive businesses. If NAFTA were to be evaluated solely on the basis of its impact during the early transition period, much of the criticism of the agreement would be valid. But even looking to the year 2000 is a short-term perspective. NAFTA's real benefits will only be felt by the generation of Mexicans who are just now entering the work force.

NAFTA accelerates a liberalization trend that has already tripled bilateral trade and could soon propel Mexico past Japan as the second biggest market for American goods. Within a decade, at present growth rates, Mexico could be buying as much from the United States as Canada does today. If, prodded by NAFTA, the Mexican economy expands at the faster annual rate of 6 percent—which seems both plausible, given the precedents of East Asia, and advisable, with a labor force expanding by 3 percent a year it could surpass Canada as an American market early in the next century. At that pace, within 20 years Northern Mexico could expect to enjoy a standard of living comparable to that of the contiguous American Southwest today.

NAFTA critics, such as the AFL-CIO, often argued that there is "no market" in Mexico because there is "no middle class." The Economic Policy Institute, which reflects union views, claimed that it is precisely "the absence of middle-class incomes in Mexico that is the big attraction [for NAFTA supporters]—the labor force of more than 30 million people willing to work for a tiny fraction of U.S. wages."

This is quite wrong. In fact, most industrial production in Mexico— indeed, most American-owned manufacturing capacity there—is geared toward local consumption, which is outpacing population growth. The Mexican workers who are satisfying this demand aren't taking jobs away from Americans. They are in effect employed by Mexican consumers, who are richer and more numerous than most Americans assume.

Many NAFTA critics echoed Ross Perot's claim that Mexico is a country with "a few extremely wealthy people [where] everybody else basically works as serfs." Indisputably, Mexico is a poor country, and its poverty is exacerbated by badly skewed distribution of income. The poor majority collects barely a fifth of the country's earnings. But the flip side of this distributionist coin is that the upper fifth of Mexican society earns about three-fifths of the country's income. That means that nearly 20 million people—more than the population of Texas—have real incomes that are three times the national average.

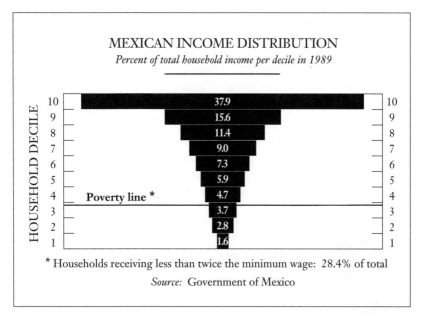

MEXICAN INCOME DISTRIBUTION
Percent of total household income per decile in 1989

HOUSEHOLD DECILE

10	37.9
9	15.6
8	11.4
7	9.0
6	7.3
5	5.9
4	Poverty line * 4.7
3	3.7
2	2.8
1	1.6

* Households receiving less than twice the minimum wage: 28.4% of total

Source: Government of Mexico

This may not be a just distribution of wealth and income, but it's plainly a market. Drive through any of the sprawling subdivisions of Mexico City, Guadalajara or Monterrey—or even the suburbs of provincial capitals like Puebla, Chihuahua, Leon or Hermosillo—and you will see a large and growing middle class that, in disposable income, is not that far behind much of the United States. They own good-sized homes, reasonably new cars, take vacations in Acapulco or Disney World, and send their kids to college. They also eat and dress better than most Americans. To suggest that American companies set up shop in Mexico for one reason alone, cheap labor, ignores the reality of this lucrative and expanding market. General Electric, for example, reported sales of $1.45 billion in Mexico in 1991—*three times the volume of its Mexican exports to the United States.* And it expects that Mexican market to double over the next five years.

Yet the impression one draws from newscasts and NAFTA critics is that Mexican cities are shantytowns populated by dollar-an-hour maquiladora workers. There are many such workers and neighborhoods. But they are not the majority, even in the overcrowded border towns, and they have American counterparts in the tin-roofed colonias of El Paso and Brownsville. The people in the upper fifth of the income pyramid live as well and earn nearly as much in real terms as the middle class of the contiguous American Southwest. That includes not just the top 1 percent—the 1 million Mexicans who are affluent by any standard—but another 8 million or so professionals and small business people with real incomes comparable to those of working-class Americans.

The long-term implications for the United States are staggering. As Mexico looks more like Texas and less like Guatemala, it would require imports of American machinery, staple foods, consumer goods, and even entire civil-engineering projects. So great are the disparities between the two economies that this dependency should persist for at least a generation. At that point, it would slowly shift towards a more stable and equitable interdependence, with a smaller income gap—and for American companies, a lucrative market of 50 million or more middle-class Mexican consumers.

Trade and Jobs

But what makes sense from a long-term policy perspective isn't always relevant to the people making those policies. In the long run, today's policymakers will be as dead as Keynes. And in the short run, some jobs—tens of thousands—will surely move south to Mexico, just as they have since the early 1980s. Fairly or not, this new emigration will be blamed squarely on NAFTA. The prospect that these losses will be made up tenfold in 20 years means little to the career of the typical Congressman.

Sooner than that, most of the people who dealt with NAFTA—the negotiators, corporate planners, committee chairmen, environmental leaders—will be gone. What matters to them is the next two or four years. That's when the needs of dislocated workers must be addressed. That's when the relocation of plants across the border would be most closely watched. The way those problems are perceived and managed would determine how the trade pact itself was judged. Politically, NAFTA's immediate impact on the American job market may be the only important question about the agreement.

NAFTA's architects brought this on their own heads. From the beginning, the Bush Administration said NAFTA was about three things: "jobs, jobs, jobs." President Bush told Congress that "all economic studies" agreed that NAFTA would boost American "exports, output and employment."

When studies by pro-NAFTA forces found that there would be little net American job creation, NAFTA lobbyists grew uneasy. That meant there was little immediate reason for American voters to support it (goodwill toward Mexico doesn't count for much). True, consumers would benefit from lower prices. But given Mexico's small share of American imports, the low current tariffs on most of those goods, and the long transition before duties are to drop to zero, the effect on the average shopping bill would be slight.

Meanwhile, NAFTA will hasten some American job losses, both from the inability of some industries to compete with duty-free Mexican imports and from shifts in production to plants south of the border. Some NAFTA supporters contended that retraining or relocation subsidies for people who lost jobs could be financed by NAFTA's boost to the tax base. President Bush complicated matters when he proposed an expanded job-training program for displaced workers, with part of that money set aside for unemployment caused by NAFTA.

Critics immediately pounced, saying this proposal was a covert admission that NAFTA would cost jobs. They argued that the funds would be severely inadequate, given the real costs of technical training and the vast numbers of projected unemployed. The Economic Policy Institute claimed that "a million U.S. workers could lose their jobs" because of NAFTA. House Majority Leader Richard Gephardt said the numbers of workers displaced by NAFTA could be so large that providing for them might force deep cuts in entitlement programs. (He might have said it would lead to further cuts in defense spending, but that wouldn't have scared people nearly so much.)

The Clinton Administration wanted to avoid this trap by making its retraining programs generic. But at organized labor's insistence, Labor Secretary Robert Reich specifically targeted NAFTA dislocations in a $657 million retraining program for 1994. So the Clinton White House is making roughly the same assumptions about NAFTA-related unemployment that the Bush Administration did. And it faces the same murky questions. Is every newly unemployed person whose former employer increases investment in Mexico a NAFTA casualty? If so, is it fair to help that person and not the job-seeker whose company moved production to Mexico before NAFTA was enacted? And why should NAFTA dislocations be favored over others? If a ball-bearing company lays off a worker in Ohio and hires a worker in Mexico, then the jobless Ohioan would presumably get federal help. If a Tennessee textile worker gets laid off because her company shifted production to China, the Tennessean wouldn't qualify. Quite apart from being unfair, such a program would perversely subsidize the relocation of jobs to Mexico.

Lost in all this is any attempt to estimate and measure NAFTA's real impact on employment, the trade balance, and the budget.

Bush Administration economists applied a common formula—every $50,000 in manufacturing exports represents one manufacturing worker—and concluded that Mexico's new openness to imports had already created 675,000 jobs and would (with NAFTA) create as many as 300,000 more a year for three or four years. Even in a complex $6 trillion economy, an employment expansion of that magnitude—nearly 3 million jobs over 10 years—would have a real impact.

Unfortunately, the standard calculus is probably wrong. Just because the equation ($50,000 in exports equals one job) is widely used by policymakers doesn't mean that it applies to the goods and services that dominate sales to Mexico. Recent American export growth has been driven by improving productivity in export industries—improvements derived from technology and capital investment. The sales-to-worker ratio of $50,000-to-1, even if accurate a few years ago, would overestimate the real employment impact of export growth today. Many American businesses—including leading exporters to Mexico—have boosted sales in recent years with no new hiring. Moreover, a growing number of exporters are in service industries, from advertising and insurance to retailing and credit cards, where standard manufacturing equations may be even more off base.

Other economists favor equally mechanical ratios. Hufbauer and Schott originally assumed that every billion-dollar improvement in the trade balance was equivalent to 14,500 jobs, or $69,000 per worker—an equation they derived by dividing 1986 direct manufactured export sales by official estimates of total "direct and supporting" export-related employment. In later revisions they used Commerce Department numbers reflecting the specific mix of manufacturing exports to Mexico, which sets the ratio at 19,600 jobs per $1 billion in exports, or $51,000 for each employee. Clyde Prestowitz at the Economic Strategy Institute based his own calculations on a "standard economic formula" of 30,000 jobs for every $1 billion in exports, or $33,333 per worker.

But while there is surely some correlation between output and employment, there is no reason to think that an increase in sales to a specific foreign market leads to a commensurate rise in production. Those sales might just as easily represent a shift away from a previous customer, foreign or domestic, to a new buyer, who may be closer, representing transport savings, or who may simply be willing to pay more. The surge in exports to Mexico must also be seen in the broader context of changing trade patterns. American exporters are increasingly looking south instead of just east and west. For many companies, this may mean different markets, but not necessarily larger ones. Sales to Mexico could also represent the temporary replacement of customers lost in the American recession. This creative use of idle capacity might reduce layoffs, but it wouldn't necessarily mean new jobs.

Sales south of the border represent a small fraction—under 10 percent—of a complex, continually changing mix of foreign and domestic markets. There is no reason to think a sale made in Mexico would not otherwise be made somewhere else. And it is simply foolish to argue that every $50,000 (or $33,000, or $69,000) in export sales to Mexico represents a worker who would have otherwise been unemployed, or to claim that every $50,000 that Americans spend on Mexican imports represents a job lost in the United States. Not every import displaces a domestic product: in Mexico's case, little of what it ships north would otherwise be made in the United States. Mexican products are already an integral part of the North American economy: bringing a Mexican-assembled Chrysler into the United States, with its American-made parts and American-directed profits, hardly has the same job-displacing impact as the importation of a Nissan or a Saab. Yet that is the logic of those who routinely equate Mexican import figures with American job losses.

A further muddling of the true picture has resulted from America's recent obsession with bilateral trade balances. Expecting the United States to maintain a surplus in cross-border trade? Then translate that into manufacturing-worker equivalents to "prove" that—presto!—NAFTA leads to long-term job gains. Think the United States would slip back into a trade deficit with Mexico? Then translate that forecast into missing-worker units to "prove" that—look out!—NAFTA destroys American jobs.

This is mercantilist nonsense. Just because Mexico ran a billion dollar trade surplus with the United States in 1989 doesn't mean there was a net loss in American jobs. Exports to Mexico had more than doubled over the previous five years to roughly $30 billion. A year later, when the United States sold a billion dollars more in Mexico than it imported, that didn't mean a sudden job loss in Mexico. In both countries, imports and exports—and the jobs they support—continued to grow.

What drives employment is the volume and vigor of the overall trade. As long as imports and exports keep growing in reasonable equilibrium—which a free trade agreement should assure—the result will be net job creation on both sides of the border.

If opening the border wouldn't destroy jobs, surely, NAFTA critics argued, it would lower wages. That fear motivated labor unions to take a strong stand against the agreement. "It's payday again for unemployed American workers," ran one anti-NAFTA ad. "Earn up to 58 cents an hour."

These fears were fed by politically reckless advertisements in industrial location magazines extolling the advantages of cheap Mexican labor. NAFTA, contended the AFL-CIO's Thomas Donahue, "is not about free trade, nor is it about development in Mexico. It is about guaranteeing the ability of American investors to move their plants to Mexico to take advantage of cheap wages and poor working conditions."

Ross Perot told *BusinessWeek* bluntly: "We can't do anything that would lower the standard of living of the American people. I'll tell you how to do NAFTA tonight. Have Mexico agree to our wage standards, our employee benefits. Have them match us and Canada. That would be a miracle in Mexico."

A miracle, indeed—but a miracle of unemployment. Mexico's wages are not the product of indentured servitude. They are the product of the lower productivity of the Mexican work force—the result of poor education, obsolete technology, and inefficient management. For decades, Mexico has protected poorly run companies with steep tariffs. With NAFTA, American companies will be able to make productive and efficient use of Mexican labor, but they will not be able to raise its productivity to American levels overnight.

Perot argued that it would be better for the United States if Mexico had higher wage and living standards. Agreed. But NAFTA is a way of making that happen. Without NAFTA, the cheap-labor export competition that so worries Perot would persist, but with even lower wages and without NAFTA's guarantees for American products and investors in Mexico.

At the turn of the century, the American work force looked much as the Mexican work force does today: barely 10 percent of American workers were skilled. Today, less than 10 percent of the U.S. work force is unskilled.

The spread of new technologies has led to a rising demand for technicians and skilled labor in manufacturing. This, in turn, has led to a rise in unemployment (and underemployment) in America's older industrial centers. Many unskilled workers have been unable to find other work, especially at pay comparable to their old jobs. The hardships they face are real—but it can hardly be blamed on the export of investment to places like Mexico.

If low wages were the key to industrial strength, then NAFTA critics might have a legitimate complaint. But it isn't. Manufacturing strength depends on many other factors—including the ability to develop and adopt new technologies, product design, and other activities that demand a highly skilled and flexible work force. America and Mexico are specializing in different parts of the manufacturing process. Maquiladora plants engage in relatively low-skilled assembly operations. On the American side, manufacturing firms increasingly specialize in the technology-intensive part of the process, which often requires workers with greater educations. American firms are becoming more competitive in global markets in large measure by cutting the costs they incur in low-skill operations. Ultimately, this should allow them to create more high-paying jobs. Average American wages should start to rise.

But for the unskilled, the picture looks very bleak. Even economists who believe that NAFTA will lead to some small improvement in median American wages expect a drop in pay for the working poor. (Stanford's Clark Reynolds sketches out a scenario for the year 2000 in which wages for the working poor could fall by as much as 2.9 percent.) But it's hard to factor out NAFTA's effect from the overall impact of low-wage import competition. Over the course of the 1980s, male high school graduates saw their earnings fall by 14 percent; their college-educated counterparts enjoyed a 4 percent income rise. If this gap is the inevitable consequence of global competition, it will continue to widen even with NAFTA.

Distinguishing the specific effect of a trade and investment pact from the general impact of Mexican trade is harder still. Rejecting NAFTA wouldn't have moved Mexico overseas. Nor would it have prevented Mexico from luring investment with unilateral liberalization measures. Even without NAFTA, Mexico would have been free to entice factories with subsidies and tax breaks. NAFTA's rejection would have been an incentive for Mexico to revert to the low-wage strategy it used to survive the debt crisis of the early 1980s, which could have affected the low end of American manufacturing pay scales even more severely.

Still, there is a natural fear that NAFTA could compound the difficulties facing the working poor. New urban manufacturing jobs are increasingly filled by new immigrants, both legal and illegal, rather than from the ranks of the native-born urban unemployed. At the same time, global market competition and international production-sharing by American multinationals have made it more difficult and less necessary for manufacturers to invest in training the high-cost, low-skill work force that is today's inner-city youth.

Low-wage competition from Mexico is a very small part of the problem. And while it is entirely possible that NAFTA could persuade even more employers to ignore the fate of this lost generation, it could just as easily lead to new forms of assistance—by forcing greater funding of job-training programs in distressed areas.[1]

Organized Labor and NAFTA

When unions complain about lost jobs, they aren't talking about employment extrapolations from trade balance figures, or even about companies forced out of business by Mexican competition. They are talking about the deliberate abandonment of the United States for a low-wage labor market. They point to boarded-up textile mills in New Hampshire and silent auto assembly lines in Michigan—and to the American plants south of the border that replaced those factories. Studies showing jobs created by import and export flows are dismissed as academic irrelevancies.

When union members look south, they see a country with no OSHA, no EPA, no independent unions, and a 10-to-1 wage differential with the United States. A caricature, to be sure, but one reinforced by tours of the maquiladora zone. NAFTA was written by an administration which said existing American work place rules weakened American competitiveness. Why, labor asks, should they expect Mexican regulatory norms to rise to American levels? Why shouldn't they be suspicious of deals negotiated by industries where the same companies—the auto industry is the classic case—control output and employment in each country?

After all, dollar-an-hour Mexicans are going to replace $15-an-hour Americans as North America's industrial labor force. Aren't they?

Hardly. Labor accounts for no more than 15 percent of manufacturing costs. And despite trends in production sharing with low-wage countries, most foreign investment by auto companies and other manufacturers is in other industrialized nations—Nissan in England, BMW in the United States, Ford in Germany—not in the developing world. Quite apart from the marketing, transportation and supply issues that keep most big manufacturers concentrated in their home markets, there are political considerations: even if a Chrysler decided it made economic sense to relocate to Mexico, such a move would be political and commercial suicide.

Even if the NAFTA battle were fought on labor's chosen turf—jobs moved to Mexico by American companies—the figures don't add up. The real number of expatriated jobs is thought by pro-labor economists to be closer to 200,000, and even that number is probably too high. (The one labor-backed effort to document such job shifts over the past 15 years could find only 96,000 relocations.)

Yet the 600,000-jobs-lost assertion has been repeated so often that many journalists and politicians assume it to be true. A typical citation appeared in a March 1993 *New York Times* article: "By most accounts, nearly 600,000 jobs have been located in Mexico that in the past might have been in the United States." The *Times* statement was repeated verbatim, without attribution, by Ross Perot in anti-NAFTA Congressional testimony two weeks later, giving the figure a new run of press citations.

The AFL-CIO estimate is based loosely on maquiladora workers— about 450,000 in all—plus Mexican employees in American subsidiaries said to be producing for the American market. Yet few of these Mexican workers directly replaced past or potential future American manufacturing employees.

Labor's interpretation of the maquiladora experience is the source of most of their misgivings about North American free trade. The AFL-CIO's Donahue, who said that NAFTA would turn Mexico "into a huge maquiladora," seems to think that virtually all 450,000 Mexican border assembly workers hold jobs that would otherwise be in the United States.

But only half these maquila plants are even American-owned. And by labor's own reckoning, no more than one in five maquiladora jobs can be directly identified as replacements for jobs lost in layoffs north of the border. Even those jobs were not necessarily replaced on a 1-to-1 basis: with production geared to the labor-intensive use of unskilled workers, many maquiladoras need more than one employee to achieve the same productivity as a worker in the United States. In other cases, the American worker was not replaced at all, but made redundant by more productive machinery. (That's no comfort to the American worker who has lost a job, but it does mean that it's quite wrong to count every maquiladora employee as a "lost" American manufacturing job.)

Much of the maquiladora growth over the past decade reflects the rapid expansion of new industries, such as personal computers and compact discs: these jobs cannot be said to have emigrated from the United States because they didn't exist before the maquila boom. Moreover, many plants that are nominally American-owned represent the relocation of final assembly operations from Asia to North America by Japanese corporate parents. Tijuana, for example, is now the source of a quarter of the color televisions sold in the United States; they are all Japanese (or

Korean) products that would otherwise be made in East Asia. This does not represent a loss of American jobs.

Still, many American companies would have stayed put, and profitable, had it not been for the easy option of the Mexican border. The maquiladoras introduced a radical cost-saving alternative for rustbelt companies that otherwise might have considered a move to the right-to-work South. A good example is the wire harness industry: spinning the spider-webs of electrical wire that keep a car humming is a painstaking, labor-intensive business, requiring close contact with customers. Once based almost entirely in the upper Midwest, now concentrated in Chihuahua, it is not a business that could be easily maintained an ocean away from the point of final assembly.

So the concerns of American unions are understandable. Not only had maquiladora investments grown most quickly when Mexico's economy was at its lowest ebb, but the influx of American investment into the border assembly belt seemed to suppress real wage growth. At the same time, the wage differential between maquiladora workers and American factory workers stayed stuck at roughly 10-to-1. With that wide a gap, unions took no comfort from studies showing a 4-to-1 productivity gap between American and Mexican workers.

| *Labor and the Clinton Adminis- tration* | From the moment he endorsed the free trade agreement in his presidential campaign, Bill Clinton promised union supporters that a Clinton NAFTA would be different from a Bush NAFTA: unlike the Republicans, the Demo- crats would attach a strict parallel agreement on North |

American labor rights.

This pleased labor leaders who wanted NAFTA to strengthen collective bargaining freedoms, workplace safety standards, the enforcement of child and penal labor laws, as well as to include sanctions against exports as a penalty for non-compliance. While the Bush Administration had allowed that these were fine and noble goals, it claimed that they had no place in a trade agreement.

Yet labor was only asking for what was once standard trade-statute language. Imports produced by forced labor have been banned by U.S. trade law since the 1930s. Developing countries cannot export goods duty free to the United States if they are held to be violating workers' rights. Even the Reagan Administration's Caribbean Basin Initiative incorporated guarantees of labor standards and collective bargaining rights. So the unions were on solid ground when they asked for a side agreement stripping duty-free provisions from any country found to be violating local labor law.

As a candidate, Clinton promised to negotiate a "tough" side agreement, requiring strict enforcement of labor standards. With amendments, that became U.S. policy. Under the side accords worked out by the Clinton team, Mexico could be assessed fines of up to $20 million and ultimately face the loss of NAFTA privileges if it consistently and egregiously failed to enforce its minimum wage laws, workplace health and safety standards, or prohibitions on child labor.

This meant little more than a codified insistence on Mexican enforcement of Mexican law. The sanctions could not be applied in cases of violations of labor contracts and other collective bargaining rights. But the unions never clearly indicated how such rights could be protected by a trade agreement—unless Canada and Mexico were also given the right to impose trade sanctions in response to domestic U.S. labor disputes.

The trouble was, the labor movement could never really decide what it wanted from the side agreements. While environmentalists were forcing Carla Hills to draft "the greenest trade treaty in history," unions were in NAFTA denial. They didn't want to improve the agreement, they wanted it to go away. Now, with Clinton's conditional support of the agreement, they had a chance to change it. Yet many labor-backed proposals were legally and economically impractical—a mandatory rise in Mexico's minimum wage to American levels over 10 years; complete compliance with American labor, environmental and workplace standards by American companies in Mexico. And internally, unions were divided over whether retraining programs should be targeted specifically at the tiny minority of workers who lost their jobs due to NAFTA.

Some Mexican laws protect employee rights more strictly than U.S. statutes—guarantees against summary dismissals, mandatory profit-sharing, paid 12-week maternity leave, double pay for overtime, protection of strike privileges, and a host of other provisions the AFL-CIO would kill for. But Mexican enforcement is, to be kind, erratic. Independent Mexican investigators have uncovered widespread evidence of abuse of child labor laws, for example, and examples of Indian peasants trapped in virtual debt peonage. But compliance is high in the big Mexican companies and multinationals against whom American workers are most directly competing.

The real problem with Mexican labor isn't Mexican labor standards: it's Mexican labor unions. Coming to terms with that reality is a challenge the AFL-CIO prefers to avoid.

For years, Mexican salary demands have been kept in check by the PRI's repressive labor monolith, the Mexican Workers Confederation (CTM). The CTM has been the principal enforcer of the rigid wage-and-price control programs that have been in effect since the early 1980s. Now, however, Mexican workers are beginning to assert more independence, and their country's and companies' new dependency on exports gives them invaluable leverage. Mexican subsidiaries of American companies once produced almost exclusively for the closed Mexican market; management could afford to wait out a strike. Now those factories are links in a North American manufacturing chain. A production shutdown in an engine plant in Coahuila can paralyze assembly lines in Michigan: companies cannot easily tolerate such interruption. Even Mexican-owned companies can be expected to react differently once they have secured significant market share in the United States. Losing customers would be more costly than a wage hike.

This drama is just beginning. The Salinas regime remains hostile to any signs of labor independence, and rarely misses an opportunity to crush a recalcitrant union or remove barriers to the hiring of non-union replacements. A 1992 Volkswagen strike led to the union's dissolution and VW's imposition of more flexible work rules; but it also produced wage hikes, as VW scrambled to keep production moving in plants that are now linked in a trans-Atlantic production chain. When wildcat strikes closed Ford's plant in Hermosillo for much of 1992, the company was left without Mercury Tracers in its showrooms when the American market rebounded.

Mexican labor could use the help. With a third of the work force unemployed or underemployed, it's hard for unions to take too tough a line, and independent leadership remains threatened and scarce. Confrontations between corrupt union chieftains and their disenfranchised membership also complicate labor relations: Mexican strikes are often deemed illegal because they break terms of a contract that the workers never knew they had accepted.

The Mexican government says with some annoyance that Mexico's autoworkers are already getting guidance and financial support from the United Auto Workers (UAW). But this aid has been limited. A few UAW locals have invited Mexican unionists to training seminars. Ford workers in Michigan commemorated a Mexican Ford employee killed in a confrontation with his own union's strike-busting goons. A group of organizers from the three NAFTA countries has been meeting annually since 1989. Outside the auto industry, Teamster locals have lobbied for better working conditions for Mexican food-packers; the United Electrical Workers has funded organizers in maquiladora plants; and, in potentially the most significant pan-NAFTA union development, the Communications Workers of America has broadened its pact with the Canadian Communications Workers to include the union at Teléfonos de México, whose leader is likely to be Mexico's next national labor chief.

Despite this, most of the limited official contact between American and Mexican unions is still triangulated through the CTM, whose leaders have enjoyed cordial working relationships with their AFL-CIO counterparts since the two confederations were founded. (CTM boss-for-life Fidel Velasquez, now 93, recalls befriending the other new cigar-chomper on the labor block, George Meany, in the late 1930s; Meany and Velasquez went on to collaborate in CIA-funded campaigns against leftist Latin American unions in the 1950s and 1960s.) In coming years, however, as the PRI's labor gerontocracy vanishes into history, pan-NAFTA unionism should evolve naturally out of industrial integration.

Industrial integration isn't the only aspect of NAFTA that is in Mexican labor's interest. Foreign capital inflows should help inflation decline naturally, while open economic borders will make rigid wage and price controls harder to enforce. Adequately funded health care and pension plans, rare in Mexico, will become more affordable for unions and employers alike, thanks to lower interest rates and financial liberalization. And as wages rise, companies become more willing to invest more in technology and training. Value creates value.

Cross-border cooperation is clearly in the interest of unions in both countries. If the AFL-CIO were to fight as hard for better Mexican pay and working conditions as it fought against NAFTA, the wage gap would diminish faster, and with it labor's concerns about jobs fleeing south.

But for American labor to cooperate with independent Mexican unionism would require a radical change in attitude. Meaningful cooperation won't be possible so long as American labor sees all American investment in Mexico as a threat.

■ The real issue for organized labor isn't jobs but the future of organized labor itself. And for the big industrial unions, whatever NAFTA's ultimate impact on overall American competitiveness and employment and wage scales, the free trade equation may well equal less than zero.

The conventional argument is that American workers ultimately profit if highly skilled, capital intensive occupations are preserved north of the border, while less skilled, labor-intensive jobs migrate south. In the long run, that should happen. But immediate job losses could disproportionately hit the unionized minority of the manufacturing work force. And long-term gains would come largely outside organized labor's ranks. Just because the pie is growing doesn't mean the unions will get a bigger slice.

Take the UAW: its membership has declined from 1.5 million in the 1970s to about 850,000 today, only half of whom are Big Three autoworkers. This decline will continue, even if NAFTA helps American automakers boost their North American sales. Most UAW autoworkers are less than 15 years from retirement: the union's loyalty is to their paychecks and pension plans, not to the health of the American auto business. And NAFTA will make it harder for unions to extract better wages and benefits from companies with factories or competitors south of the border. Far more damaging to UAW leverage than economic integration with Mexico are the successful nonunion, foreign-owned auto plants expanding across the Appalachians, and the continuing pressure from Japanese and other Asian imports. Still, anything that makes a union leader's job more difficult is something he wants to see stopped.

This also explains the strong anti-NAFTA stance of the Teamsters and Longshoremen, despite the new business for truckers and commercial ports that NAFTA will generate. That new business wouldn't go primarily to unionized workers. Furthermore, the implicit threat of Mexican wage competition—Mexican truckers earning Mexican wages could haul loads into the United States under NAFTA's rules, and Mexican stevedores would be offloading Asian and European cargo for American customers at newly privatized and modernized Mexican ports—would undercut labor's bargaining strength. For the unions, this overrides their membership's immediate interest in new job opportunities. Similarly, the UAW, while presumably committed to the survival of the American auto industry, is fighting an agreement whose terms were dictated by Detroit's Big Three in an effort to win back market share from Japan's auto makers. Steelworkers oppose NAFTA even though it guarantees permanent preferential access to the only foreign market where American steelmakers enjoy a large and growing trade surplus.

■ The simple truth that has been muddied in the job-slinging debate is that the stakes are not as huge as either side has contended; in the near-term, net effects would be quite small for the large and rich U.S. economy (although quite large for smaller, poorer Mexico). The relocation of industrial activity is not a zero sum game, as critics contend; but neither is it a painless gain, as proponents have tried to argue.

Overall, NAFTA creates jobs in both the United States and Mexico. It allows employees on both sides of the border to specialize in doing what they are best at: producing goods and services that require more skilled, technology-intensive manufacturing and services in the United States and making goods that are more labor intensive and do not require such educated workers in Mexico.

The core issue is not net job loss or job creation, or even wage differentials. It is whether the American and Mexican economies are fundamentally competitive or complementary. If they are complementary, the United States has nothing to fear and much to gain from a prosperous Mexico. But let's assume they are competitive, as labor seems to think. Logic would then have dictated opposition not only to NAFTA, but to any improvement of Mexico's business climate. One alternative would have been a No-Trade pact: just ban Mexican imports entirely. Or the rejection of NAFTA in the most baldly nativist fashion possible, in the hopes of precipitating a nationalist backlash in Mexico, which would then have reverted to its statist, protectionist past. That wouldn't have helped Mexico, or the U.S. trade balance, or employment and wage rates in either country, but it might have helped preserve jobs in the executive ranks of the AFL-CIO. The North American free trade debate dramatized a difficult truth: the interests of organized labor are diverging from—and are in many cases already incompatible with—the interests of the American work force as a whole.

American and Mexican Wages: What's the Difference?

"Follow runaway factory jobs to sunny Mexico! Paydays are great again, even if only at 58 cents an hour! It's a new beginning—and a New World Order!"

—ANTI-NAFTA RADIO AD, SUMMER 1993

Oddly, few NAFTA supporters directly challenged the claims that Mexicans work for just 50 cents or a dollar an hour. Yet the gap between U.S. and Mexican industrial wages is not nearly as great as NAFTA critics contended—and it is narrowing steadily.

A frequent source of confusion here is dollar wage rates versus real income levels. The 10-to-1 ratio that is most commonly cited is derived not from pay scales but from the per capita domestic product, which in the late 1980s averaged about $2,000 in Mexico and $20,000 in the United States. More recent GDP-per-head figures are about $3,000 in Mexico and $22,000 in the United States, a 7-to-1 difference.

But that isn't a measure of relative living standards. To make GDP figures equivalent, they must be adjusted to reflect purchasing power. In Mexico, where food, rent and services are cheaper than in the United States, that bounces real income up to $6,000 per capita, a 3.5-to-1 ratio.

And that still overstates the true differential. Any per capita calculation drags down Mexico, where half the population is under 18 and relatively few women are wage earners. In the United States, half the population is counted in the work force; in Mexico it is about one-third, including the millions of subsistence farmers who are the poorest people on the continent. A better comparison would be real adjusted GDP per industrial worker: there the gap is closing to just 2-to-1. Significantly, that is also the average difference between U.S. and Mexican productivity in advanced industrial installations. (This gap also shows up in the real world: a Connecticut factory that relocated to Mexico came back when it found its $5-an-hour Mexican workers were less than half as efficient as the $10-an-hour Connecticut workers they replaced.) And if the contrast were drawn between urban or industrial-sector incomes, rather than per capita averages, the gap would be narrower still.

For a multinational employer, however, it is the actual dollar pay rate, and not the worker's purchasing power, that determines the bottom line.

The 10-to-1 ratio cited by Perot and others faithfully reflects pay differences between the border assembly plants of, say, General Motors or General Electric, two of the biggest maquiladora employers, and their unionized factories in the United States. Some of those operations are directly equivalent in terms of job description and productivity, and the comparison is apt. But such plants are atypical. Most maquiladoras offer the repetitive, unskilled, high-turnover, labor-intensive jobs that in the United States would start at just above minimum wage, not unionized rates three times that high.

There has long been a rough 8-to-1 discrepancy between the U.S. and Mexican minimum wage. An entry-level Mexican worker earns in a day what his U.S. counterpart earns in an hour. But the maquiladoras are now paying well above minimum wage, in an effort to reduce turnover. Including benefits, the average maquiladora assembly wage is now $12 a day, with skilled jobs paying twice that; the minimum wage in the Mexican border zone is $5 a day.

But if the issue is the employment threat to U.S. factory workers, minimum and maquiladora wages are not the best comparison. The skilled factory worker against whom U.S. labor most directly competes typically earns at least $20 a day, four times the legal minimum. In many companies pay-plus-benefits exceeds $30 a day.

More relevant is the contrast between average manufacturing wages in the two countries. As recently as 1987, the gap was 13-to-1. Four years later, figures from the Bureau of Labor Statistics put it at 7-to-1. American manufacturing workers earned an average hourly wage (direct payments to employees, before tax deductions, plus mandatory employer expenditures for insurance and similar benefits) of $15.45 in 1991, compared with $2.17 for the average Mexican factory worker. This gap appears consistent with figures reported within individual firms: Ford, for example, is said by the UAW to pay skilled workers in Mexico about $2.87 an hour, not including benefits, compared with $20.21 in the United States.

But these figures understate real wages. Much of the typical Mexican industrial payroll goes toward fringe benefits (*prestaciones*) such as subsidized food, transportation, and even housing—plus mandatory profit sharing and a required Christmas bonus (*aguinaldo*) equal to an additional month's pay. (Mexican workers also get double pay for overtime, a minimum 20 days of paid vacation a year, and, for women, 12 weeks of paid maternity leave.) In all, reports Hewitt Associates, a U.S. consulting firm, the benefit package given to Mexican industrial workers equals a startling 62 percent of base pay, compared with 8 percent for American wage earners.

Multinationals claim the real price of Mexican labor is higher still because of greater spending on worker training. Some even add the cost to the employer of savings held to finance dismissals (severance payments often total three months' pay for each year of service). With all these factors added in, some companies with manufacturing operations on both sides of the border contend the real wage differential is more like 3-to-1, with the gap closing all the time. That is consistent with Hewitt's estimate that the real cost of Mexican factory labor is $5.40 an hour, about one-third the cost of American workers.

Three-to-one is still a pretty broad gap. New England's textile industry was lured below the Mason-Dixon line by much less. But that's not the whole picture. While Mexican productivity is fast catching up to U.S. standards, most Mexican plants are not modern. The country's entire industrial plant is not about to be upgraded overnight, or even within a decade. Manufacturers based in Mexico must overcome transportation bottlenecks, supplier scarcities, and other problems which can wipe out any gains from labor savings. Labor productivity is a function of technology: Mexican workers will be consistently outperformed by U.S. workers for decades to come. For low-tech manufacturers whose payrolls represent half their costs, a move to

Mexico could be amortized by labor savings in just three or four years. But for most advanced industrial installations, the productivity gap means that the huge expense of moving south could not be justified—even by savings of $20,000 per worker per year.

NOTES

Note 1: The short-run impact of NAFTA on black Americans could largely be determined by the fate of the American auto industry: five out of ten of the largest black-owned American businesses are American car dealerships, and Chrysler is the largest employer of black Americans. But the Chrysler example is instructive: it avoided bankruptcy and stayed competitive with the Japanese in part by transferring engine production from Michigan to Mexico. This assured the company's survival but reduced its Detroit payroll. So there is a paradox: while NAFTA might help major urban employers regain market share against foreign competitors, they may do so by relying less on big-city American workers.

CHAPTER 6

Oil, Cars and Mortgages: The North American Investment Agreement

Critics say that "NAFTA" is a misnomer: it's an investment agreement, not a trade agreement. They are right. NAFTA is based on the assumption that Mexico can and should get much more foreign capital than it has in the past—if its business rules are clear and fair, and if its industries have secure access to the American market.

Nobody disputes that NAFTA is ultimately about money. Mexico is willing to bury its protectionist past precisely because it expects to get a lot of cash in return—perhaps $100 billion more over the next 10 years than it otherwise would have received. These foreign funds will help Mexico unleash its own domestic investment potential, the real key to the tricky business of creating national wealth.

This means more than exploiting comparative advantage. It means building a new economic culture on a bedrock of investor confidence. This new culture envisions the market-driven reinvention of old institutions—Mexican agriculture, the state oil industry—and the provision of new economic essentials that consumers north of the border take for granted, like an efficient telephone system and a competitive home-financing market. The continuing growth and modernization of the Mexican economy can be sustained only if foreign capital continues to finance the imports that industrialization requires.

True free trade agreements are schedules for the mutual dismantling of trade barriers. NAFTA devotes most of its text to investment rules. In almost every case, its target is exclusively Mexico. NAFTA opens Mexico's doors to industries like petrochemicals and mining that were once off-limits to foreigners. It binds Mexico to strict new patent rules for pharmaceuticals and computer software. It enhances the security of investment in Mexican stocks and other financial instruments, since Mexico cannot obstruct the repatriation of profits by bureaucratic delays or punitive exchange rates. NAFTA ensures that all American and Canadian businesses in Mexico are treated in Mexican law exactly like local Mexican companies. This means, for example, that American manufacturers can no longer be ordered to maintain a positive balance in cross-border payments, a rule that forced them, among other things, to build cars for export and limit their imports of American auto parts.

Superficially, this investment liberalization seems to favor Mexico. Prohibitions against majority foreign ownership are maintained longer and in more sectors south of the border. But this doesn't mean that Mexican negotiators outfoxed the Americans. Virtually all of the liberalization is taking place on Mexico's side. The United States was already open in most industries to investment from anywhere. Mexico, which until recently had an outright ban on foreign equity control in most key industries, couldn't completely reciprocate overnight.

In financial services, for example, NAFTA's "liberalization of trade" is really a partial liberalization of direct investment rules, since NAFTA maintains prohibitions on cross-border banking and insurance sales. NAFTA's investment guidelines are carefully tailored to the real world of the Mexican market: in principle, American and Canadian banks will be allowed to acquire full ownership of any Mexican bank, but they will also be assigned aggregate market share ceilings which would in effect preclude the purchase of any of Mexico's three leading commercial banks. (This is hardly surprising: Americans would never tolerate an investment pact that permitted a foreign takeover of Citicorp, Chemical Bank, or BankAmerica.)

Even the parts of NAFTA that specifically address tariff issues can be viewed as a blueprint for investment.

The agreement's "rules of origin" are tantamount to an investment code: by requiring that duty-free goods be produced in North America—and not be assembled from imported components—the rules would promote direct investment in primary manufacturing. Even NAFTA's tariff-reduction schedules can be read as a road map for investors. Textile producers in the Carolinas will know when to begin adding new high-tech looms to supply fabric to Mexican garment companies. Mexican agriculture will be directed to get out of sorghum and into winter vegetables; American farmers will be told to stay in wheat and corn but avoid new investments in sugarcane. Automakers will get a calendar for building light trucks in central Mexico, minivans in the industrial Midwest, and electric wiring for both along the border. Oil service companies in Houston will get a signal to renovate offshore drilling rigs.

Most important, the hard currency that NAFTA is intended to attract will lead Mexico to invest its own capital more productively. Economic growth and the privatization of money-losing state industries will let the government channel tens of billions of dollars into health, education and overdue public works projects. Foreign competition and joint-venture partnerships will accelerate technological improvements in private Mexican industry. Falling interest rates and better retail financial services will make it easier for the average Mexican to buy a car or a new home. Pension funds will provide superior retirement accounts while broadening and deepening the local stock market. All these things—with investor confidence at their core—should lead to a steady rise in domestic savings and propel Mexico toward annual real growth of 6 percent or more, doubling the economy's size during NAFTA's first decade and gradually transforming Mexico into a modern consumer society.

Billions will be spent revamping Mexico's outdated infrastructure and industrial base. American companies will have an inside track for contracts to build new ports and gas-fired power plants. Mexico's capital markets, meanwhile, will offer a dynamic new playing field for American stockbrokers and investment bankers—a mixed blessing, perhaps, but one which should ultimately make the Mexican financial system more flexible and self-sufficient. And in the state-run energy sector, NAFTA will help Mexico attract tens of billions of dollars for essential expansion and modernization. Much of that money will be spent in Texas, and all of it will help safeguard American oil supplies.

Yet most of Mexico's post-NAFTA investment growth will come from more prosaic activities (home building, highway construction, fast-food franchising) driven by the growth of Mexico's domestic market. Export manufacturing—the investment most commonly associated with NAFTA—will be a minor though not unimportant part of this mix.

Paper Tigers

By keeping investment flowing, NAFTA should let Mexico continue the dramatic transformation that began in 1987, when Salinas first opened Mexico's doors to imports and investment. Over the next five years, the economy grew by more than half. Median wages nearly doubled. More dramatic still was the explosion in imports, mostly from the United States, which quadrupled from $12 billion to a projected $50 billion in 1993, and foreign investment in stocks and bonds, which soared from zero to $30 billion. These interlinked phenomena give a clear indication of how Mexico should perform under NAFTA. Under Salinas, Mexico has gone from a $200 billion economy with $15 billion in foreign investment to a $300 billion economy with $50 billion in foreign investment. Over the next 10 years, with NAFTA, it could become a $500 billion economy with more than $150 billion in foreign investment—comparable to where Canada is today.

Not everybody thinks investment in Mexico is a good thing. Some fear that we will be financing factories that will soon be churning out cheap exports, displacing American products and jobs. Others worry that a dollar sent to Mexico will be a dollar subtracted from the United States. Employment from surging cross-border exports is dismissed contemptuously as an aberration—"bubble jobs," says Ross Perot—which will vanish once Mexico gets its industrial act together.

This nightmare scenario rests on two fundamental confusions about NAFTA. The first concerns the macroeconomic profile of a typical newly industrializing nation; the second, the type of investment Mexico is likely to attract.

First, the thing to remember about those East Asian tigers which Perot and others think Mexico will emulate is that they are still running *deficits* in their trade accounts, not surpluses. And they run these deficits primarily with their principal investor, Japan. In newly industrializing Mexico, the lead investor—and prime trade-deficit beneficiary—is the United States.

Even the intrafirm trade that seems to worry people like Perot most—the commerce conducted by American multinationals with their own foreign subsidiaries—heavily favors the United States. The leading American-owned export manufacturers (the Big Three auto companies, the large electronics firms) are already shipping more to Mexico from their American plants than they are sending north from Mexico.

Still, let's assume that Perot's concern is valid—that if a Mexican investment boom were used to build up the country's export manufacturing capacity, America's trade surplus would disappear, and U.S. export jobs would tumble. Let's also assume that Mexico does reasonably well in attracting foreign investment, doubling its stock to $100 billion in NAFTA's first five years.

To begin with, export manufacturing—indeed, all manufacturing—accounts for only a minor share of the investment Mexico is now receiving. NAFTA doesn't change that. Of that $100 billion, perhaps half will be investments in Mexican stocks and bonds (compared to about two-thirds today). The other half will be direct equity investment in factories and other enterprises.

Of that $50 billion, perhaps half will be invested in service industries and non-exported consumer goods like soft drinks. Heavy manufacturing might represent $25 billion, but (again) much of this will be directed at the local market.

That leaves perhaps $10 billion in manufacturing capacity geared exclusively toward American markets. Perhaps a third of that will come from Europeans and Asians shifting production from overseas so that they can sell successfully in the new North American market.

So most of that $100 billion will be aimed at the domestic Mexican market, much of it in services and financial instruments. Less than $10 billion might otherwise have been spent on manufacturing capacity in the United States. Even there, however, the effects on the United States should be more than offset by new American investments sustained by duty-free sales to Mexico.

In fact, this is just what's been happening to Mexico under Salinas. Most of the money flowing into the country has gone into stocks and bonds, not new export factories. Moreover, much of this "foreign" investment was returning Mexican flight capital: at least $10 billion, most of it spent on privatized state companies or invested in securities. (Mexican officials expect the passage of NAFTA to lure back at least $10 billion more.) It's hard to argue that the repatriation of Mexican money from bank accounts in Zurich or Manhattan takes jobs from American workers.

The next big new capital sources are the speculative investors, companies, pension funds, rich individuals from Europe, South America, and the United States—who now hold perhaps $20 billion in Mexican stocks and bonds. Most of this money has also gone into privatized companies (banks, the phone company) that are in no sense displacing American investment or underwriting export-oriented manufacturing jobs. This first investment wave was attracted by high yields that were unsustainable; with NAFTA, more modest but dependable market growth should attract conservative institutional investors. None of this has much effect on American jobs or trade.

Despite the recent boom in the Mexican stock market, American institutional investors still have much more money in East Asia than in Mexico. Reinvesting a steadily bigger share of this foreign portfolio in a post-NAFTA Mexico will bring comparable returns—and much greater benefits to the American economy as a whole. Fund managers from London and Frankfurt (and, more cautiously, Tokyo) will likely follow the lead of their New York colleagues. If Mexico under NAFTA attracts just 1 percent of the $6 trillion managed by American and European institutional investors—a small fraction of their foreign holdings—the Bolsa might double or triple over the next few years.

Now to the one-quarter of foreign investment that most worries Perot and other NAFTA critics: direct investment by American manufacturers. It is true that with NAFTA, Mexico expects direct investment to grow faster than portfolio investment. It is also true that about three-fifths of this direct investment will likely come from the United States. But consider how this money is even now being spent. Much of it goes into the natural resource industries that used to be off-limits to foreign investors: mining, petrochemicals, natural gas pipelines, oil refineries, drilling rigs. This represents neither the displacement of American jobs nor the substitution of new Mexican export capacity for domestic production.

Even more of this direct investment is going into service industries aimed at Mexico's domestic market: retailing, insurance, fast-food franchising, financial consulting, civil engineering. Jobs are created in the United States by these ventures, but almost none is lost. As for the American investment spent on actual production facilities, most of this capacity is geared to the Mexican consumer market, not the American export market.[1]

That leaves the narrow segment aimed specifically at exporting to the American market: perhaps $10 billion of the overall $100 billion in foreign investment we have projected. Much of that industrial capacity would otherwise be in Asia, not in the United States. Indeed, some of it *was* in Asia until quite recently: Zenith, GE, AT&T and other electronics companies are all relocating production to Mexico from East Asia. Even Asian-owned companies are moving factories to Mexico's side of the Pacific. It can hardly be argued that these plants represent "lost" American jobs. Quite the opposite: to comply with NAFTA's rules of origin (which require duty-free goods to be 60 percent North American), these new arrivals from Asia will need to use American suppliers more, not less.

Agriculture is a somewhat different matter. Direct investment in Mexican orange groves and sugar plantations will eventually take a big bite out of competitors in California and Florida. Consumers will benefit, but some American growers may have to find substitute crops. Yet some of Mexico's new output will surely come at the expense of other foreign suppliers (Dominican sugar, Brazilian orange juice). Compared to other foreign suppliers, Mexican growers are far more likely to send farm products north for final processing in the United States, offsetting at least some of the agricultural job losses directly resulting from NAFTA.[2]

Insurance and Other Synergies Throughout the NAFTA debate, far too much attention was paid to narrow sectoral projections made in isolation from the rest of the economy. Negotiators themselves often seemed fixated on narrow trade-offs within and among industries, forgetting that the North American economy would prosper or suffer as an organic whole. Yet NAFTA's greatest benefits will come from the serendipitous chemistry of investment across sectoral and national lines.

As Mexico is already learning, the professionalizing impact of new businesses on markets and suppliers can have more economic importance than the businesses themselves. Much of this is hard to quantify: improved technologies, higher educational standards, better telecommunications, easier transportation, greater financial efficiency. It is impossible to measure how much business doesn't get done because the phones don't work, or because ports lack container cranes. Yet these are all crucial determinants of economic growth, and they are exactly the areas where NAFTA will both demand and facilitate improvements.

Equally important, and even harder to forecast, are the felicitous spinoffs, spillovers and multiplier effects of a modernizing financial system and a fast-moving consumer market.

One effect of NAFTA, for example, will be the upgrading of Mexico's investment ratings in the international securities markets. An investment-grade rating will be a magnet for those cautious American institutional investors who are only now beginning to diversify into foreign holdings. The specter of stodgy American pension funds making Mexican securities a regular part of their portfolios is sure to make Mexico more attractive to potential manufacturing investors.

The insurance business provides an excellent example of NAFTA's unforeseen but virtuous synergies. The trade agreement lets American and Canadian insurance companies set up wholly owned Mexican subsidiaries for the first time (transitional limits on equity and market shares are removed entirely after six years). As Mexico's consumer market matures and the overall economy stabilizes, the demand for insurance of all kinds will be certain to grow. The American International Group (AIG), a leading American insurance company, calculates that after NAFTA,

Mexico's per capita insurance spending will have grown from $30 in 1990 to $420 in the year 2000. Americans, by contrast, now spend an average of $1,900 a year. Insurance premiums in the United States totaled $480 billion in 1990, or 9 percent of GDP; in Mexico, premiums were just $2.6 billion, or 1 percent of GDP. AIG forecasts a domestic insurance market of $50 billion by the turn of the century, a fifteenfold increase in just 10 years. Given the maturing demographics of the Mexican work force and the projected expansion of the private sector, the market for personal and corporate insurance should at least double to $100 billion by 2010.

These estimates may well be conservative. Because they are based on existing trends, the NAFTA models have no way of anticipating such an enormous increase in investment. Industry analysts, however, can take more subjective criteria into account: the impact of American marketing, the experience in comparable economies, the capacity of giant American companies to absorb the increased risk inherent in doing business in a developing country. In Mexico, AIG looked not just at NAFTA's new investment provisions, but at the potential demand in a growing, deregulated economy for personal insurance (accident, health, life) and corporate services such as pension management and risk analysis. Fewer than one in five Mexican cars and one in 12 Mexican homes now carry insurance of any kind.

The invasion of Mexico by American life insurance salesmen may not be an edifying prospect, but it is a business where American companies are highly competitive and where they will get privileged access to a market of vast potential. Most of the $50 billion insurance portfolio that AIG expects to see in NAFTA's first six years will be channeled into government securities, peso cash deposits, private sector bonds, and stock investments (the Mexican stock market's entire capitalization barely reached $140 billion in 1992). This money will provide crucial funding for Mexican industry—and a sense of professional detachment rare in Mexican financial circles. The insurance industry's skill at money management and risk analysis will make Mexican capital markets more stable and efficient. That, in turn, will make banks and brokerages a more frequent source of capital for entrepreneurs not born into Mexico's business elite.

But a burgeoning insurance market is just part of a maturing financial sector. By letting American and Canadian banks and brokerages operate wholly owned Mexican subsidiaries, NAFTA will expand the supply and lower the cost of capital for Mexican business. Banking liberalization will also foster an explosion of personal and corporate credit: just satisfying pent-up demand for small business loans and consumer borrowing should drive a credit boom as big as the projected growth of the insurance market. At the beginning of the 1990s, consumer loans in Mexico came to barely 5 percent of GDP, or less than $15 billion; Mexican banking analysts say this could quadruple to $60 billion in NAFTA's first 10 years.[3] This credit expansion will help sustain the import-led consumer purchasing boom of the past five years. On the producing side, the biggest beneficiaries will be American exporters and locally based American manufacturers.

Houses of Their Own

The most dramatic example of synergistic growth from NAFTA's liberalization will come in the Mexican housing market, which is poised for dramatic investment growth that will directly benefit American lumber and construction companies.

Mexico is a country where the work force is expanding by 3 percent a year. Families are large (averaging four children) and young (80 percent of the people are under 40). The purchasing power of middle-class professionals has nearly doubled in the past five years. One would expect the home construction market to be booming. Instead, it has been stagnant for a decade. Simply satisfying the pent-up demand for housing will be a $100 billion enterprise, by one unpublished official estimate. Providing sufficient additional housing for new families will require investments of at least $15 billion a year.

High interest rates, a falling peso, and an elitist state banking system encumbered by confiscatory reserve requirements put home mortgages out of the reach of all but the most affluent families in the 1980s. Terms were prohibitively short: it wasn't uncommon to demand a down payment equal to a third of the purchase price, with full amortization required in just three or four years. (Union housing programs and state-subsidized loans filled the market gap for some workers and federal employees, which had the perverse effect of taking pressure off the state-run banking system.)

Since Salinas privatized the banks, commercial mortgage lending has jumped from $450 million in 1989 to $6.6 billion in 1992. Even so, just 15 percent of Mexico's homes were purchased with bank financing, compared to 90 percent in the United States. The typical Mexican mortgage still bears a crippling real annual interest charge of 15 percent, with repayment often required in 10 years or earlier. It's like putting a house on MasterCard. Yet Mexicans are good personal credit risks: less than 1 percent of mortgages show payment delinquencies of three months or more. That's a better record than in most American markets.

Private homes without mortgages represent at least $250 billion in illiquid personal wealth. The development of a competitive mortgage market will put a lot of this housing in play. It will give owners access to personal financing for the first time—for school tuition, home improvement, small business investments. It will also build up bank assets. Commercial banks are now financing just 100,000 homes a year. The World Bank estimates pent-up demand at a staggering 6 million units. (That's roughly equal to the entire housing stock of Texas.) By the end of the decade, at least 3 million more homes will be needed, largely to satisfy the needs of young Mexican families. Building all this housing will cost at least $200 billion—and represent an extraordinary bonanza for American construction firms and suppliers. The trick will be to arrange the financing.

The arrival of American banks as competitors promises to deepen the mortgage pool, lengthen repayment terms, and cut interest rates to less usurious levels. The growth of the home mortgage market will also be helped by NAFTA-driven reforms in the insurance business (the development of a title insurance market will remove one obstacle to the housing market's expansion), commercial lending (developers will more easily get financing for new subdivisions), additional deregulation (Mexican states and municipalities are being forced to harmonize complex and conflicting local housing rules), even rural land ownership (the sale of communal farmlands frees up sites for housing on the outskirts of fast-growing cities and puts money in the pockets of potential homebuyers newly arrived from the countryside).

The removal of import barriers will also help. Under NAFTA, overpriced Mexican cinderblock will gradually give way to competitively priced wood-frame kits made in the United States (and Canada) and brought into Mexico in bulk. Expertise will be imported as well: American real estate companies will be able to develop subdivisions entirely on their own—purchasing the land, building the houses, selling the finished product without employing Mexican middlemen.

The combination of affordable home mortgages, inexpensive building materials, and low-cost construction labor could ignite a middle-class housing boom resembling the growth of the American suburbs in the 1950s.

Again, it's the synergies that count: home mortgages in bulk drive capital markets, which finance new construction businesses, which hire workers and unleash further consumer spending, all of which is made more efficient and inexpensive by foreign investment and imports.

NAFTA is critical to every stage of this process, but not in a way easily forecast by computer models. Another example is land reform. Privatizing communal farmlands with NAFTA in force means that American agribusiness investors will drive up land prices. This will increase Mexico's national wealth, and will directly enrich thousands of farmers who would have been forced to seek jobs in the cities with or without NAFTA and land reform. NAFTA will also channel private American capital into agribusiness ventures on these newly privatized farms. Mexico had to dismantle the *ejido* system at some point. Combining this overdue reform with NAFTA makes it less disruptive socially and more productive economically.

Playing the Oil Card

In Mexico, no issue is more politically sensitive than petroleum. At the outset of the NAFTA deliberations, Salinas Administration officials insisted that oil would not even be discussed. When a deputy energy minister suggested otherwise, he was summarily fired. But he was right: Washington wanted NAFTA to enhance American energy security, and Mexico couldn't afford not to play the oil card.

It was the allure of Mexico's oil reserves that revived American interest in a cross-border market a decade ago, and it was the continuing American thirst for imported energy that gave Mexico much of the limited leverage it had in the NAFTA talks. After all, Mexican and U.S. interests were never diametrically opposed. As much as the United States needs oil, Mexico needs dollars. Despite diversification into export manufacturing, Mexico still depends on oil sales for a third of its hard currency income. And the constitutional ownership issue didn't have to be broached for both sides to get most of what they wanted.

The United States needed to achieve two things in NAFTA's energy talks. First, it needed to maintain Mexico as a reliable first-rank oil supplier for at least another decade. The way to do this is, again, investment: to channel tens of billions of dollars into new exploration and production. Otherwise, rising domestic oil consumption would eventually absorb all of an inexorably diminishing supply. To succeed, however, a bloated state monopoly—Pemex—would first have to be transformed into a modern oil company.

Second, America needed to find a way into an economic empire that has been closed to foreigners since its 1938 nationalization. The American oil industry sought privileged status in the exploration and development programs that would let Mexico achieve its primary goal—remaining a leading exporter. It wanted not only the right to bid for drilling and supply contracts that had once been reserved for Mexican companies, but also equity control of petrochemicals, power plants, and other associated businesses.

NAFTA accomplishes both American goals. If it didn't, Pemex might never be given the resources it needs to modernize, and the United States would be seeking new suppliers overseas to replace Mexico's dwindling supplies. Instead, Mexico seems certain to continue shipping out some 1.3 million barrels of crude a day through the end of the decade and beyond.

But NAFTA's biggest effect on the Mexican oil business has nothing to do with the agreement's oil and energy clauses. Simply by liberalizing the Mexican financial sector and improving Mexico's international credit rating, NAFTA will let Pemex get the financing it needs on terms comparable to those commanded by private oil companies. And by following NAFTA's procurement rules, which phase out restrictions on American subcontracting, Pemex will spend its development money much more efficiently than it has in the past. Meanwhile, oilpatch service industries will get a huge new customer, and the American economy will be assured of a reliable, market-priced supply of oil from a friendly, stable neighbor for at least another generation.

Somewhat paradoxically, NAFTA will also turn Mexico into an importer of American (and Canadian) gas, coal, refined fuels, and turnkey electric power plants. This connection with the greater North American energy grid will help Mexico use its oil resources more efficiently—and free up more crude for the export market.

NAFTA also will give American and Canadian companies privileged access to contracts awarded by the Mexican oil industry for supplies, civil engineering services, drilling ventures, and other essential expenditures. This alone could mean upward of $50 billion in new business for American oil companies over the next 10 years.

Until now, no American company has had any right to bid for any of Pemex's business. Contracts have been awarded erratically and arbitrarily. Cronyism, graft, and the clout of Mexican front organizations have been more important factors than price or quality. (The notoriously corrupt oil union had a guaranteed share of this booty.) American drilling companies, by unstated policy, were never allowed to work on mainland sites, where their visibility might inflame union sensibilities. And offshore, where American technology was essential, Mexican subcontractors would often be paid substantially more for equivalent work.

With NAFTA, however, half of Pemex's supply and service contracts will be immediately opened to public bidding.[4] American and Canadian companies could compete on equal terms with Mexican bidders. These reforms also apply to Compañia Federal de Electricidad (CFE), the public utility that is—Mexico's second largest state company. Together, Pemex and CFE spend upward of $8 billion a year on goods and services, a figure that is expected to double within a decade.

The most common American criticisms of NAFTA's energy provisions are that they don't require Mexico to spur oil development with risk contracts or, even better, force Mexico to privatize Pemex completely. But risk contracts and privatization contravene the constitutional stipulation that oil belongs to the state. And from the selfish American viewpoint as an energy importer, neither is essential to the modernization and expansion of Mexico's oil industry.

First, the risk contract controversy: outside the executive suites of the American oil majors, this is a marginal issue. Pemex doesn't need much foreign risk capital, because in most cases the risks aren't that great. Surrendering equity control of its crude reserves would be a bad and unnecessary business move.

Mexican oil country is not a hazardous, uncharted wilderness like the northern Yukon or upper Amazon. The state-run Mexican Petroleum Institute, respected for its professionalism, has thoroughly mapped the country's oil geology.[5] There is a consensus that big new finds will be concentrated in the offshore reaches of Campeche Sound, beyond the Marina region that now produces two-thirds of Mexico's crude. What Mexico lacks is the capital, technology and personnel to develop its oil fields in a cost-effective way. But the oil is there, and Mexico can afford to pay outsiders to help get it out of the ground without giving it away.

NAFTA specifically authorizes bonus payments or other "performance-related" returns to outside oil service contractors. This will let Pemex build in the financial incentives of risk contracts while retaining ultimate ownership of the reserves. Where exploration and development is technologically daunting or prohibitively expensive, Pemex may have to pay quite a bit. But it won't have to sacrifice state control.

Most of the necessary capital can be borrowed. As in the go-go 1970s, oil will again be the collateral for Mexican debt. But this time the linkage will be explicit: funds will go for oil development rather than for general revenues, and repayment will occur in the form of delivered oil. This is already happening: future exports are being pre-sold as securities to develop new production. Under NAFTA, Mexico will pay less for this financing, American investors will feel more comfortable about investing in Mexican oil securities, and the benefits of these investments will flow back—literally—to the United States.

But shouldn't the oil business simply be privatized? Unquestionably, Pemex is a bureaucratic monster, bloated by decades of corruption and mindless vertical expansion. As a creature of the state, Pemex still thinks in terms of volume rather than costs of production, of five-year plans instead of year-end balance sheets.

But selling Pemex to private owners isn't the answer. No Mexican consortium could afford to buy a firm with $50 billion in assets. Privatization would therefore mean foreign ownership. And even conservative Mexican businessmen reject that as politically unacceptable—primarily because it is economically unnecessary. After all, Pinochet's free-market Chile didn't divest state-owned copper holdings. And Pemex, unlike most privatization candidates, isn't a drain on the federal budget; in fact, it provides fully a quarter of the government's income.

Nor is privatization needed to preserve Mexico's viability as an American energy supplier. Selling downstream businesses like petrochemical plants and gasoline stations is a good idea, but Pemex is doing that anyway. Additional privatization is expected in Pemex's vast transportation network, including its oil and gas pipeline monopoly. But the core business—pumping oil—will remain in the hands of the state.

The model for Pemex isn't Texaco or Exxon, but Venezuela's state-owned PDVSA, which produces nearly as much oil as Pemex with half as many people. Professionally managed and openly at odds with its OPEC brethren, PDVSA is now sole owner of Citgo's huge American gasoline distribution network, plus sundry other oil companies and refineries and pipelines in the United States and Western Europe. It is by one estimate the fastest-growing oil company in the world and the fourth largest in the United States. Pemex's new technocrats are closely watching PDVSA's strategy of becoming, in the words of its president, "just another vertically integrated oil company, a *very big* vertically integrated oil company." NAFTA will let Pemex push this strategy faster.

What Pemex needs isn't private ownership but smart management, prepared, like PDVSA, to cooperate and to compete with the American majors. Under Salinas, Pemex has already started down this road, cutting its staff by a third (to 160,000 employees, still about 60,000 too many) and splitting into four more streamlined divisions. An increasingly autonomous and cost-conscious marketing division is beginning to behave like a real oil company, investing billions in joint-venture refining operations in Texas and Spain.

But the most dramatic change is on the ground in Mexico. In 1991, Pemex announced a $20 billion investment plan to boost production by 400,000 barrels a day over five years. This would be enough to satisfy rising domestic demand without cutting into exports. To this end, Pemex has subcontracted more than a dozen large drilling operations to American firms, which work more quickly and cheaply than Pemex's own drilling units. Under NAFTA, this sort of subcontracting will expand dramatically as bidding out these jobs becomes a matter of law.

■ Pemex isn't attracting just American money. Billions have been raised in the European bond markets. In late 1992 Pemex syndicated an $800 million loan in Tokyo, the first voluntary private Japanese lending to Mexico since the debt crisis. NAFTA, with its legal guarantees for investors and enhancement of Pemex's creditworthiness, will make this overseas fund-raising easier. But the oil that is found and pumped out with this foreign money will largely go to the United States.

In 1992, Pemex estimated its proven oil reserves at 65.5 billion barrels—nine times the reserves of Exxon, the world's largest private oil company. Venezuela is the only other Western Hemisphere exporter that comes close to reserves of that magnitude.

Estimates of Mexican reserves are often greeted with skepticism. The new conventional wisdom about Mexican oil—replacing the New Saudi Arabia school of the late 1970s—is that Pemex will cease to have an exportable surplus by the end of the century. The problem with this analysis is that it is based on data from the debt-laden 1980s, a period marked by near-zero investment in Pemex and every other Mexican public enterprise. Under NAFTA, Pemex should be able to resume investment in new exploration and production. And every time Mexico has seriously looked for more oil, it has found it.

Indeed, Mexico's reserves may be larger than officially reported, simply because of advances in drilling technology over the past decade. Deposits in the outer depths of Campeche Bay and onshore gas deposits in the northeast are too far below the surface for Pemex to tap, but

American firms are equipped to drill at such depths. One U.S. government geologist estimates Mexico's offshore deposits at more than 100 billion barrels, equal to the reserves of Iraq and Iran combined.

The real issue, however, isn't how to measure Mexico's oil deposits but how to pay for their development. Even if its stated reserves were inflated by as much as a third, Pemex would still have as much oil as six Exxons. But thanks to debt troubles, bad management, and a punitive tax burden, it doesn't have the financial resources of even one Exxon. That's why Pemex's new-breed technocrats must borrow billions, seek joint-venture investors, and cut costs by subcontracting—and why NAFTA is critical to their success.

Making Pemex more productive won't solve America's oil problems. Mexico supplies less than 15 percent of American oil imports, and even with NAFTA its shipments are unlikely to rise significantly. The Mexican government's goal is to maintain current export flows of about 1.3 million barrels a day, while keeping pace with domestic demand. The local market now also absorbs 1.3 million barrels a day, but demand could easily double over the next 10 years.

Without NAFTA, Mexico's oil exports would have inexorably declined. In the worst-case scenario, they might have ceased entirely within a decade. The United States would then have been forced to make up that shortfall with crude from the Persian Gulf. In terms of national economic security, then, there is no part of NAFTA more crucial to the United States than the provisions that help Pemex modernize and grow.

Nearly as critical, but almost totally ignored, is the other piece of the energy puzzle: CFE, the giant national power company. There will be much greater opportunities for American investment and public works contracts in electricity generation than in oil production. Projects already under way or under discussion will represent billions of dollars in business for U.S. engineering firms.

NAFTA will help keep CFE from draining Pemex's resources with subsidized fuel supplies for inefficient power plants. Under NAFTA, there will be a permanent legal and investment framework for integrating Mexico into the U.S.-Canadian energy grid. The physical and economic interconnection of natural gas markets will be the first stage, with energy-starved northern Mexico becoming a leading net importer. American gas suppliers will be permitted to negotiate terms directly with Mexican buyers, and American coal exporters will get direct, duty-free access to Mexican customers for the first time. The second stage is more complex and expensive: the cross-border unification of electric power networks. Mexico will begin as a slight net electricity importer before gradually becoming a net exporter for the continent as a whole.

While CFE decentralizes and interconnects with power companies to the north, there will be a parallel integration of the oil business across national lines. American firms will play an increasingly central role in upstream production development in Mexico, while Pemex (or its decentralized successor companies) will invest ever more heavily in downstream refining and distribution inside the United States. With NAFTA opening the production of all but eight basic petrochemical products to full American or Canadian ownership (they were all formerly reserved for Pemex), the Mexican petrochemical industry will also be reorganized on a continental basis.

NAFTA permanently exempts Mexico from any future U.S. oil import fee; in exchange, Mexico will no longer be able to set quota caps or impose punitive taxes on crude exports to the United States. In its bilateral FTA, Canada already ceded its rights to restrict cross-border oil shipments. This emerging North American energy market will allow the more efficient and profitable use of hydrocarbon resources in all three countries while lessening American dependence on Middle Eastern crude. (It also binds Mexico and Canada to the American energy marketplace, as nationalists in both countries have bitterly noted.)

Some American oil companies have been grousing about NAFTA out of greed, others out of ignorance, and some presumably as a way of concealing their glee. Before NAFTA, the Mexican oil business was closed. Now the door is open.

It is true that NAFTA does nothing to alter state control of Mexico's oil and gas reserves. But nobody ever expected it to—and, the oil majors aside, the ultimate ownership of Mexico's reserves doesn't matter that much.[6] What does matter is secure, long-term access to oil supplies on an equitable market basis.

With NAFTA, Yankee dollars will flow into petrochemicals, refineries, power plants, offshore drilling ventures, foreign marketing and refining consortia, and Pemex-backed bond issues. As Mexico's access to lower-cost capital improves, it will gradually become an efficient, long-term energy source for the United States. And that will mean billions of dollars in new business for American oil companies, which will be among NAFTA's biggest direct beneficiaries.

█ The investments NAFTA should attract into insurance, home building, and energy development are just part of a continuing economic revolution that should lift Mexico into a self-sustaining cycle where real economic growth is 6 percent a year or better. Mexico will then be able to escape the dreary choice between stultifying statism and the dead-end capitalism of low-wage assembly work. Its middle class will then expand rapidly, and its thirst for American goods will be unquenchable.

Concerns that NAFTA will divert capital from the United States are understandable but unfounded. As with everything connected with NAFTA, Mexico has the most to gain—and the United States has the least to lose.

Most of the investment flowing into Mexico in the post-NAFTA world would never have gone into American industry under any circumstances. The great bulk of this investment would have been aimed at Mexico's fast-growing domestic market, particularly the market for services. Export manufacturing—the great bugaboo of NAFTA critics like Ross Perot—is unlikely to amount to more than one-fourth of Mexico's post-NAFTA foreign investment, and even that would often represent production moved from Asia and Europe.

The Mexican economic revolution ignited by this mixture of local and foreign capital will ultimately benefit all Americans, and the resulting business opportunities will be measured in the tens of billions of dollars.

Detroit Rules

There are four important things to remember about NAFTA and the North American auto industry.

First, for better or worse, Detroit wrote NAFTA's rules.

Second, Mexico is North America's fastest-growing auto market.

Third, the North American auto business has been integrated across national lines for decades. Intrafirm trade at Ford, GM and Chrysler accounts for the biggest share of American manufacturing trade with both Canada and Mexico. NAFTA is just the latest phase in this cross-border restructuring.

And fourth, Detroit wrote the rules.

Detroit dominates the industry in all three countries, with the same three-fifths market share and more than four-fifths of all automotive production. In all three countries, the Big Three are the largest manufacturing employers. And in Mexico, they are also the three leading private export earners. So it would have been odd if they hadn't been able to dictate NAFTA's terms.

There were minor concessions to Mexican interests. Autos built in Mexico would be included when calculating fleet-based fuel efficiency standards in the United States—a stimulus for Mexican econocar production. NAFTA phases out protection for Mexican auto parts makers more slowly than Detroit would have liked, and the North American content rules are a bit less stringent than the Big Three originally sought. On the other hand, NAFTA does away with Mexico's hated balance-of-payments requirements (which accounted for much of Detroit's Mexican production in the first place) and opens Mexico's borders to American-made cars.

NAFTA's immediate effect on the auto industry will be a flood of imports—*from* the United States *into* Mexico.

Over time, NAFTA's liberalization would "clear the path for a dramatic reorganization of the regional production system," says MIT's James P. Womack, a leading authority on industry trends and an advisor to Mexico's negotiators. "By the end of the century, the entry-level products for the entire North American region will be manufactured in northern Mexico in top-to-bottom production complexes built by the multinational assemblers—U.S., European and Japanese—and their first-tier suppliers."

The United Auto Workers union says this is just what it fears: GM, Ford and Chrysler building new factories south of the border to exploit labor savings, while older American factories are slowly shuttered and finally abandoned.

The union has a point. Labor-intensive auto parts plants have been moving to Mexico for a decade. Most Chryslers already have Mexican-built engines (about the only ones that don't are the one in every nine "Chryslers" built under contract in Japan).

Auto workers have other reasons to fear NAFTA's effect on investment patterns. The integration of Mexican plants into the broader North American auto business is pulling the industry's center of gravity out of the unionized Midwest and into the right-to-work sunbelt. This changing industry geography was dramatized in 1992 when GM decided to shut 21 assembly plants in the United States and Canada. GM had two nearly identical factories specializing in broad-beamed Buicks and Chevys—one in Michigan, the other in Texas. It closed the Michigan plant in favor of its Texas operation, which relies increasingly on suppliers from the Mexican border. At the same time, it began a major expansion at one of the most efficient auto plants in the world: 200 miles south of Texas in Ramos Arizpe, Mexico. This, said UAW Chief Owen Bieber, was no accident of timing but a foretaste of the massive southward movement of jobs that NAFTA would set in—motion.

It's easy to see why Bieber would think this. The Big Three have expanded their Mexican work force at a time of mass layoffs in the United States. Between 1989 and 1991, some 50,000 American auto jobs disappeared;

meanwhile, imports of cars and trucks from Mexico—nearly all from American subsidiaries—nearly doubled to $3.3 billion.

But the truth is more complicated. In the auto parts business, where many UAW members also work, total U.S employment declined by 65,000 from 1989 to 1991. In that same period, however, exports to Mexico jumped from $2.5 billion to $4.5 billion, giving the United States a positive and growing trade balance in the sector. (Thanks to free trade, exports to Canada climbed even more dramatically, from $7 billion to $12 billion.) There are many complex reasons for the loss of American automotive jobs, but trade with Mexico is far down the list. After NAFTA, it may not belong on the list at all. Trade barriers now keep annual Mexican car and truck imports to a paltry $300 million. As Mexico opens its doors to finished American vehicles, American auto workers should reap substantial and immediate benefits.

American labor consistently underestimates the importance of the domestic Mexican market in the free trade equation. Mexican auto sales have tripled since the mid-1980s, to roughly 700,000 cars a year, and automakers expect to reach the 1 million mark by 1995. To serve this market, Nissan, Volkswagen and Ford are each planning investments of more than $1 billion over the next three years. Even so, Mexican-based output is unlikely to keep pace with Mexican demand.

There are still only about 9 million passenger cars (including pickup trucks) in all of Mexico—one for every 10 people. Across the border in California, there are more cars than people. Mexico, it should be hoped, will never reach that level of auto saturation. But within a decade the Mexican market should come to resemble the poor fringe of the European market. In countries like Ireland and Spain (where gasoline prices are triple those in Mexico), there are three people for every car. Reaching that level in the next 10 years would require a doubling of Mexican domestic production—*plus* an explosion in imports, where North American vehicles have the competitive edge. Mexico is now exporting nearly 400,000 cars a year, primarily to the United States; within five years, it could be importing nearly as many cars from the north.

It is sometimes claimed that NAFTA will be a boon for Japanese transplant shops. This is half right: NAFTA *will* bring the Japanese—not to Mexico but to the United States. For the American labor movement, that's even worse.

NAFTA's rules of origin make it possible for Japanese transplant factories *in the United States* to sell in Mexico. (During a 10-year transition, this is limited to companies like Nissan with plants in both countries; after 2004, any American-based car factory would be allowed to ship cars south.) But they will make it tougher for a new Japanese entrant in the Mexican market to aim production at the U.S. export market. Mexico, in other words, will see chains of Honda dealerships selling American-built Hondas long before it sees Honda factories in Mexico building cars for American buyers.

Built to NAFTA specs, these Japanese compacts should give American auto makers even more problems *in Mexico* than they have today. (In just 10 years, Detroit's market share there has dropped from 75 percent to less than 55 percent.) But remember: Detroit wrote the rules.

While labor leaders bemoan the attraction of low Mexican wages to U.S. investors, the real threat comes from a source closer to home: those nonunionized Americans who earn three to four times more than the best-paid Mexican industrial workers.

The average UAW auto worker makes more than $40 an hour, including benefits. The Japanese transplant shops proved that car makers can hire skilled, motivated Americans for half that amount. To their great regret, the American car companies can't hire $20-an-hour Americans: their union contracts won't permit it. But they can hire $5-an-hour Mexicans.

It is quite true that labor rates aren't the main factor in automotive invest-ment decisions. They contribute less than $1,000 of the price of the average American-made car (Japanese labor costs are similar). But labor costs aren't irrelevant, either. And for that reason alone, the UAW has reason to be nervous. In today's marketplace, unionized auto workers are grossly overpriced.

The UAW has always fought plans to hire new workers at wage rates comparable to those paid by Japanese plants in the United States. This is understandable, since labor leaders want to preserve rank-and-file benefits above all else. But it is primarily a defense of the privileges of a declining membership. It accepts the slow disappearance of American-owned auto plants in the United States as a given—even as America's competitors open new U.S. auto plants every year.

Because of the UAW, automotive investment is regularly deflected from the United States to Mexico. Take General Motors' giant auto parts subsidiary, the Automotive Components Group (ACG). Its UAW contract gives its North American division two choices: an American earning triple the average industrial wage of $15 an hour, or a Mexican earning one-third of the U.S. industrial average. It's not a difficult choice: in an integrated cross-border operation like ACG's, labor costs are a major expense and foreign competition is fierce. ACG now has half as many workers in Mexico—44,000—as it does in the United States, and the ratio tilts more in Mexico's favor every year.

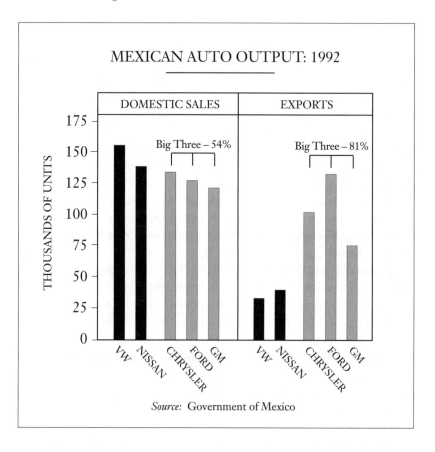

MEXICAN AUTO OUTPUT: 1992

Source: Government of Mexico

As long as the auto companies are forced to choose between $5 an hour and $45 an hour, it is inevitable that some American jobs will be lost to Mexican labor. Yet GM, Chrysler, and Ford would surely prefer the option of paying $20 an hour in the United States. American auto workers are more productive than their Mexican counterparts, American parts plants are closer to the point of final assembly, and—the critical point—it makes political sense for the Big Three to keep as many jobs as possible in the United States.[7]

To the UAW, letting GM hire new workers at lower pay scales might seem like slow-motion suicide. But the union's present strategy isn't any more promising. As things stand, the UAW is just as responsible for shipping jobs south as General Motors. NAFTA isn't the problem: it actually gives incentives to GM to boost its U.S. employment, since the auto maker could then supply the entire North American market from its modern U.S plants. NAFTA will also raise Mexican wages, narrowing the salary gap. From GM's perspective, a $10-an-hour Coahuilan is less of a bargain than a $20 an hour Tennessean.

But in the long run, if compared to a $40-an-hour Ohioan, even high-priced Mexican labor looks good.

A two-tiered union wage structure—one for old UAW members, another for the newly hired—will let American workers benefit fully from the job creation possibilities that NAFTA offers to the American auto business. The alternative—a rigid adherence to obsolete wage rates—is a prescription for pushing American-owned auto production south of the border, while European and Japanese car factories prosper in the American heartland.

NOTES

Note 1: Typical investments are in local beer and soft drink bottlers—companies that, by their very nature, have a local focus. For example, Coca-Cola, Pepsi and Anheuser-Busch have recently put $1 billion into joint-venture deals. As for the leading Mexican manufacturers (the car companies, consumer appliance makers like General Electric and Westinghouse), all are American owned, and all (except Ford) are selling more locally than they are shipping north from their Mexican plants.

Note 2: Most of the rural "job losses" projected for the United States under NAFTA are illusory, since these jobs are filled by temporary immigrant (largely Mexican) labor. If NAFTA means that some Mexican pickers will be working in American-owned orange groves in Campeche rather than in orange groves in California, it can hardly be counted as the "loss" of American jobs. Yet some of the anti-NAFTA literature did just that.

Note 3: Fears of a second Mexican debt crisis are misplaced: even with this growth, consumer debt will equal barely 10 percent of GDP, compared to more than 60 percent in the United States

Note 4: The balance of this huge procurement market—initially reserved for Mexican bidders—will be opened gradually to American and Canadian companies over 10 years.

Note 5: Pemex drilling teams in the Chiapas jungle have found more oil than private companies (such as Texaco) with contract concessions in adjacent Guatemalan fields.

Note 6: Mexico's constitutional claim to public ownership of hydrocarbons reserves seemed radical in the 1930s; today, it's the norm—even in such capitalist bastions as Great Britain and Norway

Note 7: GM's Saturn division, where the UAW permitted lower pay and more flexible work rules, is a limited and successful experiment with this sort of concession.

CHAPTER 7

The Wearing of the Green

Homero Aridjis vividly remembers the ride to his immigrant father's ancestral home in the Greek islands. The little epiphany that still defines the trip for Aridjis was the ship's escort of sleek, playful dolphins, the first the young Michoacan poet had seen. His father, a seaman, had often spoken of the dolphins when reminiscing about his youth. For Aridjis, the dolphin became a personal symbol, linking his own history to the mythos of the Mediterranean and the wildness of the natural world.

Today Aridjis is one of Mexico's leading writers. He is also its best-known environmental activist, a vocation that began with his fight to spare dolphins from slaughter in tuna nets. And to the consternation of the Mexican government, the movement Aridjis now helps lead became the most formidable early foe of the North American Free Trade Agreement.

When the Salinas Administration decided to press for a free trade pact, it fully expected fierce resistance from American trade unionists, from the leftist opposition in Mexico, and from industry lobbies and flag-waving nationalists on both sides of the border. It braced for attacks from Latin American intellectuals claiming that Mexico was abandoning its neighbors to the south. But it never expected the torrent of criticism from environmentalists on both sides of the border—or the political power they would wield in Washington.

Some Congressional nose-counters said NAFTA's fate hinged on the environmental swing vote—30 or 40 members of the House, perhaps a dozen Senators, most from states closer to Canada than Mexico, who are beholden neither to labor nor pro-NAFTA industry lobbies—but who rarely defy the greens.

That may not have been as bad for the trade pact as it seems. Quietly, many environmental activists have actually embraced NAFTA as an unexpected ally: they are using it as a lever to pry open the closed world of international economic negotiations to environmental safeguards in general and to make Mexico City and Washington raise anti-pollution standards in particular. As one USTR veteran comments, "Environmental issues will be the trade issues of the 1990s, the way intellectual property rights issues were the trade issues of the 1980s."

Nowhere has this change been more pronounced than within Mexico itself. The Salinas government's determination to get NAFTA negotiated and ratified has given Aridjis and his colleagues genuine influence over local environmental practices for the first time. Criticism from activists in both countries has forced Mexico to develop a clean-up plan for the virulent industrial contamination of border districts. This pressure has also driven Mexico to shut down polluting factories, sign on to international conservation accords, enact tougher air quality and toxic dumping rules, and expand its beleaguered corps of pollution inspectors.

The Mexican government has far to go, both in funding and political commitment. Public outrage over Mexico City's horrific air and the border's sewage-stained rivers hasn't yet kept those problems from worsening. The more rapid industrialization promised by NAFTA will put added strains on regulatory agencies that suffer from poor training, inadequate research facilities, and overly politicized management. Observers are right to be skeptical about the portrayal of the Salinas technocrats as born-again ecologists. Some of those doctorate-equipped planners believe that greater tolerance of pollution is one of the few legitimate competitive advantages of a developing economy.

But even the harshest local critics acknowledged that the NAFTA debate forced the government to confront environmental problems in a new way. The Mexican public now expects results and would likely punish the system if it doesn't deliver. So would the American conservationists who have taken Salinas at his word and publicly backed the accord. Increased intermingling of the American and Mexican economies will only increase their leverage as factories south of the border—and their exports to the north—fall under the scrutiny of the powerful American consumer lobby that environmentalists now represent.

At first, negotiators flatly rejected demands that NAFTA incorporate environmental safeguards. Ecology groups were perceived by all three administrations as naive do-gooders or willful obstructionists fighting free trade in a covert alliance with labor. Most maddening to the Mexicans was the environmentalists' apparent rejection of the commonsense proposition that ecological safeguards are more popular and more affordable in a prosperous country. As Salinas put it, "It is not automatic that with growth the environment will improve, but it is automatic that with poverty the environment will worsen."

It soon became clear, however, that NAFTA would not survive politically in the United States unless ecological concerns were addressed. The negotiators also realized that there was little harm in codifying some of the environmental pledges the three governments were already making publicly.

The Color of Money

When the negotiations concluded, Carla Hills called NAFTA as the "greenest" trade treaty ever drafted. That wasn't saying much: no previous trade pact had even the slightest tint of environmentalism, and NAFTA's environmental enforcement mechanisms are ambiguously phrased. But it isn't all empty talk: the agreement is full of provisions that oblige the signatories to take environmental issues into account.

From its opening chapter, NAFTA breaks ground in declaring its provisions subordinate not just to the General Agreement on Tariffs and Trade but to three global environmental accords: the 1973 Convention banning imports and exports of endangered species, the 1989 Basle Convention regulating cross-border shipments of hazardous waste, and the 1990 Montreal Protocol on ozone depletion. Stricter environmental regulations imposed by state or municipal governments cannot be overridden as impediments to trade or investment so long as they had some demonstrable scientific logic. Phytosanitary standards for food and agriculture will have to be maintained or strengthened.

NAFTA also formally recognizes that the three countries have a legitimate interest in the detail of environmental enforcement within each others' borders. In its most innovative provision, the signatories promise not to entice outside investment "by relaxing health, safety or environmental measures." Under NAFTA rules, environmental disputes can be referred to an independent scientific review board, which will submit its findings to a dispute settlement panel. The report, though not binding, will have to be released publicly along with the panel's decision, providing grounds for public challenge if the panel rejects the scientists' recommendations.

Outside the technical framework of the treaty itself, the United States and Mexico have begun to work on a border environmental plan. Together with Canada, they have agreed to monitor ecological protection throughout the continent with a new North American Commission on the Environment. As many environmentalists have begun to recognize, many indirect economic effects of free trade—integrated transportation networks and electric power grids, for example—will also alleviate stress on the environment. Restructuring agriculture on a continent-wide basis, to take another example, will allow a more rational use of land and water resources.

Another ecologically benign NAFTA byproduct will be a parade of salesmen offering state-of-the-art American environmental wares and services. Companies already pursuing this booming business range from small firms peddling items like solar cells, pollution detection equipment, and natural gas auto conversion kits to civil engineering powerhouses with turnkey plans for incinerators and sewage treatment plants. Lucrative contracts for the dismantling of antiquated Mexican factories and power plants are another environmentally correct growth industry (Idaho's Morrison Knudson Corp., for example, was paid $100 million to tear down an air-polluting Mexico City oil refinery). Without NAFTA, many of these contracts and products would have been unavailable in Mexico, or prohibitively expensive.

Despite this, environmentalists remain uneasy. Experts in both countries wonder if Mexico's tough new environmental rules will be stringently enforced. They worry that clauses permitting trinational reviews of specific applications of international environmental treaties could lead to those treaties' circumvention. Leaders of the moderate conservation groups that have endorsed the agreement fear that with NAFTA ratified, their leverage over Mexico will be lost.

Ecologists sell themselves short. NAFTA has already made the American environmental movement a permanent part of Mexican life. Its clout will only intensify as the two economies merge further. Virtually every large Mexico-based business will depend on the American market for an essential share of its sales and investment capital, making it vulnerable to bad publicity and, at the extreme, to consumer boycotts. The NAFTA-mandated opening to American investment in natural resource industries—mining, forestry—will give activists additional weapons (such as stockholder lawsuits) to combat environmental degradation south of the border. It isn't hard to imagine a Sierra Club campaign against, say, an American paper company getting timber from the clear-cutting of Chiapas rain forests, or an engineering firm building a border port project with inadequate sewage treatment facilities.

There's a precedent for such cross-border environmentalism: the battle over HydroQuebec's proposed Great Whale project in James Bay. Intended to provide electricity for the northeastern United States, the dam would have flooded fragile subarctic plains and displaced native communities. Canadian ecologists and Cree Indians banded together with American environmentalists to fight it. After Vermont voters condemned it in a referendum and the State of New York refused essential economic support, the project was canceled.

In 1992, Salinas pre-empted a similar controversy. After pressure from local and foreign conservationists, he halted a long-planned dam project on the southern border that would have flooded scores of Mayan archeological sites and 500 square miles of rain forest. Environmentalists fear that a future Mexican president could reverse the Salinas decision and revive the Usumacinta River dam project. But the HydroQuebec experience suggests that such a move would prompt effective resistance. (The ecotourism industry should give Mexico another incentive to keep the Usumacinta running wild.) Trade integration, despite the best efforts of the negotiating parties themselves, leads inexorably to some measure of political integration, even if it never transcends non-governmental alliances. The question is not whether American environmentalists can effect change in Mexico, but whether they will maintain their interest when the NAFTA headlines fade.

Combined with the increased political power environmentalists will wield in a NAFTA-ized Mexico is Mexico's own increased economic stake in maintaining environmental standards. The tourism industry, now Mexico's third biggest foreign exchange earner (after oil and automotive exports), is ready to expand further as NAFTA lowers restrictions on American investment in shorefront resorts. Acapulco's abject decline—a polluted harbor, an unsanitary inner city—is persuading Mexican hoteliers that their business cannot succeed without a clean environment. Pollution also undercuts the market for such critical Mexican exports as shrimp and winter vegetables.

Take the pesticide issue. NAFTA critics made much of the fact that Mexico, unlike the United States, still allows the use of DDT. They made three related points: that DDT is injurious to wildlife and farm workers, that NAFTA will open the doors to DDT-tainted produce in the U.S.

market, and that American farmers, who must use costly and less effective pesticides, will be put at a competitive disadvantage.

Mexico's response was essentially to dismiss all three complaints. Mexican officials noted that DDT is allowed only in the application for which it is still recommended by the World Health Organization: the suppression of malaria. Only non-tropical countries have the luxury of banning DDT completely, they argued, and in any event the United States clearly wouldn't want an outbreak of malaria so close to its borders. Mexican agricultural exports, moreover, are monitored for inadvertent pesticide contamination by both local health authorities and agriculture inspectors.

This is accurate, but irrelevant. Over the years there have been many reliable reports of DDT use in Mexico's coastal cotton and vegetable fields. Spraying by health authorities in these same areas makes detection of illegal DDT all the more difficult. Agricultural inspection in both countries is lamentably uneven, making it conceivable that tomatoes with trace DDT residues could make it to the American market. The best protection against that happening, though, is the growing consciousness in Mexico of the devastating impact such a discovery would have on the entire agricultural industry. Mexican farmers saw their Chilean counterparts lose hundreds of millions of dollars—and lay off some 30,000 workers—after three allegedly cyanide-tainted grapes were found by U.S. inspectors in Philadelphia. The Food and Drug Administration's swift, total ban on Chilean farm products (despite its own doubts about the evidence) stood as a warning to all Latin American produce exporters about their own vested interest in the enforcement of phytosanitary standards. By the accounts of Mexican and American agricultural experts alike, adherence to pesticide prohibitions and other phytosanitary rules is most rigorous in areas like Sinaloa that heavily depend on American export sales. The fear that chemically tainted produce could jeopardize their access to the American market gives Mexican growers a powerful incentive to maintain strict standards. Market forces are a potent environmental regulator.

The Tuna Saga

The best example of this phenomenon so far has been Aridjis's save-the-dolphins crusade.

Ironically, the treatment of dolphins by Mexico's tuna fleet was often cited by NAFTA critics as evidence of the country's unwillingness to abide by first-world norms. Some environmentalists even argued that admitting Mexico and its fishing industry into a free trade pact would undercut efforts to protect dolphins elsewhere.

But the dynamics of the tuna-dolphin controversy show just the opposite. Mexico is now reforming its tuna fishing practices to preserve dolphins and placate critics. This is all the more remarkable since its antagonists' motives are plainly suspect, and its earlier resistance to change was clearly justified by international law. Aridjis and his allies were successful only when the NAFTA debate focused criticism on Mexican fishing practices—and thus threatened both Mexico's broad trade-policy agenda and its narrower but acute interest in selling canned tuna in American supermarkets. An issue used by critics as a metaphor for NAFTA's perniciousness provides instead a greater lesson in how economic integration can force Mexico to raise its environmental standards.

At the center of the controversy is the Marine Mammals Protection Act, which was amended in 1988 to ban imported tuna from fleets that kill dolphins at rates more than 25 percent above those authorized for American ships. In 1990, the Commerce Department ruled that Mexican tuna boats exceeded that limit and banned imports of Mexican yellowfin—which had then reached a billion pounds a year.

Mexican officials were outraged. Not only was this a unilateral extension of U.S. environmental standards into Mexico's sovereign territory, but the decision singled out Mexico for punishment when even Mexico's critics acknowledged that its tuna fleet was hardly unique in its use of dolphin-trapping nets.

In Mexico's commerce and fisheries ministries, the dolphin issue had long been an irritant. In theory, Mexico had adopted rules forcing the release of trapped dolphins from purse-seine nets as far back as 1977. But they were only erratically enforced. Aridjis, rebuffed in his private pleading with the government for stricter rules and enforcement, gradually became more public. He enlisted support from 100 prominent artists and intellectuals—known now as *El Grupo de Cien* (The Group of 100) who urged stronger enforcement of environmental laws generally and an immediate end to the killing of dolphins in particular. More at home in the world of lyric poetry than in politics, the soft-spoken Aridjis was deeply resented—even vilified—by Mexican tuna fishermen and their government allies. That Aridjis had reached across national boundaries to form a coalition with American groups like Greenpeace was considered an unconscionable breach of political etiquette.

The prestige of the Group of 100 made it hard for the government to deny them a respectful hearing—and even more difficult to denounce the save-the-dolphin campaign as a foreign plot against Mexican fishermen. Privately, however, many officials in Mexico's fisheries bureaucracy saw the dolphin controversy as just the latest battle in a long, acrimonious war with the United States over tuna fishing grounds and export sales. Some even suspected that Aridjis was supported by American canneries in a self-serving effort to keep Mexican tuna out of the U.S. market. They noted that the U.S. tariff on canned tuna is a stiff 32 percent; under NAFTA, Mexican tuna would enter the United States duty-free. Import restrictions on all but "dolphin-safe" tuna would keep the canned Mexican product out while allowing the continued entry of the raw Asian Pacific tuna used by the principal American canneries. (Dolphins, for reasons poorly understood, rarely run with Western Pacific yellowtail. The American canneries began switching to suppliers across the Pacific not to save dolphin, however, but because they were pushed out of Latin America when the region began asserting control over fisheries within its declared 200-mile maritime limits.)

Investing in alternatives to purse-seining, as Mexico's critics demanded, is an expensive proposition. Mexican fishermen bitterly noted that American tuna boats had practiced purse-seining off Mexico's own shores for decades. Was it a coincidence, they asked, that this controversy over dolphins had arisen only after the collapse of the once-formidable San Diego fleet and the emergence of a competitive Mexican tuna industry?[1]

Mexico's trade ministry formally challenged the tuna ban under the General Agreement on Tariffs and Trade, arguing that the U.S. action was a non-tariff barrier prohibited by Gatt. A Gatt panel agreed. Environmentalists in the United States attacked the Gatt procedure as evidence that Mexico was insincere in its commitment to wildlife protection. The ruling was also cited as an example of supranational bureaucrats convening in private to overturn local environmental laws, a scenario often raised by critics of NAFTA and Gatt. Among trade experts, however, the consensus was that Mexico had been rightfully vindicated.

But Salinas saw that NAFTA politics made such legalisms irrelevant. A legal victory wouldn't contain the pressures that led to the ban's adoption in the first place—witness the voluntary compliance of American brand-name canners with dolphin-safe tuna, driven not by law but by the fear of boycott. Environmentalists had forced Bumblebee and others to switch to Western Pacific tuna exclusively; even without the 1988 law, they could have driven Mexico from the American tuna market. (Selling to Europe instead—Mexico's current market strategy—is a stopgap course at best, given the strength of the green movement there. Indeed, the

European parliament passed a non-binding resolution in 1991 urging the prohibition of imported purse-seined tuna.)

The bottom line for Mexico was that, Gatt or no Gatt, it could not sell tuna in the United States unless Mexican tuna boats made a sustained, verifiable effort to spare dolphins. Nor could it persuade Congressional critics of NAFTA that it was sincere in its commitment to environmentalism if it pursued its case in the Gatt.

Recognizing this, Salinas abandoned the Gatt case and reversed course. He decreed tough new purse-seining controls, including criminal penalties for violations and the immediate placement of internationally certified observers on every boat in the Mexican fleet. Salinas embraced Aridjis's cause as if it had always been his own. He smilingly announced that he "likes dolphins, too." (For Mexican marine mammals, this was happy news: in Mexico, being a friend of the president offers greater protection than a spot on the endangered species list.)

But the dolphins' protectors weren't satisfied. In January 1992, the Federal District Court in San Francisco ruled that the ban on Mexican tuna should be extended to tuna imports from all countries that imported Mexican tuna, since that tuna could (in theory) be relabeled and transshipped to American markets. Mexican officials were again outraged. In the first two years of the Salinas Administration, stricter enforcement had already reduced dolphin mortality by a third or more. The San Francisco circuit court judge was unmoved. He noted, correctly, that Mexico's kill ratio still exceeded the maximum level allowed under the 1988 U.S. law.

So in June 1992 the Salinas Administration went further. It signed an accord committing Mexico to steady declines in dolphin mortality—far below the 70 percent it claimed to have already achieved. While many conservationists remain unsatisfied, they have proved that the NAFTA process is a powerful tool for stiffening Mexican environmental policy.

The Mandate of Montreal The most powerful influences on Mexico's environmental future will not be statutes or decrees but public vigilance and market forces on both sides of the border. Staffers at the new continental Commission on Environmental Cooperation (CEC) in Montreal should keep this in mind.

In classic bureaucratic fashion, this new trilateral institution had an accepted acronym—NACE—long before before it had a clear mission. This "North American Commission on the Environment" (later fuzzed over to CEC to stress collaboration over regulation) emerged from an earlier Bush-Salinas plan for a U.S.-Mexican Joint Environmental Committee. The Joint Committee was to meet as infrequently as once a year, with the EPA Administrator and Mexico's chief environmental officer co-chairing the sessions. The committee's mandate was limited to loosely structured "assessments" of general environmental conditions and, "as appropriate," specific regulations.

The Bush, Salinas and Mulroney administrations saw the Commission as a forum for airing cross-border environmental disputes, but little else. The Clinton White House pushed to make it more: a vehicle to encourage public input into environmental policy-making in all three countries (but mainly in Mexico)—with a mandate to punish lapses in enforcement.

The CEC's chief task is to stand guard over NAFTA's most innovative environmental promise, the passage in Article 1114 stating flatly that "it is inappropriate to encourage investment by relaxing health, safety, or environmental measures." The NAFTA signatories promise not to bend or waive any such rules in an effort to encourage the "establishment, acquisition, expansion, or retention [of an investment] in its territory."

That pledge seeks to calm the principal environmentalist fear of a borderless marketplace: that the increased competition for investment dollars and export sales would drag conservation standards down to the lowest common denominator. Environmentalists complain that if one country (read: Mexico) turns a blind eye towards ecological abuse, companies elsewhere that must abide by costly environmental regulations would relocate, or use the threat of relocation to get local rules ratcheted down to the same lax levels. The NAFTA negotiators recognized this as a legitimate concern. Overriding concerns about sovereignty, Article 1114 acknowledges that people in one NAFTA jurisdiction have a stake in the environmental practices of another—even when their aquifers and airsheds are hundreds or even thousands of miles apart.

How would this be enforced? Article 1114 says only that any country persuaded that another had violated its terms "may request consultations . . . with a view to avoiding" such violations. That's it. There was no guarantee that this "consultation" would even occur, or that remedial action would be taken. The assumption seemed to be that the mere airing of a complaint would shame transgressors into compliance.

Environmentalists doubt the power of moral suasion. They pointed to the rigid procedures and penalties outlined by NAFTA for violations of subsidy codes and intellectual property rights, and demanded similar teeth for environmental protection. They argued that the Commission should have the power to conduct on-site inspections and impose penalties for non-compliance with local regulations—including punitive tariffs on goods produced by offending companies.

The Clinton USTR team met them halfway. The CEC can impose up to $20 million in fines and eliminate duty-free export privileges. But the sanctions would be imposed on governments, not polluting exporters, and even then only after a protracted consultation process. The Commission has only limited investigative authority and a small staff (early budgeting called for about 30 full-time professionals). Yet it must somehow prove that the enforcement failure was flagrant and systematic, with an identifiable impact on trade.

The CEC's usual disciplinary weapons, clearly, will not be formal sanctions, but staff reports and public hearings. That's not enough for many critics. But the environmentalists underestimate both their own strength and the capacity of protected business interests to turn well-intentioned rules into new barriers against trade.

Even if the CEC were just a talk shop, it wouldn't necessarily be toothless. The non-binding judgments of a commission whose proceedings are characterized by professional rigor and genuine autonomy would have a clear impact on companies or local authorities singled out for condemnation. Accused parties would be given some reasonable period to correct offending behavior. Failure to comply with the commission's directives would prompt a formal inquiry and the threat of fines that would come from taxpayer pockets. Few multinationals would risk the opprobrium—or the possibility of a consumer boycott or lawsuits from victims of environmental abuse (corporate lawyers won't soon forget Bhopal). Mexican companies are also increasingly sensitive to their image in the United States, which they need not just as a market but as a source of investor capital.

The commission's biggest impact will be felt within Mexico, which is unaccustomed to impartial expert review of government regulatory procedures and private business practices.

The commission's lack of direct enforcement powers will make such judgments easier. In many environmental cases, the circumstantial evidence is compelling, but there is no incontrovertible proof. Using its option to issue non-binding rulings would allow the commission to be more subjective. If there were an attempt to contravene the spirit of the pact, the commission could say so. By contrast, when the commission exercises its power to impose fines and other sanctions, it will be constrained by the narrower rules of evidence befitting a trilateral court.

With Article 1114, there are clear difficulties. Accusations that environmental standards had been relaxed in an effort to woo or retain investors are extremely difficult to document. It must be demonstrated not only that environmental rules had been violated, but that this abuse was knowingly tolerated by local authorities. Accusers would then have to show that this tolerance was part of a deliberate policy to retain or entice investment. And that would require proof that investment had occurred that would otherwise be absent, or that a factory had been kept open through lax enforcement of costly air pollution or waste disposal rules.

Obtaining such proof would be hard. There are few industries where the costs of pollution control are decisive. By one estimate, compliance with environmental standards accounts for just one-half of 1 percent of total industrial production expenditures (though up to 3 percent in such heavily polluting industries as cement and petrochemicals). Multinationals tend to build plants in accordance with the stricter environmental rules of their home markets. Standardizing plant designs is cheaper: it reduces initial engineering fees along with training and maintenance costs, while avoiding some future expense if local standards are raised closer to U.S. norms.

If low environmental standards were a significant plant-siting incentive, there should be many identifiable cases of American companies moving to Mexico for that reason in the 1980s, when regulations were easier and enforcement was even spottier. But there aren't. The example cited most frequently by NAFTA critics is the relocation of Los Angeles furniture manufacturers to Tijuana—a move they say was prompted by strict Southern Californian controls on the outdoor spraying of paints and solvents.

That claim doesn't withstand scrutiny. The General Accounting Office study that supposedly "proves" this charge found 28 furniture companies that had moved from Los Angeles County to Baja California. Of these, 22 told GAO they moved, at least in part, to avoid stringent local air pollution standards. What GAO failed to point out in its subsequent report was that these firms could have avoided L.A. spraying rules just as easily by moving to Fresno—or anywhere else in the United States. (And in fact dozens of other firms did just that.) So why did these particular firms pick Tijuana? It's no great mystery: they wanted to escape California labor costs. Twenty-three of the 28 companies told GAO that direct payroll costs were a major reason for their move, particularly the increasing burden of workmen's compensation claims. Moreover, even if these factories had moved south in search of pliant pollution inspectors, it would say nothing about NAFTA itself: companies that can't bear the costs of compliance with Environmental Protection Agency standards can move to Mexico with or without a trade pact.

Still, none of this precludes the possibility that lax environmental enforcement could be used as an investment incentive. There is anecdotal evidence that lower waste treatment costs contributed to the relocation of electronics assembly plants from the Silicon Valley to the Mexican maquila belt. And in petrochemical production, the savings from weaker health and safety rules clearly matter: a Sonora copper smelter without state-mandated scrubbers on its stacks will have a higher profit margin than a nearby competitor in Arizona. When such savings represent the difference between profit and loss, local authorities might be persuaded that strict enforcement would put the entire investment at risk.

The problem for a would-be environmental prosecutor is that cases of willful non-enforcement as an investment incentive would be few and hard to prove. If environmental violations occurred for other reasons—corporate greed or incompetence, a regulator's sloth or corruption—the offense would be a matter for national authorities to handle.

Automatic penalties for the evasion of environmental strictures raise a more serious problem. It would be impossible to keep such provisions from being exploited by Washington trade lawyers—whose interest is not in protecting the environment, but in insulating their clients from the risk and expense of competition.

Conservation activists have long argued that penalties for environmental abuse should be written into a trade pact directly, not relegated to a parallel accord. But using countervailing tariffs to penalize polluters is uncharted terrain.

If companies could use allegations of non-compliance with local regulations as a means of penalizing imports from a competitor, at least some of them would surely do so. This would create a regulatory nightmare, favoring those with the deepest pockets and cleverest lawyers. It might even dissuade local environmental authorities from keen enforcement.

Take Cemex, the huge Mexican cement company. Cemex paid some $60 million in U.S. countervailing duties after its competitors filed dumping charges in 1991—charges that Mexico insisted were false. A Gatt panel agreed and ordered the money returned. Then, in November 1992, Cemex was again hit with a fine—this time by the Mexican government, for $36 million—for failing to install appropriate pollution controls on a Mexico City plant.

Under an automatic NAFTA sanction system, Cemex's American rivals can cite that Mexican penalty as evidence that Cemex had been enjoying an unfair competitive advantage from lax environmental enforcement—an advantage for which it can be retroactively assessed additional punitive duties. If Mexican officials knew that enforcing their pollution laws would curtail American market access for one of their biggest foreign exchange earners, they would surely think twice. In the United States, the EPA has a hard time holding its own against political pressures. Mexico's environmental enforcers have far less clout, and direct linkage between pollution enforcement and trade sanctions could weaken them further.

As a practical matter, there is another crucial flaw in a commission with direct regulatory powers. Too many environmentalists see enforcement as a one-way street, with watchdogs north of the border keeping tabs on compliance in the south. Yet the Super-CEC that they would prefer would have jurisdiction over environmental affairs within the United States as well. Canadian and Mexican representatives presumably could decide, for example, that a relaxation of rules against clear-cutting Oregonian rain forests provided an illegal investment incentive for paper mills. Some American environmentalists might welcome such a ruling, but Oregon's politicians and paper companies would not.

The most critical matter is the identity and autonomy of the commissioners themselves. They should be independent figures of recognized professional expertise, with the power to review cases with the authoritative detachment that has characterized the dispute resolution boards that police U.S.-Canadian trade.

NAFTA critics often contend that the North American integration process is moving too fast. Yet here they want to move even faster. A continental commission on the environment with independent regulatory powers is a logical step in the evolution of a North American common market. To impose such an agency on the NAFTA countries now, however, would be premature.

The best course would be to get the CEC working as it is currently designed, with procedures for a five-year performance review mandated by enabling legislation. That would coincide with the elimination of most tariffs and investment obstacles, making it a logical time to reassess the entire NAFTA process. At this early stage, North America's governments have the luxury of experimentation. An independent Commission endowed with moral authority could prove surprisingly successful. If it doesn't, that failure should be readily apparent. The commission could then be retrofitted with regulatory teeth.

The one exception to the non-binding approach to NAFTA environmental enforcement should be border affairs. The fragile U.S.-Mexican frontier zone cannot be regulated under two sets of rules. Border residents drink the same water and breathe the same air. They welcome the proposal for a separate bilateral agency—staffed and headquartered *on* the border, not in the distant capitals—with investigatory resources and joint enforcement authority. On the border, the direct personal stake in health and conservation crosses national lines.

**On the
Borderline**

Should a trade agreement be burdened by environmental considerations at all?

Many pro-NAFTA business leaders reject the linkage. Prosperity is a prerequisite for environmental protection, they argue, and freer trade and investment is a prerequisite for prosperity. Typical is Jack Welch of General Electric, who dismisses the issue with a simple question: "Have you ever seen neighbors who get richer get dirtier?"

Residents of American border towns retort that this is exactly what they have seen.

The 1980s investment boom that quintupled maquiladora employment brought a commensurate rise in air and water pollution. Mexican border towns that had been small, poor shadows of their American neighbors became overnight metropolises: Tijuana is now bigger than San Diego, Juarez is twice the size of El Paso, Matamoros dwarfs Brownsville. The big Mexican border cities sport modern industrial parks and prefab suburbs filled with accountants, plant managers, and small entepreneurs. They are also ringed with shantytowns and spew untreated sewage into rivers and oceans. Smog obscures once-pristine mountain skylines, while small children cavort amid empty chemical drums. Picture the worst of North Jersey before Superfund and the Clean Air Act. Relocate it to a stark desert environment where teenage factory workers live in thousand-dollar shacks and the heat on summer nights hovers above 80 degrees Fahrenheit. This is the world that has become a metaphor for fears of life under NAFTA. Without environmental vigilance, as the border experience has clearly shown, economic growth *can* make things a lot dirtier.

Failure to crack down on these polluters was never a problem of resources but of political will. Waste disposal problems were deliberately overlooked in Mexico's rush to create employment in the depressed 1980s.

Though many maquiladora firms say that they observe stricter environmental standards than Mexico demands, the minority of egregious offenders are rarely called to account by their more scrupulous peers. To the contrary: the maquiladora associations—dominated by American investors, defended by Mexican officials—testily contend that most air and water pollution on the border isn't industrial in origin, but residential.

This is true. But it doesn't explain away industry's big direct contribution to the problem. Nor does it acknowledge that these exploding urban agglomerations without sewage treatment plants or garbage disposal systems are the home of the maquiladora work force. Border towns can't afford essential infrastructure because the businesses that should be their revenue base—the maquiladoras that lured people from Mexico's interior in the first place—pay virtually no taxes.

Many maquiladoras ignored requirements that hazardous byproducts be trucked back across the border and reported to U.S. authorities. The widely reported horror stories—disturbingly high incidences of cancer and birth defects—cannot be definitively attributed to maquiladora discharges. But that so many community leaders and health officials believe them to be true says quite a bit about the local view of Mexican regulatory vigilance.

Still, there is nothing in NAFTA itself that makes border pollution worse, and several things that can make it better. The agreement includes environmental provisions that should improve enforcement and encourage stricter regulations in the—future. The parallel environmental plan will—promote the development of cross-border national parks (the Big Bend region of West Texas and Chihuahua could be the first). In urban areas, NAFTA's investment rules will encourage build-operate-and-transfer contracts for sewage treatment projects and gas-fueled power plants.

In the biggest change for the border, the maquiladoras' special customs status will be eliminated (an in-bond factory is pointless in a free trade zone). Instead, existing plants will begin servicing both markets, instead of importing and exporting virtually everything to and from the United States. This should encourage investment deeper inside Mexico, relieving congestion on the frontier.

Lastly, the parallel border environmental plan should spur collaborative enforcement as well as cooperative long-term planning. It could also provide a framework for a new bilateral agency charged with monitoring the border environment. If handled creatively, with political autonomy and direct local funding, these new institutions could turn NAFTA into the most potent weapon for ecological improvement on the border.

NAFTA's indirect economic effects could be even more important.

Cross-border electricity grids would allow fewer, larger and more energy-efficient power plants. Industrial concentration on the border is already dissipating as investors anticipate the beneficial effects of liberalized investment rules and free trade flows in Mexico's interior. New transport rules would permit point-to-point cross-border trucking, with no long lines at the frontier for off-loading and inspection. New bridges and border crossings would also reduce air pollution. High-speed rail links, combined with point-of-origin customs inspections (Texas is planning direct service between Monterrey and San Antonio), could bypass overstressed freight crossings in Laredo and Nogales. Extending the San Diego trolley into the heart of Tijuana could have the same effect on auto traffic.

Yet the most beneficial NAFTA-induced change won't be economic but political. It's no coincidence that when American environmentalists began fighting NAFTA, Mexico doubled the ranks of its pollution inspectors and tripled funding of border clean-up projects. Enforcement today is better at the border than elsewhere in Mexico. Nearly 200 of Mexico's roughly 300 full-time pollution inspectors are deployed along the border, an indication of the government's acute sensitivity to American criticism. Environmental abuse deep in the Mexican interior has no direct impact on the public health and ecology of the United States, but on the border the impact is direct, immediate and often clearly visible.

State-sponsored Smog

Rarely do Mexico's critics allow that environmental enforcement must work both ways. Yet Mexico's environment has suffered far more abuse from American land and water practices than the American environment has at Mexican hands. Many Mexicans see this double standard as evidence that environmental concerns are a subterfuge for non-environmental business and labor interests. The AFL-CIO, after all, never showed much interest in the fragility of mesoamerican habitats before the NAFTA debate, and environmentalists never rallied to block U.S.-Canadian free trade—despite the unresolved dispute over acid rain.

It is also true, however, that the United States had never before contemplated a trade pact with a low-income country with a long history of environmental abuse. Suspicion of the Mexican government's insistence that it observes the strictest of environmental rules is well deserved, especially since so many of the worst violations have been committed by the government itself. The state petroleum company alone has been responsible in recent years for the world's largest oil spill, the toxic contamination of wetlands, and scores of calamitous accidents, including two enormous gas explosions in crowded urban areas, each claiming hundreds of lives.

Nowhere has Petroleos Mexicanos had a more pernicious impact than in Mexico's capital. With monopoly control of all fuel supplies, Pemex delayed for years the introduction of unleaded gasoline and supplied local factories with heavy, sulfurous bunker. Until recently, Pemex's biggest refinery was also the largest single stationary source of air pollution in the world's largest and most polluted city. The government's 1991 decision to close the giant Azcopatzalco complex seemed prompted not by any new awareness of the refinery's hazards but by the desire to impress environmental critics during the fast-track debate in Washington.

Despite the oil refinery's closure and other belated anti-pollution efforts—partial limits on private auto traffic, a gradual switch to catalytic converters, improvements in monitoring equipment—the air gets dirtier with each passing year. A 1992 United Nations study confirmed what Mexico City residents have long known in their hearts and lungs: Mexico's capital has the world's worst air. The UN Environmental Program and the World Health Organization (WHO) surveyed the air quality of the globe's 20 largest urban areas and found that Mexico City was by far the most contaminated. It was the only megalopolis where concentrations of four leading pollutants (carbon monoxide, ozone, sulfur dioxide, and dust) all registered at double—or more the maximum levels the WHO considers tolerable.

Mexico City is a permanent public health emergency, with schools closed routinely because of ozone alerts and hospitals reporting rising incidences of emphysema, bronchial asthma, and other chronic lung diseases. Children enter adolescence with perilously high lead levels in their blood and the lungs of heavy cigarette smokers. Given the federal government's ownership of the oil industry, direct political rule of the capital, and strict regulatory control of every aspect of the domestic auto industry, its denials of responsibility for this health emergency are laughable.

■ Yet the relevant question is not whether Mexican authorities have acted responsibly in the past, but whether a trade accord would make Mexico City's air better or worse.

Liberalized import rules have already made it easier to supply cars with unleaded gas; most of Mexico City's supply now comes from Texas.

Expanded export production in the auto industry has raised air emission standards in most model lines to prevailing U.S. levels. NAFTA opens Mexico's doors to American natural gas and to American investment in domestic gas production; many experts see a conversion to natural gas in bus, truck and taxi fleets as the city's best short-term choice. Competition from energy-efficient foreign manufacturers and the rising costs of energy at home—in itself a direct result of Mexico's NAFTA-driven market logic—should make Mexican industry cut wasteful emissions.

Most important, mass political pressure and plain personal discomfort among the country's political elite ultimately should drive the capital toward California's strict emissions standards. By 1998, for example, California will require that one of every 50 cars sold emit no pollutants at all. If greater Mexico City (now 18 million people) adopted similar rules, the size of the two markets together might virtually guarantee the availability of viable electric and natural gas car technology.

It is possible that increasing Mexican prosperity will multiply the numbers of cars on the road, making pollution worse. Still, the trade and investment liberalization under NAFTA will make it easier for Mexico to tackle the problem if it finds the political will to do so. Rising income raises expectations about personal health. Salinas aides point to a recent study by two Princeton professors showing that urban air quality in developing countries deteriorates in the first stages of industrialization, but improves after adjusted per-capita incomes climb past $5,000—the level Mexico is at today. The critical shift occurs when pollution controls become both politically necessary and economically feasible.

The concern of many environmentalists is that NAFTA (and similar pacts in the future) will be used to weaken existing anti-pollution statutes in the United States. Not surprisingly, the Bush Administration's efforts to allay this fear went nowhere. While the White House was asserting that it would insist on strict NAFTA pollution controls on both sides of the border, it was arguing in other forums that environmental rules were an unacceptable brake on American competitiveness. It was hard for environmentalists to imagine Washington pressing Mexico to enforce regulations that the president and vice president were suggesting should be softened or abandoned in the United States itself.

Now, however, with a Democratic Administration, some environmentalists are hoping that NAFTA can be used to "harmonize" Mexico's pollution laws up to U.S. and Canadian levels. In practice, this is already happening: most of Mexico's environmental rules have been rewritten since 1988 to parallel U.S. standards for water pollution, air emissions, pesticide use, hazardous waste disposal, and similar problems. And in the long run, economic integration would encourage a convergence of standards for industrial polluters and cars.

But to demand excessive harmony now would be a mistake. In poor regions just entering the age of industrialization, a factory's air emissions are apt to be dirtier than would be acceptable to the people of Denver or Pittsburgh. NAFTA recognizes that some communities would and should choose to raise their standards above required base levels. Mexico's incorporation into a North American trade zone will simply extend southward the present patchwork hierarchy of varying local standards.

Green Ink: The Bottom Line   With NAFTA and its ecological codicils now ratified, the Mexican environment will get protection it would not have otherwise received. Zealously protective of its sovereignty, Mexico would never have asked Washington for environmental aid. Even if it had, the request would likely have been squelched by a deficit-conscious Congress. As it is, direct U.S. environmental aid remains modest. The House of Rep-resentatives halved a $300 million Bush White House funding request for joint border-area sewage treatment plants, but approved $5 million from the Agency for International Development for rain forest preservation and $9 million for a Mexico City air pollution analysis. The NAFTA debate also prompted strong U.S. support for a $50 million World Bank loan to Mexico to strengthen its enforcement of environmental rules—a loan that must be augmented by Mexican matching funds.[2]

NAFTA's environmental provisions set a clear precedent for raising such concerns in the Gatt and other forums. Trade negotiators can no longer contend that issues like agricultural pesticides and auto emissions are out of bounds. In NAFTA, when environmental regulations are challenged on trade-obstruction grounds, the burden of proof is on the accuser, not on the regulator. Under previous trade rules, the opposite was true.

With NAFTA, Mexico—or the United States or Canada—can no longer contend that its environment is its own private affair. Motives are irrelevant. If the need to appease American ecologists makes the Mexican government more attentive to environmental hazards, the beneficiaries are the people who breathe Mexico's air and drink its water.

Mexico's nascent environmental movement will strengthen as the country grows more prosperous, with demands not just for anti-pollution statutes but for such first-world amenities as potable tap water and professionally managed wildlife parks. The alliance with their American counterparts that economic union is already fostering will give Mexican environmentalism money, personnel and clout beyond its borders. At the same time, greater market integration will provide the Mexican government with greater resources to enforce strict environmental laws and give Mexican business new incentives to adhere to those standards. Ultimately, the North American free trade experiment should prove that trade liberalization and environmental protection aren't incompatible.

Cleaning the Borderlands

Is Mexico's environment any of our business?

Not really—unless intentionally lax anti-pollution enforcement lures investment south and undercuts competitors north of the border. Otherwise, Mexico's environmental health should be maintained and monitored by those it directly affects, the Mexicans themselves.

The 2,000-mile exception to this rule is the border.

This thin swath of North America is home to nearly 10 million Mexicans and 5 million Americans. They breathe the same air, draw water from the same reservoirs, swim in the same stretches of surf. Border communities suffer equally when the Colorado and Rio Grande are drained dry by upstream American agribusiness, or when foundries in Sonora and Nuevo Leon pump soot out their smokestacks. What happens on one side directly affects the other. In the ecology of the borderlands, national sovereignty is an illusion.

In the world of government, sovereignty is more concrete. The border environment is regulated by two radically different bureaucracies, each with its own national personality and priorities. Even when there is a genuine desire for collaboration, the relationship is inherently antagonistic. U.S. authorities look south and see what seems to them a reckless disregard for elemental sanitation and pollution controls. Their Mexican counterparts look north and see a society that wastes far more energy and water than their own, yet lectures poor neighbors about conservation. American environmental agencies have ample budgets and expert inspectors, but are hampered by the fact that most of the border's industrial polluters are south of the border. Mexico's understaffed, underfunded environmental agencies are irked by their inability to monitor and discipline 2,000 border factories that they see—accurately—as American corporate enclaves on Mexican soil.

Enforcement methods also differ, and are mutually disdained. In the United States, reliance on precisely drafted laws and an independent judiciary, though slow and cumbersome, is generally considered effective and even-handed; to Mexicans, it can seem annoyingly protracted and expensive. The Mexican system, by contrast, lets authorities shut down suspected violators with little warning, after which they negotiate the pollution-control terms of the plant's re-opening. Considered swift and pragmatic on the south side of the border, this is viewed as excessively arbitrary and politicized on the north. When the regulating agency is Mexican and the regulated polluter is American, this clash of bureaucratic cultures can be doubly frustrating.

This fragile, overstressed strip of urbanized desert must be recognized and regulated for what it is: an organic whole. Without shared resources and responsibility across national lines, environmental enforcement won't work.

That requires a mutual cession of sovereignty, a move that could prove even harder for the United States than for proudly nationalist Mexico. Investment, inspection, enforcement and even the prosecution of offenders should be undertaken jointly by authorities given full jurisdiction over the border zone by both governments. At best, the environmental appendices of the North American Free Trade Agreement offer a unique opportunity not only to improve the border environment but to make the border a model of binational cooperation.

The one genuinely binational border agency—the century-old International Boundary and Water Commission—is confined to the hydraulic micromanagement of border rivers and irrigation projects. The commission's staff of engineers has no control over the upstream investment decisions that determine the quantity and quality of the water they manage. In 1983, Presidents Reagan and De la Madrid ordered joint action on air pollution from copper smelters, effluent discharges into the Pacific, and the supervised disposal of hazardous waste. But erratic enforcement and sparse budgets limited these programs' effectiveness.

As a direct result of NAFTA, real cooperation is already increasing. Joint investigations of toxic waste dumping have resulted in prosecutions on both sides of the border. The Bush and Salinas Administrations also proposed an "integrated environmental plan" that, while never fully funded, at least recognized the need for coordinated public works expenditures. The plan called for the systematic exchange of environmental data, including a long-overdue inventory of toxic waste sites and a comprehensive survey of border aquifers and groundwater supplies. It also set up cross-border training programs for environmental inspectors.

These proposals didn't go far enough. What's really needed is a bilateral border commission with even greater authority than the one Clinton and Salinas have proposed. This agency could become a laboratory for creative approaches to environmental problems, including market-based strategies that reward non-polluters while penalizing offenders. Taxes on effluents and carbon emissions, for example, could be collected directly by a border agency, giving it regulatory clout and an autonomous revenue base. Ideally, such an agency would be as decentralized as possible, with a border-city headquarters supervising a string of localized departments dealing with each cross-border metropolis and important watersheds.

An essential annex to the border commission would be a new regulatory body dedicated exclusively to the Gulf of Mexico. This virtual sea, plagued by overfishing and oil pollution, is surrounded almost in its entirety by Mexico and the United States. NAFTA has given the two countries a unique opportunity to impose needed constraints on the abuse of an international body of water in which both have direct economic interests.

A binational border agency would lose its effectiveness if it became excessively involved in the minutiae of specific violations. Its central task should be to set clear, attainable goals and keep track of compliance. Methodology matters less than results. Local authorities and plant managers should get the greatest possible leeway in meeting anti-pollution demands. The strategic planning of water projects and urbanization schemes will bring greater environmental benefits than the micromanagement of existing installations.

Regulation also has to work both ways.

Throughout the free trade debate, Mexico was depicted as a unilateral environmental villain, befouling the border for selfish short-term gain. NAFTA opponents sent Congressmen videotapes of fouled Mexican streams flowing into pristine U.S. borderlands. Ross Perot warned about Mexican air pollution billowing north into Texas.

Yet for decades, the greatest border-zone ecological catastrophe has been the crop-killing evaporation of Mexico's share of the Colorado River, caused by upstream diversion for hydroelectric dams and irrigation districts. The one great wetlands reserve of the arid American West—the Colorado River delta—was turned from fecund marsh to lifeless, sun-baked clay. Washington claimed to have resolved this dispute in 1974 by agreeing to build a desalination plant; but the operation took more than 15 years to get going and will only partially limit future damage.

The Rio Grande is also being drained dry by American agriculture and power plants. The choked-off water flow from the north makes industrial contamination along the river's Mexican banks all the more virulent. "The crucial problem on the border is water, and the system is already overloaded," notes Richard Bath, a border environmental expert at the University of Texas at El Paso. "If we have a major drought in the next five years, there is a good question what kind of water—if any—will be reaching Mexico from the Colorado or the Rio Grande."

To be effective, a border environmental agency would need to assert some rational control over rivers hundreds of miles to the north in New Mexico and Arizona, a prospect few locals in those valleys would welcome.

The industrial wastelands of the maquiladora belt present another bilateral challenge. By the Mexican government's own account, at least half of the 2,000 in-bond plants have had serious waste discharge problems. During the NAFTA negotiations, when Mexico was hypersensitive to criticism of its environmental practices, the General Accounting Office sent investigators to study compliance with pollution laws in the maquiladora belt. GAO looked at six recently opened plants, all in industries with a history of pollution problems. Mexican law requires new businesses to file environmental impact statements, including plans for emission controls and toxic waste disposal, as a prerequisite for obtaining Commerce and Industry Ministry permits to operate. According to GAO, not one of the plants—all of them American-owned—had prepared or submitted such a statement. Yet all six had received the necessary permits.

NAFTA worries have already prompted reform. In 1992 Mexico reorganized its inspection corps and checked 138 maquiladoras suspected of violations; 116 were ordered closed until the problems were corrected. (Still, environmentalists contend that violations often resume once offending plants are back in business.) The EPA and Sedesol, its Mexican counterpart, are assembling the first database of hazardous waste movement and storage on the border region. In December 1992, a rare collaboration between U.S. and Mexican border authorities led to the first successful prosecution of an American company for the attempted smuggling of hazardous waste into Mexico. That's the way this traffic moves: the EPA reports that the United States ships more than 50,000 tons of hazardous waste a year across the border to Mexico, while Mexico sends less than 4,000 tons—much of it the same waste reprocessed—back to the United States.

Critics of Mexico's enforcement effort often forget that the maquiladoras are creatures of U.S. economic policy. Customs exemptions were drawn up three decades ago to allow in-bond border factories. The idea was to give jobs to some of the Mexicans who had been booted back across the border after the abrupt shutdown of the bracero program, while retaining close to home the labor-intensive assembly work that was even then moving to Asia. It worked on both counts, and the main beneficiary was American business. Nearly all the materials used in maquiladora production are supplied from the United States. Most of the plants are owned by American firms that benefit from low Mexican wages and a near-complete exemption from local taxes. It was the maquiladoras that lured workers to the border towns in the first place, straining local government resources and contaminating the desert environment. The maquiladoras are a binational phenomenon, and their damage can only be controlled binationally.

Cleaning up this mess won't be cheap. The only promised outlay so far was the Bush-Salinas "billion-dollar" border plan, which actually budgeted just a third of that sum for environmental protection and rehabilitation. Nearly half of Mexico's announced $460 million contribution was earmarked for sewage systems already in the planning stage ($220 million); most of the remainder was for other long-standing projects—road construction ($118 million) and housing developments ($43 million) of questionable environmental virtue.

The Bush Administration's proposal to spend $379 million in 1993 and 1994 was gutted by Congress. Legislators slashed requested appropriations for wastewater treatment (from $200 million to $80 million) and a joint Tijuana-San Diego sewage plant (from $64 million to $32 million), and they eliminated $50 million slated for sewage treatment and potable water systems for American border shantytowns. (Northern Congressmen complained that their ailing rustbelt districts were being asked to subsidize municipal investments in the very part of the nation that will most benefit from NAFTA.)

Even if Congress had funded the entire Bush border proposal, the bilateral plan was plainly unfair. Mexico, with an economy one-twentieth the size of the United States, cannot be expected to match U.S. spending dollar for dollar. Any serious border clean-up will cost far more than $1 billion: border officials and environmentalists have drawn up a reasonable-sounding wish list for some $10 billion in sewage systems, water treatment plants, electric power connections, and border crossings. Toxic waste clean-up might ultimately double that bill.

Salinas, while agreeing to expand NAFTA-related border environmental programs, has asked Clinton to consider underwriting an environmental development fund to finance additional investments on the Mexican side.

Where would this money come from? One popular idea is a new "surtax" on border trade. Surtax advocates point out that increased border traffic demands investments in expensive border infrastructure. They argue that those who benefit from new border services should pay for them. But a new tax on trade—a tariff by any other name—could not be more hostile to the letter and spirit of a free trade pact. It would actually *raise* duties on the half of Mexico's exports that now enter the United States duty free through the Generalized System of Preferences. Penalizing Mexican imports while allowing duty free entry to similar goods from other developing countries would be the ultimate corruption of the NAFTA concept.

A better idea is to tax pollution: fines and even freely traded air emissions rights could pay for local environmental enforcement while providing new incentives for investment in cleaner technology. Toxic waste clean-up, when possible, could be financed by fines on the toxic dumpers; most have violated rules in effect since 1983, and offenders could be identified through system-atic investigation of a kind that the Mexican border zone has never seen.

Still, pollution taxes couldn't pay for billion-dollar water treatment networks and the new bridges and highways needed to relieve border traffic congestion.

Some NAFTA scholars suggested using the tariffs collected during NAFTA's phase-in for this sort of public works investment. Superficially, it is an appealing idea: it applies transitional funding—the U.S. Treasury would soon have to live without Mexican tariff revenues anyway—to NAFTA's transitional costs. The problem is, it wouldn't generate much money. Tariffs on Mexican imports peak at about $500 million in 1994, NAFTA's first year, and dry up almost completely by 2004. And there is competition for these funds: unions say this money would be better spent on worker retraining projects elsewhere in the country.

During the 1992 U.S. presidential campaign, advisors to Salinas and Clinton began discussing the possible financing of border infrastructure projects through a new bond-issuing regional development bank. Strongly endorsed by border state governors and the Congressional Hispanic Caucus, a new North American Development Bank was created by the NAFTA enabling legislation. In 1994 the "NADBank" set up shop in San Antonio, with a branch office in Los Angeles. Like other multilateral banks, NADBank is financed through commercial borrowing on a capital base of loaned taxpayer funds (approximately $400 million provided in equal shares by the U.S. and

Mexican treasuries). About 90 percent of NADBank's lending is earmarked for border-zone infrastructural and environmental projects.

The NADBank should be a lender of last resort, however. The border's binational character offers financing choices not as readily available in Mexico's interior. Viable public border projects can already tap into the state and municipal bond market. Indeed, linkage with American utilities and the creative securitization of receivables has already led to billion-dollar Wall Street deals for northern Mexican power plants and telecommunications projects. The many isolated border communities that are too small to tap the securities markets directly could have their planned new sewage treatment plants "bundled" into billion-dollar issues. Over the long run, property tax reforms and "polluter pays" provisions could make these projects self-financing. The upgrading of Mexico's investment ratings that will inevitably accompany NAFTA will make dollar-bond financing on the southern side of the border much easier than it is today.

Much of the necessary border public works investment could be financed without public funds, through such sources as privately operated bridges and toll roads. Mexico has already built a third of a planned 4,000-mile private highway network—much of it, not incidentally, with substantial American financing. All Mexican trucks will be obliged to use these private toll roads within a few years. The high tolls charged on these new highways have initially discouraged traffic, but in the long term their time and fuel savings will prove economical for users.

Other projects demand a mix of public and private financing. One example is the proposed Monterrey-San Antonio rail line, a private venture that would benefit from federal loans and grants for the upgrading of rail crossings. Another is the expansion of the Tijuana airport, paid for by Mexican government funds and private American and Mexican companies, which is providing a much-needed new air freight service for both Baja California and San Diego County (built right on the U.S. line, the airport eventually will have its own border crossing and customs post). To keep financial costs affordable for border communities, the bonds issued to pay for local infrastructure projects would often need multilateral or U.S. Treasury enhancements similar to those provided to Mexico's restructured dollar debt under the Brady Plan. In all these cases, though, the financing and the revenue would come largely from private sources.

It would be a mistake to let border spending decisions be driven by the existence of a dedicated fund. It would be wiser to identify investment needs in precise detail and then look for financing on a case-by-case basis. And *private* financing—whether directly by business itself, or by local governments tapping the private capital markets—is almost always the best choice. With private financing, the costs are borne directly by the users of this new infrastructure, not by the general taxpayer, nor by every consumer of every product that happens to be shipped into the country from Mexico. Moreover, private financing would concentrate spending on projects that business considers genuinely essential—and ensure that the work would be completed relatively quickly. This could prove not only a boon to the environment, but a low-cost, short-term growth program for struggling border communities from San Diego County to the Rio Grande Valley.

NOTES

Note 1: Though seldom noted in American press coverage, that turn-around was the direct result of Mexico's ban on freelance foreign fishing within its waters. Washington had fought Mexico's policy for years, ostensibly on the basis of philosophical opposition to national controls on migratory species. When the dwindling San Diego fleet ceased to be a political force, the U.S. government bent to pressure from its own coastal fishermen and adopted Mexico's policy as its own.

Note 2: The biggest source of funding for Mexico's air pollution program is Japan, which has contributed \$273 million to combat air pollution in Mexico City and Monterrey.

CHAPTER 8

Lead or Silver: Mexico's "Guided" Democracy

Daniel Patrick Moynihan said flatly in 1992 that a free trade agreement with Mexico "is not possible, because Mexico is not a free society." Freedom House, which judges societies largely by the fairness and regularity of elections, calls Mexico "the most authoritarian state in Latin America outside of Cuba"; it considers the country "partly free," the same ranking it assigns to the manifestly unrepresentative governments of Jordan, Thailand and Peru. Other American observers say six decades of one-party rule have led to flagrant denials of due process and other democratic rights. The USTR's Labor Advisory Committee claims that Mexican laws on child labor, workplace safety, and collective bargaining are systematically and "tragically" violated. Americas Watch, a hemispheric human rights organization, summarized the conclusion of its report on torture and murder by Mexican security forces in the title, "A Policy of Impunity."

The United States is inviting a country like this into a free trade zone?

The first question is whether Mexico can legitimately be considered a democracy.

Successive U.S. administrations have said yes. Mexico's largest opposition parties—one on the social democratic left, the other on the free-market right—both say no. They contend that the ruling party owes its permanence in power to the illegal use of public resources and continual electoral fraud, most flagrantly in the 1988 election that made Salinas president.

Recent election reforms have improved opportunities for opposition vigilance, but the PRI retains control of the autocratic Federal Electoral

Commission and all but three state election boards. Salinas is amending rules that awarded the plurality party in legislative elections an automatic Congressional majority, protecting the PRI against possible opposition coalitions. He can afford to be generous: 31 of 32 Senators and 320 of the lower chamber's 500 deputies are PRI members. On the municipal level, where election monitoring is especially weak, PRI hegemony hasn't been dented: the ruling party controls nine out of every 10 city halls. In the last presidential election, by contrast, at least half the electorate voted against the government. Even the Bush-Baker State Department conceded in 1992 that "the electoral process is still heavily weighted in favor of the PRI" and gave credence to complaints that "sophisticated manipulation and intimidation bolstered the PRI vote and denied opposition victories" in the 1991 mid-term elections.

Mexican elections are not inspiring affairs. In small cities and rural provinces the harassment, spurious detention, and even murder of dissidents remains a fact of Mexican political life. Independent human rights organizations have counted more than 100 deaths from "election-related violence" since Salinas took power. Many of the victims were partisans of the Cárdenista left, killed in confrontations over local election results.

The killings were not coordinated or condoned by the central government, Guatemala-style; indeed, they are a deep embarrassment to the Salinas regime. Some of these clashes originated in bitter, long-standing land tenure disputes and were only incidentally challenges to the PRI's rule nationally. Yet such abuses are an inevitable byproduct of the party's heavy-handed efforts to keep the Cárdenistas out of office. On the local level, where authorities are quick on the trigger and eager to enforce the perceived desires of their distant superiors, this intolerance encourages strong-armed repression. And repressive violence in Mexico is rarely punished.

Several prominent human rights activists and at least a dozen journalists have also been killed in the provinces since Salinas took office. In only a minority of the journalists' cases is it clear that their deaths were reprisals for their work as journalists, and in only a few of those cases were the killers clearly working at the behest of local authorities. Killings of reporters and human rights workers are often the work of local drug mafias and their police-force accomplices, rather than the result of any concerted effort by PRI leaders to silence critics. Still, the effect is the same: the PRI's critics are silenced. The conspicuous failure of federal authorities to halt such abuses—or even to get publicly exercised about them—makes violence an implicit tool of PRI governance. In an atmo-

sphere of generalized intimidation, with a systemic reluctance to pros-
ecute such crimes, these murders make critics think very hard about
public challenges to the established order.

Political control in the capital is a more decorous affair.

Latin American *caciques* gave their enemies a choice: *plomo o plata* ("lead
or silver"). The most effective weapon in Mexico City has long been the
latter. Political reporters are subsidized and controlled by government
handouts, both over the table (as payments to publishers for printing press
releases as news stories) and underneath it (directly into their pockets).
Those who refuse the payoffs lose not only money but access. Opposition
critics, meanwhile, are routinely offered government appointments and
contracts in exchange for silence. Under Salinas, several high-profile opposition figures have succumbed to these temptations (though many more
have resisted). In one typical example, an organizer of independent
election-monitoring missions was offered a lucrative consular sinecure in
Southeast Asia by an official who came to him with detailed knowledge of
his strained personal finances. The quid pro quo was that he would cease
public criticism of the government until Salinas left office. Both sides knew
that the offer's acceptance would permanently compromise the critic's
reputation for intellectual independence, while guaranteeing him—if he
wished—perhaps a decade of high-paid official employment. It was also
understood that by rejecting the offer, as he did, he was inviting the
scrutiny of tax assessors, personal attacks by PRI-aligned news media, and
pressures on friends and relatives with government jobs. He was also
forfeiting future chances for employment in leading Mexican companies,
which dismiss executives at any hint of antigovernment activism.

Some critics in the capital have reason to fear for their safety. In the
last administration, to cite one infamous example, the country's top political columnist was apparently killed on the orders of the chief of
Mexico's FBI—the very official who was later assigned to investigate the
crime. The real problem for most Mexico City opposition activists,
though, is the choice between co-optation and the privations of pariah
status in a society run by small, interwoven elites.

Many defenders of the Salinas regime acknowledge these realities, but
they argue that Salinas and the NAFTA preparation process itself have
made Mexico more democratic. Three of Mexico's 31 states are now run by
opposition governors; before Salinas, none was. Salinas is introducing
reforms that will require limits and public reporting on political campaign
spending. He has set up a semiautonomous commission to investigate
human rights abuses (and later elevated its director, Jorge Carpizo McGregor,

a legal scholar and civil libertarian of recognized integrity, to attorney general). There is greater professionalism in the Mexican press than ever before, an improvement due directly to economic liberalization and decentralization. Cash gifts to reporters from government press offices, a routine practice in Mexico, were recently banned by presidential decree.

Salinas's defenders also point to the president's indisputable personal popularity: his approval ratings have remained in the 80 percent range—even as he radically opened the economy and upended political taboos on issues ranging from land reform and the status of the Catholic Church to relations with the United States. The common accusation that Salinas is imposing his free trade program against the will of a rebellious populace is clearly off the mark.

Yet by the Moynihan standard—which would make NAFTA an exclusively "democratic club"—Mexico would still be blackballed.

The ultimate test of democracy is a government's willingness to be voted out of power. When Nicaragua under the Sandinistas and Chile under Pinochet were passing that test at the end of the 1980s, the PRI was brazenly rigging a majority victory for Carlos Salinas. The exact results of the 1988 election were probably never known—even by Salinas himself. But the PRI never contemplated an admission of defeat. The real challenge to the system was containing the damage: negotiating with the opposition, making the election appear credible outside the country, shoring up the Salinas presidency and halting the erosion of the PRI's electoral base. But a transfer of power was unthinkable, and seems no more thinkable today.

All the Democracy Money Can Buy

The next question: if Mexico isn't fully democratic, by most accepted Western standards, should that automatically exclude it from a free trade association?

No. It is sometimes said that an undemocratic society enjoys an unfair competitive edge in an open marketplace. That is not and cannot be the philosophy of the U.S. government. If political and economic freedoms are mutually reinforcing, as Americans have traditionally believed, then authoritarianism should be a drag on Mexican competitiveness, not an asset. Others make a more narrow point, saying that an undemocratic government can't be trusted to keep its promises in such areas as labor and environmental standards. But even if these concerns were valid, competition between American and Mexican companies will remain a daily reality—even with a free trade agreement.

So the more relevant question is whether NAFTA will make Mexico adhere more or less closely to the letter of its laws.

That, in turn, raises a broader question: will membership in a North American trade pact tend to make Mexico more or less democratic?

Most American analysts think that NAFTA will strengthen Mexican democracy. Many say the economic opening catalyzed by NAFTA will lead directly to the PRI's disintegration. Freedom House argues that "foreign investment dollars now come with democratic values . . . which, as they take hold, exert increasing pressure on the pyramidal structures of Mexican politics." The Heritage Foundation believes that since single-party authoritarianism and free-market capitalism are "incompatible," capitalism will gradually extinguish authoritarianism. The Inter-American Dialogue, a private Washington organization that supports the trade agreement, warns that "for NAFTA to succeed . . . Mexico must open its politics, end electoral fraud, and fully respect human rights." The Dialogue's liberal Democratic leadership also contends that economic integration with the United States will naturally undermine corporatism, embolden the opposition, and put Mexican elections under the unforgiving spotlight of the American media.

There is evidence for all these claims. It isn't a coincidence that the northern border states hold the only consistently competitive elections in the country. The north is the most prosperous part of Mexico, and the least dependent on government spending. The opposition is rooted in an independent-minded (and deeply conservative) middle class, proportionately the country's largest. The economic and cultural influence of the United States is pervasive; the Mexico City political class is considered a distant anachronism. Monterrey, the undeclared capital of Mexican private enterprise, three hours from Texas by car, is the home of Mexico's most independent and professional newspapers. Although Salinas is personally popular in the north, as are his economic programs, the PRI is losing its grip on state and local governments. Many of its traditional levers of power—subservient union bosses, the artful redistribution of tariff exemptions and state contracts—no longer function in a privatized, liberalized economy. The north is also simply more urbanized and literate than the national norm, making for a more independent electorate.

With NAFTA, much more of Mexico will resemble the north. The areas where the PRI remains strongest—the rural backwaters of the central Sierras, the heavily Indian south—are a diminishing part of an increasingly urban, industrialized nation. This traditional Mexico will disappear even faster.

Still, many thoughtful Mexican critics say that the free trade pact will artificially perpetuate the life of a one-party state. Like the Washington-backed foreign debt bailouts before it, NAFTA is seen as another example of Washington's putting stability and economic interests ahead of principles.

Without the foreign capital influx from the free trade deal, the PRI might well have been as vulnerable in 1994 as it was in 1988. And free markets alone do not inexorably lead to multiparty pluralism. Prosperity is a friend to incumbency. The past decade's biggest economic successes—Singapore, South Korea, Taiwan, all countries admired by Mexico's technocrats—are only beginning to edge away from rigid authoritarianism. Many Mexican businessmen attribute Mexico's recent success to the fact that its political system resembles Singapore's more than it does Costa Rica's. Traditional Mexican politicians find the United States excessively democratic—too unpredictable, too decentralized, too undisciplined, too susceptible to mass whim and the influence of an unrestrained press. The conversion of Mexico's elites to free-market capitalism doesn't imply a newfound faith in freestyle Western politics.

But their conversion may be unnecessary. New media outlets, new sources of revenue for opposition fund-raisers, a new sense of regional release from the oppressive hand of the capital—all these forces will profoundly reshape the state of Mexican politics. Blocking NAFTA in the name of democracy assumed that economic hardship would stimulate political reform. That hasn't been true in the past. Indeed, the defeat of NAFTA might have bolstered the most retrograde elements of the ruling party.

Still, it would have been foolish to support the free trade accord on the ground that its Mexican architects are committed democrats. The PRI leaders who embraced the NAFTA cause did not intentionally sow the seeds of their own demise. And so far, they have had no reason to fear that American economic support for Mexico will be contingent on democratic reform. Nor have they been under any pressure to democratize from their most powerful and supportive constituency, local businessmen. To the contrary: democratization is actively opposed by the Mexican business elite.

When Salinas decided to disband the government's newsprint monopoly and curtail its politically corrupting advertising budget, he was fiercely opposed by the newspaper publishers who had profited from those subsidies. When his administration proposed an end to old corporatist rules requiring companies to join government-licensed trade associations, it ran into a firestorm of criticism from Mexico's chambers of commerce and industry. These proud private sector organizations were terrified at the prospect of having to recruit and provide real services to members whose dues now flowed to them automatically.[1]

Most business leaders keep a conspicuous distance from the political opposition—even from the business-minded National Action Party (PAN). (In one celebrated case, a top executive at a Monterrey conglomerate who dared to support a local PAN campaign was forced by his bosses to quit.) The powerful, secretive Council of Mexican Businessmen, a private forum for 36 of the country's richest industrialists, informed Salinas in a closed-door meeting in late 1992 that they disapproved of his practice of negotiating with the opposition after contentious local elections. This willingness to seek negotiated solutions to local political conflicts "is a symptom of weakness," the business leaders reportedly told Salinas.

The Council's views are crucial: it has far more political clout than such formal pillars of PRI corporatism as the senior union leadership and the national farmworkers federation. The Council was one of the few groups consulted by former President Miguel de la Madrid about his choice for a successor; their favorite, Salinas, who got the job, would later institutionalize this consultation, sending his own cabinet's presidential aspirants to be vetted in Council question-and-answer sessions. Many of the winning bidders in privatization sales have also been Council members. Throughout the NAFTA negotiations, the Council was highly successful in protecting its interests, achieving permanent or transitional advantages for its banks, breweries, glassworks, cement factories, and broadcasting operations.

In February 1993, many of the Council members, plus a few select outsiders, attended a now-notorious dinner party at the home of Antonio Ortiz Mena, a former finance minister and past president of the Inter-American Development Bank. Each dinner guest was asked by Salinas to contribute an average of $25 million to the party's 1994 presidential campaign. According to the PRI, pledges from the 29 guests ranged from $4 million to $70 million—the last from Emilio Azcarraga, the multi-billionaire television magnate—for a reported total of $750 million.[2]

Such huge requests may have seemed reasonable to men whose fortunes had doubled or trebled during the Salinas years. By some estimates, the holding companies controlled by the PRI's dinner guests generate one-quarter of Mexico's gross domestic product. More startling than the amounts solicited was the PRI's unapologetic public defense of the event as an integral part of the Salinas reform package: private fund-raising is necessary, party officials explained, to "separate the party from the state." Still, when the local furor about the "millionaires' banquet" was reported in the *Wall Street Journal* and on the front page of the *New York Times,* one week after a Mexican business daily broke the story, the PRI reversed course and announced self-imposed limits on individual campaign contributions of 1 million pesos (about $300,000).

The incident was a nice example of the NAFTA paradox: economic liberalization has further concentrated economic power, even as the linkage with the American political system has led to greater transparency. In the past, the PRI would have simply taken $600 million from the federal Treasury. Now it is under pressure to find legal alternatives. Ten years ago most Mexican newspapers wouldn't have printed the story about the fund-raising dinner, and most American papers wouldn't have cared. In 1993, it made headlines on both sides of the border. As a result, the PRI was forced to separate itself a bit farther from the public purse.

'El Derecho Ajeno'
Mexican officials realize that a greater worldwide emphasis on elections and human rights makes such press scrutiny unavoidable. Yet few believe that Mexico's political "idiosyncrasies" are a legitimate subject for foreign inquiry.

This is a point of principle for Mexico. Meddling in a country's internal affairs is not an abstract issue for a nation whose modern history is defined by conflicts with a superpower neighbor. Salinas, criticizing the "extraterritorial" projection of U.S. law in his meeting with President-elect Clinton, pointedly cited the Benito Juárez dictum that is emblazoned on hundreds of Mexican state offices: "Among nations as among individuals, peace comes from respect for the rights of others." The 19th century message remains clear: hands off—and on that basis, maybe we can get along.

For half a century Mexico has opposed intervention in the internal affairs of numerous countries around the globe, even when this stance forced it into an uncomfortable confrontation with the United States. In the late 1970s and early 1980s, this position was modified—to Washington's further annoyance—as Mexico began staking a claim to third world leadership and urging accommodation with leftist insurgents in Central America. Under Salinas, Mexico has reverted to its traditional anti-interventionism, opposing not only the U.S. invasion of Panama but also multilateral efforts to impose sanctions on unconstitutional regimes in Peru and Haiti. When the Organization of American States voted in

December 1992 for the automatic suspension of members who overturn democratic rule, Mexico cast the sole dissenting vote.

This is more than philosophical consistency. The bedrock issue is self-preservation. With the PRI beset by electoral challenges of unprecedented scope and vigor, and the economy increasingly dependent on foreign capital and markets, the government feels acutely vulnerable.

There is no global trend more worrisome to Mexico's government than the routine dispatching of international election monitoring teams. Especially infuriating to PRI stalwarts is the notion that "minority parties"—their reflexive term for the opposition—could appeal to foreigners to resolve local political conflicts. That strikes at the heart of the Mexican system, which functions on the assumption that the PRI-backed president is the ultimate arbiter of all important political and economic disputes.

When Jesse Helms chaired harsh Congressional hearings on Mexican electoral practices in the mid-1980s, the outrage in the Mexican political establishment crossed ideological lines. Conservative businessmen and leftist academics bridled equally at this "interference" in Mexico's internal affairs, which most saw not as impartial fact-finding but as American right-wing retribution for Mexico's Central American policies (which, of course, it was). Even the rightist PAN, the most conspicuous victim of voting fraud, was divided; a few PAN officials cooperated with Helms, but most refused.

Today, when American criticism of the political system comes mostly from the left, it is often dismissed in Mexican government and business circles as a calculated campaign against open trade, rather than a genuine concern for human rights.

The cynicism is understandable. The AFL-CIO now decries the limitations on collective bargaining inherent in a government-aligned union movement; before the NAFTA debate, it was an uncritical ally of the PRI's Mexican Workers Confederation. Human rights organizations didn't scrutinize Mexico's domestic record too closely when Mexico was a reliable supporter of sanctions against rightist regimes in Chile, South Africa, and El Salvador. It was only when Salinas ended this activism, in a rightward tilt against conflicts with Washington, that human rights groups began treating Mexico as fair game.

Mexico's own human rights activists welcomed the new criticism, as did Mexican intellectuals who had long rejected outside scrutiny—especially from the United States. After advocating energetic human rights investigations and election monitoring in Central America, some feel obliged to support similar missions to Mexico as a matter of consistency. Many have also reluctantly concluded that foreign pressure is the most effective way to force domestic reform.

For most American critics, unbroken single-party rule in the three federal branches of government plus almost all states and cities is inconsistent with representative democracy. Mexican officials challenge that assumption, pointing to similar political monopolies elsewhere. Once those analogs were found in the now-unfashionable third world, such as India's Congress Party. More recently, the favorite comparison has been with Japan's Liberal Democrats. Salinas Administration spokesmen note that even the bitterest American criticism of Japanese trading practices rarely extended to attacks on the 38-year LDP stranglehold on political power. Nobody suggested that LDP corruption scandals or its systematic abuse of incumbency privileges should disqualify Japan from membership in the G-7 club of industrial democracies. Is the PRI's situation so different?

Mexicans also note that there is little consistency in American concerns about democratic practices in the developing world. They recall that Washington gave significant financial aid to Central American countries where labor organizers and community activists were decimated by officially sanctioned killers who still enjoy immunity from prosecution. Why impose tougher human rights standards on a country that is requesting trade, not aid?

Some NAFTA critics answer by pointing to Spain and Greece, which had to adhere to Northern European standards of electoral behavior and collective bargaining before gaining entry to the European Union. Mexican officials reject the EC analogy, noting that Mexico is asking only for a tariff and investment deal, not for admittance to a bloc that is openly seeking political unity. That is true, but irrelevant. Washington is making democratic procedures a condition for preferential economic treatment in most of the world (with China the great exception). There is particular pressure to institutionalize these conditions in Latin America, so that a coup or blatant electoral fraud would automatically sever trade privileges and multilateral economic assistance. This linkage is now an explicit tool of U.S. policy in Haiti and Guatemala. Mexico cannot be a blatant exception.

Other Latin Americans have long complained that Mexico was enjoying a U.S. double standard on human rights and election practices. Inviting Mexico into NAFTA without insisting first on real democratic reform could make it hard for the United States to impose such conditionality elsewhere. But too much consistency could be foolish. Rejecting

NAFTA wouldn't have made Mexico more democratic. But it could have made Mexico poorer and more resistant to U.S. influence. NAFTA will speed Mexico's modernization and give the opposition greater access to the court of American opinion. That won't guarantee democratization, but it will make democratization less difficult.

Ultimately, NAFTA is a strategy for Mexico's modernization. It's right to raise questions not just about the agreement's effects on trade and investment flows but about its broader social repercussions. Modernization isn't purely economic: NAFTA's impact on Mexican civil society will be far more significant in the long run than cross-border trucking or an expanded foreign banking presence.

It would have been a mistake, however, to make "democracy" a formal condition for NAFTA membership. Codifying acceptable standards of democratic procedure is difficult, and a genuinely rigorous attempt would probably keep Mexico out. But it would be equally mistaken to ignore the issue in a post-NAFTA world. If the Mexican government consistently fails to honor its own election laws and its promises of political reform, it would amount to a breach of an implicit contract. The United States might well respond by withdrawing from NAFTA. The reason is straightforward: NAFTA is a relationship not just among governments but among peoples. American officials should be able to assume that they are dealing with a government that fairly reflects the popular will.

This hasn't been a big U.S. concern in the past. Indeed, one strong argument for regular scrutiny of democratic standards is the need to persuade the Mexican left that Washington does not have a vested interest *against* Mexican democracy. That was the conclusion of many Mexican observers after the 1988 elections. When the right-wing National Action Party was cheated out of election victories in the mid-1980s, complaints from Capitol Hill and the U.S. Embassy were common. But when the left-wing Cárdenistas became the principal opposition threat, official Washington fell silent. It seemed to the Cárdenistas that by questioning the terms of Mexico's opening to American trade and investment, they had reinforced the natural tendency of the U.S. government to let the PRI dictate the terms of political participation. Many Washington policymakers would privately agree (and approve). The PRI has, after all, given the country decades of stability. And the bias against the Mexican left runs deep in American business and diplomatic circles. At its core is an archaic caricature of Cárdenas and his followers as rabid nationalists intent on expropriating privatized businesses and rebuilding protectionist walls.

But investors have less to fear from Mexican democracy than they have been led to believe.

As a practical matter, potential investors should want to know whether IMF-vetted economic reforms enjoy the consent of the governed. The 1988 election suggested that they did not, raising the issue of their permanence. In the 1991 by-elections, however, Salinas overwhelmed the anti-NAFTA Cárdenistas while reclaiming the anti-statist north. The evidence now is that Salinas and his programs are broadly popular—far more so than either the PRI or the PRI's opponents.

But will his reforms survive? NAFTA's intent is to ensure that they will. Yet that still depends on political support in Mexico. The PRI should win more easily and cleanly in 1994 than it did in 1988, having co-opted the northern right and ridden roughshod over the scrappy but fractious left. And the PRI's candidates will adhere to the Salinas free-market party line. But even if a leftist coalition were to stage an unlikely upset, the foundation for lasting change is in place. In the second half of his *sexenio*, Salinas was able not only to conclude the NAFTA negotiations, but to amend radically the constitution, giving legal status to the Catholic Church, liberalizing foreign investment rules, and ending Revolutionary-era land tenancy laws. None of these measures is likely to be rescinded by a future government. As in the rest of Latin America, there is a broad consensus that there is no alternative to more open markets and greater reliance on private investment. Social democrats returning to power in the region have fought to re-order tax and social spending priorities, not to retreat into economic nationalism.

The best evidence for this is the way the Cárdenista opposition has muted its critique of Salinas's professed goals. Their target is not the Salinas economic program as such but its pace, price and methodology. The most prominent leftist critics of Salinas say that they see deeper economic integration with North America as inevitable. Cuauhtémoc Cárdenas himself echoes this view.

Any viable national opposition challenge, moreover, would require a coalition with small-business elements of the antigovernment right. The common centrist agenda would be democratic reform, not xenophobic protectionism.

Again, the most pertinent question is whether such a coalition will be weakened or strengthened by North American free trade. And the best way to answer that question is to examine the record of Mexico's current free-market government.

An Enlightened Despot?

The democratization controversy is centered on the contradictory public personae of Carlos Salinas himself.

Is he a familiarly "American" good government type, the Harvard man extolled in American editorial pages who sees free-market capitalism as a necessary foundation for democracy? Or—as many Mexicans assert—is he an unapologetic authoritarian who has braked political reform and reconcentrated power in a near-imperial presidency?

"All of the achievements for which Mr. Salinas is praised and respected in U.S. political, financial, corporate and academic circles have been possible only because he has preserved, toughened and enhanced all the authoritarian features of the one-party system," writes Adolfo Aguilar Zinser, a harsh but careful critic of the Salinas regime.

In the same way that Friedmanite free trade purists and Cambridge industrial-policy advocates are both convinced that the Mexican technocrats are kindred spirits, the Salinas government has skillfully projected incompatible political images. Those Wall Street investors who think capitalism must precede democracy welcome what they see as Salinas's Asian-style authoritarianism and his rejection of the freewheeling politics that hampers market reforms in Russia and Brazil. Washington policy analysts, by contrast, tend to view Salinas as a Yankee-style reformer, struggling to democratize despite resistance from a corrupt PRI old guard.

The latter image pervades American editorial praise of the Salinas regime, but the former is closer to the truth. In his first years in office, Salinas often criticized Gorbachev for what he viewed as the historic error of undertaking political reform before the Soviet economy was restructured. The analogy was intentionally clear. Mexican commentators began referring to the Salinas program as "perestroika without glasnost." His most knowledgeable American allies—people like Wayne Cornelius, the University of California-San Diego Mexicanist who was Salinas's Harvard doctoral advisor; Robert Pastor, a former National Security Council director for Latin America and Harvard classmate of the Mexican president; Bruce Babbitt, who became a student of Mexican politics and friend of the Salinas generation as Arizona's governor—spoke candidly about the strategy of consolidating economic liberalization while postponing (or eschewing) political liberalization. Salinas himself repeatedly said that swift democratization would make it harder to forge a political consensus for economic change.

"If you are at the same time introducing additional drastic political reform, you may end up with no reform at all," he told one American interviewer. "We want reform, not a disintegrated country."

The Mexican historian Enrique Krauze, who is in many ways an admirer of the free-market technocrats, likens the Salinas governing style to 19th century enlightened despotism, which "made many changes in the right direction without the participation of the people." For decades PRI leaders openly referred to Mexico's political system as a "guided" democracy, acknowledging that it was not fully representative. What Mexico wants, and doesn't yet have, in Krauze's pleading phrase, is "a democracy without adjectives."

Editorial writers and other American opinion leaders paint quite a different portrait of the Salinas regime. After almost every local election, the new Mexican technocrats are lauded as devotees of pluralism, struggling to introduce democracy along with capitalism. The "new PRI" consistently gets the benefit of the doubt: electoral chicanery is ascribed to old-line party bosses, while offers to review disputed election results and negotiate with the opposition are presumed to be the corrective response of the Salinista reformers.

This has been enormously helpful to Mexico's image in Washington, but it distorts the true nature of the technocrats' rule. Few of the Salinas technocrats would willingly abandon their power, particularly to impose market reforms, simply because of popular resistance. And even fewer of their ardent business supporters would want them to. The technocrats understand that the sacrifices of free trade come disproportionately before the rewards, with all the risk of political upheaval that implies. In the long run, the economists who run Mexico expect free trade to bring prosperity and a permanent consensus that open markets are in the national interest. Genuine democratization could then be introduced by a future administration with little economic risk. Until then, the government's vote-soliciting and vote-counting apparatus will remain under the president's direct control.

And that is the way that Salinas wants it. He was misunderstood from the start, not only by *gringo* academics and editorialists but by many Mexican political sophisticates. It often seemed from press accounts that "Harvard-trained" was his given name. But Salinas was never a Yankee egghead. He rose to power precisely because he was a consummate Mexico City politician. A skilled bureaucratic infighter, steeped since childhood in the culture of the PRI mandarinate, Salinas has worked hard to make both the party and the economy more competitive. Even his

Harvard doctoral research was a thoroughly practical inquiry into the political effects of pork-barrel spending in the countryside.

Carlos Salinas did not become President of Mexico to preside over the dissolution of the PRI's electoral empire.

An irony of the Salinas vote in 1988 is that his strongest support came from the backward Mexico of state-owned communal farms, a system he would later abolish. Areas that exemplify the new market-driven Mexico—the automaking exurbs of Mexico State, the maquiladora districts of Tijuana—voted for Cuauhtémoc Cárdenas, whose surname is a continuing reproach to the Salinas experiment.

The paradox is easily explained: the rural vote is still a delivered vote, while the new industrial voters are more independent and less tolerant of the worsening distribution of wealth. Liberalization and industrialization might be undermining the PRI power base, but that didn't deter Salinas from pursuing his economic goals. And that alone was evidence for some that Salinas was moving toward democratization.

This is not an analysis widely shared within the Salinas government itself. The PRI's technocrats see their challenge as "modernizing" the party, not eliminating it. No political system anywhere has wittingly reformed itself out of power, and the PRI doesn't plan to be the exception.

In the first four years of the Salinas Administration, the PRI faced serious gubernatorial challenges in just six of Mexico's 31 states. In two, the opposition easily won; in the remaining four, where the PRI declared victory, the elections were so clouded by fraud and coercion that opposition protests after the balloting were better attended than their rallies during the campaign. In three of the four cases, Salinas told the proud new PRI governors-elect to pack their bags; he then appointed interim governors (two from the PRI and one from the left opposition) to serve until new elections could be called.

These interventions quelled the opposition protests that had threatened to embarrass the regime abroad. It was quintessential Salinas: bold, astute, effective, and not overly concerned with precedent or legal nicety. Abroad, he was widely applauded for advancing the cause of democracy. Yet he had annulled ostensibly legitimate local elections by executive fiat, reinforcing the pernicious tradition that governors are ultimately presidential appointees. The Mexican government's central failing—its unwillingness to stage credible elections—was implicitly acknowledged but not corrected.

The decision to intervene was based on cold-eyed risk analysis: the inconvenience of lingering political crises during the NAFTA negotiations outweighed the cost of discord within local PRI fiefdoms. But in no significant case did Salinas order investigations into the allegations of fraud or move to punish those responsible. From a president who didn't hesitate to make criminal examples out of corrupt union bosses and insider-trading brokerage owners, this omission sent a mixed message to the party faithful.

In the two cases where the rightist PAN actually elected governors—in Chihuahua and Baja California—the margins were too great to subvert. Any attempt to concoct PRI victories would have prompted mass protests along the U.S. border in the midst of the NAFTA negotiations, a risk that Salinas couldn't afford. The PAN victors were also vocal supporters of the president's economic policies, reassuring investors that pluralism didn't threaten free trade.

The government has not been so broad-minded about challenges from the Cárdenista left. In the many local elections with limited opposition, the PRI still feels compelled to pad slim majorities. The party's famed alchemists—experts at turning the lead of dissent into the gold of eternal incumbency—freely practice their black electoral arts. The difference, mirroring the transformation of Mexico itself, is that their wizardry has been modernized, with subtle computer tricks replacing the polling-place thuggery of the past.

With Cárdenas expected to be the leading challenger again in 1994, any legerdemain needed to ensure another PRI succession would enjoy the unspoken support of local and foreign businessmen and, perhaps, of the conservative leadership of the PAN. The greater danger would be Washington's reaction. President Clinton has promised to make support for democracy a linchpin of U.S. foreign policy. It would be hard to exempt Mexico from the scrutiny that will presumably be applied to other governments in the hemisphere. The anti-NAFTA coalition in the United States will closely monitor the Mexican presidential campaign in 1994, the year the pact is scheduled to take effect. Evidence of systematic ballot-rigging would lead inevitably to demands for NAFTA's abrogation. That threat alone will make the leaders of the "new PRI" more careful than their inward-looking predecessors.

"You have to have a system in which economic integration and modernization runs parallel to political modernization," says the novelist Carlos Fuentes, a member of Mexico's government-appointed human rights commission. No longer, Fuentes notes, can the government rig elections "with impunity, with the attitude that these are our local traditions, and nobody cares what happens in Mexico in any case. Today a Mexican election triggers worldwide attention, even in remote states like Guanajuato and San Luis Potosí. So you can't get away with it anymore. President Salinas will sooner or later have to accept the need for a clean democratic system."

Analysts who view Mexico from afar, including both critics and admirers of the Salinas regime, often put too much emphasis on the power of the president and the governing elite, and too little on the strength and demands of forces outside the system. This is in part the legacy of Mexicanist scholarship, now outdated by a generation, that describes a disciplined pyramidal system topped by corporatist cadres and supported, if only by acquiescence, by a largely rural, semiliterate work force. It also slots nicely into more recent simplifications of Mexico as an economic and political laggard being dragged into the future by a technocratic elite.

But at every point in the past decade where the system has moved in a democratizing direction—by acknowledging an opposition victory, granting more television time to minority parties, revamping the voting register—it has been a belated and reluctant concession to grass-roots pressure. When the opposition solidly wins a state or municipal election, despite its overwhelming disadvantages in campaign funding and media access, overturning that result is more trouble than it is worth especially when the foreign press is watching.

"The Mexican political system is an anachronism," Fuentes says. "It's archaic, it's immoral, it's self-defeating. And it's easy to remedy: one person, one vote, and be sure that that person and their vote are registered, and that there are no other ballots cast from the graveyard. We have to clean up the electoral system, or we will get in trouble economically. There will be greater attention from the world whether we like it or not. So it is up to us to reform ourselves, instead of having others dictate reform."

The Other Chicago Boys

As democratizers, the technocrats benefit from the contrast with their elders. The PRI's founders came to power by force of arms; later, they viewed elections as staged referendums legitimizing the perpetuation of corporatist rule. The idea that renegade ex-PRI leftists could take control of a state government by winning at the ballot box is anathema to the older generation.

Some of these PRI "dinosaurs" still lumber about the political landscape, but it is a myth that they are the technocrats' implacable enemies. They are canny survivors, characterized by servility, not ferocity. Most prominent is the redoubtable Fidel Velázquez, the 93-year-old union boss, whose refusal to die during the Salinas *sexenio* has helped the president limit wage increases and postpone the inevitable implosion of the government labor bloc. The few labor chieftains who dared to challenge Salinas and his team were crushed by jailings, political coups, tax audits, and even military intervention. Resistance was tellingly slight, and more disciplined subalterns were quickly installed in their place.

The real problem with the PRI old guard was not that it was undemocratic but that it couldn't deliver. Corruption and ossification, plus the unfamiliar demands of the media age, had weakened their control of their own constituencies.

It's no coincidence that the labor sectors where Salinas cracked down hardest—the oil workers, the national teachers union, northern border bosses—had been unwilling or unable to turn out the vote for candidate Salinas in 1988. Salinas has since methodically replaced these dysfunctional powerbrokers with grass-roots committees and business-led political coalitions. A barrage of professional television advertising—for the party and for the president's economic programs, a distinction often lost on the viewer—has given the Salinas presidency the culture of a permanent campaign. The PRI machine has been modernized, not dismantled.

The facile dichotomy between repressive dinosaurs and reformist technocrats has little relevance to the real world of Mexican politics. At the end of 1992, for example, Salinas ordered a change at the Ministry of Governance, the command post for micromanagement of the Mexican political system. The Ministry's functions range from internal security (political surveillance, federal police, detective agencies) to media control (broadcast licensing, circulation supervision, censorship of film scripts, monitoring and massaging news coverage) to electoral engineering (supervising registration and vote counts, trouble-shooting as the executive's liaison with PRI campaign staffs, negotiating afterwards with disgruntled losers).

The original Salinas appointee, Fernando Gutiérrez Barrios, in his late 60s, was one of just two members of the PRI old guard in the cabinet, with a long background in national intelligence services and important political posts, including a state governorship. The 40-something new Governance Minister, Patricio Gonzales Garrido, though also a former governor, has the profile of a Salinista technocrat, with a graduate degree and close relationships with his generational peers in the financial elite. Yet the switch at the top was universally understood to be a move toward a tougher political line in preparation for the 1994 presidential elections. Gutiérrez Barrios was known throughout his career for his conciliatory approach to the disaffected left. Gonzales Garrido is a very different character. As governor he tried to ban unfavorable press coverage and presided over some of the bloodiest local election conflicts in recent years; now, as Governance Minister, he suggested that opposition parties lacked the "maturity" to participate in election supervision.

Francisco Ruíz Massieu, a leading PRI political strategist and very much a part of the inner circle, is another representative hard-liner. As governor of Guerrero in 1988, he delivered that crucial coastal state to Salinas in what appeared to be a brazen reversal of a Cárdenas victory. (While national PRI leaders were conceding defeat in the state, the governor and his local apparatus "reclaimed" Guerrero with a late rural vote swollen by multiple voting and purged of opposition ballots.) Ruíz, whose technocratic authoritarianism is admired by business leaders, argues that continued PRI rule is essential if Mexico is to succeed in its quest for capital. Foreign "confidence" in Mexico is based not just on economic performance, but on the "permanence" of its political system. As he told visitors to his state in 1991: "Mexico is a reliable country because it is predictable."

Many new-generation PRI politicians accept the need for electoral accountability. Yet even they usually defend the concept of continued rule by one party. The real question for this more idealistic faction is whether that party will be kept in power by corruption or by votes. Mexican cynics would retort that in the PRI's case, the answer is both. For true-believing PRI reformers the choices are mutually exclusive: any mobilization of state resources to win elections is thought to be a fair use of the perks that sustain incumbent regimes everywhere. So if the PRI wins elections with real votes, it is by definition no longer corrupt.

A little finagling is still permitted, however. In U.S. law, evidence of pervasive fraud is reason enough to call a new election. From the PRI's viewpoint, fraud should invalidate an election only if and when it so blatantly pervasive that ordinary citizens are persuaded that the opposition was cheated out of a likely win. If the fraud simply enhances an otherwise inevitable PRI victory, that calls for apologies, perhaps, but not recounts. What matters isn't the election's numerical outcome but its perceived legitimacy.

The obvious American analog to the PRI is a big-city political machine, with its complex web of patronage relationships, district organizations, union affiliates, and electoral rules designed to frustrate challengers. Aguilar Zinser, in a sardonic reversal of the usual bilateral vote-monitoring roles, led a Mexican delegation to observe the 1992 U.S. general election in Chicago. Precinct captains told the Mexicans how the city enforced party discipline by skewing municipal services toward districts with strong Democratic turnouts. In Mexico, similarly explicit linkage between public spending and pro-government voting is often denounced by oppositionists as prima facie evidence of electoral manipulation. Aguilar wryly concluded that there were "remarkable resemblances" between Chicago's "one-party system" and Mexico's own.

The superficial resemblances help put the modern PRI in context: as the Chicago of Richard M. Daley is to the Chicago of Richard J. Daley, the Salinas administration is to the PRI monolith of a generation ago. Whether any of those models is a full-fledged democracy is debatable, but they unquestionably share many of the same vices and virtues.

There are also crucial differences. The Chicago Democrats run the ground floor of a triple-tiered edifice. State and federal authorities are often their opposition. They have only marginal control over local media and no influence at all at the national level. If the Cook County machine were national in scope, with the open support of a media conglomerate operating several leading dailies and all three networks, it would more closely resemble the apparatus that Salinas had at his disposal in the most critical electoral test of his presidency: the 1991 mid-term legislative election.

The 62 Percent Solution

It was the final evening of the most intense Congressional campaign in Mexico's recent history. At stake was not only the composition of Mexico's next legislature, but the reputation of the Salinas Administration at home and abroad. The PRI was banking on a solid recovery from its near defeat three years earlier, and the president needed to prove that he had solid support in his quest for a free trade deal with the United States. The vote would be the first and last national referendum on Carlos Salinas and his economic program.

Jacobo Zabludovsky, the veteran anchorman for Televisa, Mexico's only commercial television network, stared stiffly ahead as he opened his nightly news broadcast. His desk was cluttered with the heavy rotary-dial telephones that are among the symbolic trappings of the senior Mexican official.

The lead story that Friday was a bland bulletin from the president's office urging voters to go to the polls. Zabludovsky recited the text verbatim. For the accompanying visual the cameras slowly panned the press release, starting with the presidential seal and finishing with Salinas's flourish of a signature. There was no analysis of the election's importance, no mention of the opposition, no hint that the president had any personal interest in the outcome. Televisa had again offered up a living caricature of a government-controlled press.

For Mexican critics, everything that is wrong with the political system is encapsulated in Zabludovsky's election coverage. Even more than in the United States, television is the country's main source of political news. Televisa's market share is virtually the market itself: all its competition combined, from local and federal government channels to American networks piped in by Televisa-controlled cable, captures less than 10 percent of the national viewing audience. Televisa's iron-willed owner proudly describes himself as a PRI loyalist; as a result, the evening news is dominated by fawning coverage of the daily doings of the president and his ministers. The problem isn't competence: Televisa's international reporting is usually balanced and professional. The problem is the political culture of which Televisa is an integral part.

The print press, though far more diverse than radio and television, is equally compromised, headlining the government's recommended story of the day and living off state ad budgets and under-the-table payoffs to reporters. In election campaigns this complicity is magnified, with opposition leaders receiving only perfunctory coverage. Substantive criticism of government policies is scarcer still. Mexico abounds with articulate, attractive critics on both the right and the left, but their commentary is familiar only to readers of elite journals of opinion—and, in those rare moments when Mexico is in the spotlight, to readers of the foreign press. When the government undertakes radical policy changes like the abolition of communal farm property or the end of anticlerical strictures on the Catholic Church, these decisions aren't debated on the Mexican equivalents of "Nightline" or "Meet the Press." There are no Mexican equivalents to "Nightline" or "Meet the Press." When an opposition candidate scores a historic upset gubernatorial victory, he never receives the media attention that might make him a viable national political figure. When the PRI outspends its rivals by 10-to-1, the press rarely demands an accounting of its funding, or a rationale for the partisan use of government offices, vehicles, aircraft and personnel. The question of fraud in Mexican elections goes beyond the mechanics of voter registration and vote results. Even if Swiss accountants tabulated the ballots, Mexico's elections would take place in an informational void.

Still, with all these advantages, the PRI nearly lost the 1988 election. What was universally acknowledged at the time was the truth in Salinas's pained admission that "the era of one-party rule is over." It seemed inconceivable that Salinas would ever enjoy the power of his PRI predecessors to rule by rubber-stamped decree and hand-pick a successor with minimal public discussion or party input. Yet by the halfway point of his six-year term, Salinas had become the most powerful president in Mexico's recent history, with all the traditional prerogatives of his office restored or enhanced.

From the earliest returns in the 1991 Congressional election, it was clear that predictions of the PRI's demise and Mexico's reformist rebirth were premature. In its 62nd year in power, Mexico's Institutional Revolutionary Party celebrated its longevity by claiming 62 percent of the vote—exactly the margin it had been forecasting with mysterious precision for weeks in advance. Election participation by registered voters also reached about 62 percent, according to the first government reports, remarkably high for mid-term legislative elections in a presidentialist system. This figure was later ratcheted up to almost 70 percent, or 23.5 million voters.

The PRI announced wins in 290 of the country's 300 Congressional districts. It also picked up 30 of the additional 200 seats allotted by proportional representation to second- and third-place finishers. In all, the PRI majority in the 500-member lower chamber jumped from 254 to 320—close to the two-thirds margin Salinas needed to amend constitutional strictures on foreign investment and land reform. The PRI also immediately claimed victory in all six gubernatorial contests that year (including two where it faced attractive, well-organized opponents) and all 32 Senate races. A system ostensibly moving toward open multiparty competition had reverted with a vengeance to its classic formula: *de todas, todas*—winning all of all of them.

The opposition immediately claimed that the PRI's margin was the result of fraud. They also claimed to have won two of the six contested statehouses. No doubt the election was plagued by the familiar vices of Mexican realpolitik: coercion, pliant media, multiple voting, purged and padded electoral rolls, the flagrantly partisan use of public resources. Suspicions increased when it took a full week for the computer banks at the gleaming new Federal Electoral Institute to complete the ballot count. And then when at last it did so—a week late—the figures suggested that 5 million more people had ostensibly turned out in an off-year election for a rubber-stamp Congress than had voted in the presidential race three years earlier.

The PRI couldn't have it both ways: if the 1991 count was accurate, then the opposition was probably right to have claimed that millions of antigovernment ballots had mysteriously vanished in 1988. Subsequent analysis of the 1991 results by independent Mexican experts showed systematic inflation of the government vote in PRI strongholds. Yet the exaggeration of the PRI's support in 1991 seemed to be of a far lesser magnitude than the rigged reduction of the opposition vote in 1988. If in 1988 the panicked PRI had opted for a makeshift "fraud by subtraction," as political scientist Juan Molinar concluded, in 1991 it had reverted to the subtler and more traditional methodology of fraud by addition.

Internationally, the mid-term elections were praised as a vindication of the Salinas program and a tentative step toward democratization. Foreign observers noted that the official results were close to the predictions of independent surveys; in Mexico City, where the government allowed exit polling for the first time, the tallies of pollsters and official ballot counters also closely matched. Complaints about fraud focused almost exclusively on the gubernatorial races in Guanajuato and San Luis Potosí, two states with strong opposition candidates and independent vote monitors.

By the time the *Wall Street Journal* and the *New York Times* published editorials questioning those results, Salinas was already engineering a quiet coup. He quickly replaced the PRI "winner" in Guanajuato with an oppositionist of his own choosing. In San Luis Potosí, he replaced the declared winner with a PRI Senator and scheduled new elections. Though the PRI retained control, the gubernatorial change was a victory for the scrappy 77-year-old San Luis opposition leader, Salvador Nava, who had been challenging one-party rule since Salinas was a teenager. Nava's broad opposition coalition was the biggest threat to the government since the 1988 Cárdenas candidacy. When Nava, battling cancer, announced his retirement from politics in May 1992, Salinas visited his bedside and praised the veteran dissident's tenacity and commitment to nonviolence. Nava's death later that month removed perhaps the only figure capable of uniting Mexico's opposition across ideological lines.

In the legislative contest, most observers shared the State Department's later assessment that "an election devoid of fraud would not have significantly altered the PRI's strong showing." Opinion polls showed that Salinas was genuinely popular, much more so than the PRI itself, with voters responding perhaps more to his vigor and decisiveness than to the content of his reform program. Salinas had also become an adept and tireless campaigner. Equally important were the construction projects, factory expansions, and other visible signs of growth. After a decade of stagnation and drift, Mexico had a new sense of forward motion.

The 1991 election was also the first great test of the community-level public works program known as "Solidarity." Funded by proceeds from privatization sales, the National Solidarity Program brought schools, hospitals, roads and potable water to poor districts that had been ignored during the harsh recession of the 1980s. In contrast to past patterns of bureaucratized largess, local residents helped decide which projects to pursue and were required to contribute both money and labor.

Lauded on the *Wall Street Journal* editorial pages as a "politically neutral" alternative to old-line PRI pork-barrel patronage, Solidarity was anything but: run directly out of the president's office with a $3 billion annual budget, it was expressly designed to recapture the grass-roots support the PRI had taken for granted and lost. Solidarity's origins could be traced back to Salinas's Harvard doctoral thesis, which seemed the work not of an academic economist but of a political scientist—and an unusually pragmatic one at that. His research, conducted in the 1970s, zeroed in on the disturbing (for the PRI) lack of correlation between the government's local spending programs and the strength of its local political support, as measured in polls and in election turnouts. Salinas concluded that these projects failed to help the PRI because they rarely reflected local priorities, didn't involve local leadership, and were mismanaged or abandoned by officials in the distant capital.

Solidarity was designed to remedy this political defect, while providing a personal political base for Salinas. The new program was ceaselessly promoted through billboards, brochures and national television with the president's name and visage, accompanied by a stylized revision of the PRI's tricolor logo. The party's initials, however, were nowhere to be found: this was a presidential program, not a PRI program. In many states, Solidarity had a bigger discretionary public works budget than the local governor (making it easier to cede statehouse control to the occasional successful oppositionist). Salinas advisors boasted about Solidarity's success in luring community leaders away from the left and back into loyalist ranks.

So identified was Salinas with Solidarity that critics claimed to see an emerging cult of personality. Yet they grudgingly acknowledged that it was the most effective recruiting effort in the PRI's recent history. Solidarity was the soul of the new Salinas machine, and presidential aides dropped orchestrated hints that it could be mobilized in the future, if necessary, as the nucleus of a new political party.

The Forgotten Issue

Salinas had set the machinery of the state and party to work building an overpowering and internationally visible mandate for the second half of his sexenio. The results of what his aides advertised in advance as a referendum on the Salinas presidency assured the continuation—and acceleration—of the radical march toward deregulation, privatization and free trade. Yet NAFTA was barely even raised as a campaign issue by the Cárdenista opposition, which concentrated its attacks instead on electoral fraud and the reconcentration of wealth. Opinion polls showed that most Mexicans supported NAFTA. Cárdenas questioned the agreement's timing, detail and negotiating procedures—but not the logic of economic integration itself. The free trade agreement also enjoyed the whole-hearted backing of the second opposition bloc, the National Action Party, which repeated its 17 percent showing of three years earlier. Holding the balance of the non-PRI vote were the tiny *partidos paleros*—the rent-a-party stick figures of old-line Mexican politics—who can be counted on to support any policy promoted by the regime in power.

There was little interest in Washington or on Wall Street in asking hard questions about the legitimacy of the election. Analysts who feared resurgent Mexican populism took comfort from results showing support for Cárdenas plunging from 31 percent in 1988 to 8 percent in 1991. Both those numbers understated the left's true support; the 1991 Cárdenista percentage was also cut by the defection of coalition partners who still exploited the Cárdenas message and name. But the election had exposed the central Cárdenista weakness: the failure to articulate a coherent alternative to the Salinas free-market program. It also underlined the generic difficulties of keeping an opposition coalition energized and intact in a monopolistic political system.

Foreign investors immediately grasped the election's economic message. The securitized Mexican debt instruments known as Brady Bonds traded the week after the elections at a record 62 percent of face value, a gain that erased the losses suffered by creditors when they reluctantly signed Mexico's landmark debt reduction accord 18 months earlier. The de facto endorsement of the Salinas program in the secondary market for

LDC debt was paralleled by the falling yields and rising volume of new Mexican Eurobond issues.

Most spectacular of all was the ascent of the Mexican stock market. In the eight and a half months leading up to the August 1991 balloting, the Mexican Bolsa index climbed by 86 percent—despite a summer slow-down as local investors awaited election results and foreign speculators diverted funds to the roaring exchanges of Buenos Aires and Sao Paulo. At the close of August, with Salinas's hold on power solidified, the market would continue its spectacular rise without interruption until the second quarter of 1992. Much of this expansion was fueled by the biggest out-pouring of American portfolio capital ever channeled toward a single foreign market.

Like Mexican voters, foreign investors were looking at the numbers. The economy was growing at 4 percent a year, after a decade of stagna-tion. Inflation, which hit triple-digit levels in the early 1980s, had dropped below 20 percent. The peso had stabilized; the threat of big devaluations had seemingly disappeared. The trade deficit was growing, but the short-fall was covered by the foreign capital that had been attracted not just by economic fundamentals but by the promise of a free trade pact with the United States.

After NAFTA

Critics say Salinas and the PRI decided to "win the 1988 elections in 1991," and in some brute sense they suc-ceeded. They were also trying to win the 1994 elections in 1991. With a dispirited opposition and a recharged PRI, the odds that Salinas could keep his economic program on track and dictate the selection of Mexico's next president went instantly from even money to a sure bet. And the pressure on Salinas to reform the PRI from within evaporated almost overnight.

Given the weakness of the opposition, the most profound and lasting political reform in Mexico today would be the democratization of the PRI's nomination procedures, beginning with the selection of its presi-dential candidate. Now, the only really important process takes place inside the president's head. Salinas, like his predecessors, runs the PRI like a one-man nominating convention, picking not only his own succes-sor but virtually every governor and most members of Congress.

Here, then, is a fundamental change, long overdue, that Salinas could have implemented unilaterally. All he had to do was relinquish his tradi-tional prerogatives and convene a PRI convention or primary election.

Practically, however, it would have been easier to decree a return to the gold standard. Salinas, like all Mexican presidents before him, realized that without that power he couldn't govern. Otherwise, he would have been a lame duck from the moment he took office. In a system where presidents emerge from a dense party bureaucracy, with almost no independent political identity or personal power base, and are then limited to a single six-year term, they need extraconstitutional powers to command the loyalty of their subalterns. The president's complete control over his lieutenants' political future keeps his troops in line. The cult of the *destape* is what sustains Mexican presidential power. Democratizing the selection of the presidential candidate cannot be undertaken in isolation. It would require a whole package of fundamental reforms, including basic changes in the PRI itself (making it a genuine political party, not a ministry of elections) and an end to the constitutional prohibition of re-election (ostensibly, an anti-dictatorial measure that grew out of the Revolution and that still enjoys strong popular support).

Salinas may be a reformer, but he is also a prisoner of the system which placed him in power.

The 1991 PRI landslide reassured NAFTA's supporters that Salinas's chosen heir would triumph in 1994. But there were dangers lurking in the rubble. The great achievement of the Mexican political system over the past 20 years has been its success in channeling dissidence—including most of the radical left—into the conventional currents of electoral politics. The resultant political stability has helped Mexico survive the economic shocks of the 1980s and build a foundation for future growth. Now, the claim of a monolithic election victory persuaded many oppositionists that the government would never cede power at the ballot box. The Cárdenas forces, regrouping for 1994, are already contending that Salinas is engineering a succession that will perpetuate his own influence in the next PRI administration, keep foreign-investor-oriented economic policy as the government's main concern, and indefinitely postpone democratic reform. "When President Salinas cautions about the dangers of implementing radical political reforms *before* his economic reform program has had a chance to take hold, he is not really suggesting that once the economic transition is accomplished he will proceed with democratization," Aguilar Zinser argues. "In fact, economic liberalization is consistent with and dependent on the preservation of political authoritarianism."

That's debatable: liberalization should ultimately undermine single-party rule, despite efforts to mimic the command-and-control capitalism of the East Asian tigers. It is crucial to distinguish between what Salinas and his lieutenants want and expect to happen after NAFTA, and what is likely to happen. Mexican opposition forces will continue to press for a more open and accountable political system. Economic dynamism and decentralization should make their quest less difficult.

But Aguilar is surely right to say that democratization—defined as an end to one-party rule and a genuine commitment to the separation of powers outlined in Mexico's constitution—has never been Salinas's intent. PRI technocrats freely admit that an open economy would unleash forces that may be difficult to control. But their only response has been to make the party so formidable that it can withstand the stresses of a modern economy.

The counterpart to this political strategy can be found in Mexico's industrial policy. Through "directed" deregulation, the Salinas government has deliberately encouraged the formation or restoration of dozens of near monopolies—both regional and sectoral—that have the potential to become centers of Mexican power in an integrated North American economy. Single companies control industries such as broadcasting, brewing, glass-making, cement, copper-mining, shipping, aviation and telecommunications. In other critical sectors—banking, steel, construction, forestry—the market is dominated by just two or three firms.

These private-sector giants have been nurtured by state intervention: licensing agreements, government sales orders, assistance in debt workouts, trade policy favors, and lucrative privatization deals. Some are old dynasties that survived the debt debacle of the early 1980s; others are new business groups that emerged later. All are in the front ranks of the PRI's new corporate contributors. What they also have in common is that they are seen as viable players in the new North American marketplace. All have a clear willingness to divest deadwood, acquire technology, pursue strategic alliances, and crush local competitors. Some of these companies would still succumb to the competition inherent in a bigger, more dynamic marketplace. Others would likely seek shelter in mergers. Most of them, though, have the necessary skills and critical mass to survive the challenge of American capitalism, and Mexican leaders see no reason to hasten their demise.

Similarly, the Salinas government knows that a corporatist party cannot survive the systematic dismantling of subsidies, regulations, and state industry. There will be fewer jobs and contracts to hand out. Subservient media monopolies will begin cracking apart. Stultifying centralization will gradually give way to a more regionalized and spontaneous brand of politics.

Salinas is preparing the PRI for this new reality with sophisticated media campaigns, better candidate recruitment, and grass-roots organizing. Business donations should underwrite up to $1 billion in election expenses—enough to run 10 U.S. presidential campaigns. The ruling party still demands the loyalty of schoolteachers, the military, all primary industrial unions, and the vast civil service. Government officials are still working overtime to divide and discourage their amateurish opposition.

Mexico's sexagenarian is gearing up for a few more turns of the wheel: free trade may make its task of perpetuating its power more difficult, but it won't make it impossible.

Salinas versus Cárdenas: What Really Happened? The July 1988 presidential election was a watershed event in modern Mexican political history, but it still isn't clear exactly where the waters parted or which way they are flowing. What is certain, though, is that the election provided unflattering insights into the nature of PRI rule, and indications of what could be in store if the 1994 succession proves unexpectedly difficult.

Just as there is a benevolent myth about the democratizing intentions of the Salinas technocrats, there is a black legend about the perfidious PRI of old. When press reports about Mexican vote-rigging started surfacing in the mid-1980s, many foreign policy sophisticates assumed that this was nothing new: the interest of American editors in Mexican politics might be a novel development, but not the system's recourse to blatant, systematic fraud. In 1988, when the PRI handed Carlos Salinas de Gortari the presidency in an election marred by hundreds of polling-booth irregularities and a suspiciously delayed vote count, pundits and diplomats commonly reported that this was Mexican business as usual.

It wasn't. In the past the PRI machine had routinely inflated victory margins to disguise low voter turnout and discourage future challengers. But fraud wasn't essential to those victories. It had been four decades since the PRI faced a serious national opponent. The 1982 presidential contest offered one lackluster opposition candidate; in 1976, the PRI had no opposition at all.

All that changed in 1988. For the first time since its foundation the ruling party was under attack from well-organized opposition forces on both the left and the right. The PRI's central ideological conceit—that all normal democratic discourse took place under its big tent—was damaged irretrievably even before the balloting took place. The party's aura of invulnerability faded further with the designation of Salinas, who had alienated PRI unions as the government's free-market economic strategist. Several disgruntled labor leaders encouraged rank-and-file defections to the dissident candidacy of Cuauhtémoc Cárdenas, the son of the president who had nationalized Mexico's oil industry.

Salinas said he wanted a clean victory, but party bosses concluded that it would not be—possible.

It is difficult to see how Salinas—or any PRI designee—could have won a majority legitimately. Mexico was then in its sixth painful year of zero growth. The oil market had collapsed, bringing the peso and wages down with it. Mexico was battling the unfamiliar demons of South American-style hyper-inflation. In 1985, Mexico City had suffered the worst earthquake in its 800-year history. The government was roundly blamed for lax building-code enforcement, inadequate disaster relief, and seemingly deliberate underesti-mates of the death toll (about 30,000 died, triple the number officially reported).

Compounding these troubles was the government's political clumsiness. President Miguel de la Madrid had won praise in world financial circles for doggedly maintaining Mexico's debt payments and setting the economy on its new privatizing course. But at home, his economic orthodoxy was far less popular. De la Madrid seemed stiff and aloof, governing by decree and disappearing during crises like the earthquake. Narcotics scandals and ballot-rigging had tarnished his carefully nurtured image as a moral crusader. His increasingly rare public appearances elicited whistles and catcalls, and PRI union bosses publicly criticized him in a way they had never dared with his predecessors. By tolerating messy electoral frauds in the north, De la Madrid had re-energized the right-wing opposition. By enacting overdue economic reforms, but with little apparent concern for their impact on the working poor, he drove the PRI's nationalist left into the arms of the opposition. And Salinas, as De la Madrid's handpicked heir, was burdened with the unavoid-able pledge of "continuity."

Few experienced observers ever believed the PRI's claim to a 50.4 percent victory. Fewer still believed official reports of a 50 percent voter turnout, an inexplicably steep decline from recent national and local elections.[3] Accounts of irregularities—from tampered voter rolls to the wholesale theft of ballot boxes—were too numerous and credible to be dismissed. More persuasive still was the stunned gloom in PRI headquarters on election night. Party functionaries thought that Salinas received fewer votes than the official tally would eventually show, and that Cárdenas did better than the 31 percent later reported. Many knowledgeable people felt that Cárdenas won; others believed that Salinas had managed a narrow plurality, but that the PRI feared the margin was too narrow to make the victory credible.

To believe that the PRI resisted its own deepest instincts, that it stood virginally aside while the voters almost dispatched it to oblivion, requires an act of faith. Like most vices, fraud is addictive. Even elections that can be won cleanly invite intervention. Results must square with previous fraud-inflated tallies. In the PRI's case, as with many political monopolies, votes are often fabricated not merely to win elections, but to rack up margins formidable enough to sustain a mythos of invulnerability. That makes the habit hard to break: if the vote-rigging machinery is switched off from one election to the next, the results will show a sharp drop in pro-government turnout and a parallel surge in opposition support.[4] And since the opposition suspects the system of fraud anyway, their presumption even in a tight loss is that they really won—or at least came close enough to expect victory from an all-out campaign next time.

As the country entered new election six years later, nobody could say what the real results of 1988 were. Many thousands of ballots were stolen. Those that survived were locked in the basement of the PRI-controlled Congress and later incinerated, making a recount impossible. Cárdenas victories in states like Guerrero, which the PRI had originally conceded, were reversed in the final tally. His surprisingly broad national appeal was evident in first-place finishes in places like Tijuana, Toluca and Mexico City, not the natural constituencies of an agrarian populist but areas with unusually thorough opposition poll-watchers.

The key to 1988 was the north, where the PAN alleged widespread PRIista fraud in PAN strongholds. Salinas was far more popular in northern Mexico than the PRI itself. He attracted broad support among voters who had been casting protest votes over the previous five years for the conservative, anti-government PAN. Even so, it's hardly likely that Salinas carried virtually every border-state district east of Baja, as the PRI claimed. And the PAN probably did better than its 17 percent official showing. Particularly question-able was the 39 percent turnout reported in the PAN's Chihuahua stronghold, which compares poorly with the 60 percent turnout reported in the 1991 Congressional elections.

This pattern was mirrored in Michoacan, the Cárdenista bastion, where turnouts were reported at 38 percent in 1988 and 68 percent in 1991. Nationally, in the hardest-fought presidential election in the country's history, only 18 million people were officially reported to have voted, compared with 23.5 million in the less important 1991 by-elections. If the 1991 legislative election was as squeaky-clean as the government contends, then the 1988 presidential vote was even more crooked than critics have claimed.

It is commonly asserted that "most Mexicans" think that Cárdenas actually won. In truth, most Mexicans believe that there was fraud but that Salinas still placed first. In independent polls, consistently more voters say they voted for Salinas than for Cárdenas. Voters in states where Cárdenas won handily—Michoacan, Mexico, Morelos, Guerrero, Baja California—may also think that Cárdenas won nationally. But in the conservative PANista north, many people find it inconceivable that the Cárdenas message would have broad national support.

In the election's messy aftermath, the PAN briefly held the balance of power: a strong third-place finisher. It also had the best opposition vote-monitoring network. If the PAN had declared at that point that its independent results showed that Cárdenas was the clear victor, the momentum against the PRI might have been unstoppable.

The PAN said no such thing. Instead it blandly claimed victory for itself, tarnishing the credibility not only of the official vote count, but of the independent assertions of the opposition. Privately, senior PAN leaders said their own numbers indicated that Salinas won, albeit narrowly. This reading may have been skewed by the PAN's concentration in northern middle-class districts where Salinas support was unusually strong and Cárdenas's unusually weak. But the PAN's attitude may also have reflected their deep antipathy toward the southern, union-based, anti-clerical populism that Cárdenas personified. Given a choice between Salinas the free-market capitalist and Cárdenas the tribune of the poor, the PAN leadership would opt overwhelmingly for Salinas.

And that's just what they did. Within a year the PAN had abandoned its combative stance and embraced the Salinas agenda as its own. That's because it was: the PAN had always advocated freer markets and better relations with Washington and (especially) the Vatican. The PAN gave Salinas the congressional votes he needed to amend the Constitution; it even embraced his electoral "reform" plan, under which the plurality vote-getter in Congressional elections (read: the PRI) would be automatically assured of a majority. PAN elders boasted privately that they were "governing from within."

The post-electoral alliance of Salinas and the PAN led to a revisionist view of the 1988 vote as an endorsement of free-market economics. But the election wasn't contested primarily on economic policy grounds. It was a referendum on continued PRI rule. But the opposition was fatally divided, ideologically and geographically. And once Salinas took office and began gaining real popularity, fewer and fewer Mexicans were inclined to question the legitimacy of his presidency.

The lesson learned by the PRI in 1988 is that a narrow majority in a credible election is far more useful—domestically and internationally—than a fraud-tainted landslide. Hence their new willingness to tolerate independent poll-watchers (including foreigners!) and campaign spending limits. This reformist resolve will vanish if an unexpectedly weak economy and strong opposition again combine to threaten the PRI with defeat. The PRI wants cleaner elections if and when it is sure it will win, not because it is committed to pluralism.

Mexico's New Left

Too frequently, American support for Salinas and NAFTA was predicated on fears of a resurgent, economically irresponsible anti-American left.

During the 1988 presidential elections, the nearly victorious Cárdenistas were widely depicted as nationalist demagogues exploiting mass discontent after a decade of recession. In the 1990s, as NAFTA focused new attention on Mexican politics, the demonization of the left continued apace. One often-quoted commentator, M. Delal Baer of the Center for Strategic and International Studies, warned in the *Wall Street Journal* that "a cast of anti-*gringo* grudge bearers, socialist holdouts, and drug lords waits in the wings" hoping that Salinas and NAFTA would fail. (The slanderous implication that anti-NAFTA activists were backed by cocaine dealers betrayed willful ignorance of both the opposition and the police-protected drug cartels.) Liberal Democratic champions of the agreement, such as Senator Bill Bradley and U.S. Trade Representative Mickey Kantor, warned that NAFTA's failure might bring to power a recalcitrant anti-Yankee left. Even those Mexiphiles who welcomed the emergence of a vibrant left-of-center opposition tended to see the Cárdenistas as anachronistic populists waging an otherwise admirable campaign for democratization.

There was a Washington consensus, then, that NAFTA's defeat would have been a victory for xenophobic nationalist ideologues, who once in power would have shut the door to free trade and have re-expropriated privatized industries.

That consensus was wrong on two counts.

First, as a practical matter, NAFTA's defeat would not have propelled the left into power.

True, NAFTA's collapse would have been a victory for Cuauhtémoc Cárdenas, in that he opposed the accord and argued that Salinas had become irresponsibly dependent on Washington. But Mexican business opposed Cárdenas fiercely, and Salinas and his operatives had a firm grip on Mexico's electoral machinery. Disarray within the Cárdenista coalition since 1988 tarnished Cárdenas's credibility as a manager and leader, and he failed to articulate a compelling alternative to Salinas's ambitious free-market strategy. If NAFTA had been rejected by the U.S. Congress it would most likely have provoked a nationalistic backlash. But that wouldn't have made the PRI any more inclined to surrender power. Nor was the right-wing opposition ready to back the Cárdenista left in a unified anti-PRI coalition.

Second, even if Cárdenas had a chance to be elected, he would have been unable—and probably unwilling—to pursue economic policies radically different from those of the Salinas government.

In countries as diverse as Venezuela, Chile, Argentina and Colombia, politicians with solid social democratic credentials have also been cutting subsidies, selling off state industries, and lowering trade barriers. In these days of global competition for markets and capital, they don't have much alternative.

That is not to say that a Cárdenas government wouldn't have done some things differently. Throughout Latin America, there is an emerging consensus that the privatizers of the 1980s neglected health and education and haven't adequately regulated newly autonomous industries like telecommunications. A Cárdenas government would have applied correctives, but within a competitive capitalist context. The era of import-substituting, deficit-financed, state-directed growth is over, and the Latin American left knows it.

In 1990, in an open letter to the Mexican Congress, six center-left opinion leaders criticized NAFTA in terms that closely reflected Cárdenas's views. They were careful to say that they didn't oppose freer cross-border trade in principle. But they objected to the NAFTA negotiations on domestic political grounds: there was no legislative oversight, they complained, and almost no informed public debate of the issue. They also feared that the agreement would make Mexico a cheap labor source for an otherwise dynamic North America. And though they didn't say so explicitly, they revealed deep misgivings about any development strategy that relied on the long-term cooperation of Washington.

The letter's authors were writers Carlos Fuentes and Carlos Monsiváis; academic commentators Adolfo Aguilar Zinser, Jorge G. Castañeda, and

Lorenzo Meyer; and Jesus Silva-Herzog, the respected former finance minister (1982–86), who was later named ambassador to Spain and minister of tourism under Salinas. All save Monsivaís are, like Salinas, bilingual cosmopolitans who move easily between Ivy League faculty lounges and Mexico City political salons. They are to varying degrees left of the Mexican center, but they resent being caricatured as knee-jerk nationalists.

Most of their concerns are strikingly similar to those later expressed by Clinton and other pro-NAFTA Democrats. "We fully agree that closer and expanded integration of the American and Mexican economies is inevitable," the six stated in their 1990 letter. They urged that NAFTA "be pursued slowly, carefully and responsibly," with the addition of a "social charter" addressing labor rights, workplace safety, environmental issues, and consumer protection.

Immigration should also be on the NAFTA agenda, they argued, "since labor is our main competitive advantage in the area of services."

Like many American critics, they said NAFTA would be a failure if it didn't narrow the gap between American and Mexican incomes: "Low Mexican wages cannot be a permanent feature of North American economic relationships. That comparative advantage is too costly for everybody involved: too humiliating and unproductive for Mexican dignity and economic development; too costly in jobs and welfare for American and Canadian workers; too destructive for our common environment and civilization."

Those concerns were partly addressed by the many studies showing that NAFTA would elevate Mexican wages and by the side agreements on labor and environmental standards. Cárdenas said he no longer objected to the agreement itself but to what he viewed as its undemocratic ratification process at home. His 1994 presidential platform was no longer expected to call for NAFTA's abrogation.

A decade ago the left's political task was easier. The election of 1988 was a referendum on the past. All three presidential campaigns shared the premise that the Mexican economy had been badly mismanaged for at least a decade. Private sector supporters of Salinas and the PAN said things started going wrong under the unabashedly "statist" Echeverria administration (1970–1976). Critics on the Cárdenista Left focused on the López Portillo (1976–1982) decision to make Mexico a leading oil exporter. They reminded voters of their insistent (and prescient) warnings that foreign-financed oil development would lead to debt and dependence on volatile world markets. But everyone agreed that the economy was in a shambles.

Salinas, by boldly upending trade barriers and political taboos, was striving to make the next presidential election a referendum on the future. That forced the Cárdenistas to identify not just what they were against, but what they were for. And on that, there was little consensus. When the Zapatista National Liberation Army stormed out of the hills in January 1994, they represented for the democratic left both an opportunity and a threat. By spotlighting the broken promises of the institutionalized revolution, the Chiapas radicals put the issue of social justice—the left's trump card—back on the electoral agenda. But they challenged Cardenas's assumption of moral leadership and forced him and his allies to either condemn or condone armed insurection. Either way they lost—by alienating part of their own core following, or by frightening urban moderates angry at the PRI but even more disturbed by the prospect of civil disorder. There were more of the latter than the former, and most ended up voting for the right-wing opposition instead.

The poor third-place finish by Cardenas in 1994 effectively ended the career of the only unifying force in Mexico's democratic left. The strong second-place showing by the conservative National Action Party seemed to consolidate the PAN's traditional position as the only viable opposition alternative. But there is a vacuum on the port side of the Mexican spectrum that will be filled by some new restructuring of the post-socialist left, and its leaders will have a real chance to make a run for power in the year 2000.

Outside Mexico, Cárdenas voters were incorrectly assumed to form a not-quite-literate rural bloc in rebellion against Mexico City technocrats and nostalgic for the PRI's paternalistic, corporatist past. Salinas supporters, by contrast, were thought to be motivated by their comprehension and endorsement of the need for free-market economic reform. Yet in 1988, poor rural voters were the only solid Salinas faction, while the white-collar urban vote was split between Cárdenas and the pro-business PAN's Manuel Clouthier. Union voters, meanwhile, were divided between Cárdenas and the PRI. Ernesto Zedillo did better in 1994 with the educated, urban vote, and the PAN won support that had gone to cardenas six years earlier, but the pattern basically held: the PRI won where people are poorest and least educated, and where the opposition still can't field credible local candidates and experienced election officers.

As Mexico becomes steadily more literate and urbanized, the left should regain lost ground. There will be more independent union support for an opposition alternative as the PRI labor bloc disintegrates. The left should also get aid from another seemingly unlikely source: the Catholic Church, now allowed by Salinas's reforms to engage in more open political activism. In the north the Church is staunchly conservative. But in Chiapas and the rest of the poor rural south the Catholic hierarchy's foes are PRIista landlords, and the enemies of their enemies are becoming their friends. Just as the collapse of communism is ridding liberation theology of its fellow-traveler taint, an alliance with reformist bishops could at last remove the stigma of rabid anti-clericalism from Cárdenism. The PAN, paradoxically, will remain limited by its legacy of confessionalism. It is harder for the PAN to transcend its rigid Catholicism than it is for the left to abandon Marxist dogma.

The Cárdenas coalition stretches from its working-class base to the liberal professional class (Cuauhtémoc's father, Lázaro, the president who national-ized the oil industry, remains as mainstream a historical figure as Franklin Roosevelt). It also includes a small but critical corps of ex-Marxist activists. Like the left everywhere else, it is struggling to redefine itself as something more than the opposition to the free-market right.

The demise of Soviet Communism was a windfall for the PRI: the notori-ously fractious Mexican Marxists had only recently regrouped as a modern Eurocommunist opposition when they threw in their lot with Cárdenas. Then the Berlin Wall fell. The theoreticians who once saw Cuba or East Germany as a credible model now started reassessing West Germany and newly prosper-ous Spain. Others shunned overarching ideologies entirely and began concentrating on grass-roots community organization. No longer could a vaguely defined affinity for socialist ideals unify the Cárdenas forces in an electorally useful way.

Still, the business-government alliance of the Salinas PRI leaves room to the left that only the heirs of the Cárdenas alliance can fill. Even the government's pollsters give the left a solid hold on at least a quarter of the electorate. Nineteen ninety-four was not Cárdenas's year, but it is only a matter of time before his supporters coalesce into a viable social democratic opposition. When they do, they will represent a real threat to the PRI, but not to the United States. To the contrary: as the experiences of countries as diverse as Chile and Korea have shown, a change in political command that redirects but doesn't reverse economic policy reinforces the sense of national consensus that is a requirement for stability and progress.

NOTES

Note 1: Their rebellion succeeded: the law mandating business association membership was renewed for another five years. The trade-off was that the government could continue to limit these groups' political autonomy with little need for apology.

Note 2: By contrast, the Clinton and Bush campaigns cost about $100 million each. The largest single Democratic donation in 1992 was $400,000 from the Steelworkers.

Note 3: Both those 50 percent figures were leaked to foreign reporters at a time when the government was still telling the local press and opposition that it hadn't yet counted initial returns.

Note 4: This happened early in the De la Madrid administration, which chose not to deploy vote-padding squads in its first round of municipal elections. The result was a jarring string of PRI defeats.

CHAPTER 9

The

Tex-Mex

Axis

When President Bush organized a ceremonial signing of the North American Free Trade Agreement in October 1992, he summoned Carlos Salinas and Brian Mulroney to San Antonio. When President-elect Clinton decided to reiterate his support for NAFTA in a pre-inaugural meeting with Salinas three months later, he held the talks in the governor's mansion in Austin. Both meetings were hosted and applauded by Texas business and political leaders from both parties and all of the state's huge and diverse regions. From the beginning, NAFTA was an economic and foreign policy priority for the two men who were then the dominant political force in both Texas and Washington, George Bush and James Baker. And later, when NAFTA began faltering owing to the doubts of the Democratic Congressional majority and the disengagement of the Democratic White House, supporters looked for leadership to the two most powerful political figures in Texas Democratic politics, Governor Ann Richards and Treasury Secretary Lloyd Bentsen.

NAFTA owes its political life to the Lone Star State. And for good reason. The impact of Mexican trade on the American economy divides the United States neatly in two: Texas, and everywhere else. Mexico now accounts for about a third of total sales by Texas companies outside U.S. borders. In no other exporting state does Mexico's share of foreign markets even break into double digits.

More impressive still, Texas provides virtually half of all American exports to Mexico. Since it began removing import barriers in 1987,

Mexico has become by far the fastest-growing market for American goods, and the Texas share of those sales has never been less than 44 percent.

In all, counting imports, Texas-Mexico commerce should reach $40 billion in 1993, more than total American trade with Korea or France. In less than 15 years, especially with NAFTA, Tex-Mex trade could pass the $150 billion mark, equal to current total American trade with Japan.

NAFTA boosters like to say that the agreement's benefits will be felt as far away from the border as Seattle and Boston, and they are right. But the fact is that Texas, above all other states and regions, gets by far the biggest slice of the NAFTA pie.

By itself, the Texas windfall doesn't make NAFTA unfair or disadvantageous. Any trade pact will invariably have different effects in different regions. But there is a specific American prejudice against Texas: it has already benefited from two hugely resented transfers of domestic wealth—the energy crisis of the 1970s, which boosted flagging oil and gas fortunes, and the savings and loan crisis of the 1980s, which sucked billions of taxpayer dollars into the black hole of Southwestern real estate. To a cynic, NAFTA may seem another sop to a politically powerful state at the expense of the rest of the country.

Yet the part of Texas that gets the biggest boost from NAFTA—the state's southeastern swath—includes the poorest counties in the country. And the trade agreement coincides with military cuts that will hurt San Antonio, Corpus Christi, and other south Texas cities. NAFTA-prompted investment in Mexico's oil industry, moreover, would not only help Houston, but reduce America's dependence on the Persian Gulf. And industrial exports to Mexico would diversify and stabilize the notoriously cyclical Texas economy, making it a firmer anchor for the entire south-central swath of the American economy.

More than half the U.S.-Mexico border is Texan—the half that is the most populated, the most productive, and the most densely intertwined with communities to the south. For that reason alone, Texas has a far bigger stake in Mexico's prosperity than any other state. Mexico's share of the state's exports rose from 25 percent in 1987 to 32 percent in 1990 and continues to climb. If the duty-free provisions of NAFTA had been in place in 1991, one University of Texas economist estimates, the Texas trade surplus with Mexico would have doubled to $9.4 billion. A 10-year projection based on the same assumptions shows NAFTA boosting sales and services by $80 billion. Under this scenario, Texas would gain an additional $1.4 billion in tax revenues and add 240,000 new jobs to private payrolls.

Even without NAFTA, this $40 billion cross-border interchange created a vibrant new regional economy, with profound effects on both Texas and Mexico. This new region's industrial capital is Monterrey, the northeastern Mexican city where the country's strongest conglomerates are headquartered. In Mexico's protectionist past, Monterrey companies looked only to the south; now, as they prepare for NAFTA, they are looking north—and they like what they see.

The central Tex-Mex trading axis connects Monterrey to San Antonio, within the broader arc of an expanding Dallas-Mexico City relationship. To the east, a parallel oil industry and shipping corridor runs from Houston down Mexico's Gulf Coast to Coatzacalcos. Out west, where Texas ends, Greater Juarez/El Paso is a north-south crossroads for the auto business, producing transmissions, headlamps and wire harnesses for the Big Three and Japanese transplant factories in both countries.

■ But it isn't only business opportunities that bind Texas and Mexico together. For many Texans, northern Mexico is less "foreign" than New England—and the affinities go beyond a shared weakness for nachos and accordions. Texas's quasi-national sense of cultural identity is thoroughly Mexican in origin—not only the Anglo cowboy culture, where virtually every term and technique came up from the south, but also the overtly Mexican architecture, cuisine and music. Joe Carrasco and Freddie Fender share an obvious debt to *la madre patria*, but so do Willie Nelson and Doug Sahm.

This kinship extends to political culture as well. American politicians who sniped at NAFTA often said it should be a "democratic club"—implying that Mexico failed the test of membership. Police abuses, media coercion, electoral chicanery, the often blurry line between government and business—all were cited by NAFTA's critics as evidence of Mexican unworthiness.

The PRI didn't get this guff from Texans.

Eligio "Kika" de la Garza, the veteran congressman from McAllen, grumbles that it shouldn't matter to Americans whether Mexico is run by "a president, a pope or a dictator." De la Garza, who rarely faces even token opposition in the border seat he has occupied for 30 years, is not about to give lectures on multiparty pluralism.[1] De la Garza enjoys hobnobbing with his PRI counterparts with an openness that irritates the Mexican opposition. At a 1991 Veracruz State campaign stop with his friend Miguel Alemán (a billionaire PRI senatorial candidate), he was taken by local reporters to be a member of the ruling-party entourage.

That doesn't mean de la Garza supports NAFTA unconditionally: he has fought hard to protect his region's sugar and peanut growers from Mexican competition. He also fights for bigger budget allotments for border-area roads and bridges. But his demands are directed at Washington, not Mexico City.

An earlier beneficiary of 15th District politics was Lloyd Bentsen, the son and heir of one of its largest landholders and its representative in Congress from 1948 to 1954. Bilingual since childhood, at ease with both Mexican culture and power politics, Bentsen is said by Mexicans to display an instinctive, nonjudgmental grasp of how Mexico works. (But then Mexico works a lot like Texas.) As chairman of the Senate Finance Committee, Bentsen was a dominant force in Texas politics and one of the most influential members of Congress on economic matters. In the Senate, Bentsen was careful to condition his support for NAFTA on Administration funding of parallel environmental and worker retraining programs, stressing the economic self-interest of the United States. Yet there was never any doubt about his basic sympathies.[2]

But the cross-border rapport has been strongest in the executive branch. The Salinas Administration would never have pressed for the pact if it had lacked the support of the Bush Administration's "three Texans"— Secretary of State James Baker, Secretary of Commerce Robert Mosbacher, and the President himself. Like many rich Texans, all had some direct business experience with Mexico. Seen from south of the border, they cut familiar figures. Mosbacher, the well-placed friend and fixer, an outer satellite of the inner circle, had followed the classic *camarilla* route to power. A cabinet star like Baker had a special appeal from a Mexican perspective: a consummate insider, he managed to project himself as a credible presidential prospect without dirtying his hands in the pursuit of elected office.

But no American political career has a more classic PRIista profile than that of George Bush himself, who proved his utility in top-level appointments and then dutifully submerged his own identity to become an ex-rival's faithful lieutenant. In 1987, a leading Mexican politician chastised me for suggesting that the PRI's nominating procedure—the *dedazo*, or knighting by incumbent fingertip—was undemocratic. "What's the big difference?" he demanded. "Anyone can see that the next president of the United States will be George Bush. That's not because people are clamoring for him, but because he is Ronald Reagan's designated heir, pure and simple. Isn't *that* a *dedazo?*"

Bush had the closest personal connections to Mexico of any modern

American president. One of his first business partners was a Mexican oilman who later headed Pemex. As a Houston politician and later as head of the CIA, he paid close attention to Mexican economic development and border security issues. In 1979, when he was a presidential candidate, he chaired an American Enterprise Institute study group that advocated a more open trading relationship with Mexico. On a personal level—and this is a man for whom such things count a great deal—he had three Mexican-American grandchildren.

He also enjoyed genuine rapport with Salinas and other members of the Mexican policy elite. Salinas was the first foreign leader Bush conferred with after his 1988 election. The Mexican president still cites this courtesy—and Bush's offer to work for a comprehensive new trade agreement—as the beginning of the new era in bilateral cooperation that is reflected in NAFTA. The desire for closer cross-border ties expressed on both sides is referred to by Salinas's official chroniclers as "the Spirit of Houston," after Bush's adopted home town, where the meeting was held.

Claims by rich Anglo Texans that they "understand" Mexico, as if by proximity and osmosis, can be deeply annoying to Mexicans. But Texans are comparing themselves with other Americans, and the conceit has merit. The tie between Texas and Mexico is especially strong in the ranching culture of south Texas and the Mexican north and in the oil business of the greater Gulf Coast. Like many of their generation, Bush, Baker and Mosbacher made their money in oil, while aspiring to the lifestyle of the gentleman's ranch. Salinas, in an interview for this book, said that this Texas background made the Bush Administration "more sensitive to the way that Mexicans think and act, which has been reflected in the care and tact with which President Bush has managed relations with Mexico, and that is something we appreciate."

Salinas has a similar regional perspective. Long before his graduate studies at Harvard, his border region roots allowed him to view the United States with an openness and complexity that is rare in the Mexican political elite. Though raised and educated in the capital, Salinas returned often to his family's home in the tiny ranch town of Agualeguas, near the Rio Grande. In Mexico City, critics saw a studied contrivance in the efforts of the intensely political Salinas family to maintain and advertise its Norteño ancestry. (His father was a cabinet officer, senator and presidential aspirant, his mother an early PRI proto-feminist.) But to the gentry of nearby Monterrey, Carlos Salinas is plainly one of their own. His economic policies have restored the city to its former prominence as the nation's business capital. To the extent that Mexican history can be seen as a struggle between the Creole, entrepreneurial north and the *mestizo*, hierarchical south, the Salinas Administration represents the reascendancy of the north.

The free trade agreement is seen by both critics and supporters as an effort to make that ascendance permanent. This implies not only economic union with the United States but some degree of emulation—a matter of less concern in Monterrey than in Mexico City. Many northerners pride themselves on thrift, hard work, and self-reliance—traits they associate more with their American neighbors than with their fellow countrymen to the south. This stereotyping persists in part because northern Mexicans know Texas better than they do Oaxaca. Yet the positive attitude towards the United States is genuine. Salinas says that because of his home state's "economic closeness to the United States, it has learned to compete, to be innovative, to change, to take risks and act decisively." These are, as he knows, also attributes often ascribed to Salinas himself, suggesting something of his own attitude towards American influence.

■ Texas—unlike California, say, or New York or Florida—has long benefited from its almost national sense of common purpose. Texas politicians can almost always be counted on to present a united front when promoting their state's interests. Whether pursuing supercollidor contracts or defending the oil-depletion allowance, Democrats and Republicans usually behave as Texans first. NAFTA was no exception.

As a result, Texas backing for NAFTA was broad and bipartisan. Active supporters included Mexican-American Democrats in Austin and Washington, conservative businessmen like real estate magnate Trammel Crow and natural-gas tycoon T. Boone Pickens, liberal academics from the University of Texas, farmers in south Texas, and electronics manufacturers in the Dallas metroplex. When Democratic Governor Ann Richards introduced Carlos Salinas to a historic joint session of the Texas legislature in the spring of 1991, the Mexican President received a tumultuous welcome. President Bush's request for fast-track negotiating authority for NAFTA received only four "no" votes from the 29-member Texas Congressional delegation. Mexican-American leaders like Raul Yzaguirre of the National Council of La Raza were critical in assembling national Hispanic support for NAFTA. The conspicuous exceptions—fast-track opponents in Congress included Henry Gonzalez, the crankily contrarian San Antonio populist—only underscored the near unanimity with which Texas politicians have embraced free trade.

Not that NAFTA lacked opponents in Texas. Sagebrush leftists like Jim Hightower, black leaders in Dallas and Houston, sugar growers in south Texas, Austin environmental activists, AFL-CIO organizers in border cities like Brownsville and El Paso, old-line nativists suspicious of Mexico and Mexicans—all spoke out against the accord. Statewide polls in the spring of 1992 showed broad support for the agreement, but also a widespread anxiety that it would nonetheless spur the emigration of jobs south and do little to boost Mexican living standards. Six months later suspicion of NAFTA had increased: exit polls in the November presidential election indicated that more Texans disapproved of NAFTA than supported it.

Yet these misgivings found little echo in the state political and business establishment. The most prominent exception to that rule is Ross Perot of Dallas and Texarkana, who declared his opposition to NAFTA during the same February 1992 CNN call-in program in which he launched his bid for the presidency. Since then he rarely missed an opportunity to claim that NAFTA would "implode the tax base" as American companies moved jobs south of the border. Perot's down-home protectionism still has wide appeal in his native state, especially in its emphatically non-Hispanic northeast corner.

NAFTA supporters, meanwhile, continued to argue that NAFTA was a good deal for Texas, primarily because it was a good deal for Mexico. As Texans knew from Mexico's oil-boom days, anything that promoted prosperity in Mexico would create a ready market for Texas goods—and a steady stream of Mexican shoppers and tourists crossing north to sample Texan wares. Texas had also been shocked by the economic devastation of the early years of the Mexican debt crisis, which bankrupted scores of Texas border retail outlets and real estate firms.

The business communities of San Antonio, Dallas and Houston all began promoting themselves as the natural hubs of this new cross-border economy. All have good claims: San Antonio as a marketing and service center, Dallas for manufacturing trade, Houston in the oil business—and in Gulf Coast shipping lanes. Mexican officials like to tease American audiences with a trivia question: what is Mexico's leading cargo port? Veracruz? Tampico? The answer is the Port of Houston. Several of Houston's biggest rivals for the Mexican cargo business are also in Texas. Brownsville and Corpus Christi have become de facto Mexican ports, replacing Tampico as the port of preference for many Monterrey shippers. And Galveston is building both a new rail link and a container port dedicated to two-way Mexico trade.

Texas's exports to Mexico include the expected grain, beef and gasoline, but they are dominated by a diverse range of high-tech manufactured goods. In 1989, for example, the state's biggest sales to Mexico (of a total $11 billion) were in electronics ($3.2 billion), computers and industrial machinery ($1.19 billion), and transportation equipment, from helicopters to auto parts ($1.13 billion).

The dominance of capital goods is evidence of another welcome phenomenon: the broadening of Tex-Mex trade beyond the immediate border. One LBJ School study of NAFTA's impact on manufacturing employment concluded that the most dramatic rise would take place in Dallas, while cities closer to Mexico like El Paso and San Antonio would actually lose a few hundred jobs. In all, a fully operational NAFTA today could give Texas another 67,000 manufacturing jobs, of which nearly 27,000 would be in Dallas-Fort Worth.

All this action is spreading Mexico-generated business away from the border itself. When Mexican liberalization was confined to the maquiladora industry, much of the business activity between Mexico and Texas was confined to a fragile, overloaded sliver of territory paralleling the Rio Grande. With freer trade, that narrow border strip is already losing importance.[3]

Although agriculture in the border area will be hit hard by NAFTA, Texas ranchers are generally supportive of NAFTA: they see new markets across the border—and lots of room for profitable cooperation in grazing, meat-packing and marketing. One might also expect farmers in the Rio Grande Valley to have opposed the agreement; the region's sugar and winter vegetables earnings are dependent on protection against tropical competition. Yet they, too, see market opportunities in once-protected Mexico. Some even talk about the Tex-Mex equivalent of coals to Newcastle: the exportation of jalapeno peppers to Mexican retail outlets. Despite a similar crop base, south Texas farmers were not as fiercely opposed to NAFTA as their colleagues in South Florida—largely because of their knowledge of the Mexican market.

Mirroring this change is the growth of trade with Texas in areas several hours south of the border. In Monterrey and its industrialized hinterland, it is now common to speak of Texas, rather than the rest of Mexico, as the region's natural market. It is a relationship that northeastern Mexicans openly welcome.

At the time of its secession from Mexico in 1836, Texas was a sparsely populated extension of the great arid expanse of the Mexican north. Its belatedly appreciated resources—in pasturelands, oil fields, natural gas—

were matched or bettered south of the border. Yet today, with barely one-sixth as many people as Mexico and one-third the land, Texas boasts a much larger and more diverse economy. In 1990, the Texas gross state product was estimated at $364 billion; Mexico's gross domestic product is now about $300 billion.

It may seem paradoxical that some Mexicans feel most at home with those Americans whose forebears gave their country its gravest humiliation. But Texas is not simply territory that Mexico lost in a bloody neocolonial war. For unreconstructed Mexican nationalists, it remains a bitter reminder of riches and geographical reach that are rightly Mexico's own. For many of its capitalist-minded northerners, it is a continuing reproach to the statist economic model that their compatriot Salinas is now abandoning. And for less ideological sorts, Texas affluence is simply an object lesson in the advantages of affiliation with the colossal market of the north.

For the hard-driving dynasties of Monterrey, it is difficult not to see Texas as an example of what might have been—and what still might be. The *regiomontanos*, as Monterrey natives are called, are, like Texans, often contemptuous of their country's older centers of political and financial power. And they have similar biases: for engineers and against lawyers, for the privileges of capital and against the power of organized labor, for profits and against taxes, for action and against contemplation. They are confident that NAFTA will let Mexico—or at least Greater Monterrey—catch up to Texan standards.

■ The border with Mexico—once stigmatized as a source of crime, migrants and congestion—is fast becoming Texas's biggest asset.

Recall that the integration of Mexican plants into the broader North American auto business is pulling that industry's center of gravity out of Detroit and into the sunbelt. Juarez, across the Rio Grande from El Paso, is already North America's largest auto parts manufacturing center outside Michigan. Mexico is the biggest supplier of engines for Chrysler and Ford; General Motors, with some 70,000 employees in Mexican assembly plants along the border, is the biggest single maquiladora employer.

A decade ago, proximity to Mexico wouldn't have played a part in the General Motors decision to keep open its Buick-Chevy plant in Arlington, Texas, while closing a similar plant in Michigan. This time it may have been decisive. That lesson has not been lost on Texan politicians and business leaders. With the opening of Japanese transplant shops in the right-to-work states of the Appalachian south, the industry had already begun to move away from Detroit. Now Mexico was exerting a new southwesterly pull, with Texas as the beneficiary.

Tex-Mex interdependence also extends deep into the oil patch. The Texas contractors who made fortunes during the 1977-1981 Mexican oil boom can already taste the prospects of a new investment cycle.[4] By prying open Pemex development and service contracts, and opening Mexico to Texas natural gas exports, NAFTA would initiate the development of complementary energy grids. Coal fields in northeastern Mexico would suddenly be available to Texas utilities. Over time, Pemex would let American companies compete on an equal footing with Mexican suppliers. For Texas, this means a dramatic jump in machinery exports for oil and gas extraction, transportation and refining, as well as the more extensive use of entire American drilling crews and technical support teams.

Texas oilmen have also realized that oil-rich Mexico will soon be a major energy importer. One of the most prominent is T. Boone Pickens, whose Japanese investment adventures once made him the state's feistiest protectionist. Now Pickens is a NAFTA cheerleader, extolling the accord in speeches and press releases.[5] Big natural gas distributors like Enron and Valero Energy have proposed extensive new pipeline links across the border, and investors in Texas electric utilities have suggested new binational power plants.

Mexican protection of its state oil industry has long artificially constrained cross-border trade in the energy industry. Texas exports to Mexico in the oil and gas sector, including equipment sales and refined fuels and service fees, are now barely 5 percent of the state's total Mexican sales. Under NAFTA, that share would grow dramatically.

The Texas energy business would benefit in other unexpected ways. While the USTR worked overtime to pry open Mexican refineries and pipelines to American investment, NAFTA would have a more immediate impact on Mexican investment in underused Texan refineries and pipelines. Pemex, unable to satisfy domestic demand for unleaded gasoline and short on capacity for processing heavy crude, is already relying on Texas and Louisiana refineries. The market reforms introduced by NAFTA—including competitive bidding for procurement contracts, an end to downstream monopolies in petrochemical production and gasoline sales—would tend to make Pemex behave more like a normal oil company. And once Pemex starts making decisions on a bottom-line basis, the cost of building new refineries in Mexico will look daunting compared to new investments in idle capacity in Texas.[6]

Buying refining and distribution outlets in its principal export market would make good business sense even if Pemex didn't face domestic refining shortfalls. In lean years it is a safeguard against price and market share declines; in good times a boost to the foreign-exchange bottom line. Most of Pemex's interest as an investor in the United States logically centers on Texas. Any important new bidder for refining and transport facilities would help boost oil patch employment and industrial property values. A company that comes complete with its own crude supply is a double blessing for a region of depleted local reserves but a surfeit of downstream infrastructure, talent and market demand.

For political as well as business reasons, Pemex can be expected to move quietly and incrementally, preferring joint ventures to outright takeovers. Mexican critics hostile toward Salinas's pro-U.S. tilt say Pemex should invest locally, not in the United States, and consider any decision to the contrary an attempt to curry favor with Washington. For example, Pemex chairman Francisco Rojas was careful to insist that a recent deal in which Pemex bought half of a Shell refinery that it will supply with crude oil "would not affect Pemex's plans for other refining investment within Mexico." But the expansion of Pemex across the border would be extensive, probably reaching a scale similar to that of Venezuela's state-run PDVSA, which is now doubling its American investments to an estimated $4 billion.

Throughout the NAFTA debate, too much attention was paid on both sides of the border to demands of the oil majors. Mexico was never willing to compromise on state control of crude production, transportation, and marketing. The Mexican government may one day loosen its hold on the oil business unilaterally, but never as part of a mandatory arrangement with Washington. The political costs would be too high, the financial rewards too few. For the Texas-based oil service and supply industry, including wildcat drillers, the majors' demands that Mexico offer risk contracts, complete with a share of any found oil, had little real business relevance. Far more important were changes in Mexican state procurement policies and investment opportunities downstream of the wellhead.

The energy sector, now conspicuously underrepresented, should soon be the most dynamic single element of the Texas-Mexico business relationship. Simply to maintain current export levels and domestic self-sufficiency, Pemex plans to invest upwards of $20 billion over the next five years. A lot of that money would be spent in Texas.

With a new bilateral oil business added to NAFTA-propelled growth in consumer manufacturing south of the river and high-tech capital goods to the north—and in farms and auto factories on both sides of the border—Texas-Mexico commerce could easily reach $60 billion a year in NAFTA's first five years and pass the $100 billion mark before trade is to become fully free 10 years later. The Tex-Mex trade axis would become nearly as big as the entire U.S.-Japanese trade flow is today—with the critical difference, for Austin as well as Washington, that Mexico would be running a deficit.

The imports that Mexico brings in from Texas would be purchased disproportionately in the north, which would in turn provide the biggest share of Mexico's manufactured exports. From the perspectives not only of Monterrey and Dallas, but of Altamira and Galveston and Agualeguas and Crystal City, the Mexican northeast and Texas are becoming a single economic region—the fulcrum of the Yukon-to-Yucatan free zone.

NOTES

Note 1: Nor on electoral fraud: the 15th District is one of many in Texas with a storied history of ballot-stuffing, including its gift of a 1948 primary victory to Senate aspirant Lyndon Johnson.

Note 2: The leading non-Texan in Mexico's Congressional corner is New Mexico's Bill Richardson, whose district ends in the Sangre de Cristo mountains—culturally as well as geographically the northernmost extension of historic Mexico. Raised in Mexico City, the 45-year-old congressman has spent more of his life south of the border than in the state he represents. Richardson moved to New Mexico from Washington in 1978 as a Democratic Party functionary, became a congressman four years later, and soon began urging a U.S.-Mexican trade pact. With his unapologetic carpetbagging and elite professional training— a degree from the Fletcher School, stints at State and Senate Foreign Relations— the bilingual Richardson bears striking similarities to his generational counterparts in Mexico's political elite.

Note 3: This is not unmitigated good news: on the Texas side, shoppers from nearby Mexico once accounted for perhaps a quarter of the entire state's retail sales. Now, with Mexicans able to buy the same goods in their own department stores, the border shops are losing business.

Note 4: Mexico's emergence as an important crude exporter in the late 1970s was led by oilman Jorge Díaz Serrano, who had earlier amassed a fortune in a Houston-based drilling business; among his earliest partners there was a youthful Yankee emigré, George Herbert Walker Bush.

Note 5: No doubt the prospect of a bonanza in natural gas sales helped persuade Pickens of NAFTA's merits—just as the loss of opportunities for quick stock profits made him a fierce opponent of Japanese financial regulations. When it comes to political consistency, Pickens is all Texan.

Note 6: The first evidence of this strategy came just after the NAFTA talks concluded: Pemex and Shell announced a new joint venture in Deer Park, along the Houston Ship Channel. For an undisclosed price, Pemex bought half of Shell's 225,000 barrel-a-day refinery, which it will supply with crude and rely on for unleaded gasoline. A billion dollars will be spent overhauling the refinery so it can handle more of Mexico's thick Maya oil. Shell said its new Pemex partnership should ensure the survival of a 63-year-old installation with 2,400 employees, an annual payroll of $115 million, and a property tax bill of $28.5 million a year. Similar ventures are being pursued by Chevron at its Port Arthur refinery and by Dupont in Houston; in each case, Pemex is trading heavy crude for refined products.

CHAPTER 10

What Will the Neighbors Say? Latin America After NAFTA

On June 27, 1990, George Bush unveiled his Enterprise for the Americas Initiative—an ambitious if sketchy program for lowering debt, boosting investment, and clearcutting trade barriers throughout the Western Hemisphere.

Buried in the business pages and ignored by the networks, the Bush address drew little attention at home. In Latin America, however, it was hailed as the most constructive U.S. proposal for the region since the Kennedy Administration's Alliance for Progress. Galvanizing the region's attention was the audacious heart of the Bush plan: "a free trade zone stretching from the port of Anchorage to Tierra del Fuego." Bush called on all the countries of North, Central and South America—a region of more than 700 million people—to join as "equal partners" in the world's biggest unified market.

The proposal generated more enthusiasm than the Bush Administration ever expected or intended.

Foreign ministries from Mexico City to Santiago found it hugely refreshing to hear a U.S. administration addressing the region not as an aid supplicant or insurgency threat, but as a colleague and an economic asset. Bankers welcomed its promise to cut payments on debts owed to U.S. government agencies, while investors applauded the pledge to spur privatization and deregulation with a $1.5 billion investment fund. Even environmentalists had something to be pleased about, with the inclusion of a debt-for-nature swap provision. Happiest of all were local and foreign advocates of economic reform, who watched as the unexpected offer of a trade pact with the United States set still-protected economies scrambling to cut tariffs and liberalize investment rules.

The Bush initiative won bipartisan support throughout the Americas, with praise from Latin American governments and opposition leaders, as well as from such mainstream Democrats as Bill Clinton. It was lauded by foreign affairs professionals as a creative fusion of economic and foreign policy ideally suited for the post-Cold War era. Bush's policy address "immediately changed the psychological context of the hemisphere," said Viron Vaky, a Latin America policy-maker in Jimmy Carter's State Department. "This was an offer to substitute the old security framework of U.S.-Latin American relations for a new economic framework. Nobody had articulated this before."

But no details were spelled out. There was no timetable. The implications for American trade policy were left unexamined. Nor were other basic questions asked. Did the United States have the political will to deliver on this bold promise? Did the concept itself make economic and diplomatic sense?

When Bush left office two and a half years later, the Enterprise program remained little more than a broad conceptual promise. But an uncritical acceptance of its basic premise continues to shape U.S. policy toward Latin America, and Latin American policy toward the United States. Even with this acceptance, it is still unclear whether the policy makes sense, and whether Washington will ever implement it—two quite different questions.

At his December 1992 economic conclave in Little Rock, President-elect Bill Clinton listened intently as a Chinese-American businesswoman attacked the idea of a free trade zone for the Western Hemisphere. This is "exclusionary," she insisted, and strategically ill conceived. Does Washington really want to turn its back on Asia, she asked? Doesn't the United States plan to remain a Pacific power? Isn't a better GATT more important than an expanded NAFTA?

Good questions, Clinton responded.

They still are. Yet hers was a rare dissenting voice, and the Clinton Administration quickly and uncritically embraced George Bush's hemispheric trade plan. Clinton's conversion was signaled early, at his pre-inaugural meeting with Carlos Salinas, when he said he saw NAFTA as the beginning of a broader free trade relationship with the rest of Latin America. He reiterated this position throughout the 1993 NAFTA debate, and then had the United States host a pan-American summit in Miami in 1994 designed to further the cause of hemispheric integration.

How did a Democrat elected on promises of sweeping change come to take his Republican predecessor's policy as his own? The answer lies in the hard work of a small group of Democratic Latin Americanists, who applied steady pressure during the transition period to keep the Bush plan alive. Their first salvo was a weapon common to Washington interregnums: a perfect-bound treatise aimed at the undefined heart of the incoming administration. Entitled *Convergence and Community: The Americas in 1993*, and published by the nonpartisan Inter-American Dialogue, the report offered the expected mix of semi-opaque grandiloquence, turgid bureaucratic analysis, and multipoint policy prescriptions. But it laid the groundwork for what would soon become Administration policy, while showing—albeit inadvertently—how hard it is to make the case for that policy on the grounds of American economic self-interest.

The report's authors knew the usual objections to an exclusive pan-American trading bloc. So they began their recommendations with a ritualistic endorsement of Gatt. They admonished area governments to "steer clear of any new restrictions to extra-hemispheric imports," and suggested that "even the appearance of laying the foundation for a 'fortress America' should be avoided." They even conceded that a hemispheric trade group was "perhaps debatable on strictly economic grounds"—a remarkable caveat for an economic policy proposal. But they then went on to recommend that post-NAFTA free trade deals be "restricted to the nations of this hemisphere"—but only "for the time being."

According to the report's high-minded authors, the ultimate purpose of economic integration is not "a mere search for commercial advantage" but nothing less than political union—the laying of a foundation for "a genuine Western Hemisphere Community of Democracies."

The Inter-American Dialogue is a decade-old Washington think tank dedicated to the worthy proposition that the two Americas should talk more to each other. Latin American members include Mario Vargas Llosa, the Thatcherite Peruvian novelist; Luis Inacio "Lula" da Silva, the Brazilian socialist labor leader; Enrique Iglesias, the head of the Inter-American Development Bank; Lorenzo Meyer, the liberal Mexican historian and political critic; Raul Alfonsín, the former Argentine president; Marcos McGrath, Panama's archbishop; José Francisco Peña Gómez, the Dominican social democratic party boss; Pedro-Pablo Kuczynski, the waspish Peruvian investment banker; and Javier Pérez de Cuellar, the former United Nations secretary-general.

On the less-diverse American side, the group is top-heavy with former diplomats and dominated by Democrats. At the time the report was issued, the group's president was Richard Feinberg, a Clinton advisor on Latin American policy before his appointment as the National Security Council's chief Latin American policy analyst. Interior Secretary Bruce Babbitt, who polished his Spanish as a young geologist in the Andes, was the Dialogue co-chairman. Another leading member was Henry Cisneros, Clinton's Secretary of Housing and Urban Development. Paula Stern, a former chairman of the International Trade Commission, who lobbied for pan-American trade at Clinton's pre-inaugural economic seminar in Little Rock, also took part, as did Peter Tarnoff, now an Undersecretary of State.

It was only natural, then, that the Dialogue's case for the Bush initiative would get a Democratic spin. So the report called for keener attention to environmental protection and labor rights. It advocated automatic sanctions against undemocratic governments as an integral part of a hemispheric trading system (though not so draconian that they would exclude Mexico or Peru). The Reagan and Bush Administrations, now safely consigned to history, were chastised for failing to consider the impact of their economic policies on the distribution of Latin America's wealth. This was all fairly predictable.

What was surprising was that the essence of the Enterprise for the Americas Initiative would be endorsed almost without change. The Dialogue report advocates extending NAFTA gradually southward until it becomes a Western Hemisphere Free Trade Area. Only then, say the authors, should the United States open its free trade doors to countries outside the hemisphere.

One can hardly complain that the Inter-American Dialogue would advocate special U.S. trade treatment for the Western Hemisphere. The group's express purpose is to foster closer relationships within the Americas. Half of its members are Latin Americans, and the North Americans, by dint of their participation, are a self-selected group with a professed interest in the region.

But it is certainly surprising that the globalists—among them Jimmy Carter, Robert McNamara, A.W. Clausen, McGeorge Bundy and others—didn't insist that the report consider the global implications of a hemispheric trade bloc, or even the implications for U.S. relations with the rest of the world.

Nowhere did the Inter-Americanists explain why a hemispheric economic community is a good idea—why it is a better strategy for all concerned than, say, a Pacific Basin trade area, or a push for global liberalization without regional trade blocs. Nor did it address Bush's own suggestion that NAFTA be expanded on a country-by-country basis—east (Poland, Hungary) and west (Singapore, New Zealand) as well as south.

The group endorsed the Bush position that NAFTA's next member should be Chile, largely because Chile was told by Bush that it would be next. That invitation was formally extended to Santiago at the 1994 Miami summit meeting. The Dialogue report simultaneously supported moves to blunt NAFTA's trade-diverting damage to the countries of the Caribbean. Yet the contradictions in those two positions were never addressed. Look at NAFTA from Santiago, then take another look from Santo Domingo. Chile, on the far side of the globe, hasn't suffered from NAFTA at all. The Dominican Republic, an overnight sail from Florida, was hurt immediately by the preferential American market access given to Mexican sugar, textiles, and light manufactured goods. There are a million Dominicans in the United States and few Chileans. Chile is Latin America's most successful economy; the Dominican Republic is one of its poorest. Most capital investment in the Dominican Republic comes from the United States, and most of its exports go to the United States. Chile's export markets and investment sources are widely diversified, with the United States accounting for a small minority share. Policymakers can differ on whether trade preferences should be assigned on the basis of altruism or self-interest, but making Santiago a bigger priority than Santo Domingo cannot be justified on either ground.

Abandoned by the Clinton Administration, but illustrative of the thinking of its policy-makers, was the Dialogue's proposed "new multilateral organization to guide and coordinate progress toward a Western Hemispheric Economic Community." This new organization would encompass not only national governments but private groups (labor unions, environmentalists) and the existing hemispheric agencies: the Organization of American States, the Economic Commission on Latin America and the Caribbean, the Latin American Free Trade Association, and the Inter-American Development Bank (with its adjunct, the Inter-American Investment Corporation), plus the coordinating bodies of Mercosur, the Andean Pact, Caricom, CACM, and other subregional groups. As this list should make painfully clear, the last thing the Western Hemisphere needs is another multilateral bureaucracy.

Equally worrisome was the Dialogue's suggestion that this organization should grow out of NAFTA's planned governing secretariat—again, making the United States the managing partner of the hemispheric union.

Tellingly, the few dissents were lodged by the South Americans in the group. Sergio Bitar, a prominent Chilean economic strategist, said Latin America should pursue trade accords with Europe and Japan as well as the United States. Former Brazilian Foreign Minister Celso Lafer, a conservative, worried about "the trade and investment diversion consequences of NAFTA." His socialist compatriot, Lula, said "asymmetries" between North and South would make a hemispheric economic union inherently inequitable. It would be better to seek integration within subregional groupings like Mercosur, the future presidential candidate argued.

And that is exactly what is happening. Despite all its pan-hemispheric rhetoric, Washington is still not ready to expand NAFTA, but Mercosur and the other regional trade pacts are smashing barriers to commerce within Latin America. Will the vision of an all-American free trade zone ever be realized? Should it be?

■ Oddly, in the final months of the Bush presidency, the hemispheric common market idea was quietly interred—not by Clinton—but by Bush himself. In the principal economic policy speech of his campaign, delivered to the Detroit Economic Club in October, Bush portrayed NAFTA not as the first link in a hemispheric free trade chain, but as the first in a series of such pacts scattered randomly around the world. Chile was mentioned as a candidate. But so was Poland, Australia and Singapore. The latter countries spurned the Bush offer; Chile still patiently awaits. The problem, as the Bush speech inadvertently revealed, is that the free trade offer to Santiago was never part of a coherent strategy. NAFTA's passage further complicates matters, since a pact with Chile (or any other country) would have to be sold not just to Congress, but to Canada and Mexico as well.

The last-minute Bush abandonment of the hemispheric project went largely unnoticed outside trade policy circles: it was, after all, a brief passage in a long speech in a losing campaign. But the Detroit address had been designed as an overarching policy vision for a second Bush term. Its chief architect was Robert Zoellick, a top aide to White House chief of staff James Baker, who in his previous job at the Baker State Department had been one of the few forceful and visible Administration advocates for the Enterprise policy. Zoellick's abrupt reversal of that policy reinforced impressions that the Enterprise Initiative was a hastily improvised NAFTA adjunct that had never enjoyed the Administration's full support.

**The
Enterprise
Surprise**

The Enterprise for the Americas Initiative had been crafted quickly and quietly by David Mulford, the Undersecretary of the Treasury for International Affairs, with the collaboration of Roger Porter, Zoellick's predecessor as the chief White House domestic and economic policy advisor. The purpose of the program, said Bush at the time, was to "create incentives to reinforce Latin America's growing recognition that free-market reform is the key to sustained growth and political stability."

But the Initiative also had more immediate diplomatic motives. First, Latin America needed reassurance that it had not been forgotten amid the excitement provoked by the dissolution of Soviet communism. "The United States will not lose sight of the tremendous challenges and opportunities here in our own hemisphere," said Bush.

Second, and more important, South and Central Americans needed to be persuaded that they would not be penalized by NAFTA. Countries making the painful transition to free-market economics worried that investment would now be diverted to Mexico, which would also enjoy privileged access to the all-important American market. Don't worry, Bush was now saying: the U.S.-Mexico pact is just the first step toward a hemispheric free market.

This was news to Mexico. Just 17 days before, Salinas and Bush had stood side by side in Washington to order formal negotiations for a bilateral free zone. For 10 years, the White House had been preaching the virtues of a unified economy from "the Yukon to the Yucatan." Now, quite suddenly and with no private warning, the United States was proposing to extend NAFTA from the Arctic to Antarctica.

In Mexico City, the Salinas team kept its reservations to itself. Mexico could hardly be seen opposing freer trade for the rest of Latin America, especially since it had long championed the virtues of regional cooperation. Yet some Mexican officials clearly were disgruntled by the news that Washington might not be cutting an exclusive deal with Mexico.

As Canada had earlier, Mexico had assumed that the invitation to join a U.S. free trade zone implied some measure of exclusivity. Salinas Administration officials knew that preferential access to the American market would be an important domestic selling point in overcoming the inevitable local opposition to a North American free trade deal. Now the Salinas team was served notice that Washington, unlike Mexico City, had never surrendered any autonomy in its pursuit of a continental trade accord. The Salinas team's only choice was to hope that the Bush Administration would not extend its trade pacts south too quickly. In the interim, Mexico would pursue a kind of Beginomics: "creating facts" during the negotiation process with an ambitious privatization drive, the rapid dismantling of foreign investment barriers, the forging of its own hemispheric trade links, and the assertion of some control over the pace and conditions of future NAFTA membership.

The Mexican government was hardly alone in its surprise at the new Bush policy. The Inter-American Development Bank had been designated by Bush as the coordinating agency for the Enterprise Initiative. Yet it had not even been consulted about the policy. Even bank president Enrique Iglesias had been unaware of the plan's scope until the day of the speech. "I had some idea about the Initiative beforehand, but I was not aware of the magnitude of the proposal," he said later. "I was very surprised, because the proposal went beyond my expectations, especially regarding trade."

Bush's own State Department fared no better. Senior officials with responsibility for Latin America first learned of the initiative when they were called for comment by colleagues from Canada. Bernard Aronson, the Assistant Secretary of State for Inter-American Affairs, had not been included in the Treasury-led group that devised the new policy. Nor had Carla Hills, the U.S. Trade Representative, who was still immersed in the Gatt talks and who had only recently and reluctantly agreed to start working on a North American trade agreement.

The Canadians hadn't been informed beforehand, either—even though they had already been blindsided three months earlier by the news that Mexico was planning to join the North American trade alliance. The Mulroney government took some grim comfort in the knowledge that so many senior American policymakers had also been left in the dark. "We were surprised to hear about it," one Ottawa trade official drolly noted, "but no more so than the State Department."

Also out of the loop were responsible officials in Brussels and Tokyo. In his speech, Bush said he wanted the European Union and Japan to contribute $500 million each to a murkily defined $1.5 billion investment fund. EC officials learned of this only through an account of Bush's speech in the *Financial Times*. Even weeks later, Japanese officials were complaining that they had been unable to obtain basic details about the fund's purpose. With such sloppy beginnings, it was perhaps no surprise that when Bush left office two and a half years later, the fund had not yet begun to function.

In Canada's case, special access to the American market was promised

explicitly by the Mulroney government when it began pushing for domestic acceptance of its bilateral trade accord. Now, citing provisions in
the U.S.-Canadian FTA that called for consultations in the event of trade
agreement with third parties, the Mulroney Administration began insisting on a role for Canada in the U.S.-Mexican negotiations, despite
Mexico's deep-seated reluctance to include a third party in the discussion
and the White House's fears that trilateral talks could fatally complicate
both binational deals. Canada got its way, but only after pledging that it
would neither disrupt the U.S.-Mexican negotiating calendar nor back-
track on trade liberalization commitments already negotiated with the
United States.

After the Launch

At the Bush White House, domestic policy advisor Roger
Porter contended that the Enterprise Initiative hadn't
superseded or obstructed the push for a pact with Mexico.
"We are making Mexico a special case, in that they are
first," Porter told me at the time. "All we have with the
other countries at this point are framework agreements." Porter claimed
the proposal was the result of a Bush request for "a comprehensive
program for Latin America" combining "democratic political institutions
with economic arrangements that will produce prosperity."

Yet Porter's own account of the policy's origins suggested that the
Bush Administration had never fully examined the potential conflicts
between a hemispheric trade plan and an exclusively North American
initiative—perhaps because it never expected Latin America to take its
offer seriously. "The Enterprise for the Americas Initiative is less a
government program than it is a set of principles which are designed to
move us toward a vision of what economic life in this hemisphere can be,"
Porter explained.

That was not how Latin Americans saw it. To their eyes, the Initiative
was clearly a U.S. government program, one that unambiguously invited
countries to the south to link economies in barrier-free trade. Uruguayan
President Roberto Lacalle called Bush immediately after the Enterprise
speech to volunteer his own economy as a test case. President Patricio
Aylwin in Chile also offered to sign a trade accord virtually on the spot.
But the Chileans and Uruguayans were told to wait until NAFTA's
conclusion. As a practical matter, Administration officials said, that would
be sometime in Bush's second term.

Two months later, when Bush suddenly canceled a scheduled Latin

American tour, doubts began arising about America's commitment to the hemispheric plan. White House spokesmen cited budget negotiations with Congress as the excuse. But skeptical Latin American observers noted that the Bush Administration wasn't pushing Congress for the appropriations or discretionary debt reduction authority it needed to implement the Enterprise Initiative. Then came the Iraqi invasion of Kuwait. Preparations for the West's military response soon precluded any serious consideration of the Bush trade plan. The Enterprise Initiative became a collateral victim of the Persian Gulf war.

When the Middle East hostilities ended, the Administration was pre-occupied with getting fast-track negotiating approval for Gatt and NAFTA. Latin American officials began to wonder if the Initiative's promise would ever be realized. As details of the plan began trickling out, it was clear that debt reduction would be marginal, environmental preservation minimal, and the $1.5 billion investment fund more of a concept than a funded reality.

By contrast, the Administration pressed forward on the U.S.-Mexico pact, formally notifying Congress of its intention to negotiate and dis-patching Commerce Secretary Robert Mosbacher on a week-long, five-city NAFTA road show with his Mexican counterpart, Jaime Serra Puche. "It was really extraordinary to have that kind of cooperation with the U.S. administration," a gratified Serra said at the time. When Bush at last rescheduled his Latin American trip, Salinas—acutely sensitive to the political ramifications of putting NAFTA into a broader hemispheric context—specifically requested that Mexico be kept off the president's itinerary. Bush agreed, instead taking most of his cabinet to a separate cross-border summit in Salinas's home state in November 1990, drama-tizing his commitment to the pact.

When Bush flew to South America in December, he was received cordially, even enthusiastically. But little hard news was generated by the trip—no trade pacts, no debt accords—and daily American press cover-age focused exclusively on Bush's comments about the Persian Gulf. Latin American leaders were disappointed. They had hoped there would be an opportunity for Bush to build American public support for his regional trade plan. It wasn't to be. "In Washington, it was almost as if he hadn't gone at all," a senior Latin American official remarked.

In January 1991, Bush made a brief mention of the Initiative in his State of the Union speech. But he left little doubt that his priority was Mexico. "With the Mexican Free Trade Agreement and our Enterprise for the Americas Initiative, we can help our partners strengthen their

U.S. TRADE PATTERNS
(1992: $ Billions)

	Exports	Imports	Total Trade	% of Total US Trade
NAFTA*	131.2	133.8	265.0	27%
Canada	90.5	98.6	189.1	19%
Mexico	40.5	35.2	75.7	8%
OTHER W. HEMISPHERE**	35.2	33.5	68.7	7%
EUROPEAN COMMUNITY	102.9	94.0	196.9	21%
EAST ASIA	124.4	208.4	332.8	34%
Japan	(47.8)	97.4	145.2	15%
WORLD	448.2	532.7	980.9	100%

* NAFTA = Canada + Mexico

** Latin America and the Caribbean, without Mexico

Source: Department of Commerce

economies and move toward a free trade zone throughout the hemisphere," Bush said. The real test of the Administration's intentions came a few months later. Bush had to request the extension of the president's fast-track authority to negotiate trade accords. Fast-track rules prevent Congress from amending trade pacts after they are submitted by the executive; they would be essential for the negotiation of NAFTA and a new Gatt deal. That made the floor fight in Congress over fast-track's extension a proxy for the larger debate over the Administration's trade policy. Bush aides made it clear that they would use their fast-track authority sparingly, and limit their negotiations to the essentials—Gatt and NAFTA—plus, perhaps, a single token nod towards the Enterprise concept: a free trade agreement with Chile, which was already the most free-trading economy south of the border.

Mexico's southern neighbors had first begun to get anxiety pangs in March 1990, when the *Wall Street Journal* reported that Salinas was actively seeking a free trade deal in Washington. In the past, Mexico had always publicly spurned such offers. Now, barely a month after it had succeeded in restructuring its debt, Mexico seemed ready to gain the open access to the American market that the rest of Latin America had only dreamed of.

Alarm bells started ringing throughout Central America and the Caribbean. Governments were especially worried about light industry that had been lured by U.S. customs and tax incentives: would American garment factories relocate from Santo Domingo to Oaxaca, from San Pedro Sula to Ciudad Juarez? In the debt-strapped capitals of South America, finance ministers fretted about their bond issues and stock markets: would American institutional investors they were courting now redirect their funds into Mexico? Tropical agribusiness also braced for a shock: would Mexican produce displace Colombian coffee, Brazilian orange juice, Nicaraguan cotton, Panamanian bananas, Dominican sugar? Would all the region's economies be forced to prepare for their own free trade deals, whether or not they were ready? If so, would they need Mexico's prior support?

The answer to all these questions, on balance, was yes.

Bush Administration officials gamely sought to persuade Latin Americans that it wasn't so. But they had a weak case. There was no getting around the fact that NAFTA could have a devastating impact on several industries—including sugar and apparel—that are critical to the Caribbean Basin economies.

And while it was true that NAFTA might be Gatt-legal—in that it doesn't impose new barriers on products from outside North America—that's irrelevant to companies worried about Mexican competition in the American market. NAFTA is explicitly designed to heighten Mexico's advantages for American importers and investors. Mexico's southern neighbors would inevitably pay a price for this favoritism.

Throughout the NAFTA debates, few advocates conveyed any sense that the pursuit of a North American trade agreement involves choices—between bilateralism and multilateralism, and about priorities among trading partnerships. NAFTA raises fundamental questions of international political commitments. Is Washington putting its North American relationships on a higher plane than its dealings with the rest of the world? Is

NAFTA the underpinning of a true continental common market, as the European Coal and Steel Community was a generation ago? Or is it merely a limited mechanism for phasing out minor local trade barriers, with Canada and Mexico enjoying temporary privileges as Washington widens its free trade web across South America, the Pacific, and beyond?

These are not abstract issues but hard questions of economic policy and international law. The first fork in the road came immediately after the announcement, in June 1990, of Washington's intent to negotiate a Mexican deal.

The United States could have said clearly that it was committed to Gatt, with the pursuit of NAFTA—given the long land borders and dense economic integration among the three countries—as the one prominent exception. That would have implied that NAFTA would eventually mutate into something beyond a simple free trade area. And that acknowledgement would have been consistent with Gatt, which allows exceptions for incipient free trade areas on the assumption that they will evolve into some form of common market, complete with supranational political institutions. America's principal trade partners would scarcely have objected, since they accept that the economies and cultures of North America are uniquely connected.

But the stated U.S. intention was different: NAFTA was not an incipient common market, Bush officials said, but the first link in a chain of bilateral trade deals to be struck throughout the hemisphere.

This new policy was immediately embraced by economic analysts and political leaders who had been skeptical about Gatt—and who were sure that the world was fracturing into huge, competitive trading blocs. Senator Max Baucus (D-Montana), chairman of the Senate Finance subcommittee on trade, said he welcomed the prospect of a pan-American bloc as a counterweight to the EC and a means of applying pressure on the Europeans in Gatt. Several prominent economists—ranging from Chicago's Milton Friedman to Rudiger Dornbusch of MIT—broke ranks with their multilaterally inclined colleagues to argue that trade barriers could be cut more quickly through regional trade arrangements. Critics of U.S. trade policy toward Japan embraced the new Enterprise Initiative as a way to keep Japan from using Latin America as a low-cost back door to the American market.

This warm reception made some U.S. officials nervous. Trade Representative Carla Hills, a convinced multilateralist, stressed the primacy of Gatt and said the Enterprise plan called "only for a free trade area, not a common market." But Bush's language had been clear. He was not simply reiterating U.S. advocacy of freer trade. He was proposing the creation of "one economy" from Alaska to Patagonia.

Within the Americas, the Bush plan raised difficult logistical and diplomatic questions. Would the sequence of accession to the free trade zone be dictated by geographical proximity, by standards of democratic behavior, by degrees of dependence on American trade and investment, by the depth of commitment to free-market economics, or by a more random application process?

Outside the hemisphere, Bush's Americas-first policy provided convenient cover for Asian proponents of an exclusive East Asian trading bloc and for Europeans favoring stiff EC trade barriers. And it made life difficult for U.S. diplomats dispatched to chide Danes and Malaysians about their own restrictively regionalist aims.

Ironically, the Bush Administration's commitment to hemispheric free trade was largely rhetorical. Hill's considerable negotiating energies were directed almost exclusively towards NAFTA and Gatt. But her boss's speeches pushed events in the opposite direction—reinforcing the trend towards trade-bloc formation and undermining support for Gatt.

How Exclusive a Club?

It also raised false hopes in the countries to Mexico's south. The negotiation of a North American Free Trade Agreement never merely meant that Mexico is "first in line," as too many U.S. officials glibly assured their South and Central American counterparts. NAFTA would make Mexico an arbiter of the regional free trade process, with an institutional voice in determining whether similar access to the North American market should be extended to other economies.

The agreement's terse "accession clause," Article 2205, says that "any country or group of countries" are welcome to join the bloc, providing that they negotiate mutually agreeable terms that are then ratified by each NAFTA country's "standard approval procedures." Freed of the bureaucratic language, this means that, if NAFTA is ratified, any future free trade suitor would no longer be proposing to Washington, but to North America as a whole. Canada and Mexico would have effective veto power over new applicants, as would the U.S. Congress.

Many NAFTA supporters had pushed for a more detailed accession clause, which would have granted membership to almost any qualified applicant. Among the institutional advocates of such clear-cut "docking" rules were the Heritage Foundation, the Institute for International Economics, and the Inter-American Dialogue, all of whom had endorsed the notion that NAFTA should evolve into a hemispheric trade area.

The case for a detailed accession clause is superficially appealing. By spelling out trade and investment guidelines and basic macroeconomic criteria—similar to the requirements for membership in the OECD, for example, with ceilings on inflation and deficits and commitments to realistic exchange rates—potential applicants would have known exactly what policy steps were expected of them. It would have also sent an unambiguous message to the rest of the world that the United States was prepared to go around Gatt and cut its own trade-and-investment deals with all willing allies. Equally important, clear accession rules in an agreement ratified under fast-track procedures would have protected the rest of Latin America against future Congressional misgivings or a drastic change in the American political climate.

But this is exactly why a detailed accession clause would have been a mistake.

First, it would have kept Congress out of the trade negotiation business. As appealing as that prospect might seem, the clumsy and irksome process of obtaining Congressional approval is the best way to build a consensus for a policy that has no automatic mandate. There are reasons why the Constitution specifically assigns to the legislature the right to regulate commerce.

Second, it would put control of U.S. trade strategy—which in Latin America's case is now the core of U.S. foreign policy—in the hands of foreign applicants. The terms and sequence of free trade pacts would be determined not by U.S. interests—the security of the Panama Canal, say, or concerns over Caribbean emigration—but by the domestic economic policies of the petitioners. Uruguay, for example, would get in line far ahead of Nicaragua, despite Washington's long history of involvement in Central America and continued stake in its stability. The Reagan Administration's Caribbean Basin Initiative—which targeted investment incentives toward poor nearby economies of recognized U.S. strategic and economic importance—received bipartisan support precisely because it recognized these selfish national priorities.

Third, a mechanistic approach to NAFTA membership would undermine other subregional trade groupings that Washington has long and rightly supported. Latin American economic integration is not a new idea. The multiple attempts to create common markets and free trade networks over the last 30 years have provided some valuable lessons. The most important is that grandiose hemispheric experiments tend to founder ingloriously, while modest subregional pacts—the Central American Common Market is the best example—can make surprising headway. Washington should make clear that it favors the development of all regional trade pacts, not simply the expansion of NAFTA.

But that's not the signal Washington has been sending. Shortly after beginning free trade negotiations with Mexico, Washington signed a framework agreement with the Mercosur countries—Brazil, Argentina, Paraguay and Uruguay—to encourage the new bloc's internal integration and alleviate commercial frictions with the United States. Mercosur officials saw the framework agreement as a prelude to a pact with NAFTA, sometime after Mercosur concluded its own internal integration at the close of 1994.

Then, in May 1992, fulfilling a pledge he had made in Santiago a year and a half earlier, President Bush promised that Chile would be the next country favored with a free trade agreement.

The promise to Chile highlighted the inconsistencies of the Enterprise for the Americas policy. Chile is the only significant Latin American economy that has spurned regional trade groupings. It abandoned the Andean Pact in the early 1980s and declined invitations to join the Mercosur Group in the early 1990s—because, authorities explained, the Chilean economy was far more liberalized and freed of distorting subsidies than its neighbors. In truth, Chile feared being dragged down by its stagnant, inflation-ridden neighbors. It may not have really needed a free trade pact with Washington, but by any strict economic policy standard Chile was clearly eligible. Its distance, small size, contrasting growing seasons, and lack of a developed industrial base also insured that Chile would not arouse the intense opposition in American labor and farming circles that Mexico inspired.

The NAFTA accord does not explicitly preclude the negotiation of parallel bilateral trade accords outside North America. Indeed, Mexico has already set up its own direct trade pact with Chile, among others, while the United States has a free trade agreement with Israel. But for the United States to enter into its own agreement with other Latin American countries at this point would violate the spirit of NAFTA. It would anger the Canadians, who were none too happy about the expansion of the North American trade zone into Mexico. And Mexico, while unwilling publicly to challenge the petition of a sister republic, is in no hurry to see its own relative advantages under NAFTA diluted by southern competition.

Simply delaying the entry of other countries would have enormous advantages for Mexico: American garment manufacturers in the Dominican Republic say that even if they knew that their Dominican exports would get duty-free American treatment two or three years down the road, they would still strongly consider immediate relocation to Mexico. The lag would be too long and the Mexico-based competition too fierce. In the interim, Mexico would benefit from its own network of new bilateral free trade agreements, stretching south through Central America and Colombia to Bolivia and Chile, and east into most of the Caribbean. Mexican officials have been quite frank in their pitch to foreign investors: Mexico may soon be the only country in the Americas offering duty-free export access to both the North and South.

Diminishing Returns: Pushing NAFTA South

The Enterprise Initiative was praised by pro-NAFTA forces, but privately it made them nervous. It gave fresh ammunition to critics who felt NAFTA should be debated not just on its own merits, but as a precedent for free trade throughout the hemisphere.

From a domestic American political perspective, there were persuasive arguments for a trade deal with Mexico: the obvious U.S. stake in border security, the long-term easing of immigration pressures, and the advantage to American business of concentrating subsidiaries in a nearby economy that is overwhelmingly dependent on American imports. None of these arguments applies to more distant countries like Uruguay and Ecuador—which raise no potential security issues, have never been major exporters of immigrants, and have long enjoyed far more diversified foreign trade and investment patterns. In fact, including such countries would only dilute free trade's impact on Mexico, thereby reduce NAFTA's benefits for the United States.

But there was another problem: the Initiative's unstated premise was that the Western Hemisphere is a natural market unit. This is debatable at best.

In 1990, when Bush unveiled his plan, trade between the United States and Latin America amounted to barely $100 billion a year. Mexico alone accounted for more than half of that. U.S.-Canada trade, by contrast, surpassed $170 billion a year, similar to the scale of commerce between the United States and the entire European Union. Commerce with the second biggest single American trading partner, Japan, reached $140 billion.

Within the hemisphere, trade patterns vary widely. The United States accounts for 70 percent of Mexico's foreign trade and nearly half of the total commerce of the Caribbean Basin economies. But the U.S. share of Latin America's foreign trade shrinks to less than 25 percent south of the Equator. In the giant Mercosur zone the Europeans have long been bigger trading partners than the North Americans. For Chile, the biggest export market and foreign investor is Japan.

Only a third of American trade occurs within the Western Hemisphere. And of that more than two-thirds takes place inside North America. Trade between the United States and Canada alone is nearly triple the volume of all American trade with Latin America and the Caribbean, excluding Mexico. The country's two NAFTA neighbors account for 26 percent of total American trade, compared with the rest of Latin America's 7 percent.

It is true that Latin America has been the fastest-growing American export market in recent years. But that's because the region is climbing out of the trough of the debt crisis, which forced drastic import-slashing currency devaluations. Even so, American exports to Latin America and the Caribbean ($63.5 billion in 1991) account for just 15 percent of American sales worldwide ($421.8 billion). Mexico alone accounts for half of that market and for more than two-thirds of its growth over the past five years.

The overwhelming Mexican preference for American goods—consistently more than 70 percent of its total imports—isn't shared by the rest of the region. Of the larger economies, Venezuela comes closest, buying half its imports from the United States; in neighboring Colombia the figure is 38 percent. Further south, American market share drops off fast: 28 percent in Argentina, 24 percent in Brazil (the same as South Korea), 21 percent in Chile (the same as the Philippines).

From a U.S. trade viewpoint, Latin America without Mexico is a marginal player. Internationally, it is even less important. In 1990 the three NAFTA countries together generated 18 percent of total world trade flows. The rest of the Western Hemisphere combined—from Central America and the Caribbean down through Brazil to the southern cone—contributed less than 3 percent.

The United States is the region's single biggest market, buying $57.6 billion from Latin America in 1991. But that is just two-fifths of the region's total exports. And even that apparent dependence is statistically skewed by Mexico, by far the region's biggest exporter. With American sales accounting for a huge 73 percent of its total exports, Mexico is in the same acute dependency league as Canada, which sends 80 percent of its exports directly across the border. By contrast, countries in the nearby

LATIN AMERICA AS A MARKET

The Major Latin Economies:
U.S. Exports as a share of their Imports (1991)

Mexico: 71%

Venezuela: 49%

Colombia: 38%

Argentina: 28%

Brazil: 24%

Chile: 21%

Source: International Monetary Fund, 1992

Caribbean Basin typically send less than half their exports to the United States (Costa Rica, 46 percent; Guatemala, 38 percent; Jamaica, 39 percent). Venezuela is the exception at 55 percent, because of oil shipments. South of the equator the American market accounts for less than a quarter of all export sales (Brazil, 23 percent; Peru, 22 percent; Chile, 17 percent; Argentina, 14 percent).

In the early years of the European Economic Community, trade within Europe already accounted for more than half of its members' aggregate foreign trade. Three decades later that intraregional market share has risen to 70 percent.

Such self-containment could never be reached in the Western Hemisphere, even under the most optimistic visions of trans-American economic integration—unless, of course, the region's trade rules were intentionally diversionary.

Today, the great motor of extra-hemispheric trade is the Pacific Basin. It's no accident that Western Hemispheric integration efforts mirror trade pact proposals in East Asia, where regional cooperation is tempered by the reality of dependence on markets outside the region.

Some analysts look at these parallel regional relationships and conclude that there is little harm in formalizing them, with a U.S.-dominated Americas Enterprise Zone on one side of the Pacific trading with a Japanese-controlled East Asian consortium on the other. Businessmen in Mexico talk of benefiting from a broader Tokyo-Washington trade axis, with Mexico assuming a role analogous to Korea; down the line, Singapore and Chile would sign on, while Thailand, Malaysia and Indonesia became the rough equivalent of the Mercosur. The problem with this vision is economic and political autonomy. In each region, the issue becomes more acute as the trade web moves south. Do the Thais and Malays want their relationship with North America to be defined by Tokyo? And even if they do, should U.S. policy encourage it?

Similarly, why should Chilean or Brazilian economic ties to Japan be run through Washington? That's not in Santiago's best interest, or Brasilia's, or Tokyo's. It would be equally inadvisable for Washington to assert some proto-colonial pride of place among South America's trading partners. When viewed from Mexico City, such bloc-to-bloc mediation is simply an institutionalization of economic realities. In South America, however, trade and investment sources are far more diverse. A set of trade blocs framing the Pacific would only promote the unnecessary dependence of Southeast Asia on Tokyo and of South America's southern cone on Washington.

If these new regional relationships are to succeed, they need to evolve naturally from mutual self-interest. On those grounds, there is a better case for a post-NAFTA deal for countries that already enjoy broad duty-free access to the American market under the Caribbean Basin Initiative. The CBI countries can tap a reservoir of goodwill in Washington, as well as a sense of self-interest and historic responsibility.

Ties of history and immigration must also be considered, as they are in the EC-Eastern European relationship. Half of what was Mexico is now the southwestern United States. The historic connection is real. Mexico is the culture of origin of more than half the Latino electorate; it is the birthplace of at least half the country's undocumented workers. Most of them live in a region that was Mexico for half its recorded history.

Like Mexico, the 24 CBI countries are linked to the United States by geography, history, immigration and immediate security concerns. They depend on the United States for almost half their trade and investment, and include such permanent foreign policy headaches as Nicaragua, Panama and Haiti. The leading Caribbean islands all have large and growing emigrant colonies on the U.S. mainland, as does Central America. The Caribbean Basin countries sent 1.35 million legal immigrants to the United States in the 1980s, a proportionately larger outflow than Mexico's 1.67 million. A quasi-colonial relationship with the United States has been a constant part of their lives as independent nations. To give these economies special consideration is not exclusionary, nor would it be seen as such elsewhere in the world.

Happily, the Caribbean Basin economies are manageably small. As a group, the CBI beneficiaries (the Caribbean and Central American common market members plus Haiti, the Dominican Republic, Panama, Surinam, Turks and Caicos, and the Cayman Islands) have an economy one-third the size of Mexico's, with a little over half the population.

Their economies are not terribly complex, either, thus simplifying the task of trade negotiators. A revised CBI deal with new sectoral agreements on sugar and textiles would shield the Caribbean from most of the damage threatened by NAFTA. Bolstering the economies of the Caribbean would also help Puerto Rico, which worries that NAFTA could hurt its service industries, including transshipment ports and banking.

These accords ideally would be negotiated not bilaterally with Washington, but between the NAFTA bloc and the two regional associations: the anglophone Caribbean Community (Caricom) and the Central American Common Market (CACM). Special arrangements would be needed for Hispaniola and, probably not too far into the future, Cuba. But to go further, into a full-fledged NAFTA-style trade and investment pact with the Caribbean region, would require parallel agreements on the environment and labor rights and some basic certification of democratic procedure. Strict application of these standards probably would disallow every country in the region except Costa Rica and the former British colonies of the Caribbean.

The next logical tier of free trade candidates would be Colombia, Venezuela and Ecuador, which recently formed a customs union. Together, they are slightly more than half the size of Mexico in population and economic activity. They all depend on American trade and investment and offer safe, abundant supplies of the most crucial American import: oil. South America's northern trio could first strike sectoral trade agreements—but only if Colombia manages to restrain its cocaine trade, which is already spilling into and out of Venezuela and Ecuador.

Mercosur is another matter entirely. The vast territory taken up by Uruguay, Paraguay, Argentina and Brazil has an economy and population equal to two-and-a-half Mexicos. The Mercosur bloc is not an important supplier of goods or labor to the United States, nor a first-rank customer. The North American economies are essentially complementary, but Brazil and Argentina offer stiff competition in agriculture (soybeans, citrus, wheat, sorghum, grapes) and high-tech industry (small aircraft, military equipment).

The political reality is that South America has fewer friends in Washington and on Wall Street than Mexico. Brazil's intellectual property rights rules have alienated computer hardware and software companies. Bankers have been frustrated by long, difficult debt negotiations. They aren't eager to go to bat for either Argentina or Brazil, much less Peru. Steel companies are more afraid of competition from Brazil than from Mexico. And Detroit auto makers have nowhere near the commitment to South America that they do to Mexico, where their factories have been continually modernized and integrated into regional production lines.

Mexico's foreign investment boom—focused on the development of export-oriented manufacturing—has swollen the ranks of its corporate advocates in Washington. By contrast, most American investment in Brazil and Argentina dates back to the 1960s and 1970s and is aimed at the region's domestic market. The numbers are telling: the American share of direct foreign investment in Mexico—almost 70 percent—is equivalent to its share of foreign trade. In Brazil and the Southern Cone, the former is almost twice as high as the latter: 40 percent versus 20 percent. Despite the conventional wisdom, trade does not always follow investment. Multinational subsidiaries in South America are mostly dedicated to local sales. It is only natural that they are more interested in pushing internal economic reforms than in improving South American access to their own home markets.

The South American countries also don't have the history of continual U.S. political and military intervention that typifies the Caribbean Basin. One indirect consequence is immigration flows: the United States received just 466,000 legal immigrants from all of South America in the 1980s, compared with 3 million from Mexico and the Caribbean. Illegal immigration amplifies all those numbers, but it doesn't change their proportions much.

Nor is Washington the overwhelmingly dominant foreign player that it is in the Caribbean Basin. Argentina has long cultivated a special relationship with Italy, as has Brazil with Portugal and southern Africa. Chile is cementing new economic partnerships in the South Pacific. Peruvian President Alberto Fujimori was elected in part on the strength of his promise of closer ties with Japan.

Even assuming the most optimistic scenario, the United States is unlikely to be ready for a true free trade pact with America's southern hemisphere until late in the 1990s. Reforms to brake inflation, spur investment, and settle outstanding debts have yet to be implemented in troubled economies like Brazil and Peru. Once the trade debate moves south of the Equator, its dynamics markedly change.

The Chilean Option

Chile has been lauded for years as Latin America's great free-market success story. It was the pioneer in privatization, debt reduction, and trade liberalization—virtually all the economic reforms that were later adopted by Mexico. Chilean securities are now ranked as investment-grade by American risk assessment agencies, another first for the region. In Washington as well as on Wall Street, Chile is cited as a model to be admired and copied. But the harsh truth is that there are few compelling reasons for President Clinton to honor George Bush's promise to make Chile the country's next free trade partner.

To begin with, there are practical problems. The dispute between the United States and the European Union over Gatt would probably keep Chile off the agenda until late 1994 or beyond. Even if NAFTA and a new Gatt accord could be concluded quickly, conflicts with other American trading partners—China, Japan, the poor countries of the Caribbean— inevitably would take precedence over talks with Chile, as they should. In all those cases, the stakes for the United States are far higher.

Advocates of a pact with Chile have been helped by the absence in Washington of organized resistance to such a deal. But the corollary is that there is no natural coalition of American interests willing to do battle on Chile's behalf. The fundamental question—whether a bilateral free trade accord is in the long-term interest of both Chile and the United States—has never been thought through in either country. If a free trade pact is seen as a gift to the deserving, rather than as an exercise in job creation, it is unlikely to win Congressional support. So for Chile, virtue may be its own—and only—reward.

Unless, that is, a deal with Chile is concluded simply as a demonstration project for the rest of Latin America. From the moment Bush proposed a free zone "from Alaska to Tierra del Fuego," it seemed clear that there would be just one practical way for him to realize this goal. First he needed to conclude his real priority, the agreement with Mexico and Canada. Then he could try to strike a separate deal with Chile, which was too small and distant to be a threat to American labor, and too open and liberal to be easily refused. The straits of Bering and Magellan would thus be linked in duty-free commerce, fulfilling the formal promise of the Enterprise for the Americas Initiative. The rest of the pan-American trade map would be sketched in with subregional trade pacts and a network of bilateral framework agreements with Washington. Unifying these arrangements in a coherent hemispheric whole would be somebody else's problem.

The cynical view of the Enterprise for the Americas Initiative, expressed by some U.S. diplomats in the region at the time, held that since most of Latin America was plainly incapable of meeting U.S. demands for economic reform, there was no real harm in extending the offer. At worst, it would encourage countries to keep moving toward freer markets. The concept of a hemispheric trade bloc was also seen as a useful (albeit empty) threat towards Europe and Asia. If Paris and Tokyo started worrying about the implications of a Fortress of the Americas, the thinking went, they might go along with America's proposal for a radical liberalization of global services and agricultural trade under the Gatt. A deal with Chile would make this strategy credible, since there were few objective economic requirements for membership that Chile had not already surpassed.

From the viewpoint of North American economic self-interest, the most persuasive argument *for* a trade agreement with Chile is that it wouldn't do any harm: free trade is better than fettered trade, and Chile is too small to pose an industrial threat to American workers. But that is hardly enough. In times of economic stress, a trade accord must be sold as a solution to domestic problems, be it illegal immigration or excess grain production. Chile neither poses nor resolves such problems.

A good case can also be made for extending NAFTA privileges to countries hurt by trade diversion into Mexico. Clear examples include the Dominican Republic (sugar), Costa Rica (coffee), Venezuela (petrochemicals), Colombia (flowers), and Brazil (orange juice and steel). In Chile, by contrast, there is no export sector clearly penalized by NAFTA. Another argument, from a Washington viewpoint, is that a trade pact is needed to help a country rise above acute, potentially destabilizing poverty, or to preserve a fragile democracy. Chile, a victim of its own success, doesn't have these problems.

Chilean Finance Minister Alejandro Foxley, frustrated by Washington's foot-dragging, hinted in mid-1992 that if Chile wasn't welcomed into a free trade pact with the United States, it might pursue its own accord with its Asian trade partners. Japan, Foxley pointedly noted, had recently surpassed the United States as Chile's biggest single export market. If the Minister's remark was intended as a threat, it was remarkably inept: few American opinion leaders care whether Chile gets a free trade pact, and of those few who have actually thought about it, most tend to see it as a favor, nothing more. If they knew that Chile did more business with Japan than with the United States, they might think it a wasteful favor. It could even be argued that a Chilean alliance with the Pacific would make Chile a natural ally of U.S. efforts to prevent such a bloc from becoming an ethnically exclusive Asian enclave. It could also help speed the formation of parallel links between NAFTA and East Asia. It might even attract Japanese portfolio investors into South America, a long-standing U.S. goal.

A few voices have been raised in Washington against a free trade agreement with Chile. It is argued that the Caribbean countries are closer, poorer, and more deserving. Other critics fear that regional trade blocs could hinder progress towards trade liberalization under Gatt. Still others oppose bilateral deals with Chile and other countries precisely because they threaten regional trade groupings. MIT's Rudiger Dornbusch, though a vigorous advocate of a pan-American trade zone, argues that it should be built out of NAFTA and other subregional blocs, not bilaterally. A U.S. pact with Chile, he argues, would undermine the Mercosur and encourage other Southern Cone countries to strike their own deals with Washington.

Those concerns are justified: Argentina's rising trade deficit with Brazil has led Buenos Aires business leaders to urge withdrawal from Mercosur and the negotiation of a bilateral pact with the United States. Argentina's problem is not "contamination" by Brazilian inflation, as it sometimes contends, but an antiquated, ingrown industrial base. Brazil, despite its fiscal chaos and political uncertainties, has a dynamic, competitive capitalist core. On a level trading floor, the state of Sao Paulo will thrash greater Buenos Aires every time. It would be ironic if the pursuit of a free trade deal with Washington allowed Argentina to evade direct, healthy competition with its Brazilian neighbors.

It would be even more ironic if a hub-and-spoke expansion of NAFTA ended up creating a U.S.-Latin America trade network without Brazil—which is, after all, half of Latin America. But that would be the probable consequence of Mercosur's dissolution.

The Brazilians consider their country the natural economic anchor of South America, with trade alliances reaching into Europe and Japan as well as north to the United States. Diplomatically, they have long oscillated between China-like insularity and American-style globalism. They do not easily see themselves as part of a "hemispheric community."

New Age Imperialism?

Another risk in spinning a hemispheric web of economic alliances is that it may lead to hegemony with a human face. American dominance was once encoded in regional defense pacts; now it may reassert itself in trade agreements. Even when the economic benefits are genuinely mutual, the imbalance of power guarantees that the rules will be enforced by and from Washington. Access to the American market is the free trade carrot, the threat of denial the stick.

The danger is that this new pan-American trading system may perpetuate old patterns of dominance and resentment. That might be a risk worth taking if the economic rewards to all involved were overwhelmingly apparent. But they are not. Prohibitive duties and non-tariff barriers blocking South American exports are much more of a problem in Western Europe and East Asia than in the United States.

Many economists who profess to favor multi-lateralism and abhor bloc-based regionalism nonetheless endorse the idea of hemispheric free trade. Some argue that with Gatt's eternal political difficulties, it is better to dismantle trade barriers regionally than not at all; with luck, they say, local progress will spur global liberalization—through both threat and example. All parties insist that these new free trade groupings would be Gatt-legal, with no new external trade barriers to third-party products and investments. Yet there are clear philosophical and tactical differences between pursuing trade liberalization on a regional basis and pursuing it through Gatt.

There is a telling parallel between the trade policy experts who prefer regional liberalization to an exclusively global approach and the foreign policy experts who would rather appeal to hemispheric agencies in regional conflicts than to the United Nations or other world bodies. In each case, the assumption—often inchoate, rarely directly stated—is that Latin American nations generally accept and benefit from U.S. tutelage, falling as they do within the natural sphere of U.S. influence. With foreign policy directives increasingly enforced by trade sanctions, these regional economic and diplomatic mechanisms are not just analogous, but mutually reinforcing.

Facing the Washington mall is a symbol of this linkage: the pillared, Romanesque headquarters of the Organization of American States (OAS). Its architecture—and its place among the marble monuments of American federalism—reflect its origin as something like a neocolonial office for the hemisphere. Its ragged grounds and grimy walls, like the second-echelon envoys who gather inside, show the results of decades of neglect. In the 1980s, with Central America torn apart by war and all of Latin America struggling with its deepest economic emergency in half a century, the OAS was conspicuously irrelevant. Civil conflicts were addressed within the region by such ad-hoc assemblages as the Contadora Group. This revived old demands within the region that the OAS either disband or reform itself with an exclusively Latin American and Caribbean membership. Financial battles, meanwhile, were fought either bilaterally or within the multilateral lending agencies.

In the 1990s, however, some of the same U.S. policymakers who favor a hemispheric free trade zone are trying to remake the OAS into an enforcer of Latin American democracy. The OAS provided the umbrella for sanctions against Haiti after the coup against President Jean-Bertrand Aristide. It was also the forum in which Peruvian President Alberto Fujimori felt obliged to promise new elections. It has been urged to convene its own military force—to attack drug cartels and back up economic sanctions against coup leaders. The OAS has also become a formal sponsor of vote-monitoring missions, with stature to condemn—though not invalidate—national elections.

In Washington, this vision of a brave new OAS is making strange bedfellows: Democrats in the best tradition of Wilsonian interventionism, Republican cold warriors looking to battle leftist insurgencies, and former adversaries of both in the human rights movement, who want multilateral election-monitoring and tough sanctions against military *golpistas*. The common thread binding all together is a desire to protect elected governments against internal threat without resorting to unilateral force by the United States.

Proposals to revive the OAS are simply the latest phase in a reshaping of hemispheric relationships which began with debt restructuring pacts and which is now continuing with free trade arrangements. The economic relationships of the future will include explicit demands that poorer trading partners conform to U.S. expectations on environmental protection, labor rules, due process, and other sorts of domestic behavior. The linkage is increasingly direct. Any country singled out by the OAS for violating democratic procedures risks the loss of favorable trade treatment from the United States—and so might any country challenging American policy within the OAS. In an era of capital scarcity, the promise of a trade pact with a leading industrial economy is a powerful enticement, and the threat of trade sanctions is a powerful stick.

The end of the cold war has made the United States less concerned about security and more predisposed towards pragmatic, respectful cooperation with its neighbors. The conditions Washington would attach to normal trade and diplomatic relations are things that most Latin Americans want: free elections, a clean environment, economic growth. But efforts to promote these goals are unlikely to work if they are seen as resulting from foreign pressure, particularly U.S. pressure, rather than growing naturally out of domestic politics. In addition, such pressures are not likely to be applied consistently, reflecting instead the prevailing political fashion in Washington.

The deep-seated didactic instincts of the United States, combined with the desperation of its neighbors for capital, could easily lead to a new form of American hegemony. As in the past, U.S. efforts to make the world safe for democracy—and now also for the environment, entrepreneurial capitalism, and other fine things—can be counted on to create tension and instability on both ends of the relationship.

Things would be different if the United States were willing to play by new pan-American rules. But there isn't the slightest chance of real reciprocity.

The U.S. Congress is not about to let outsiders pass binding judgment on U.S. foreign investment rules, or immigration policies, or on the clearcutting of Oregonian rain forests, or electoral rules and practices. A 1992 Congressional primary election in Texas was staged for a second time—on the orders of a U.S. federal judge—after the loser presented circumstantial evidence of fraud. If the evidence had been presented to a hemispheric panel dominated by Latin Americans, would Texans have heeded the verdict? Strangest of all to contemplate is the United States bowing to foreign demands for fiscal discipline and increased domestic savings—exactly the kinds of reforms Washington has routinely demanded in Latin America over the past decade.

The end of the cold war has let the United States see Latin America as an economic partner, not a security problem. This opportunity to rise above the paternalism of the past could be lost, however, in the creation of new hemispheric bureaucracies where U.S. power predominates. It would be ironic if the advocates of environmentalism, democratic reform, and market freedoms cleared the way for a New Age imperialism.

NAFTA First

The first priority has to be the consolidation of the North American trade area—a process that has already begun with NAFTA's ratification. At the same time, the countries of Central America and the Caribbean should renegotiate their special relationships with the expanded North American bloc. Not just Washington is involved: Mexico has its own tentative free trade deal with Central America, and Canada has long had a special relationship with the Caribbean.

Does that mean leaving South America out? Yes, most of it—at least for the rest of the decade. If global liberalization stalls and regional blocs begin diverting trade and investment, the pan-American trade plan could be revived. If not, there would be no need for a hemispheric economic alliance.

In the meantime, South America can build on its traditional strengths of trade and investment diversity. The distraction of "hemispheric" rhetoric could derail the difficult Mercosur trade integration process, slated to conclude in 1994. It would also keep the South Americans from directing their free trade fire at Europe and East Asia. By fighting together as allies within Gatt, where North and South America share an interest in liberalizing agricultural trade, the NAFTA and Mercosur blocs could forge a more realistic partnership than they could within the artificial confines of a hemispheric trade zone.

There are other arguments for hemispheric free trade. One is simply that it keeps the pressure on for economic reform, to the ultimate benefit of all the countries involved. But that pressure is already acutely felt: tariffs and foreign investment restrictions are dropping quickly everywhere in the region, even without a new trade pact. As in Mexico and Chile, and the East Asian economies before them, most of what has to be done can and should be done unilaterally. Economic virtue is its own reward: sound fiscal and investment policies will attract and multiply capital. The United States is more open to Latin America's products than those from any other important industrial market. It is hardly obliged to respond to overdue liberalization with trade concessions.

A more compelling argument is that a free trade agreement is a guarantor of permanent market access. Potential investors in Brazil's citrus industry, for example, could justifiably worry that a cannery shipping orange juice to New York today might be hit with prohibitive U.S. tariffs in the future. Stock markets would remain forbiddingly volatile, with any sign of resurgent U.S. protectionism prompting swift capital withdrawals.

Eliminating that risk, however, doesn't necessarily require a comprehensive free trade accord. Building on its network of framework agreements, Washington could negotiate bilateral and multilateral prohibitions on future trade barriers. This would assure market access and prevent protectionist backsliding. Similar pacts could be struck with trading partners in Europe and Asia.

Though well intended, the Enterprise for the Americas Initiative was another example of Washington raising expectations that it could not fulfill. It potentially jeopardized one solid trade integration accomplishment—the accord with Canada—and called into question the depth of U.S. commitment to an agreement with Mexico.

For its original proponents, a purely North American common market had a logic based on the reality of interdependence. The volume and patterns of U.S.-Canadian and U.S.-Mexican trade over the decades has proved that the three economies are more complementary than competitive. The hemispheric free zone idea, by contrast, is rooted in common misconceptions about regional and global trade flows. Formally inviting Mexico into a North American market is a recognition of market reality: since World War II the United States has consistently accounted for two-thirds of Mexico's foreign trade and investment, despite a continuous Mexican effort to diversify both. That is not true of Latin America's southern hemisphere.

South Americans are not clamoring for special access to the United States but for a fairer crack at all the markets of the industrialized world. Confining themselves to a hemispheric system would imply reciprocal privileges for American products and companies, which would discourage Japanese and European investment. It is not at all clear that this would be in South America's interest.

The United States should also assess the plan on the basis of its own self-interest.

There is nothing sacred about the boundaries of the Western Hemisphere. On most pertinent grounds—economic interdependence, ethnic and historical ties, security interests—a better case could be made for the inclusion of Korea in an expanded NAFTA, or the Philippines, than for Argentina or Bolivia.

There are also questions about the viability of a trade bloc dominated by heavily indebted commodities producers, a category that includes the United States. There are clear synergies and few areas of direct competition between the United States and Mexico; this is less true of wheat-exporting Argentina or airplane-exporting Brazil. And the United States will probably always have stronger business interests in East Asia and Western Europe than it does in South America.

To be successful, trade integration efforts must follow market reality. The three nations of North America are a natural economic unit. "The Americas" are not.

Discount Foreign Aid?

Even if it were a good idea, building a hemispheric trade zone is beyond the reach of the Clinton Administration. But Clinton could make a quick, constructive impact on the region by reviving the forgotten debt reduction and investment fund components of the Bush Enterprise for the Americas Initiative.

Designed as an Alliance for Progress for the debt age, the Initiative has considerable virtue of being relatively cheap. The only direct U.S. financial commitment was to have been a $500 million contribution (spread over five years) to a $1.5 billion investment fund. In addition, the Bush Administration said that it would forgive up to $5 billion of the $12 billion owed by Latin America to U.S. government agencies. Yet when Bush left office, the investment fund remained unfunded and Washington had less than $500 million from Latin America's debt obligations.

When he announced his Enterprise plan, President Bush said that the Japanese and Europeans would put up the other $1 billion for the $1.5 billion fund. Neither Tokyo nor Brussels was informed about their largess beforehand. Neither was the Inter-American Development Bank, which Bush proposed as the fund's administrator. It wasn't until more than a year later that Washington officially asked for Japanese and European contributions, and even then it wasn't clear to the designated donors exactly what this new fund was expected to do.

The 1992 Bush budget request said only that the fund would promote privatization, foreign investment, and unspecified "investment regime reforms." White House briefing papers said the fund would provide money for technical assistance and job training. All those worthy goals, critics noted, were already supported by programs financed by the World Bank and the Inter-American Development Bank itself. Some IDB insiders also questioned their organization's capacity to run a new fund when it was struggling to manage a loan program that had recently doubled to more than $5 billion a year.

In early 1993, the Europeans reluctantly pledged $130 million, and the Japanese at last agreed to put up the entire $500 million if the United States came through with its own contribution. The Congress ultimately authorized $90 million of the requested $100 million, but made U.S. appropriations contingent on disbursements from other donors.

Somebody has to go first. Washington has a firm promise of Japanese matching funds for U.S. aid to Latin America. The Clinton Administration shouldn't squander the opportunity. But the fund needs a clearer purpose. One sensible application would be cost-efficient investments in public services—hospitals, schools, potable water projects—which suffered from neglect in the privatizing 1980s.

Clinton could also make an immediate difference with official debt. The loan forgiveness proposal raised expectations throughout the region. Treasury Secretary Nicholas Brady's commercial debt securitization and reduction plan, though initially opposed by most bankers, has doubled the market value of Latin debt and stabilized the finances of beneficiary economies.

The architect of the Enterprise Initiative was Bush's acerbic but respected Undersecretary for International Affairs David Mulford. Unfortunately, the Mulford debt reduction plan was hamstrung by U.S. budget constraints. Its strict conditionality—demanding fiscal reforms, privatization and trade liberalization—barred many poorer countries where loans from governments are a big part of the overall debt. Even if every penny of the scheduled $5 billion had been forgiven, Latin America's total foreign debt would have fallen by just 1 percent.

All this became irrelevant, however, when Congress balked at authorizing even such modest forgiveness. The 1992 Bush budget proposed erasing $216 million in Latin American and Caribbean debts to the U.S. Agency for International Development; Congress approved $50 million. Bush asked to cancel $70 million in outstanding food loans; Congress agreed to forgive $40 million. More loans were erased later in Central America, but the reduction still fell far short of the original promise.

Congressional critics of NAFTA and the Caribbean Basin Initiative say that these trade pacts don't address the underlying problem of the region's foreign debt. Clinton could change that by reducing eligible official debt more quickly and on easier terms than Bush proposed. It's not a lot of money: the debt is mostly long-term, low-interest loans, producing little annual income for the Treasury. After all, the Bush Administration wiped out $5 billion owed by Egypt and Poland without imposing economic conditions of any sort.

Official U.S. credits have the greatest relative weight in five struggling low-income democracies of the Caribbean Basin: Jamaica, Costa Rica, Honduras, El Salvador, and the Dominican Republic. All will be hurt by NAFTA, and they need and deserve U.S. support.

CHAPTER 11

The Hidden Target: NAFTA and Japan

Just a century after the Spanish Conquest, galleons were ferrying silver and spices from Acapulco to the Philippines and on to Japan. Europe's path to the Orient traversed Mexico, and its commerce became Mexicanized en route; the capsicum chili peppers that ignite Szechuan and Thai cuisine are among the legacies of this trade.

Not only goods crossed the Pacific. Emissaries from the viceroy made careful entreaties to the shoguns, while Franciscans from Cuernavaca embarked on proselytizing missions to the Japanese peasantry. The viceroy's men were courteously welcomed; the Franciscans were not. St. Felipe de Jesus, the first Mexican to be canonized, died a grisly martyr's death in Nagasaki in 1597.

Noblemen from the Edo court, emerging suddenly from their fierce insularity, received a warmer reception when they visited the colonial palaces of Mexico City. They saw Mexico as a rich new market and a conduit for coveted European technology, and were generously entertained by *criollo* merchants eager for commerce outside the control of Madrid.

These early contacts are sometimes elegized by Mexican and Japanese officials in sake-and-tequila toasts to their ancient friendship. But Mexico never became a Pacific nation. Japan shut its doors to foreigners in 1640 and kept them closed for two centuries. When they reopened, independence from Spain had long since severed Mexico's ties with Manila, its door to the Orient.

Mexico looked north and east, not west. Early industrial development centered on Mexico City and Monterrey, each linked by railways to Gulf ports and the Texas border. Beginning in World War II, government-led import substitution added to the glut of industry around the capital and its northeastern rival. Later, in the 1960s and 1970s, Mexico underwent the longest period of sustained industrial expansion in its history, while southern California emerged as the most dynamic region of the world's biggest economy. Yet the contiguous Mexican Pacific remained a neglected backwater, dotted with tourist resorts and humble fishing towns.

Throughout industrialized Mexico, outside investment has always been overwhelmingly American, with U.S. companies consistently holding about two-thirds of the total direct foreign equity in the country. Next, in a pattern little changed since the 1950s, are the British and the Germans. The Japanese have been a sluggish fourth.

Mexico wanted the North American Free Trade Agreement to change all that. Instead, NAFTA has pushed the Japanese even farther away—increasing the pressures for an East Asian trade bloc and decreasing the prospect that fat East Asian trade surpluses will be channeled toward the cash-starved economy south of the Rio Grande.

■ The Salinas Administration has long seen Japan—along with its Pacific neighbors—as Mexico's biggest potential source of new financing, technology and markets. Despite early frustrations, Salinas himself insisted that NAFTA would ultimately make it easier for Mexico to attract Japanese investment south of the border. Many American critics of NAFTA said this is exactly what they feared.

Yet the evidence suggests that the hopes and fears of both sides are equally misplaced. From the standpoint of American self-interest, Japanese investment in Mexico would be an asset, not a problem. But the Japanese have never been terribly interested in Mexico, and NAFTA is likely to make them even less interested. Instead, ironically, NAFTA will encourage greater Japanese investment in the United States—particularly in job-producing manufacturing activities. Any incremental gain in Japan's Mexican investment is likely to take the form of portfolio investment or be concentrated in natural resource industries. The first makes Mexico richer and better able to afford American imports. The second provides equal or greater opportunities for American energy firms to exploit what has long been a carefully protected preserve of the Mexican state. Either way, America benefits.

In broad terms, NAFTA should hold the same appeal for Japanese companies that it does for American investors. Yet the pact includes provisions expressly meant to deter East Asian trade and investment. The strict "rules of origin" require most products to be at least three-fifths North American—making it impossible for most goods in Asian-owned final assembly plants to qualify for duty-free access to the American market. Japanese television manufacturers in Tijuana, for example, would be forced to build or buy their picture tubes in North America, instead of importing them from Asia.

The content rules are even tougher in the two industries where Asian competition is most feared: textiles and autos. In the apparel and textile business, NAFTA imposes a "yarn-forward" rule that essentially requires that qualifying garments and fabrics be woven out of North American thread; the practical effect will be to disqualify clothes made from Asian fabric. Nearly as strict is the 62.5 percent North American content rule for cars, which will keep Japanese manufacturers from using Mexico merely as an assembly and exporting site for the American market.

None of this has been lost on the Japanese government, which worries that the anti-Japanese impetus behind much of NAFTA will aggravate anti-U.S. sentiment at home, making bilateral trade relations even more difficult. In December 1992, a few days after NAFTA's signing, Canada's Brian Mulroney took a call from Japanese Prime Minister Kiichi Miyazawa, who sought assurance that NAFTA wouldn't close North America to Japanese goods.

Miyazawa was clearly hoping to avert domestic pressure for a stronger official reaction to NAFTA from Tokyo. That was asking for a lot: NAFTA's own American architects were hailing the agreement as a way to keep Asian-owned factories out of the Mexican market.

The anti-Japanese impulse behind the U.S. negotiating strategy represented an ironic mutation of U.S. policy. When Washington first began contemplating a trinational trade zone, it was in part as a response to the challenge of an integrated European Union and as a way to improve the security of the country's southern border. On both counts, an alliance with Japanese capital seemed to make sense. Indeed, U.S. officials repeatedly urged Tokyo to recycle its trade earnings into the developing world, claiming that such investment was in the interest of both the United States and Japan.

Now those interests were felt to conflict. With Japan commonly seen as the main U.S. rival in a post-Communist world, and Mexico struggling to shift its focus to the Pacific, the dynamics of the negotiations were quite different. Confronting the challenge of Japanese trade and invest-ment—by courting, containing or copying it—became a pervasive subtext in the NAFTA debate. Clinton trade chief Mickey Kantor claimed that failing to enact NAFTA could "open up opportunities for the Japanese and other countries to come in and take advantage of what we will not take advantage of."

Many American commentators appear convinced that Tokyo strate-gists have settled on Mexico as a low-wage, resource-rich back door into the American market. Buttressing their views are official Japanese state-ments of support for NAFTA and Tokyo's willingness to lend billions on soft terms to the Mexican treasury. But there is a critical distinction between the Japanese government and the Japanese private sector. Japa-nese business is far less interested in a NAFTA-ized Mexico than Ameri-cans seem to think.

When Salinas took office, American corporate holdings in Mexico had reached $14.9 billion, or 62 percent of all direct foreign investment there. Great Britain was a distant second, with $1.8 billion (dominated by pharmaceuticals), followed by Germany with $1.6 billion (half of it Volkswagen). Japan came next with $1.3 billion, just 5.4 percent of the total. Japan's stake in Mexico represented a scant 0.5 percent of its foreign holdings, a share roughly in line with Mexico's minuscule fraction of Japan's international trade. Buying just 0.7 percent of Japan's exports and supplying 0.8 percent of its imports, Mexico was barely a blip on Japan's strategic radar.

Salinas wanted to make those numbers rise. In his first year in office he slashed trade barriers, making Mexico an attractive market for Japanese consumer exports. The foreign debt was virtually eliminated as a mana-gerial and diplomatic problem by the Brady Plan refinancing. But the biggest enticement for the Japanese was supposed to be the announce-ment that Mexico and the United States would begin crafting a free trade deal. That, it was hoped, would be taken by the Japanese as proof that the United States was committed to Mexico's growth—not just for Mexico's sake, but because Mexico was an opportunity.

It hasn't worked out that way.

By the end of 1991, a three-year investment boom had nearly doubled overall foreign holdings in Mexico, from $24 billion to $40 billion. The Japanese share, however, had fallen below 5 percent. In 1989, Salinas's first full year in office, Japanese direct investment increased by a slight $36 million, less than a quarter of the $149 million gain of the year before. This represented barely 1 percent of the total $3 billion net increase in foreign direct investment in Mexico in 1989. Japan's attention was elsewhere: that same year it invested a record $8.2 billion in its fast-developing Asian neighbors, $14.8 billion in Europe, and a huge $32.5 billion in the United States. This pattern has continued, with the Japanese still contributing a meager 1 or 2 percent of net foreign capital flows into Mexico.

In portfolio inflows the meager Japanese share was especially striking, given Japan's soaring investments in comparable securities markets in Asia. More than $8 billion in foreign funds flowed into Mexican securities in 1991, smashing the previous record $3.4 billion in 1990. The bulk of this money came from the United States (much of it repatriated Mexican capital); there were also substantial investments from European institutional investors. Yet almost none—less than $200 million—originated in Tokyo. Nor was there any Japanese interest in the huge Mexican privatization deals that attracted bidders from around the world, disappointing officials who had hoped that Japanese capital and technology would help upgrade Mexico's steel and telecommunications industries.

Some analysts concluded from these numbers that Mexico would reluctantly abandon its courtship of the Orient and embrace NAFTA in a belated recognition of its North American economic destiny. Salinas himself rejected that analysis, stressing his continued determination to strengthen economic ties to the Pacific. One reason a North American free trade accord is worth pursuing, he said, is because it can be used to lure investment that would otherwise stay in East Asia. Mexican officials noted that the prospect of NAFTA had already led companies like Zenith and AT&T to relocate manufacturing operations from Singapore to Tamaulipas and lured Korean and Taiwanese textile and electronics factories to Baja and Sonora. Mexico is also joining Asian-dominated economic confederations like the Pacific Economic Cooperation Council.

Mexican cynics said this pro-Pacific posture was simply a cover for Salinas's true intention: a complete economic merger with the United States. Yet Salinas insisted that he had consistently advocated an open NAFTA, one receptive to extraregional trade and investment, as opposed to the continental fortress envisioned by some NAFTA boosters in the U.S. Congress—and by many wary observers in Tokyo. "The concerns expressed in some sectors in Asia would be well founded if the agreement were creating a closed economic zone, but this is not the case," Salinas argues. "Closed blocs are the prologue to trade wars and would be the worst possible scenario for the end of the century."

Japan's appeal is not only economic. Japanese capital carries little historical baggage, so it's less of a political problem in Mexico than American investment. That's a big asset for a government that wants to triple or even quadruple the total foreign investor stake in the country. There are also intangible attractions: Japanese business practices have a strong appeal to the big Mexican industrial clans, who fear a turn toward American-style antitrust enforcement. And then there is Japan's politics, which in practice long amounted to one-party rule, and which PRI apologists often used to justify their own domination of Mexican politics. Businessmen and politicians alike see in Japan an attractive alternative to the United States—a different path, politically and economically. If Japan's presence in Mexico could be increased, Mexico might be able to make that path its own.

In pursuing Japanese investment, Mexico faced deep skepticism. Tokyo businessmen questioned the depth and future of Mexico's economic reforms and its access to an increasingly protective American market. One of his closest advisors expressed Salinas's frustration: "It is never the right time for the Japanese. In the early 1980s they told us they needed to wait until inflation was controlled and the debt problem resolved. In the late 1980s they said they wanted to wait until our privatization and deregulation and trade liberalization programs were all put into place. Now in the early 1990s they say they need to wait and see how NAFTA will affect them."

Mexico's NAFTA proposals were designed to allay Japan's concerns. Mexican negotiators fought hard to keep content requirements from becoming even more restrictive than the final 60 percent compromise. In interviews for this book, Salinas stressed that a fundamental goal of Mexico in the NAFTA process was to diversify its international economic relations. The president's press office later delivered a typewritten transcript of one conversation in which the article "a" had been altered to "the," emphasizing that diversification was "the fundamental point" of his trade strategy—an editing change made, an aide said, at Salinas's behest. "We are extremely interested in Japan and the Pacific Rim," Salinas said. "Economic dynamism, technological capacity, financial resources, and markets are all concentrated there. We cannot remain outside this area." Mexican leaders have long eyed Japan as a potential counterweight to the United States, but no one has looked more closely than Salinas. As budget minister during the debt crisis, he became the leading government proponent of closer trade ties with Tokyo, a posture that seemed rooted as much in cultural admiration as in economic necessity. As press reports about Mexican-Japanese relations rarely fail to note, Salinas even sent his children to a Japanese-run primary school. This is not as exotic as it sounds: the educational norm among the Mexican gentry is the foreign-language private academy, be it a lycée, the American School, or a German-curriculum gymnasium. The Japanese school attended by the three Salinas children happened to be the closest elite private school to the southern Mexico City condominium complex where the Salinas family moved a decade ago. Yet the Japanese school is a unique institution, with direct Japanese government funding and curricular supervision, plus a no-nonsense faculty rotated in annually from Japan. Most students are the sons and daughters of expatriate Japanese or Mexicans of Japanese ancestry; though popular with upper-middle-class professionals, there are few children of cabinet ministers or captains of industry. It seemed characteristic of Salinas to choose schooling for his children that was more rigorous and meritocratic than the traditional upper-class alternatives—and at the same time good for his career and, eventually, for his country.

Once inaugurated, Salinas made Japanese relations a diplomatic priority. The interest was reciprocated. In Salinas's first nine months in office, Japan sent five high-level missions to Mexico to discuss aid and investment plans. The last and most important of these was headed by Prime Minister Toshiki Kaifu, marking the first state visit by a Japanese head of government. At a September 1989 reception in Los Pinos, the three young Salinas children greeted the prime minister in fluent Japanese, charming Kaifu and his traveling Japanese press corps. The gesture didn't hurt Salinas's image: he had already flattered Tokyo with his open admiration for Japan's economic success—and impressed its money men with his hard-headed anti-inflation and trade liberalization policies.

Two months later, as Salinas's first year in office drew to a close, Japanese officials signaled their approval of the new government by underwriting a $49 billion debt-reduction-and-refinancing deal. The debt workout was the first accomplishment of the so-called Brady Plan, under which direct bilateral support came not from the U.S. Treasury but from Tokyo. A $2.05 billion Japanese loan bankrolled the purchase of U.S. zero-coupon bonds, which served as collateral for the "Brady Bonds" issued by Mexico in exchange for old bank debt.

This early success led Salinas to believe that Mexico's transpacific ties could be tightened. Yet, perversely, the Brady Plan has proved to be the biggest obstacle to Japanese private investment.

Mexico has long disdained traditional foreign aid from the United States and other nations. It tells them that it wants investment, not charity; trade, not aid. But in Tokyo financial circles, Mexico is still seen as a supplicant. The Brady Plan was supported by the Japanese government but criticized bitterly by Japanese banks, which considered the debt-reduction scheme both financially and philosophically objectionable.

The stigma on Mexico is proving hard to erase. Mexico is now the biggest debtor to the Japanese Export-Import Bank—not because of the volume of its Japanese trade but because the Bank subsidized the last two Mexican debt bailouts. More recently, it has begun to underwrite Mexican environmental programs, providing loans with minimal Japanese purchasing requirements. This is a sharp departure from past Japanese foreign aid practices—and one which has done nothing to build a constituency for such aid in Japanese business. Outside East Asia, a country's attractiveness to private Japanese capital may be inversely proportionate to its success in getting Japanese government aid.

Washington feeds this syndrome by pressuring Tokyo to subsidize aid to Latin America while spurning its natural desire to influence how that money is spent. The Japanese recently agreed to U.S. requests to give billions to the Inter-American Development Bank and $500 million more to a murkily defined Enterprise for the Americas investment fund. In neither case did Washington seek Japanese views beforehand regarding the uses of the money. Japanese bankers were reminded of the Brady Plan: a foreign policy package crafted by and for Washington—but bankrolled by Tokyo.

This disgruntlement echoed the widespread resentment over American demands for Japanese contributions to the 1991 Gulf War, and heightened Tokyo's concern that it was being treated as a cash-filled handbag, not a true ally. Now, with NAFTA often touted as an anti-Japanese defense system, Japanese opponents of Tokyo's acquiescent posture toward Washington on Mexico are claiming vindication.

A little unabashed selfishness might help Japan deal with Mexico and the rest of Latin America more objectively—without Washington's mediation. Take, for example, Japanese investment in Mexico's oil industry. In the 1980s, Mexico became one of Japan's few reliable non–Middle East oil suppliers. Its crude oil sales to Japan jumped from 35,000 barrels a day in 1980 to 180,000 barrels by 1986, and have stayed at or above that level ever since.

Mexico would have happily sold more oil to Japan (and other Pacific buyers) when it first became a leading exporter in the late 1970s. But it lacked one essential: a Pacific supertanker port. Japan promptly came to the rescue. As part of the pre-Brady Mexican debt rescheduling of 1987, the Japanese Export-Import Bank loaned Mexico $500 million to build new pipelines and loading facilities on the Tehuantepec Isthmus. Although Mexico was not obliged to spend the money on Japanese materials or contractors, the ultimate beneficiary was plainly Japan. By 1990, oil from the Gulf of Mexico was flowing across the Isthmus to Yokohama-bound tankers at the Pacific port of Salina Cruz. The new 550,000 barrels-per-day pipeline, together with deepwater loading facilities also financed by Japan, gives Mexico the capacity to triple its oil shipments to East Asia. Mexico gained a world-scale Pacific oil port, while Japan secured access to a long-term supplier inside the Pacific Rim.

More recently, Japanese banks loaned $800 million to Pemex—their first voluntary commitment of capital in Mexico since the debt crisis—for development of the new oil fields that will fill that pipeline.

This is just the kind of Pacific relationship Mexico wants NAFTA to foster. Opening Mexico's oil industry to foreign investment would create opportunities for Japanese engineering firms and energy importers alike. Already, the giant C. Itoh company is discussing the construction and financing of a $2.5 billion Pacific Coast refinery for Pemex—a turnkey project that would be paid for by processed fuel exports to Asia. Sumitomo, Marubeni, Mitsui and Mitsubishi are all pursuing joint-venture agreements with Pemex for production of petrochemicals that had been reserved exclusively for the state.

The development of joint energy projects could stimulate other strategic partnerships with Japanese heavy industry, or so Mexico hopes. The unanswered question is whether the impression of an anti-Japanese NAFTA will dissuade Japanese companies from pursuing such ventures.

■ American critics who fear Japan invariably focused more on direct investment than trade. They dislike Japanese-owned factories in Tennessee and Tijuana equally, and suspected that NAFTA would be good for both. They argued that NAFTA would accelerate the decline of American manufacturing industries like textiles and electronics, and they often viewed the agreement as part of a general surrender to America's (largely Asian) economic competition. There were even a few displaced Cold War analysts who saw NAFTA as a Trojan Horse that would help Japan breach the innermost walls of the American empire.

There were those who praised NAFTA as a powerful weapon in a new economic Cold War. Economically, this makes no sense: adding Mexico to the North American economy expands the regional GDP by less than 4 percent, the equivalent of just one year of robust American and Canadian growth. If Canada and the United States do not already form a globally competitive bloc, the addition of Mexico does not make them one.

It was not exactly a surprise to hear this sort of defense of NAFTA from Congressional Japan-bashers like Montana's Senator Baucus. Portraying NAFTA as a retaliatory response to Japanese trading practices could have won badly needed votes—and provided political cover for wavering Democrats. What was surprising was to see them joined by traditionally anti-protectionist opinion leaders on the right. The Heritage Foundation, for example, contended that the United States needed NAFTA "to confront and, if necessary, economically defeat Japan." That sentiment was often echoed by U.S. negotiators, despite their public reassurances to the contrary. During the NAFTA negotiations, State Department officials warned darkly about extracontinental "free-riders" profiting from the agreement. Treasury Department officials said it would be "unfair" for investors who "have never been interested in Mexico" to reap the benefits of duty-free access to the American market. Backed by Washington, the Detroit car makers—who also dominate the industry in Mexico and Canada—won restrictions that would keep new (read: Japanese) investors from enjoying the agreement's short-term benefits.

This assumes, of course, that Japan sees NAFTA as an opportunity to do well (in trade) by doing good (recycling its surplus into impoverished Latin America). Yet there is no evidence that this is so. The prospect of a NAFTA deal lured new investors into Mexico from many countries—Spain, Switzerland, Holland, Venezuela, Korea, Taiwan, India—but not Japan. The Japanese seemed to have been actively repelled.

Apart from Nissan of Mexico, which has increased its Mexican stake in response to Detroit's success in keeping other Japanese auto companies out, most Japanese companies have responded to NAFTA by holding the line on their existing level of investment. Some are even retrenching, shuttering plants that were designed for a closed local market.

One would think that if NAFTA were clearly in Japan's interest, a substantial body of opinion in Japan would realize it, and money would already be flowing to Mexico. Of course, it's possible that American NAFTA critics see advantages for Japan in North American free trade that the Japanese themselves cannot. But it isn't likely: in the past, the Japanese rarely have had difficulty in discerning such opportunities on their own.

Corporate Japan realizes that it is the hidden target of the free trade experiment. While Ottawa, Washington and Mexico City all ritually decry protectionism, the signals from the NAFTA negotiating table were, to the Japanese, disturbingly enigmatic. "What exactly do you want from Japan?" asked the head of Toshiba's Mexican division during a closed-door discussion of NAFTA with American colleagues. "Tell us—do you want Japanese investment or not?"

There were no ready answers.

■ Tokyo is characteristically reluctant to comment on U.S. policy toward a traditional area of U.S. influence. Japan's neighbors are not so discreet: they suspect that NAFTA is a barrier to Asian goods and investors. Some are already urging Tokyo to formalize its own regional trading web into a kind of NAFTA East. Malaysian Prime Minister Mahathir and Singaporean Prime Minister Goh Chok Tong have argued that a North American trade bloc requires the creation of a formalized yen bloc in response. Goh, backed by Thailand, prefers a strengthening of trade within the ASEAN framework. The more provocative Mahathir favors an ethnically exclusive East Asian Economic Group (EAEG) that would exclude Australia and New Zealand and negotiate as a "caucus" within Gatt.

The East Asian caucus proposal has been strenuously denounced by the United States: Michael H. Armacost, the former U.S. ambassador to Japan, has argued that it "would draw a line down the Pacific" and "create negative impressions in the United States and perhaps invite emulation by countries in our hemisphere." The Malaysians say that this is the U.S pot calling the Asian kettle black: after all, the caucus was formulated as an explicit response to Washington's plans to extend the free trade area throughout the Western Hemisphere. This invitation was not extended to Pacific nations like Korea and the Philippines—despite their equally close economic and strategic ties to the United States.

Even Asian critics of Mahathir's plan resent the U.S. suggestion that a pan-American bloc would remain open and Gatt-compatible, while an analogous Asian grouping would be closed and trade-diverting. Washington complains that commerce within East Asia is increasingly dominated by interchange within and among the *keiretsu* and their offshore subsidiaries. Yet American trade with Latin America is equally dominated by intracompany business, the result of an American investment presence built up over more than a century.

This entire debate makes Japan uncomfortable. Tokyo is afraid that formalizing its Asian trade links would antagonize the United States and make the North American economy more restrictive. It is also wary of institutional arrangements that would bolster the bargaining power and Japanese market access of its East Asian partners; today's dense but informal web of intracompany trading relationships suits Tokyo's purposes just fine.

Akira Urabe, a Japanese Foreign Ministry coordinator for Latin American and Caribbean affairs, bluntly says that Japan disapproves of preferential trade treatment for any "specific region" of the developing world. Alluding to both NAFTA and the Caribbean Basin Initiative, Urabe emphasizes Tokyo's preference for multilateral trade liberalization. He argues that intraregional initiatives undermine Gatt and distort trade and investment flows, and warns against concentrating on the American market. Latin America, he says, should pursue "every possible trade opportunity" in East Asia.

■ The Mexican officials who have avidly followed Urabe's advice profess surprise about U.S criticism of their entreaties to the Japanese. After all, they say, isn't this what Washington always said they should do—open their doors to the world, seeking trade and investment opportunities from whatever source? And isn't this just what Washington has long urged Japan to do—invest more of its export earnings in the economies of the developing world, especially those within the U.S. sphere of influence?

This is disingenuous. Mexican negotiators know very well that the Japanese electronics assemblers on the border are cited by U.S critics as proof that Mexico is a back door for Japanese exports.[1]

Nor are the Mexicans entirely consistent. Jaime Serra, the politically astute trade minister, rarely misses an opportunity to tell American industrialists that NAFTA's prime objective is to enhance "North American competitiveness" in the world marketplace. (He doesn't need to name the competition.) At the same time, Serra tours Europe and the Orient trying to persuade potential investors that a Mexico-based manufacturing plant is the ideal way to penetrate the American marketplace—that is, to enhance *their* competitiveness *against* the North Americans. This isn't necessarily hypocritical: as a true free trader, Serra believes that greater competition within North America will improve the region's competitive edge in dealings with the rest of the world. But in terms of American public opinion, he is playing by turns to two very different visions of how NAFTA should operate.

In Japan, Serra emphasized his opposition to strict North American content rules that would bar most Japanese manufacturers from the Mexican market. Again, his position is genuine: he believes in the long-term benefits of Japanese investment for job creation, technology transfer, and trade diversification. But Serra didn't tell his Tokyo audiences that he preferred far stricter local content rules than Japanese investors (and other East Asians) would like. After all, Mexico wants to maximize NAFTA's foreign investment incentives. Light assembly operations like those in the maquiladora belt have only a minimal economic impact beyond their direct low-end payroll. What Mexico needs is integrated manufacturing operations offering a full range of employment opportunities and making extensive use of a diverse local supply network. Without NAFTA's local content requirements, much of this manufacturing production would have remained offshore.

Serra says his task in the rules-of-origin struggle was to strike a balance between the extreme local-content demands of American manufacturers and the unrealistically low levels suggested by some Japanese. Call it "the Serra curve": grabbing a piece of scrap paper, he sketches an arc from 0 to 100 and jabs his pencil roughly in the middle. Somewhere near here, he says, is the optimum level—*if* your intention is to attract investment from outside the region.

That optimum level would vary not only from industry to industry but from manufacturer to manufacturer. In most cases, it would be close to the 50 percent content levels required by NAFTA and the U.S.-Canadian pact before it—the same level set by the European Union in its national-origin test for auto imports. In autos and other sensitive industries, such as textiles, Washington pressed successfully for higher levels, though not to such an extreme as to make new non-North American investment impractical.

Despite their sometimes opposed investment goals, the Mexican and U.S. positions on local content were never irreconcilable. For that reason, U.S. officials sometimes mistakenly assumed that Mexico shared their vision of a predatory Japan. One telling example: in discussions over financial services, Mexico was willing to go along with the U.S. argument that subsidiaries of banks based in any of the three countries be given equal or "national" treatment under local law. First, however, negotiators had to define a "North American" bank. In Mexico, where foreign investors are barred from holding more than 30 percent of a financial institution's equity, the issue is straightforward: Mexican private banks are by definition owned by Mexican nationals. In the open-market United

States, however, where many second-tier banks are controlled by over-seas investors, the question of national origin is rather messy. So Mexican negotiators proposed a simple definition: if an independent bank is legally registered and conducting the bulk of its business in Country A, it would be considered to be a bona fide Country A bank. Their U.S. counterparts were aghast: did Mexico really want Sumitomo Bank of California to be counted as a North American bank?

The Mexicans replied mildly that they were only being practical. Global capital fluidity would make it nearly impossible for trade officials to moni-tor the capital-origin status of hundreds of banks—even if they could agree on a definition of national origin. The exchange was a bit of negotiating gamesmanship: Mexico knew that each national government would ulti-mately set its own standards for determining a bank's home. But the basic U.S. question was off the mark. Mexico would be delighted to see Sumitomo of California considered North American under NAFTA rules.

Mexico's goal in liberalizing its financial market is to channel lower-cost international credit into local business. The giant Japanese city banks are the biggest potential sources of such funding. Yet they are wary of addi-tional Latin American exposure. To the extent that NAFTA might prompt Japanese lenders to assess Mexico from a North American risk perspec-tive (rather than an exclusively Mexican one), it will spur the flow of capital to projects where their Japanese corporate clients have potential interests as partners, suppliers or contractors.

Sumitomo of California is just the kind of Japanese company Mexico wants NAFTA to attract. As one of the leading commercial banks in the state, Sumitomo has a direct stake in southern California, with which northwestern Mexico is increasingly interdependent. It played midwife and financier to the most successful transpacific private business partner-ship to date: the association of Mazda with Ford. The Mazda-designed Ford Tracer factory in Hermosillo, near the Arizona border, not only is Mexico's biggest single manufacturing export earner but is recognized as one of the highest-quality car production lines in the world.

Even if NAFTA were more open, Japanese investment might be slow in coming. Japanese manufacturers pointedly remind questioners why they crossed the ocean in the first place. It was politics that drew them to America, not economics. The goal was to circumvent import quotas and blunt American hostility through local job creation. Building plants in Mexico does nothing to build a political constituency in the United

States. Granted, there were also marketing justifications: products aimed at American consumers were improved by moving design and retailing staffs to the United States. But Mexico offers no advantage in that department, either.

Until recently, Japanese direct investment in Mexico was aimed exclusively at a protected local market. Now, with Mexico slashing tariffs, Japanese manufacturers find it more efficient to supply the local market with imports. While welcomed philosophically, trade liberalization has savaged the bottom lines of many Japanese investors. So Mexico is still a hard sell in Tokyo boardrooms. A classic example is Honda. The only prominent success story in Mexico's campaign to attract Japanese investment in the stagnant mid-1980s, Honda set up a small plant in Guadalajara to challenge what had been a monopoly market for small motorbikes. After Honda suffered paltry sales in a debt-deadened market, local demand picked up at the end of the decade. But it was too late: as Mexico's economy expanded, its import restrictions shrank. That opened the door to Harleys and Kawasakis—foreign-made motorcycles built in plants with greater economies of scale. Honda says bravely that it will find new markets for its Mexican bikes in Central and South America. But Japanese business consultants report that Honda considers its Mexican venture a costly mistake.

Japanese industrialists say they foresee a limited role for Mexican operations as labor-intensive extensions of their American transplant companies. They see the American transplants benefiting from the incorporation of a growing market south of the border that was once walled off by prohibitive tariffs.

Even giant Nissan is turning its domestically oriented Mexican subsidiary into an appendage of its Tennessee facilities. The company's new billion-dollar engine plant in Aguascalientes will ship most of its output to Smyrna, three days away by truck. This cross-border integration was not prompted by NAFTA, but by strict Mexican rules requiring auto companies to finance import purchases with export earnings—rules that NAFTA eliminates. Without that trade-balancing requirement, Nissan probably would not have proceeded with its last big Mexican expansion. The company stresses that a siting decision based simply on cheap labor—and moving production farther from suppliers and the target market—would, from its perspective, be a bad decision. Even Mexico's vaunted transportation advantage is questioned: it is cheaper, Nissan says, to ship its cars to Los Angeles from Yokohama than from Cuernavaca.

Future growth in its North American manufacturing operations, Nissan officials suggest, is more likely to take place in the United States than in Mexico. Moreover, under NAFTA, sourcing for its Mexican auto operations probably will move north to the United States. The Mexican content of Nissan's vehicles has dropped steadily from more than 70 percent a decade ago to barely 45 percent today—the inevitable result of the need to build sales in a more open local market and still make engines and vehicles that can be exported competitively. In Nissan's view, Mexican parts are too often overpriced and technologically obsolete; indeed, the company's policy is to lower its Mexican content to the minimum levels that Mexican law allows. Under NAFTA, that minimum drops immediately to 30 percent, and will be eliminated entirely by 2003.

Shoichi Amemiya, the stocky, outspoken president of Nissan's Mexican subsidiary, had warned Mexican negotiators beforehand that unless NAFTA's rules of origin required a high level of Mexican content, he and other foreign auto makers would turn increasingly to suppliers based in America or Canada. (In Nissan's case, many of those suppliers would be the subsidiaries of Japanese companies supplying Japanese transplant clients.) He also noted that without Mexican content rules, Honda, Toyota and Mazda could all penetrate the now-restricted local market directly from their plants in the United States; currently, all three build autos with North American content of 60 percent or higher. NAFTA's 10-year phase-out of Mexican content rules—the result of the protectionist desires of Nissan and the Big Three—only postpones the inevitable.

This turns on its head the conventional American view of Japan using Mexico as a low-cost springboard into the American market. Instead, Japan may well use its American installations as an efficient, capital-intensive launching site for exports into Mexico—and beyond, if Washington concludes broader hemispheric free trade accords. Overall, NAFTA may have the unexpected effect of making the United States—not Mexico—more attractive to Japanese direct investors. To the more limited extent that NAFTA does lure Japanese manufacturing operations to Mexico, they are likely to be integrated subsidiaries of American transplants.

There is a precedent in the maquiladora industry, the focus of heavy Japanese investment in recent years. Concentrated in Tijuana, maquiladoras are mostly low-tech plants that have been moved south from California or elsewhere in the United States. They remain an integral part of the Japanese parent's North American operations, with the same supply network and the same target market. The Mexican economy is only tangentially involved: the Japanese maquiladoras use Mexican products for barely 1 percent of their output, despite Mexican incentives to boost local content. The second largest Japanese investor in Mexico, Yazaki, a Tokyo-based auto parts company, has some 7,000 employees in the state of Chihuahua assembling wire harnesses for American-made Nissans, Hondas and Toyotas. Yazaki also supplies harnesses to Ford in Hermosillo, as well as to Chrysler and GM in Michigan. With its 6,000 workers in the United States, Yazaki now has more employees in North America than it does in Japan.

The Japanese say their Mexican border plants are essential to making their overall North American operations competitive. But they point out that the electronics companies that run the biggest maquiladora plants— Toshiba, Hitachi, Sony, NEC, Matsushita—are expanding faster within the United States than along the border. Indeed, the American chairman of Minolta has publicly criticized American companies like Zenith for relocating entire divisions to Mexico, a decision the Japanese consider a short-sighted preference for labor savings over investments in quality and productivity. The head of Hitachi in Mexico relates how his superiors decided to do just the opposite to remain competitive: they shut down all but one of their Mexican plants in the 1980s while expanding their presence in the United States. This synergy is exactly what many advocates of NAFTA originally had in mind: a continental corporate restructuring allowing more efficient use of labor and greater economies of scale.

Within the Mexican business elite, there is broad acceptance of the notion that the Pacific Basin is becoming the world's main economic engine. The success or failure of NAFTA will be judged in good part by the extent to which it links Mexico to this yen-dominated world, which includes Los Angeles and Vancouver as much as it does Kuala Lumpur and Taipei.

Julio Millan, a businessman who represents the Mexican private sector committee in the Pacific Economic Cooperation Council, impatiently dismisses the popular notions that a North American trade zone could be an alternative to Pacific Basin trade or, alternatively, that Mexico should directly pursue trade and investment links with Japan in competition with the United States: "The most important trading relationship in the world is and will continue to be the relationship between the United States and

Japan. That is the axis through which Mexico will develop trade with Asia. On our own, we are simply the southern part of the North American economy, just like Thailand and Malaysia are southern extensions of the Japanese economy. The two regions mirror one another: they shouldn't conflict with one another."

With NAFTA, the improved investment climate should attract Japanese interest. The dynamic business relationship between East Asia and the American West Coast has already reached deeply into northwestern Mexico. As Mexico becomes more thoroughly integrated into the North American economy, it is likely to get a bigger share of Japanese capital simply as spillover. During the past 30 years, Japan has directly invested $120 billion in the United States—compared with the paltry $1.85 billion it has in Mexico. That gap is certain to narrow.

In the long run, Mexico should attract substantial Japanese investment in areas where it enjoys clear competitive advantages: processed foods, agriculture, petrochemicals, tourism. Direct penetration by other Asian investors—Korea in civil engineering, Taiwan in computers, India in steel, Singapore in textiles—should pique the interest of their Japanese competitors. Mexico's own trade accords with the rest of Latin America make it the site of choice for manufacturers who conclude that the region is served most efficiently by local production. By the end of the decade, Mexican factories could have duty-free access to virtually every market in the hemisphere. NAFTA's rules of origin and other restrictive provisions could be overcome—if Asian investors were willing to relocate primary production facilities along with their own supply networks.

In the short run, however, NAFTA will deter Japanese investment, both because of its specific protectionist restrictions and because it will be interpreted as a signal from Washington that Japan should steer clear of the American hinterlands. To compete in the North American market, Mexico needs an immediate infusion of cash and manufacturing expertise. Yet if American business efficiently exploits NAFTA's long transition periods to bolster market dominance in Mexico, many Japanese companies may conclude that it is easier to supply the market from world-scale plants in Asia. That would be good news for many American companies but not for Mexico, or for the overall American economy. When Japanese capital creates jobs south of the border, about 15 cents of every dollar spent by those new wage-earners goes north to pay for American consumer products; barely a penny returns to Japan. If the factories are in Asia, those spending patterns are reversed. A direct Japanese investment presence would spur Mexico's technological and economic growth, which would directly benefit its northern neighbor and main import supplier. It would also help to slow emigration: American companies alone could not employ more than a fraction of the million people who enter the Mexican job market each year.

Mexico and Japan are a good strategic fit, which is why Mexican officials cringe when Japan is portrayed by American politicians as a rapacious economic enemy and when Japanese politicians attack the United States as a decadent empire. Every time public opinion leads American buyers to cancel orders for Japanese steel or subway cars, Mexico sees irrational damage done to a dynamic trading partnership that it hopes to join.

Mexico would not be the only victim. It is difficult enough for Latin American leaders to persuade Japan that their market-oriented reforms are profound and permanent. A further souring of the U.S.-Japanese trading relationship—particularly if it was followed by a turn to protectionism by Washington—would make the region's sales effort harder still.

As disturbing as it may be to Latin Americans, Japanese investors frankly admit that they view Mexico and the rest of the region as little more than the backyard of the United States. They remain profoundly skeptical about Latin America's regulatory environment, political stability, work force quality, labor relations, infrastructure assets, and cultural idiosyncrasies. On every count, they prefer their Asian neighbors. Japanese investors are unlikely to overcome these prejudices and invest without an implicit invitation from the United States.

But just the opposite is happening: NAFTA supporters and critics in the United States are sending an increasingly explicit signal to stay away. The Japanese government has contributed billions in aid to Mexico, more than any other government in the world, including the United States. Mexico now has the most open trade and investment rules in the region and is openly solicitous of Japanese capital. If Japanese industrialists conclude that because of American fear and mistrust they still aren't welcome in Mexico, they might shun Latin America entirely, concentrating instead on their existing East Asian supply and assembly networks. In that case, NAFTA, portrayed as an inevitable response to a world mutating into trade blocs, will have provoked just what American policymakers have long sought to avoid: an insular Asia hoarding a swelling trade surplus, and an impoverished Latin America dependent on a United States burdened with its own debt and deficit problems.

Staring at the Rising Sun

A few years back, a Tokyo business consultant was talking to friends in Mexico City about his work with a small Sonora fishing cooperative. With Japanese capital and training, the co-op's inefficient coastal shrimping fleet was being transformed into an offshore long-lining enterprise. The Mexican fishermen worked on a schedule and pay scale that would drive their American counterparts to mutiny. But around-the-clock hours and meticulous packing during journeys of a month or more had made the co-op a competitive supplier to the Japanese market, the most demanding in the world.

A success story? The consultant didn't think so.

"Sometimes I wonder if this country is ever going to progress," he sighed. "These Mexican fishermen—after 20 or 30 days at sea, they get restless, they want a drink, they want to see their women. They just aren't like Japanese fishermen."

Failure to satisfy Japanese expectations is hardly peculiar to Mexico. Prime Minister Miyazawa's public disparagement of American labor productivity reflects what Japanese industrialists say privately about many countries. But in Mexico, desperate for investment and eager to see the Pacific Basin as a new font of capital, these blunt judgments inflict a special sting. Japanese opinions of Mexican workers tend to be more caustic than their views of Americans. Away from local ears, Japanese executives openly disparage the local work ethos, griping about chronic absenteeism traced to freely admitted boredom, sloppy craftsmanship defended as "improvisation," production-halting political gamesmanship disguised as union militancy.

The prejudice goes beyond the shop floor. In the executive suites of Japanese companies, Mexican nationals complain that they advance through the hierarchy much more slowly than their peers in American and European multinationals. Mexico's reluctance to fully repay foreign debts is taken as an unwillingness to accept responsibility. And while Japanese companies thrive amid the unapologetic corruption of Indonesia and Thailand, the Mexican culture of the petty *mordida* is considered alien and offensive.

The Mexican view of the Japanese couldn't be more different. The Mexicans admire Japan more than they admire any other country in the world. Japan is seen as offering all the advantages of modern capitalism—cutting-edge technology, competitive finance, access to difficult markets—without the foreign policy entanglements of a military superpower.

Many Mexicans have also enjoyed the spectacle of Japan besting the

United States in industry after industry. (In language that must have made her readers wince, an *Excelsior* columnist once praised the Japanese for proving that there are no limits to the potential of *morenos y chaparritos*—people who are short and dark.) Asian manufacturing success demolished the notion once common even in Mexico that capitalist enterprise was the exclusive franchise of Northern European Protestantism. The Japanese are admired for beating the *gringos* at their own game—and for doing so while retaining their cultural integrity.

Japan's emergence as the world's leading manufacturing exporter revived Mexican hopes for a counterweight to U.S. influence. Not only did Japan seem to offer a less meddlesome style of capitalism, but it began to look to many Mexican strategists like an ideal role model.

There were similarities between the Japanese and Mexican ways of doing business: close cooperation with labor and institutional investors, with an entrenched government technocracy at the strategic pinnacle; clans of industrial conglomerates interconnected by complex supplier and equity relationships; a preference for long-term market share over short-term profit, coupled with a disdain for U.S. vigilance against antitrust and insider-trading violations. Japan's success suggested that Mexico's idiosyncratic private sector could be refined and modernized, rather than revamped completely along alien U.S. lines. Not that there has been any rush to emulate other relevant traits of Japanese business, like the dedication to consumer service and technological innovation, or the commitment to real competition within the confines of the national market. But from the vantage of the old Mexican industrial clans, the *keiretsu* system seems comfortingly familiar.

More disturbing, from an official U.S. policy perspective, is the appeal of a system of governance that puts little emphasis on electoral democracy. Multiparty pluralism, a vigorous free press, the citizen's right to vote the bums out—these are not the prominent characteristics of East Asian political culture.

Mexican single-party corporatism resembles the factional, consensual Japanese system more than it does the technocratic authoritarianism of a Malaysia or a Singapore, or the army-constrained rule of Thailand and Korea. Yet the PRI has more in common with all these varied Asian regimes than it does with the Westminster-derived parliaments of the British Commonwealth or the freewheeling, separate-powers federalism of the United States.

Many American commentators have urged Latin America to democratize not simply as an end in itself, but as a precondition for capitalist growth. Yet they also hold up Japan and the Asian tigers as economic role models. This contradiction hasn't passed without notice in Mexico. If industrial success is the ultimate job of the nation-state in the post–Cold War age, it cannot be argued that squabbling grass-roots democracy makes the task easier. Indeed, the growing democratization and labor militancy of South Korea is held up with relief by other Asian competitors as the cause of the country's recent relative exporting decline.

Many defenders of the Salinas and De la Madrid governments freely concede their adversaries' angriest charge: that genuinely representative democracy would have precluded the painful wage suppression, debt repayment, and trade liberalization policies that laid the foundation for Mexico's current growth. But this says more about how they value democratic purity than it does about any second thoughts concerning the social cost of economic reform.

This makes Japan doubly appealing. In dealings with Tokyo, Mexican leaders are often subjected to harsh scrutiny regarding debt and investment policies. But they are rarely if ever bothered about electoral fraud or environmental despoliation or human rights violations—the common subjects of U.S. Congressional inquiry. The pragmatic Japanese seem to share the Mexican view that political and environmental matters are domestic affairs that have no place in bilateral discussions.

The Japanese also embrace the Mexican view that stability and predictability are more important than a government's willingness to leave office. The PRI, warts and all, has given Mexico enviable stability since the 1920s. Now it must persuade Japan that its cyclical habits—feinting toward populism in one *sexenio,* backpedaling toward business in the next—have given way to permanent commitment to economic liberalization. The most compelling guarantor of these policies, Salinas believes, is a trade and investment treaty with the United States.

The Tokyo Backlash against Debt Relief

Without Japanese aid, Mexico's landmark debt restructuring would have been impossible. In all, Tokyo bankrolled a $2.05 billion investment in U.S. zero-coupon bonds, which served as collateral for the Brady Bonds issued by Mexico in exchange for old bank debt. This was not an entirely charitable effort: Japanese creditors held about 20 percent of Mexico's public-sector commercial debt, roughly equal to the share booked in American banks. Neither the United States nor any other government provided any unilateral contribution to the Mexican refinancing.

Japan's support of Mexico in the Brady Plan was once seen as a precursor to broader financial and commercial cooperation. Unfortunately, it's had just the opposite effect, undermining Mexican efforts to project a positive business image and tainting Japanese impressions of the free trade accord. In the small, closed world of *keiretsu* commerce, the biases of bankers have a powerful impact on industrialists. Tokyo's ambassador to Mexico, Tsuneo Tanaka, crisply summarizes the prevailing private sector view: "One, those of us who have been in Mexico have lost a lot of money; two, our banks don't want anything to do with it; three, NAFTA is being written to increase the advantages for American companies."

Tokyo's support for the Brady workout was chiefly motivated not by a concern for the welfare of Japanese banks, nor by admiration for Mexican economic reforms, but by the more familiar desire to placate Washington. Japanese leaders realized that Mexico's stability and prosperity were critical to the United States. So the Brady deal made geopolitical as well as financial sense.

But Japanese bankers were unenthusiastic, even though many felt the reduction-plus-securitization formula ultimately would enhance the value of their Mexican assets. After all, Mexico's debt was not a particularly urgent matter: even an outright default wouldn't threaten their solvency. For the five leading Japanese lenders, Mexican exposure equaled one-twentieth of equity and one-half of 1 percent of total asset value; for their top five American counterparts, Mexican loans totaled more than half of equity and almost 3 percent of assets. (Before the recent puncturing of the Japanese real estate bubble, the Bank of Tokyo, by far the most vulnerable Japanese creditor, could have covered the loss of its entire Mexican portfolio simply by selling its small downtown Tokyo guest house.)

The U.S. Treasury had long pressed Japan to redirect more of its trade-surplus earnings to the indebted countries of the developing world—especially in regions beyond East Asia. But only here did it press Japan hard for a specific contribution. Many Japanese leaders saw it as a chance to prove Japan's value as a U.S. ally, while at the same time aiding its own commercial banks. Or as a leading Japanese banker put it, "We see our role in Mexico in a trilateral rather than bilateral context."

Still, Japanese private bankers never disguised their dislike of the Brady Plan. Not only did they share every banker's distaste for debt relief, but they objected strongly to Mexico's request for fresh loans. Why, they asked, extend new credits to a country that is making you write off a third of its existing debts? The attitude was summarized by Sashio Kohjima, who represented Japanese banks in the Brady negotiation: "In Japan, if we have a national debt, everyone—even every primary school child—thinks it is our responsibility to pay it back. If we don't, it is a blot on our character. It is hard for us to understand a country not paying."

But what rankled most was the Brady Plan's American authorship. Japanese commercial bankers saw it (correctly) as a scheme imposed by Washington to address the peculiar financial problems of American banks, while at the same time buttressing U.S. foreign policy interests in a region of little strategic importance to Tokyo. In 1989, when the plan went into action, Japanese banks held $45 billion in Latin American debt, even more than the $42 billion booked by American banks. Japanese bankers felt their input into the Brady formula was hardly commensurate with their risk; it was, in their view, a philosophically and financially flawed scheme they had neither devised nor needed.

In the end, of course, Japanese banks fell in line behind the Ministry of Finance, which took its cues from the U.S. Treasury. And from a commercial creditor viewpoint, the Brady Plan worked: it lowered Mexico's interest payments while enhancing the principal's real value.

But Japanese banks remain hostile toward new Mexican lending. Mexico recently raised billions by placing scores of new bonds in New York, Vienna, London, Frankfurt and other markets; tellingly, not a single new issue was placed in Tokyo. One Japanese executive, exploring financing choices for a Mexican expansion, said his Tokyo banker told him curtly that he "couldn't even mention Mexico to the board."

With NAFTA giving new competitive advantages to American banks and brokerages, Japanese distaste for Mexican finance could well increase.

NOTE

Note 1: Of course, this entirely misconstrues the structure of the maquiladora: maquiladora components, by definition, are either American-made or enter the United States from elsewhere paying full standard duties. (Maquiladora tariffs are assessed only on the value-added part of the product, mainly labor.) The only duty-free products that maquiladoras can export to the United States are those made from materials that were originally imported from the United States.

CHAPTER 12

Toward a Common Market: The New North America

Americans don't warm to the notion of a common market. To conservatives, it conjures up images of aloof Eurocrats imposing new rules and taxes on overregulated entrepreneurs. Liberals are more fearful still, envisioning supranational rule by Gatt-trained trade potentates deaf to environmental and labor concerns.

The idea of a common market with Mexico arouses more specific objections, some practical, others rawly ethnocentric. Ronald Reagan, the North American market's first prominent champion, didn't help his case when he said he envisioned the free movement of not just goods and services, but labor as well.

Canadians and Mexicans are even warier. A continental common market can sound unnervingly like a United States of North America, with Washington its unchallenged capital.

Yet a North American common market is both inevitable and desirable. Economic integration cannot and will not stop with the adoption of a freer trade and investment regime. A common market structure is needed—and in fact is already being developed—to resolve the inevitable conflicts of economic integration and to capitalize fully on its inherent advantages. This has already required moving beyond trade and investment issues into environmental protection and the enforcement of labor standards. Monetary policy, immigration and many other areas can also be constructively addressed within a collaborative trinational framework. At its best, a common market can be a laboratory for policymaking that is impossible when all parties are also setting precedents for their dealings with the rest of the world.

For the United States, Mexico occupies a special place among developing nations, just as Canada holds a special case among industrialized nations. NAFTA acknowledges and institutionalizes these relationships. The real NAFTA—the North American Free Trade Area that is being established by the North American Free Trade Agreement—provides an essential forum for further policy coordination and economic liberalization. There are critics in each NAFTA nation who consider their neighbors competitors, not allies; for them, economic integration and policy coordination is inherently pernicious. But if North America's economies are fundamentally complementary, the three countries have nothing to fear, and much to gain, from refining their areas of competitive advantage and expanding their areas of common ground.

■ When NAFTA was first proposed, critics in all three countries claimed that its hidden agenda was the development of a European-style common market. That was the original Reagan proposal, after all. Didn't Europe also start out with a limited free trade area? And, given the Brussels precedent, wouldn't this mean ceding some measure of sovereignty to unelected bureaucrats? Even worse, wouldn't this lead to liberalization and collaborative policymaking in many other sensitive areas, from monetary policy and immigration to labor and environmental law?

NAFTA's defenders said no. They argued that the agreement is designed to dismantle tariff barriers, not build a new regulatory bureaucracy. NAFTA, declared one Congressional backer, "is a trade agreement, not an act of economic union."

In his 1988 presidential campaign, Salinas had explicitly rejected calls for a North American common market, and he was always careful later to describe NAFTA in much narrower terms. Mulroney, campaigning for a bilateral FTA in the early 1980s, had also insisted that the free trade area wasn't a nascent North American Economic Community. President Bush, backing up his Canadian and Mexican colleagues, also depicted NAFTA as something more modest than his predecessor's vision of a borderless continental economy. This was not only sound diplomacy, but good politics. The Bush Administration recognized that fears about unelected trade commissars and limitations on national autonomy would be shared by people who might otherwise favor free trade.

Yet the critics were essentially right. NAFTA lays the foundation for a continental common market, as many of its architects privately acknowledge. Part of this foundation, inevitably, is bureaucratic: the agreement creates a variety of continental institutions—ranging from trade dispute panels to labor and environmental commissions—that are, in aggregate, an embryonic NAFTA government. Border environmental and public works problems are being addressed by new regulatory bodies, and new financial mechanisms are being developed within the NAFTA framework. These institutions won't be just concepts, or committees, but large buildings with permanent staffs. The environmental commission is to be housed in Canada, the labor commission in the United States, and the coordinating NAFTA Secretariat in Mexico. With their trinational personnel and a mandate to work collectively and independently, these agencies should develop a distinctive NAFTA corporate culture.

Externally, the NAFTA group is already behaving like a classic trade bloc, attempting to replace imports from third parties with local products. This trade diversion strategy, a fundamental characteristic of any true common market, encourages direct investment in Mexico as an alternative to investing or simply buying in East Asia. Internally, by forcing Mexico to reform its investment rules, NAFTA creates a common set of rules for all North American business, not just importers and exporters. It reinforces and accelerates a process of interdependence which over time should lead to increasing coordination of environmental and labor rules, fiscal and monetary policies, immigration and naturalization procedures, and other areas of common concern. NAFTA and the economic integration it will foster will make it impossible to avoid these issues. It will also provide structures to address them—structures that will evolve and expand as integration deepened.

These structures will not resemble Europe's. The European Union has given common markets an undeservedly bad name. The NAFTA market will be indigenously North American: less officious, more spontaneous and diffuse, yet clearly oriented towards the practical business of trade and investment. That's not merely because Americans have a deeply ingrained anti-bureaucratic bias that Europeans lack (though it helps). It's also because North America doesn't need elaborate institutions to achieve real market integration.

In Europe, the impetus behind integration was always more political than economic. Jean Monnet wanted to break a pattern of cyclical warfare by giving every European power a stake in European stability and prosperity. Unifying the continent's coal and steel industry, as he did in 1951, was only a means to this visionary end. Real unification needed a complex multilateral structure where no single nation (meaning Germany) could ride roughshod over others. That demanded, in turn, a neutral, quasi-federal administrative center. The overlapping structure of NATO— helped by the absence of Paris and the presence of Washington—provided some formal coordination of security policies. A few ambitious European business groups sought unification as a way to emulate the marketing breadth and economies of scale enjoyed by their American competitors. But the "common market," as it was colloquially known, was always something of a misnomer: a true tariff-free trade zone didn't emerge until 1992, two decades after the Community first expanded beyond its original six members and long after it had built up a complex regional political infrastructure. Politics drove the economics of European integration, not the reverse.

NAFTA, by contrast, has no Brussels, and no Bonn, because it already has Washington. And it has no Ecu, because it has the dollar. NAFTA, its national security implications and labor and environmental codicils notwithstanding, is ultimately a business proposition, not an attempt to forestall intraregional conflict or supersede the authority of national governments.

Real political integration has no future in North America. While Mexicans and Canadians no longer fear armed intervention, they do not want America's military and economic power enhanced by an EC-style formal unification, with the trappings of a parliament and a trinational civil service. Americans, in turn, see no reason to cede domestic policy-making authority to any institution where Mexico and Canada— or any other country or group of countries—might enjoy a collective veto. That's why negotiators from all three countries readily agreed that the parallel agreements on labor and the environment would only address the national enforcement of national law—and then only if and when it could be demonstrated that allegedly lax enforcement had a demonstrable and injurious impact on trade.

Europeans, despite resistance to monetary unification and other aspects of the Maastricht package, have shown extraordinary willingness to cede real political power to civil servants ensconced in remote Belgian office towers. Like their parallel acceptance of American generals in Bonn, this enlightened acquiescence is a legacy of the second world war, and it has no North American parallel.

European integration required layers of formalized liberalization, centralized vigilance, and the delicate crafting of new political institutions. Merging two bordering economies into an already-unified megamarket is a simpler affair. NAFTA, at bottom, is the codification and regulation of an integration process that is already well advanced and that would have continued (though more slowly and unpredictably) even without a free trade agreement. In North America, regulatory reality still lags behind market reality—just the opposite of Europe, where market integration was forced as a conscious act of political will.

The contrast is telling: in terms of formal liberalization, NAFTA will put the North American market about where Europe stood a decade or so ago. With NAFTA fully phased in, North America will still have more internal barriers than the borderless economy decreed in Europe in 1992. Yet informal market unification—the real business of cross-border trade and investment—is in most industries already more developed in North America than in Europe. And it is the real integration of the marketplace, not the bureaucratic structures directing that integration, which is the true measure of a common market.

North America's political and demographic structure encourages such decentralized integration. Each NAFTA partner is a continent-wide as-semblage of industrially and culturally distinct population centers and geographical districts. Unlike any other international trade grouping, the member governments are all organized federally: NAFTA is a consor-tium of 92 states and provinces, plus scattered federal districts, territories and dependencies.

This peculiarly North American tradition will ease local alliances across national lines. The Canadian provinces and U.S. and Mexican states cover the same range of size and population and are reasonably analogous juridi-cally. The provinces have far more autonomy than U.S. states, while the Mexican states, by dint of tradition (though not by law), have far less. Still, the Mexican states are getting greater independence in environmental affairs, investment promotion, educational management, and, along the border, in relations with their American neighbors. Opposition govern-ments in several states—a Mexican first—are accelerating this trend. So are tax provisions and pollution codes discouraging additional industry in Mexico City. Economic deregulation and belated electoral reforms are gradually loosening the capital's chokehold on the body politic.

Mexico isn't alone in its rediscovery of federalism. In Canada, what-ever the outcome of the next round of constitutional reform, Ottawa will devolve still more power to the provinces. Indeed, one reason that Que-bec is the province most favorably disposed towards NAFTA is that Quebecers see it as a way to consolidate local autonomy within the quasi-federal context of an integrated North America. In the United

States, meanwhile, the states are seeking a greater voice in the design and implementation of federally mandated social welfare policies, even as they are acting as local laboratories for those policies.

Trade liberalization removes an artificial barrier to cross-border cooperation. Whether in Canada, the northern United States, the southwestern United States, or northern Mexico, local political units often have more in common with their counterparts across the border than they do with other regions of their own country. The tradition of bicameral federalism in all three national legislatures also helps maintain a balance between democratically allocated power (Americans are three-quarters of NAFTA's voters) and respect for the sovereign rights of smaller states. The checks and balances built into North American political life are more of an opportunity than a problem. They will let a North American common market evolve organically, not bureaucratically.

The New NAFTA Power Elite   NAFTA's dispute resolution panels will be the first layer of North American common market governance. Judging by the experience of the U.S.-Canadian panels, which have won respect for their objectivity and professionalism, their staff judges and trade experts will gradually become less parochial, and more constructively trinational.

The labor and environmental commissions, while potentially more contentious, should also ultimately encourage more cooperation than confrontation. Both commissions will start life with less power than President Clinton originally envisioned. In his October 1992 NAFTA campaign address, Clinton said that the proposed North American environmental commission should have "the power to provide remedies, including money, damages, and the legal power to stop pollution." He also proposed to apply binding trade sanctions for local violations of domestic labor laws. But Mexican and Canadian negotiators refused to go along, agreeing only to more limited environmental and labor-policy agencies, without direct spending or enforcement powers. The new commissions will be empowered to impose trade sanctions only after warnings and fines and when two of the three NAFTA countries agreed there was a clear pattern of deliberate nonenforcement with a demonstrable impact on the price of traded goods. (It also occurred to Clinton's advisors that the NAFTA commissioners from Canada and Mexico could have used this supranational authority against the United States.)

Yet both commissions should gradually acquire authority and prestige—as well as an expanding staff and budget—if they professionally and independently investigate complaints and recommend action against persistent abuses of environmental rules. They should also facilitate cross-border cooperation. The environmental commission's work could lead to common NAFTA standards on pesticide use, for example, while the separate new binational border agency would cooperatively monitor the border-zone watershed and air pollution management. The labor commission, meanwhile, will provide a useful forum for communication and cooperation among unions and other organized labor groups across national lines.

The loyalties of NAFTA staffers will ultimately be to their home countries and regions, since the various commissions and panels employing them will remain strictly subordinated to the three central governments. For that reason, Mexico and Canada fear that an EC-style system will amount to their annexation by the United States. ("Unity would mean that everyone would go to Washington with their problems instead of coming here," said a high official in Salinas's Mexico City office. "Think about monetary policy: do you think the Fed would follow *our* advice?") The Clinton and Bush Administrations each accepted the idea of limited action against NAFTA members, but only when that action was supported by the other two countries. Yet even with NAFTA in effect, few congressmen will accept a Mexican-Canadian veto over any purely domestic U.S. law or practice. North America isn't ready for genuine reciprocity.

Not every step towards the consolidation of a common market will require further layers of bureaucracy. As tariffs disappear, so—eventually—will much of the customs bureaucracy that tabluates and collects those tariffs. As market integration advances, the frivolous filing of dumping suits and countersuits might also diminish, both because of fairer trinational enforcement and because more and more of these once-fierce conflicts will involve present or potential business partners and clients. Further reforms, as in Europe, could eventually eliminate internal dumping cases entirely: in a true free trade area, a dumping suit filed by Mexico against the United States would be just as unthinkable as a dumping suit filed by Michigan against South Carolina. This alone would eliminate most of the work of the dispute resolution panels.

NAFTA's evolution into a customs union—the next logical step in a common market's evolution—could lead to enormous savings on both borders, as customs inspectors were freed to concentrate on air and seaports. Ultimately, North American content rules and food safety regulations could be enforced at the point of origin, just as the USDA inspects meat at the packing house, not when it crosses state lines.

Mexico could turn NAFTA into a de facto customs union all by itself: all that's required is for Mexico to lower its tariffs unilaterally on non-NAFTA products to levels in line with American and Canadian norms. American and Canadian external tariffs are already closely aligned, and on average are triple Mexico's duties. If external tariff differences were eliminated, any port on the continent could become a legal point of entry for the entire NAFTA market.

Common external tariffs would be opposed by many Mexican companies. Some American companies would also fight for continued preferential access to a Mexican market where they are more protected against Asian and European competition than they are in the United States itself. Yet there would be powerful countervailing pressures from Mexico-based exporters. Trading partners abroad already point to high import barriers as justifying reciprocal restrictions on Mexican goods. So the dynamic is toward openness: as shown over the past five years, as the Mexican economy becomes more internationalized, its most competitive industries begin naturally to favor additional trade liberalization.

Harmonizing standards on a continental basis would also simplify enforcement.

Fears that these standards would be "harmonized down"—that is, reduced to the lowest common NAFTA denominator—are misplaced. The muscular consumer and environmental lobbies in Canada and the United States have proved quite able to block any relaxation of health or safety standards—even when the governments in power actively favor such measures. By encouraging the three countries to adopt equally strict pollution and phytosanitary standards whenever possible, the North American environmental commission could make training, monitoring and enforcement cheaper and more effective throughout the region.

Still, anyone with philosophical objections to North American unity— a category that includes principled nationalists in all three countries— should not only have opposed NAFTA, but the U.S.-Canadian FTA and every other common market structure. The reason is straightforward: despite denials all around, NAFTA implies a partial surrender of national sovereignty in exchange for greater market access and regional stability. The United States, with by far the biggest and freest market, gives up proportionately the least; Mexico, as the poorest and most protected of the NAFTA economies, suffers the most acute loss of autonomy, though it also gains the biggest relative economic benefit. But for all three, there are new limits on economic policy prerogatives. Under NAFTA, neither Canada nor Mexico can unilaterally redirect oil exports to markets outside North America. Similarly, the United States can't ship its surplus wheat to Russia if that means hardships for Mexico. All three countries are be barred from manipulating environmental rules to attract investment. And no country can stiffen current rules for the entry of goods or investments from any NAFTA neighbor.

In theory, this is all reciprocal, with the United States surrendering an equal measure of its own sovereignty. For Canada and Mexico, the only practical way to counterbalance U.S. power is to insist on a one-nation, one-vote system at the top of the NAFTA pyramid: ensuring, at least formally, that together they can thwart Washingtonian unilateralism. The NAFTA dispute panels will operate under this two-nation veto, as will the parallel environmental and labor commissions. Yet some pro-NAFTA Republicans in Congress had cautioned that they might have opposed the pact if the parallel labor and environmental agreements ceded too much to some supranational authority. And some anti-NAFTA activists challenged any North American system that did not accommodate the larger population and overwhelming market dominance of the United States.

In practice, however, these limitations will affect Mexico and Canada more than they will the United States. In the real world of geopolitics, Washington is surrendering virtually nothing. The United States holds the ultimate trump card: it can always walk away. By virtue of sheer scale and global reach, the American economy could easily have survived NAFTA's demise. The Mexican and Canadian economies, densely intertwined with American markets and investments, could not have.

American withdrawal is not an empty threat. NAFTA's terms let any country pull out with six months' notice. If the darkest predictions of NAFTA critics ever came to pass, the U.S. Congress would surely jump to give notice. For the United States, the consequences of withdrawal would be minimal; for Mexico and Canada, the impact would be devastating. The disparity of power alone means that Mexico, especially, would be increasingly constrained by the reality of economic dependence. In the past, Mexico could afford to chart an independent foreign policy course. It could ignore Washington's economic advice, even when bilateral friction threatened to spark punitive retaliation (the Nixon and Reagan Administrations both briefly paralyzed Mexican border trade in the name of narcotics control, for example). With NAFTA, however, the economic pain from any conflict with Washington would be far more intense. As noted astutely, if undiplomatically, by John Negroponte, the Bush Administration's ambassador to Mexico, NAFTA forces Mexico to recast its foreign policies in a North American mold.

The limitations on Mexican and Canadian sovereignty flow from the practical consequences of economic integration. A good example is the so-called Torricelli Amendment—a 1992 Congressional edict requiring the foreign subsidiaries of American companies to honor the U.S. trade embargo against Cuba. The measure was protested bitterly by Ottawa and Mexico City. Lawmakers in both countries insisted—not surprisingly—that businesses operating in their countries would be expected to abide by Canadian and Mexican law, including their own national foreign policy strictures. Canada and Mexico have always openly conducted business with Castro's Cuba: it's their small way of demonstrating foreign policy independence of the United States. Yet the American companies that dominate major manufacturing sectors in Mexico and Canada are unlikely to defy a Congressional order, even if they are legally entitled to do so. Mexican and Canadian firms would also think twice about exporting to Cuba if it meant alienating investors and customers in the United States.

Progress through Resistance

In perhaps the greatest single irony of the NAFTA debate, it was the fiercest critics of the free trade experiment—insisting on ever more stringent requirements for NAFTA membership—who insured that NAFTA would transcend the limited scope of a trade pact. The more the agreement was attacked, the more it expanded a defensive web of commissions and institutions, all complete with acronyms and job descriptions, and most only passingly related to trade.

Environmentalists, in the first and most significant broadening of the NAFTA agenda, forced the creation of a trinational environmental commission, with the power to review anti-pollution enforcement in all three countries. Labor unions then pressed successfully for a parallel agreement on labor and workplace safety standards, which would in turn shelter its own trinational bureaucrats.

So far, the NAFTA umbrella covers trade, investment, labor and environmental concerns. But most critics want even more.

Some opponents have advocated a NAFTA equivalent to the European Union adjustment funds that channel billions of Ecus into Ireland

and Greece. This North American Development Bank, or NADBank, with a proposed paid-in capital base of $5 billion, would give the incipient common market an off-the-shelf public works department. Many NADBank proponents also favor a tough EC-style "social charter" mandating the harmonization of labor laws.

A national coalition of Hispanic-American political organizations said it would support NAFTA only if it were accompanied by immigration reforms, including guarantees that Mexicans applying for work visas will be treated at least as liberally as Canadians. Proponents of immigration controls, meanwhile, say Mexico should keep Mexicans without U.S. work visas inside its borders as part of the NAFTA deal.

Exchange rate policy is another proposed area of conditionality. Ross Perot and other NAFTA opponents, fearful of the effects of a sudden peso devaluation, insist that any free trade agreement should include a monetary policy clause with restrictions on sudden currency fluctuations.

With diehard NAFTA enemies like Perot succumbing to this creeping Maastrichtism, it is hardly surprising that true-believing free traders were also proposing complex new NAFTA codicils. Columbia University economist Jagdish Bagwhati, who also serves as a Gatt advisor, says American factories in Mexican territory should adhere to EPA and Occupational Health and Safety Administration rules—exactly the kind of conditionality and extraterritoriality that Bagwhati would normally deplore. Hobart Rowen, a *Washington Post* columnist and another staunch NAFTA partisan, suggested that NAFTA have been made contingent on an expansion of Mexican family planning programs—though this would have imposed far more demanding trade standards on Mexico than are asked of other, less important trading partners. (It's also off the mark: Mexico's widely praised population control program has cut growth from more than 3 percent to less than 2 percent a year, despite pressure from the Catholic Church and a 12-year funding cut-off by the Reagan and Bush Administrations.)

If all of these had been prerequisites for NAFTA membership, NAFTA would never have happened. For many NAFTA critics, that is exactly the point. Yet these are all legitimate issues that can be systematically addressed within the NAFTA framework. Even their complexity testifies to the need for an overarching strategy to regulate the U.S.-Mexican relationship, which by its nature transcends issues of tariffs and investment rules.

But asking Mexico to resolve these problems unilaterally before it joins a free trade area is not only demeaning, but impractical. In every specific instance—environmental enforcement, immigration policy, monetary management, and a host of other areas—NAFTA makes it easier, economically and politically, for Mexico to address these issues constructively.

These issues will not go away—and would not have, even without NAFTA. Mexico will remain hard by the border, thoroughly dependent on American trade and investment. It will continue to be America's largest source of immigrants. Air and water resources will still be shared. But there would have been differences: without NAFTA, Mexico would have become poorer and less able to cope with its problems. And it would have had less reason to listen to Washington about anything.

Everything doesn't have to be done at once. American leverage over Mexican behavior doesn't end with the adoption of NAFTA. The more Mexico becomes economically intertwined with the United States, the more vulnerable it becomes to American political pressure. Indeed, this is the fundamental Mexican opposition complaint about the agreement. For Mexico, this negotiated cession of sovereignty can be justified by NAFTA's compensating economic benefits, and by the new U.S. obligation to at least communicate and coordinate economic policy changes. But NAFTA doesn't somehow diminish America's status as the hemisphere's sole superpower or lessen Mexican dependence on American money and customers.

Critics frequently complain that NAFTA is moving too fast—that North America is trying to do in three years what Europe did in 30. Yet the pace of regional economic integration is quite comparable: the 1965 auto pact between Ottawa and Washington was the foundation of the U.S.-Canadian FTA, as Europe's 1951 steel and coal agreement led directly to the six-member European Economic Community. Mexico started on the path to trade integration in the early 1980s, with its debt negotiations and bilateral framework accords. With a fully phased-in NAFTA, at the end of the next decade, North American trade and investment will still be more restricted than trade in Europe today.

There is both hypocrisy and inconsistency in these complaints. Many of those who say North America is being pushed toward integration too hastily also argue that NAFTA is flawed because it lacks an EC-style commitment to harmonize wage levels, workplace rules, and environmental standards. Yet in Europe, those goals weren't fully codified until the 1993 Maastricht treaty. Maastricht requires constant financial transfers to bring the EC's poor periphery up to the norms of the industrialized center. This leveling of the economic playing field is seen in Europe, correctly, as a final stage in the move towards true unification, consolidating the permanent removal of barriers to goods and immigration. Whether Europe will ever reach that point is anybody's guess. But NAFTA critics cannot argue that North American integration is moving too fast and demand at the same time the simultaneous ratification of a whole series of sweeping measures that took the Europeans decades to enact.

Still, the European experience—as with U.S.-Canadian trade—shows that economic liberalization and integration tends to move more quickly than originally negotiated. Businesses adjust beforehand to scheduled changes, and become more willing to trade off accelerated cross-border market access for more rapidly diminished protection at home. Ideally, while North America's external barriers were reduced and harmonized, internal trade barriers would also be dismantled. Not all of this intramarket liberalization is required by NAFTA. But NAFTA's effect on internal North American import and export patterns will be more profound than is generally recognized. And these changing trade patterns will in turn drive the evolution of the market over the next decade.

Over the next decade, as economic interdependence in the NAFTA triad intensifies, further liberalization will be needed to speed this natural evolution. As with NAFTA now, these efforts will amount to playing catch-up with the marketplace, rather than telling the market where to go.

Ironically, the most important area for further liberalization is trade, where NAFTA leaves much work undone. In some industries, this simply means cutting tariffs more quickly. A 15-year timetable for eliminating duties on orange juice is indefensible when most goods will be crossing the borders within 10 years with no hindrance at all. A greater anomaly is the maintenance of antidumping provisions within a free trade zone. These should eventually be eliminated, despite fierce, rear-guard resistance from Washington trade lawyers. With NAFTA, endless dumping litigation within a unified market will ultimately be seen not only as a logical inconsistency, but as an indefensible drag on economic efficiency and competitiveness.

Rather than warring internally, North American industries should set their sights jointly on markets and import opportunities beyond NAFTA's borders. In many specific product categories, the three countries could fix joint external tariffs, simplifying tariff collection and international trade negotiations. (This has already been done with computers.) The United States and Canada could easily adopt common tariffs for most non-NAFTA products within a few years, creating a customs union in everything but name. Mexico could then align its own much steeper external tariffs with those of its NAFTA partners before North America's internal trade barriers were fully dismantled.

This is another way in which NAFTA represents a step toward a common market: it provides a structure for dealing collectively with other trading groups. Now with NAFTA adopted, it would contradict the spirit of the agreement (and in some cases the letter) for Washington to resume strictly unilateral negotiations with Europe, the emerging East Asian bloc, or other trading associations in our own hemisphere.

Ideally, the NAFTA countries should strive for simultaneous, harmonized tariff reductions with other trading partners under Gatt. Failing that, NAFTA representatives could negotiate bloc-to-bloc tariff harmonization schedules with the European Union and with the East Asian economies. Either way, the gradual alignment of non-NAFTA tariffs could be used as leverage to benefit North America as a whole.

By behaving unabashedly as a trade bloc the NAFTA countries escape the most-favored-nation trap: they can do favors for each other that they are not prepared to offer trading partners elsewhere in the world. This would make it easier to liberalize trade in industries that NAFTA leaves untouched. It makes no sense, for example, for air routes within a unified North American economy to be configured nationally rather than geographically: Air Canada should be able to fly passengers from Boston to Buffalo, Aeromexico should be able to do the same from Los Angeles to Houston, and American Airlines should be able to work a direct route from Toronto to Acapulco. With NAFTA, market realignments such as this can be negotiated without triggering demands for equivalent local cabotage rights from carriers in Asia and Europe.

Continental deregulation could also be profitably applied to telecommunications, coastal shipping, satellite broadcasting, oil and gas pipelines, and other protected industries. The key to these breakthroughs, however, would be the assurance that such concessions would not then be extended globally under a new round of Gatt talks, or even hemispherically through a pan-American free trade zone. Even such hyperprotected businesses as coastal shippers—protected ferociously and expensively in all three countries—might be persuaded to accept such a restructuring if it were phased in slowly and confined to North America.

As always, the incentive for such liberalization would be reciprocal market access. And the net effect would be to deconstruct a continental economy shaped for centuries by national borders and rebuild it along more natural subregional lines.

In the 19th century Mexico was in the West. Now it is in the South. NAFTA will reinvigorate traditional north-south trade corridors from Canada to central Mexico. And these, in turn, will further stimulate economic integration within the many natural regions of North America that spill across national boundaries. Anticipated by Joel Garreau's *Nine Nations of North America*, this internal regionalism is already evident, culturally and politically, in both border regions.

More important than formal trade reforms will be the informal progress towards market unification, with revamped transportation networks, new trade corridors and population centers, and new industrial specializations. Electric power grids will be interconnected; so will broadcasting and telecommunications networks. "National" parks will cross national borders. Fiber-optic information highways will connect telecommuters in all three countries. Bullet trains will link Dallas to Monterrey and New York to Montreal. New airports and seaports will be built along borders to draw customers from both countries. All this will naturally encourage new subregional economic relationships across national lines. And this, in turn, will transform a regional free trade zone into something denser, more integrated, and more stimulating.

The U.S.-Canadian free trade agreement has already deepened this subregional consciousness in the northern United States. In the Pacific Northwest, the growing trade with British Columbia has made "Cascadia" a standard marketing and industrial planning concept. More important than the exchange of goods is the perception—in Victoria, Spokane and Eugene—of common regional interests: in the timber and fishing industries; in high-tech education; in environmental practices; in expanding trade with Asia. On issues ranging from Gatt to wildlife preservation, Vancouver and Seattle have more in common with each other than they do with Montreal and Cleveland.

At the border's midpoint, entrepreneurs and local governments are promoting a "Red River" district uniting Minnesota and the Dakotas with Manitoba and western Ontario. Many of the same commodities are produced on both sides of the border (iron and wheat, machine tools, and auto parts) with surprisingly little direct overlap. Manufacturers and merchants who had once restricted their business to their own country— often at great distances—are now finding markets and suppliers directly across the border.

Similar subregional affinities can be found to the east, where Windsor is virtually part of greater Detroit, and Buffalo has been willingly pulled into

Toronto's orbit. Quebec is increasingly dependent on markets in New York state. In New England and the Maritimes, squabbles over fishing rights obscure a deeper sense of community that can be seen when the coastal shelf is threatened by oil drilling or factory fishing fleets from Europe.

NAFTA imposes new subdivisions on the continent, with northern Mexico and its contiguous neighbors coalescing into four distinct subregions—a more diverse and differentiated area than Garreau's "Mexamerica" monolith, which embraced everything from Texas to California, with most of Mexico thrown in.

But for new cross-border economic and political alliances to develop, the continent's transportation networks must first be rearranged. Historically, the United States had a natural north-south economic orientation, with Atlantic seaboard trade of manufactures from the north and raw materials from the south paralleled by the later Mississippi corridor. Federal policy encouraged nation-building east-west alternatives: first the transcontinental railroad, then the interstate highways, and even the air corridors linking the coasts. This phenomenon was much more exaggerated in Canada, which had to subsidize east-west roads, rail and air freight to make it practical for British Colombia to trade with Ontario and the Maritimes. The Canadian economy is a strip of North America 3,000 miles long and only 300 miles wide: promoting commerce within this narrow field required expensive public works and heavy tariff inducements. With the U.S.-Canadian FTA, however, a series of new north-south rail and shipping lanes are spurring fresh trade links within these northern border regions.

Mexico was always the exception to this coast-to-coast orientation. Its principal transportation—networks run along north-south lines. This isn't coincidental: the country was developed as a natural-resource cornucopia, opening to the developed north. All the important railways were built before the revolution, when Mexico was fast becoming an economic colony of the United States. Mexico's trunk rail lines were southern spurs of American railroads. Its first highways, developed for truck traffic to the border, paralleled the rail lines. And the one major east-west causeway led to Veracruz, Mexico City's seaport, which was in turn a northern-oriented gateway to markets on America's Eastern seaboard.

After the Revolution, this north-south network was frozen in protectionist amber. With foreign trade officially discouraged, these traditional transportation lines became a feeder system for the capital, pushing labor and raw material into Mexico City from the provinces. Mexico's industrial and political centralization was fostered by the closed doors of the import-substitution model; all roads, literally, led to Mexico City. This inward-looking strategy prompted new interest in east-west transport links. But in a protected, state-directed economy, there were few compelling reasons to make such an expensive investment: everybody inside the Mexican market was laboring under the same disadvantages. Now this neocolonial legacy is proving useful. Though they require billions of dollars in expansion and modernization, these north-south routes plug naturally into the different subregional economies that will define the post-NAFTA bilateral relationship.

These emerging NAFTA border regions correspond naturally to North America's time zones. (Mexico, Baja excepted, keeps all its clocks on central standard time, but that will change.) They are all bisected by a 2,000-mile border zone that is too slender and varied to form a coherent natural subregion. McAllen is closer to Chicago than San Diego, and closer to Little Rock than El Paso. Baja California has long been a free trade zone for its entire thousand-mile length; La Paz, at the peninsula's southern tip, has more of a classic "border economy" than Monterrey, which is just a three-hour drive from Texas. Border communities share many bureaucratic problems and sociological traits, but they aren't linked latitudinally by commerce or political alliances. They relate to their natural hinterlands to the immediate north and south, which belong in turn to the four natural subregions of the Mexican north and the American southwest.

Moving from west to east, they are:

LAS CALIFORNIAS

The two Californias, upper and lower, are linked by culture, history, and immigration. Los Angeles is the second largest "Mexican" city in North America. The central Californian valleys that form the country's highest-yielding agricultural district have depended for generations on Mexican labor. The second biggest city on the North American Pacific Coast, Tijuana—edging past San Francisco and San Diego—is the definitive border metropolis, a sprawling gateway where an Americanized Mexico intermingles with a Mexicanized America. The rest of Baja California is a winter playground for American Californians. Wealthy Mexicans, meanwhile, favor vacation stays in La Jolla, and UCLA undergraduate educations for their bilingual children.

Despite this, the Californias are the cross-border region that will be least affected by NAFTA. That's because almost all of it, demographically and economically, is in the United States; California doesn't have much of an immediate Mexican hinterland. Baja south of Tijuana and Mexicali is mostly empty desert. It is already a free trade area, and has been for decades. The border maquiladora zone is nearing saturation. And with NAFTA, the border free trade zone and the maquiladora industry lose their legal advantages over the rest of Mexico, diminishing Baja's relative industrial importance.

The California economy—three times bigger than all of Mexico's, and far more diverse—is no more dependent on Mexican trade than is the United States as a whole. Mexico represents about 8 percent of the state's foreign markets; after NAFTA, that share is unlikely to rise much above 10 percent. The California connection to Mexico is immigration, not commerce. The future of California's export economy will continue to be the Pacific Basin, not the Western Hemisphere.

Still, NAFTA will bind the Californias closer together. Long Beach is already Mexico's biggest Pacific port; a proposed Tijuana desalination plant could become San Diego's biggest new source of electricity and fresh water. The privatization of Mexican farmlands and NAFTA's foreign investment reforms will lure California agribusiness to Baja's fertile northern valleys. The expanding Tijuana airport, hard by the border, will be southern California's big air freight hub. In Tijuana, NAFTA's open cross-border trucking regime will give this isolated city efficient access to important domestic markets for the first time: the U.S. interstates that parallel the border make the drive to Mexico City and Monterrey a day shorter.

This economic integration will take place even faster if NAFTA can avoid discouraging Japanese investment in Mexico. The big Japanese-owned Tijuana electronics plants are an integral part of their parents' Californian operations; increasingly, these are also headquarters for Mexico and the rest of Latin America. Asian investment in both countries is concentrated along the Pacific, and greater intracompany trade among these North American subsidiaries will knit the American and Mexican coasts closer together. By incorporating the resources and low-cost labor of Mexico, the greater Californian economy will be a strong magnet for Japanese investment that would otherwise be channeled to Southeast Asia. Western Mexico and the American Pacific coastal states have a shared interest in an open NAFTA—one that is genuinely receptive to Asian goods and capital.

THE ROCKY MADRES

The trade corridor where NAFTA will have its biggest impact is east of the Californias, along the continent's mountainous spine: the great ranch-

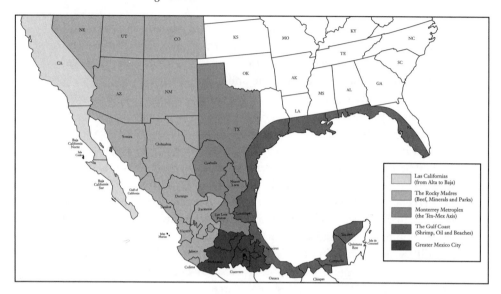

ing and mining badlands from Alberta to the Bajio that are North America's real West. Despite their obvious similarity, the Mexican and American sides of this region have never had much to do with one another. There are few good road and rail crossings and—on both sides sparse industrial development and little agricultural exchange. NAFTA changes that.

The western slope of the Rocky Madres is dominated by Sonora and Arizona, with their Nevadan and Sinaloan nether regions. Its shoreline is the Sea of Cortez, the Southwest's undiscovered Pacific Coast. Guaymas, four hours from Arizona, already has the basic outline: a fledgling industrial port, an improved highway, and new beachfront hotels, including a Club Med catering to the horse set. With NAFTA facilitating financing and promoting demand, and removing obstacles to cross-border trucking and tourist buses, Guaymas will become a port and resort, first for Tucson and Phoenix, and eventually for the entire Southwest. Three hours farther south, the deepwater harbor at Topolobampo will be developed into an efficient alternative rail port with direct overland service to west Texas and Denver. The region's emerging industrial center is Hermosillo; its anchor, the $2 billion Ford Tracer plant. With NAFTA's domestic content requirements gluing the North American auto industry together, Sonora and Arizona are well placed. Both states are also benefiting from the congestion of their west coast neighbors: just as real estate costs and labor costs are driving businesses from California to Arizona, Sonora is luring industrial development that would have gone in the past to Baja California.

Below Hermosillo, into the state of Sinaloa and in adjacent agricultural valleys, agribusiness entrepreneurs from California and Arizona are investing in properties with growing seasons that complement their properties in the north: when Sinaloans are harvesting, fields in the Imperial Valley are ready for planting. Agriculture in this traditionally productive Mexican winter vegetable belt could easily be integrated with farming interests in the north.

On the eastern side of the mountains is one of the continent's oldest trade corridors, running from Torreon through Chihuahua, with a border stop at El Paso del Norte, up past Albuquerque and into Santa Fe. Over the past century this route's northern leg was redirected along the railway and stockyard path to distant Chicago. As this central swath of North America becomes more urbanized and industrialized, manufacturing trade will bind the region together just as cattle and immigration did in the past. The pivotal cities are Juarez and Denver. The largest North American auto parts supplier south of the Great Lakes, Juarez is attracting increasingly high-skilled factory investment. Chihuahua's new PAN state government is working to replace the old maquiladora assembly economy with higher-wage, high-tech industrialization, all of which will require closer ties to markets and suppliers in the United States.

MONTERREY METROPLEX

The crux of the new NAFTA trading relationship is the connection between greater Monterrey, the capital city of private Mexican industry, and the eastern Texas triangle bounded by Houston, San Antonio, and the Dallas-Fort Worth metroplex.

Cross-border traffic naturally funnels through this corridor—it's already the conduit for a third of all U.S.-Mexican trade. High-speed rail service and borderless information services will revolutionize this route before the NAFTA transition period is over. Monterrey is the headquarters for Mexico's cement, glass, brewing, petrochemicals, plastics, and steel industries, and three of its top five banks, and two of its top five retailers, and for franchise chains of everything from Blockbuster Videos to Domino's Pizza. Texas, meanwhile, sits directly athwart Mexico's principal population centers. Eastern Texas is the center for U.S.-Mexican marketing, shipping and export-import financing. It's also Mexico's main supplier of goods ranging from helicopters and customized computer software to refined gasoline, cotton clothing, and advanced machine tools. It's the gateway to Mexico for Washington state apple growers, and the entrance to the United States for Guadalajara computer manufacturers. The slow but inexorable opening of the Mexican oil and gas business to foreign investment will expand the Tex-Mex trade and investment relationship still further.

That the east Texas-northeastern Mexican region should benefit more from free trade than any other part of the North American economy is neither surprising nor disproportionate. Tex-Mex cultural and ethnic connections are ultimately stronger than those uniting the Californias. A new Mexican-American leadership class in Texas—a group with no real counterpart in California, where the Mexican-American community has more immigrants but fewer voters and political activists—is emerging as an important player in the cross-border relationship. In Texas, the ties that bind are personal as well as economic.

THE GULF COAST

The final border region is essentially maritime, sweeping from Tampico to Tabasco and around to Tampa and Galveston. The big industries on all sides are oil, shrimp and shipping. Fertilizer and petrochemical plants are an integral part of the Gulf economy. The coasts are fringed by the same lowland subtropical agriculture: cotton, citrus, sugar, Brahma beef, winter vegetables. This is the most predictably protectionist of the NAFTA regions. It is also the most polarized environmentally: the fishing industry, a leading employer in all Gulf coastal states, is everywhere at odds with oil drillers and shippers. But there is a growing sense of common interest in the protection of the Gulf's fragile ecology, both offshore and along what remains of the original mangrove coastlines. There will also be increasing intraregional maritime trade as corrupt, inefficient union monopolies are driven out of Mexico's newly privatized ports. The endless delays and brazen pilferage at ports like Veracruz were an artificial constraint on what should have been a natural trade flow among the American and Mexican Gulf Coast states.

At the eastern mouth of the Gulf, the collapse of Castroite Cuba would herald the reunion of Havana, the Yucatan, and South Florida, all of which shared close commercial and even family links in the 19th century. Yucatan ports are beginning to be linked to Florida by overnight ferry service; NAFTA will increase cargo demand for such services and ease transportation paperwork. Miami will feel closer to Merida than Boston does to Halifax. The Yucatan is where Mexico competes directly for the Caribbean tourism and light manufacturing trade. NAFTA will make it more competitive still, and Florida is its natural outlet to the American market. In the long run, the Cancun-Havana-Miami tourist corridor could easily become the busiest yachting and diving region in North America.

But petroleum is the most important regional business: under NAFTA, the Gulf of Mexico will be the natural hub of a new North American energy market. Already in the works are billions in new joint venture projects along Mexico's Gulf shore with American energy companies and billions in joint investment projects on the Texas Gulf coast with Pemex and private Mexican investors. More important, NAFTA sets the precedent for preferential access within the North American market for the natural customers of the region's oil and gas reserves. This change alone will have an immediate and binding impact. It is already widely forgotten that Washington paid Mexico hundreds of millions of dollars in the 1980s to pump oil out of the southern end of the Gulf of Mexico and ship it to Louisiana, where the U.S. government then pumped it back into the ground at great expense. These strategic reserves of Mexican crude—still sitting there in subterranean salt domes deep beneath the bayous—were a far more expensive way of safeguarding American energy security than NAFTA's oil and government procurement provisions. With a common market, these are common resources, regardless of who had formal title.

Inside Looking Out

If we are going to be a common market, we should start acting like one. Leaders in all three countries should openly acknowledge that they expect to be working toward further economic integration. They should also frankly admit that the complexity of this process—not to mention its political delicacy—precludes adding new full members to this market anytime soon. Extending the new market too quickly south, or through bilateral pacts arrayed randomly around the world, might easily lead to the creation of more protectionist-minded trade blocs in East Asia, while diluting NAFTA's own advantages.

Trade diversion won't work if it is spread too thin: the central argument for NAFTA was that it is better for American workers to have American companies investing in Mexico than in Thailand. Wages and work rules are under siege by competition from low-income producers around the world. This brutal reality cannot be wished away. Although they are considered the most visible and pernicious symbol of this phenomenon, American factories in Mexico are, paradoxically, the best possible protection against it. NAFTA concentrates industrial production in Mexico that would otherwise flow to Asia and other export centers less dependent on American imports. It will also lure portfolio capital that would otherwise go to other emerging stock markets overseas. This investment will help Mexico export not just within North America, but to newly liberalized South American economies, which like Mexico have long required all goods sold domestically to be produced there. These sales and the jobs they create will in turn deepen the Mexican domestic market for manufactured goods. By consolidating production to the greatest extent possible within North America, North American companies will benefit, and so will their employees.

Indeed, the most compelling economic argument *against* NAFTA was that this regional production strategy conflicts with the tenets of free trade. While NAFTA doesn't put new tariff barriers on goods from outside North America, it does create systemic advantages for local producers through content rules, investment preferences, and other legal means. In theory, these trade-diverting devices are tolerated by Gatt members only because common markets are considered transitional steps toward some form of political union, as in Europe. But in North America, the aims of integration are unapologetically commercial.

President Clinton, in a February 1993 address on trade policy, dismissed the argument between bilateralism (or trilateralism) and multilateralism as "a false choice." Yet NAFTA is a tactical choice against multilateralism, even if its practical effect is to help spur progress toward a successful conclusion of Gatt. No country has a greater stake in multilateral trade liberalization than the United States. So it's in the national interest to make North America the exception to the multilateral rule. NAFTA should remain a specific, geographically limited experiment as long as progress towards global trade liberalization can be maintained.

Even without explicit aims of political unity, this strategy is quite defensible. The dependence of Mexico and Canada on the United States is well understood in the rest of the world, as is Washington's national security interest in maintaining open and stable relationships with its neighbors. The United States, after all, has only two borders. And the economic integration of Mexico—what NAFTA is ultimately all about—makes the North American common market qualitatively different from other trade blocs. Never before have an industrial superpower and a struggling middle-income nation opened their doors to one another. The success of this experiment is based on economic triage: Mexico can raise its living standard closer to the North American norm only if it attracts jobs and investments that might have gone to even poorer neighbors to the east and south. The alternative—distributing American investment and import orders over the widest possible horizons—may seem superficially more equitable, but it would have little cumulative impact, and it would deprive Mexico of the critical economic mass it requires to rise to the next level of development.

The emergence of a North American common market does not mean the world is about to fragment into three or four major trading blocs. The fear that America might find itself caught between such blocs plainly helped give birth to NAFTA. The EC was then months away from a borderless marketplace. Japan was pulling back from Latin America as a market and production center, and was receiving serious proposals from the Southeast Asian economies for a formalized yen bloc arrangement. The apparent breakdown of the Uruguay Round enhanced regionalism's appeal, making the formation of a protective North American bloc seem inevitable. As the University of Texas trade expert Sidney Weintraub observed when NAFTA was proposed: "With the addition of Mexico to a North American preferential trade grouping—assuming this comes to pass—there is no longer any basis for denying that the world is divided into regional trading arrangements."

But as multilateralists warned at the time, there are reasons to be wary of trade blocs, in North America or elsewhere.

If freer world trade would maximize global prosperity, groupings that divert trade and investment would deter natural economic interchange and growth. If the goal is local or regional competitiveness, the concern is the inevitable decay of overprotected economies. The North American common market would have to strive to avoid these traps by seeking further liberalization on a parallel basis with other trading blocs or, better, within the global framework of Gatt. Otherwise, the North American market could provoke the formation of retaliatory blocs in East Asia and a defensive restructuring of the European Union. This, in turn, would make an inward-looking pan-American trade zone an unfortunate inevitability.

Under NAFTA, the greater North American economy will combine the cross-border integration of natural resource industries (like energy and steel) that has long been the hallmark of Europe's Common Market with the regional production-sharing arrangements in advanced manufacturing industries (like autos and computers) that have been pioneered by East Asia. Because of its size, diversity, resources and interdependence, a North American common market could combine the best aspects of both systems. A North America free of tariff and investment barriers would be the most unified major market in the world. Even without NAFTA, North America conducts proportionately more of its business within its borders than the European Union or East Asian yen bloc do today. And externally, the North American free trade area would be the most open common market in the world, giving it good reason to demand better access to markets overseas.

Resettling the Continent	It was exactly a century ago that Frederick Jackson Turner warned that the West was won—that is, the territories seized from Mexico were being tilled and populated—and the great pioneering era of American history was coming to a possibly traumatic close.

Turner was a bit premature. Faith in manifest destiny soon drove a southward expansion of American might: Theodore Roosevelt's resuscitation of the Monroe Doctrine and Woodrow Wilson's good-governance crusades made the Caribbean the new focus of American ambitions. Pacific conquests and two world wars then turned the United States into a global power, with investments and dependencies reaching into Asia.

Yet throughout this period, the settlement of the West continued to absorb the nation's domestic energies. Indeed, it was the natural wealth and Pacific projection of the American West that made the country the superpower that it is. Westward expansion remained the great industrial, agricultural and demographic story of the United States until late in the 20th century.

Until now, that is. The 1990 census confirmed that the westward expansion is over. The national center of demographic gravity is no longer marching towards the Rockies. California's population is still rising, but that is the result of immigration (Mexico being the principal culprit), not citizens relocating west. The fastest growing state in the 1980s was Florida, the first time in generations that distinction had been held by an eastern state. Californians are looking back east for work, cheaper housing, and the greener spaces they bypassed on the way out. Southern California is as crowded and costly as the northeastern corridor; its air is warmer but also dirtier. Defense industries are shrinking; subsidized desert agriculture has hit its economic limits; the region's old strength as an energy supplier is foundering amid tapped-out reserves and new environmental constraints. The West, accustomed since birth to constant growth, is becoming just another region, with the same cycles of growth and decay that the rest of the country has long endured.

Its westward expansion finally complete, the United States is again trying to push south into Mesoamerica. The difference this time is that, by mutual assent, Mexico is wedding itself to the United States—and laying subtle claims to the lands that Santa Ana lost. NAFTA will restructure the continent, with lines of people and goods running north-to-south as well as east-to-west, and once-fixed borders blurring in overlapping spheres of economic influence and political power. Economically, Mexico ultimately will be nearly the size of Canada, and a bigger and better trading partner than Japan. Mexican immigration will diminish over time as Mexican prosperity rises, while the immigration that remains could be regulated and legalized within a common market system of preferences. The North American Free Trade Agreement is the framework for a relationship that would restructure much more than mere trade.

Because of NAFTA, the 21st century will be marked by the consolidation of a new North America, an economic community with common goals and standards, and one of the richest unified markets in the world. This unity will be economic, not political. But it will also be cultural, with American popular culture permeating Mexico ever more deeply and Mexican culture seeping north into the United States.

Long before the Salinas Administration, the lines were blurring between north and south. The Mexican border never made a clean division between capitalism and corporatism, or between the Protestant ethic and mystic Catholicism. Now the distinctions are fading even faster. In both countries, there is a growing recognition that the border is just one point on a continuum of economic and cultural change.

Mexico's own regional differences mirror those within the United States. In the north, and in Mexican business circles generally, traits once disdained as "Anglo-Saxon" are openly admired: punctuality, blunt speaking, an unsentimental concentration on the bottom line. The United States, meanwhile, is overtaking Argentina as the fourth-largest Spanish-speaking country in the world. By the end of the decade, the largest American state will have a majority "minority" work force, with the descendants of Mexicans comprising the largest single group. New Chicano pride and old-fashioned regionalism have made southwestern Anglos aware of how much of their own heritage is Mexican: "Spanish" architecture, "Tex-Mex" cuisine, the cult of the cowboy—all mark the survival of northern Mexican culture in a region owned and governed by recent arrivals from the English-speaking east.

Even the language divide is blurring: much of Monterrey and Tijuana, and much of Los Angeles and San Antonio, is now bilingual. The cultures of electoral democracy also range over a continuum of time and place. Just as American elections today are cleaner than they were a generation ago, so too is Mexican politics cleaner and more competitive than ever before. The contrasts within nations are nearly as stark as the contrast between nations: just as Minnesota politics is cleaner than Texas politics, Chihuahua politics—the frauds of the 1980s notwithstanding—is cleaner than Chiapas politics.

The sharpest regional demarcation after NAFTA won't be the line between Mexico and the United States, but the line between the new industrialized Mexico of the north and the rural economy of its poor south.

■ Some NAFTA opponents dispute the notion that Mexican economic development is in America's interest. They fear an Asian-style export juggernaut shipping goods from high-tech factories with low-wage workers. Aside from overestimating Mexico's industrial potential and vastly underestimating American strength, this paranoid analysis departs from the premise that Mexican growth leads inexorably to American decline. What such critics really oppose is the notion of an economically developed Mexico: if they could decree Salinas out of existence, they would. These critics—ranging from the nationalist right to the formerly internationalist left—seem to long for the status quo ante, with a poor but self-sufficient and self-absorbed Mexico having little economic impact on the United States except as a supplier of cheap oil, stoop labor, and tropical vacations.

Other Americans, however, readily grasp the advantages of a stable, prosperous Mexico. The problems that are associated with Mexico in the popular mind—illegal immigration, drug trafficking, environmental despoliation, the exploitation of cheap factory labor—are clearly more easily addressed if Mexicans have more economic opportunities than they do now. It is equally apparent that in most respects the two economies are inherently complementary: in agriculture, in energy, in capital-intensive machinery and labor-intensive assembly work, each country is a natural market for the other's products.

Ross Perot was right about one big thing: NAFTA should have been ratified only if it was in the long-term interest of the American worker. It should not have been backed as some fuzzy strategy for hegemony in the Western Hemisphere. Nor should it have been construed as an altruistic experiment in trade preferences for a deserving neighbor. Arguments that NAFTA should have been passed as a show of support for Mexico's pro-American president were equally ill-conceived: fears that a NAFTA-less Mexico would succumb to rabid anti-Yankee nationalism have no basis in Mexican political reality.

The United States ratified NAFTA because economic integration with Mexico will create new markets and more and better jobs—and not just next year, but 10 and 20 years from now. Mexico, overcoming deeper visceral objections to economic integration, had already concluded that the economic advantages of a North American common market far outweigh the political disadvantages.

This is as it should be: a common market cannot work unless every party believes that it is in its own rationally calculated interest. When I first moved to Mexico as a reporter in 1981, Mexico was still flush with its new oil wealth, and enjoying its self-assigned role as a spokesman for the poor south against the industrial north. It seemed inconceivable that Mexico would ever seriously entertain the common market proposal offered by the new American president. A year later, with oil prices halved, loan payments stopped, and the Mexican economic miracle in inglorious shambles, it seemed inconceivable that the United States would ever seriously pursue Reagan's idea. But in the wreckage of the debt crisis, Washington and Mexico City realized that they were partners, as the U.S. ambassador remarked at the time, in "a marriage without the possibility of divorce." When Salinas decided that the relationship should be consummated, what had been unthinkable—borderless trade and bilateral free-market investment rules—suddenly seemed inevitable.

Now that Mexico has become an integral part of North America, not only Mexico will be transformed, but the rest of the continent will as well. The benefits would be abundant and permanent. Fifty years from now NAFTA could be seen as the start of a new phase of North American economic expansion, and the bitter opposition to the agreement may be viewed much as we now see contemporary criticism of the Marshall Plan or the annexation of Alaska.

With NAFTA, the 21st century will mark North America's emergence as one of the largest and richest unified markets in the world. North America will begin thinking of itself as an economic community with common standards, a shared history, and compatible goals.

Even without a trade agreement, the continent would have remained economically interdependent. Mexico would have needed to stay on its present investment-driven path—even if it hadn't been obliged to do so by a treaty with Washington. But by having brought Mexico into the North American market formally, as a political partner and an acknowledged economic asset, the United States has the historic chance to make its relationship with its most populous neighbor more equitable as well as more profitable. There is no aspect of that relationship—financial, diplomatic, political, cultural or environmental—that progress toward a common market will not improve, just as there are no bilateral conflicts that NAFTA's rejection wouldn't have aggravated. NAFTA won't automatically resolve Mexico's problems or erase the legacy of centuries of cross-border friction. Nor will it guarantee North American success in the global quest for markets and capital. But in all these things, it will help. And that is reason enough to do it.

Immigration: NAFTA's Unfinished Business

There can never be a true common market in North America if goods and capital can cross borders freely but workers cannot. Yet NAFTA carefully avoided the contentious issue of labor mobility. While the pact makes it easier for executives in all three countries to get temporary business visas, the real issue—the hundreds of thousands of Mexicans seeking work legally and illegally in the United States—was sidestepped entirely. By failing to address immigration as an integral aspect of their new North American partnership, both countries virtually guaranteed that it would become the single most divisive and emotional issue blocking the constructive development of this relationship.

Despite the decision to keep it out of the agreement itself, immigration was always central to the NAFTA debate. President Salinas told Americans that NAFTA is a way for Mexico "to export goods, not people" to the United States. His critics retorted that NAFTA's economic reforms would actually send more people north.

In fact, for the rest of the century, NAFTA will have little noticeable impact on immigration pressures in either direction.

In the long run, NAFTA-driven economic development will accelerate existing trends towards smaller families and higher wages. Incentives to seek work in the United States will gradually diminish. Mexican demographers say the "push" factor of Mexican population expansion and economic distress has already peaked.

The more powerful "pull" of American labor demand has not ebbed, however. In the 1990s freer trade and investment will do little to slow the flow of labor across the border. What the NAFTA framework does offer in the short term is a chance for Washington to deal with Mexican immigration constructively and realistically—and in partnership with Mexico.

When NAFTA was first discussed, critics and advocates in both countries urged that it be broadened to address mutual immigration concerns. Mexico, despite its misgivings, ultimately needs American investment. The United

States, despite its own misgivings, ultimately needs Mexican labor. Officials in Mexico assumed that American common market plans implied a *quid pro quo:* guaranteed access to Mexican oil and better treatment for American investors south of the border, in return for Mexican access to American markets and better treatment for Mexican workers north of the border.

Salinas himself originally wanted NAFTA to address the immigration concerns of both countries. But the Bush White House warned that any overt linkage to more open immigration would kill the pact in Congress. It urged Salinas to sell NAFTA instead as a *solution* to Mexican immigration. And that is what he has tried to do—even though it undercuts Mexico's traditional claim that immigrant labor wasn't a problem for the United States but rather an underpriced asset. In Mexico's view, the real problem was the widespread tolerance of illegality—a byproduct of American political culture (which resists tough employer sanctions and identification cards) and population trends (where an aging middle class increasingly depends on low-cost immigrant labor). When immigration opponents in the United States decry tolerance of "illegal aliens," their assumption is that an insistence on documentation would prompt an exodus of the undocumentable. The Mexican premise is quite different: knowing as they intimately do the historic dependence of the American Southwest on migrant labor, Mexicans assume that a legalization campaign would inevitably mean providing working papers to tens of thousands of gainfully employed illegal immigrants.

When Clinton insisted that NAFTA be broadened to embrace environmental and labor concerns, Salinas again asked that immigration be included in the discussions. It was too late. Stagnant incomes and high unemployment had made too many Americans hostile to new immigration. Most original proponents of free trade with Mexico—from free-market Republicans to Good-Neighbor diplomats—had urged more open immigration policies. Now many NAFTA advocates wanted the agreement tied to new restrictions on immigration, such as requiring Mexico to patrol its own northern border. But Mexico could hardly consent to Cuban-style emigration controls, especially as part of a pact that removed incoming barriers to American goods and investors. Demands for formal collaboration on border security only made real cooperation more difficult. When Californians voted to deny schooling and basic health services to even the children of illegal immigrants, the furor in Mexico ensured that the tone of future bilateral discussions on the issue would be more confrontational than cooperative.

There is still room for constructive cooperation, however. America's present immigration system gives Mexicans two choices: illegality or permanent residency. This has the perverse effect of causing many Mexicans to stay in the United States longer than they themselves would like. Illegal workers are reluctant to return home between jobs or growing seasons because they know that legal re-entry is impossible. And workers with green cards lose their legal status if they return to Mexico for prolonged periods. So they stay—and often their families join them. The result is that Mexico loses highly motivated workers who are accumulating capital and skills while the United States absorbs the costs of caring for dependents of workers who might rather be in Mexico.

Labor traffic across the border will continue to be a fact of North American life for some time to come. Mexico will remain the continent's chief supplier of migrant labor, from Juárez construction workers who work by day in El Paso to Oaxacans who spend half the year on California's harvests. The Immigration and Naturalization Service says about a third of the 300,000 people who immigrate illegally every year are Mexicans. Many eventually return home. But most settle permanently in the southwestern states that were once Mexican territory and that are home now to millions of legal Mexican immigrants. This constant influx has already made Mexican-Americans the majority of what will soon be the country's biggest minority: the descendants of Spanish-speakers. The sheer size of that community and its concentration along the southwestern border—where it was the first and is often still the dominant culture—assures that Mexican immigrants will be welcome in the United States for many years to come. As a practical matter, it would be impossible to stop illegal Mexican immigration without fierce—and possibly unconstitutional—discrimination against American citizens of Mexican ancestry.[1]

The challenge is not to halt immigration, however, but to reduce the exploitation of immigrant labor, and attempt to align immigration more closely with America's economic needs. Immigration critics and advocates agree that illegality exposes undocumented workers to intolerable conditions and drags down wages and standards for the entire low-end of the American labor force. Both sides also agree that Mexican immigration is a special case due to the numbers involved and the unique character of the cross-border labor market. Both sides say further that immigration ought to be dealt with bilaterally.

The NAFTA relationship presents alternative means to do just that—without setting automatic precedents for other immigrant groups. The NAFTA countries could build on the precedent of their white-collar visa reforms to establish a broad-based system of temporary work permits—from month-long stays to renewable multiyear visas—with the understanding that these permits would not lead inexorably to permanent residence. (Mexico could use its new system of photo identification cards for voters to provide documentation for temporary workers.)

Temporary or "guest-workers" programs have a bad name in both countries due to the mistreatment of Mexican farm workers in the *bracero* program of the 1950s and the current H-2 program for temporary harvest labor. But with more labor inspectors and a bilateral commitment to better enforcement, these abuses could be stopped. And the principle under which the H-2 program operates—linking the volume of temporary farm-worker visas to predetermined labor needs—could in theory be expanded to other industries.

Coordination will be easier as pressure subsides from the Mexican baby boom of the 1960s and 1970s. While the full demographic effects of NAFTA won't be felt for decades, education and urbanization have already lowered Mexico's annual birth rate from 3 percent to less than 2 percent. With NAFTA, there will be more nonagricultural jobs in the Mexican countryside, attracting people who otherwise would migrate out of boredom or frustration with subsistence agriculture. At the same time, the growth of new provincial industrial centers will provide an alternative for emigrants who now head straight to the border. Mexican industrialization will gradually draw people away from the densely settled rural south to the industrial districts of the arid north. NAFTA will accelerate this process—to the benefit of both countries. At the same time, the economic restructuring of the United States that NAFTA will hasten will eliminate many menial jobs that now pull immigrants north of the border. The narrowing gap between industrial pay scales—now about 6-to-1 and likely to shrink to half that over the next 10 years—will also make emigration less seductive and more selective.

But NAFTA will complicate Mexico's own immigration problems. Rising wages will lure more Central Americans into Mexico, just as American pay scales attract Mexicans to the United States. There are already 1 million Guatemalans and Salvadorans living illegally in Mexico. Most are concentrated in the rural south and in the poorer outskirts of Mexico City, where they suffer deprivations at least as acute as those suffered by Mexicans illegally in the United States. Mexican immigration officials are notoriously abusive and corrupt, and Mexican immigration law is restrictive and arbitrary (as shown by Mexico's summary expulsion of would-be refugees from China). In the border zone, Mexican police routinely round up and deport Central American immigrants with no pretense of due process, despite protests from human rights activists. ("Our immigration policy is far worse than U.S. policy," a Mexican diplomat once remarked to me. "I don't know why they don't ever throw it back in our faces, but they don't.") Mexico would be in a better position to urge American immigration reforms if its own house was put in order.

Mexico can't afford to stop emigration overnight. Its American-employed workers send home more than $3 billion a year. That's equal to Mexico's earnings from tourism or the entire maquiladora trade. Any sudden change in American immigration policy would create deep nationalistic resentment in Mexico, where tens of thousands of Mexican families have sent temporary workers north for generations. And for American workers, there's another consideration: freer cross-border migration would be a check on exploitative wages within Mexico. That would reduce the incentive for factories to move south while also broadening the pool of potential U.S. union members.

Eventually, common market rules might permit dual citizenship in NAFTA countries. As it stands, NAFTA could also open the way for experimentation with border-zone pass systems in binational metropolises like Juárez-El Paso and Windsor-Detroit (which had such a system during the second world war). Real immigration reform needs to be binational. Otherwise, frictions will intensify and Mexico will permanently lose many of its most productive citizens. In immigration, more than any other issue, Mexico will always be a special case, and NAFTA offers a chance for both countries to address that reality.

NOTE

Note 1: Mexican immigration is nothing new: Mexicans have consistently been among the three or four largest immigrant groups in the United States since the 19th century, though rigorous border statistics weren't kept until recently. Since the 1960s Mexicans have led all immigrant groups. The 1990 census counted 7.4 million new legal immigrants over the previous decade—the most in any 10-year period in American history. Mexicans, at 1.67 million, were by far the biggest single group. Many were legalized through the amnesty provisions of the 1986 Immigration Reform and Control Act (IRCA). Seventy percent of the 1.76 million IRCA applications for legal residency were filed by Mexicans. In the separately administered program for seasonal agricultural workers, 80 percent of the 1.2 million amnesty applicants were Mexican.

SUBJECT INDEX

About the Author

William A. Orme Jr. has covered Latin America as a journalist for the past fifteen years. While based in Mexico City from 1981 to 1988, he served as a correspondent for *The Economist* and the *Journal of Commerce* and as a special correspondent for *The Washington Post*. He also contributed regularly to the *Financial Times* and the *International Herald Tribune*. He was the founding editor of *Latin Finance*, a Miami-based monthly specializing in regional debt and investment issues. He is currently executive director of the Committee to Protect Journalists in New York City.